labor politics

in a

democratic

republic

BY VAUGHN DAVIS BORNET

California Social Welfare (1956)

Welfare in America (1960)

Labor Politics in a Democratic Republic (1964)

Contributor to:

Ideas in Conflict
(American Association for State and Local History, 1958)

The Heart Future
(American Heart Association, 1961)

LABOR POLITICS IN A DEMOCRATIC REPUBLIC

Moderation, Division, and Disruption in the Presidential Election of 1928

by *VAUGHN DAVIS BORNET*

Southern Oregon College

1964

Washington, D.C.
SPARTAN BOOKS, INC.

London
CLEAVER-HUME PRESS

iii

Library of Congress Catalog Card Number 62-21137
Printed in the United States of America.

Sole distributors in Great Britain, the
British Commonwealth and the Continent of Europe:
CLEAVER-HUME PRESS
10-15 St. Martins Street
London W. C. 2

To

EDGAR EUGENE ROBINSON

Preface

THIS IS THE STORY of labor and politics in the United States in the Presidential Election of 1928. It is a picture of trade union leaders and political figures working in alternative patterns to change and (as each thought) to improve the nation. One intent of the book is to display in sequence the colors of the ideological spectrum of that day and time. Here may be seen Herbert C. Hoover and the Republicans, Alfred E. Smith and the Democrats, Norman M. Thomas and the Socialists, and William G. Foster and the Communists, all engaged in framing appeals designed to woo laboring men, labor organizations and leaders, or abstract groups like "workers with hand and brain" or "the proletariat." Here also are orthodox trade union leaders like William Green of the American Federation of Labor, Daniel Tobin of the Teamsters, and the leaders of many well-known unions during a time of prosperity, seeking to be influential in helping to decide the final score in the great game of politics.

It was a noteworthy year, 1928—midway between two world wars, yet prosperous, confident, and forward-looking. It was a time when reactionaries and radicals minced no words in expressing what was on their minds. For this and other reasons, the nature of the Socialist and Communist programs for redesigning the American economy and body politic stand revealed in their true light—free of the oddities of linguistics and the alterations in outward conduct that were to come to each group in later decades. Thomas and Foster, both dynamic leaders, were destined to retain throughout their lives their prominence among adherents to their respective ideologies. In Hoover and Smith the two major parties had high-minded and articulate leaders of noteworthy previous experience who were capable of much consistency in appeal.

Certain issues placed before the public in 1928 by single-minded persons were not normally part of American presidential politics. These hotly controverted matters—religion and prohibition, each highly personal—had the effect of burying for contemporaries and posterity a good deal of what otherwise would have been included in headlines—and later become part of comprehensive historical narratives in school textbooks. The sources for this account are unpublished letters and papers, typed minutes of closed meetings, interviews, magazines and pamphlets of limited circulation, and daily newspapers. The solid books and articles from the hands of historians, political scientists, and labor economists listed in the Bibliography were of the utmost value, especially in permitting concentration on the main task.

The nature of American labor and politics in 1928, far from being of antiquarian interest, will have meaning for decades to come, because the issues revealed on that political and economic battleground are enduring in our nation. What kind of party system should we have in the United States? What gradation in a capitalist economic system should we seek—or oppose? Should we consider patterns of economic and social control urged by radicals of several hues? These were basic questions for leaders in 1928; today, despite the years of New Deal, war, uneasy peace, and the technological changes that have followed, they still remain fundamental.

Since the United States is now worrying through her most critical decade since the 1860s, the present story might be thought to have only a limited service to render. But most observers will agree that the long American record of orderly self-government accomplished routinely by choosing leaders from nominees of multi-interest political party organizations is almost unique in a world where unrest, chaos, and dictatorship have been all too frequent. Our functioning party system, and the restrained conduct of leaders of large economic groups in our democratic republic, ought to have poignant meaning for many less fortunate peoples overseas. They certainly have meaning for the people of our own nation, who for the past hundred years have entirely accepted the idea that election results are final—until the next constitutionally scheduled election. It was in the hope of furthering, in some small way, the efforts of men and women to govern themselves through freedom of electoral choice that I wrote this book.

VAUGHN DAVIS BORNET

Ashland, Oregon
April, 1964

Acknowledgments

THIS BOOK is affectionately dedicated to Edgar Eugene Robinson, Professor of American History, emeritus, and formerly Director of the Institute of American History, Stanford University, whose suggestion, aid, and guidance have been for many years the source of my greatest inspiration. Many of his revealing and influential works on American political history are cited in the Bibliography and relied upon in the text.

Professor Thomas A. Bailey of Stanford was a constructive reader of the doctoral dissertation which, eleven years ago, formed the early outline for much that appears in the present work.

The close friendship and keen political wisdom of Thomas Barclay, Professor of Political Science, emeritus, Stanford University, have had special value for the present writer—as they have for countless other persons.

Florence Thorne, former secretary to Samuel Gompers, gave access to the seldom-used American Federation of Labor archives in the old headquarters furnace room, Washington, D. C. Clifford Lord, then director, State Historical Society of Wisconsin, and members of his staff, made available the Hillquit, Simons, and Wisconsin Federation of Labor papers. Theodore Mueller and Frederick Olson facilitated exploration in the manuscript holdings of the Milwaukee County Historical Society. Norman Thomas generously permitted access to his papers at the New York Public Library, and Duke University librarians granted the opportunity to read in the Socialist Party's official papers. Lucile Kane and others at the Minnesota Historical Society made available the Teigan and Hall papers. Officials at the Manuscript Division, Library of Congress, and particularly Katherine Brand, facilitated convenient access to the Coolidge papers and other collections.

Various officials of the National Archives gave helpful advice on the contents of Department of Labor and other pertinent papers housed there.

At Hyde Park, New York, Director Herman Kahn and the staff of the Franklin D. Roosevelt Library located correspondence that provided an intimate look at the Democratic Party of the 1920s. Communist Party maneuverings were traced in the pamphlet and newspaper collections of the Hoover Library, Palo Alto, Calif., and the Jefferson School Library, New York City. Herman K. Murphy of National Industrial Conference Board courteously opened files, and officials of the New York Public Library made available the papers of Theodore Debs, the Frank Walsh papers, and other collections. Many other librarians assisted the research effort—for example, at Milwaukee Public Library, Chicago Public Library, New York University Library, San Francisco Public Library, and the University of California Libraries at Berkeley and Los Angeles. Eloise Giles at the American Federation of Labor Library and members of the Federation staff were very cooperative. Stanford University librarians, particularly in the reference, periodical, and government document divisions, performed many cumulatively important courtesies. Dean Albertson, Oral History Project, Columbia University, provided guidance to pertinent transcribed materials.

Many national and state labor leaders wrote letters about particular matters; William Green, Daniel Tobin, John Frey, Matthew Woll, Edward Keating, and others granted interviews. Constructive comment in letters came from Professors Selig Perlman, Leo Wolman, Louis M. Hacker, Eric Goldman, Clarence A. Berdahl, Harold F. Gosnell, Allan Nevins, and John Troxell. Advice from Herbert R. Northrup, Morton Leeds, Brother Potamian, F.S.C., Henry J. Browne, Manoel Cardozo, Louis Stark, and others helped at various stages; Alfred H. Kirchhofer of the Buffalo *Evening News* loaned rare pamphlet materials. A seminar with Ralph Henry Gabriel on intellectual trends in the 1920s was a rewarding experience. John Hazard and Kenneth Templeton made important suggestion about the preliminary version of Chapters 5 and 10—which appeared as "The Communist Party in the Presidential Election of 1928" in *Western Political Quarterly,* XI, September, 1958. Funds from the Ford Foundation financed a postgraduate year of research and travel to manuscript depositories. Personal friends were helpful at many stages; I particularly want to thank Clarence McIntosh, Herman Bateman, Milton and Marion Holmen, Lisette Fast, and Lorraine Lang. The skilled advice of John Hogan and Dorothy Stewart, and the encouragement of Edward T. Lowe, friends at the RAND Corporation, meant much during many months of editing and polishing the manuscript. Arthur S. Taylor, my kindly predecessor as Chairman, Social Sciences Division, Southern Oregon College, shared his extensive memories of the 1920's. Mary Yanokawa, Jessie Hausner, and Jo Ann Chamorro typed the manuscript with efficient accuracy.

It is a special source of gratification that this book has been published in the capital of the United States of America by an enterprising new publisher, whose president Robert Teitler, has displayed personal interest in the manuscript.

As I conclude this pleasant opportunity to thank some who helped in many ways, there is the disquieting feeling that others who went out of their way to be of service have been left unmentioned; I would avoid this if I could. The members of my family, my wife, Beth Winchester Bornet, and our children, Barbara Lee Bornet and Stephen Folwell Bornet, showed inexhaustable patience, helped me with the Index, and thereby aided in bringing this work of many years to final completion.

Contents

LIST OF ILLUSTRATIONS

Chapter 1

Unions in a Prosperous America

MOST AMERICANS FELT a certain sense of security in the year 1928 as they reflected on their past progress, surveyed their present situation, and looked ahead to a clearly predictable future. Most citizens viewed with satisfaction their traditionally democratic way of life. The economic benefits that had come through several centuries of national expansion across a new continent of vast resources had encouraged general faith in the merits of an almost unfettered capitalist system. Leaders in political life tended to assume that the nation (and most of the planet) would be governed increasingly in accordance with the obviously benevolent experience which mankind had gained through countless years of upward movement in Western civilization. Thus there was widespread belief that whatever festering problems of social and economic democracy remained in the nation could eventually be solved by orderly means in progressive stages. The passage of a reasonable period of time would do wonders, even for knotty problems of old. Would not the deserving of the land at length be satisfied and happy? Critics of such concepts as these lacked appeal for the masses of Americans, for whatever the fog in the crystal ball, this was the pervading spirit of the day.

1

I

Many thoughtful persons assumed in 1928 that the practical application of scientific discoveries by American industrial genius, reinforced by the sheer magic of mass production in American industry, would surely make poverty an evil of the past. While some critics called this mode of thinking cross materialism,[1] others —like the distinguished author of the best-selling volume knowingly entitled *The Rise of American Civilization*—preferred to call it humanitarianism.[2] And Charles A. Beard also contended in an essay in *Recent Gains in American Civilization* that there had been genuine improvement in the national welfare in his own day. There had been the general reduction in governmental corruption, improved labor legislation in the states, far more efficient municipal government, and the uneventful daily functioning of a multitude of obscure government bureaus. Had not such progress been realized, significantly, by "the processes of democracy"?[3] An oriental philosopher highly respected in the Western World, Hu Shih, even found in such concentration on material things true spirituality, saying:

> . . . That civilization which makes the fullest possible use of human ingenuity and intelligence in search of truth in order to control nature and transform matter for the service of mankind, to liberate the human spirit from ignorance, superstition, and slavery to the forces of nature, and to reform social and political institutions for the benefit of the greatest number—such a civilization is highly idealistic and spiritual.

A "materialistic" civilization, he said, was one limited by matter and incapable of transcending it.[4] What if the Socialist Party candidate for governor of Ohio called the national musical instrument of America "the cash register"?[5] In retrospect, Norman Thomas would say, thoughtfully, ". . . we had what seemed like dazzling

---

[1] See Paul Arthur Schilpp, "Is Western Civilization Worth Saving?" *World Tomorrow*, XI (September, 1928), pp. 369-371.

[2] Charles A. Beard in his introduction to a volume he edited, *Whither Mankind?* (New York, 1928).

[3] In Kirby Page, ed. (New York, 1928), pp. 3–24.

[4] Hu Shih, "Civilizations of East and West," in *Whither Mankind?* pp. 40-41.

[5] Joseph W. Sharts, April 13, 1928.

prosperity in the twenties . . .," [6] and a keen observer looking back from 1932 judged, "The period from 1922 to 1929 constitutes a clearly defined epoch, bounded on both sides by severe depressions. . . ." [7]

It was by no means known in 1928, of course, that the future held depression, rampant fascism, a major war, and thermonuclear threats—or worse. Yet a few close observers did not miss the menace to self-government posed by the warning of Benito Mussolini to the Italian Senate: "To give power to the masses and abandon them to themselves—which amounts to giving them over to groups, parties and demagogues—signifies practically the ruin of the State and anarchy." [8] Adolph Hitler was then unknown to all but his intimate associates. The Soviet Union seemed torn within by Trotskyite dissention. Rumors of a retreat in that country from the early communist objectives of the Bolshevik Revolution, plus her observable inability to force her ideologies on other nations by strength of arms, tended to reduce earlier world interest in the Russian "experiment." While civil liberties were being infringed in the U.S.S.R., and private economic enterprise—except in agriculture—had almost been eliminated, it did not seem at that time a matter for general concern, except among those residing under the Red Flag of Communism. [9] Said a top government official, "the mass of the peasantry, as yet, does not at all embrace our . . . plans for developing the economy and socialist construction, and is not inspired by them." [10]

An effort of the Red Chinese to capture power on the Asiatic mainland in the name of Communism had failed in the middle of the twenties, and it was in 1928 that Hirohito, 124th of the im-

[6] Thomas to Oral History Project, Columbia University, Spring, 1949 (a typed transcript), p. 72.

[7] Charles Merz, reviewing Frederick C. Mills, *Economic Tendencies in the United States* (New York, 1932), in *New York Times,* January 8, 1933.

[8] *New York Times,* November 9, 1928.

[9] Roger Baldwin of the American Civil Liberties Union gave the Soviet government the benefit of nearly every doubt in his book, *Liberty Under the Soviets* (New York, Vanguard Press, 1928), but in January, 1930, he inserted a new "author's note" which warned that the book should be modified by the reader "in order to shift more emphasis upon the machinery and policies of repression, less upon the liberties." (Page xv.) On the Soviet economy, see Oleg Hoeffding, *Soviet National Income and Product in 1928* (New York, 1954), a RAND Corporation study.

[10] Quoted in *ibid.,* 89 n.

perial Japanese line, began his day of enthronement by kneeling before the shrine of the Sun Goddess and invoking her aid in guaranteeing perpetual prosperity and happiness. If Great Britain faced a period of steadily worsening economic stress, few persons recognized all of its larger causes or future consequences; still, the rise of its Labour Party entranced many of the class-conscious overseas. The World War seemed to be an aberration of the past, for had not the Kellogg Peace Pact promised a future in which war would be forever outlawed?

If some financiers and businessmen had been engaging in sharp practices in those years, the facts gained few headlines. If certain bankers (behind the scenes) had carried their trust too lightly in the blind belief that evil days would come no more, neither they nor their depositors seemed aware of the disaster latent in such myopia. If a hierarchy of interlocking directorates and a maze of sometimes mythical holding companies had muddled the nation's financial waters, the handful of uncertain protesters were virtually unheard. There was little demand for strong governmental regulation of Wall Street—or of anything else. If the farmers of the nation protested that they were not sharing fully in national prosperity, urban citizens were unable to get unduly alarmed over the alleged plight of those who had cried "wolf" too often.

One day late in 1929 it would become evident to those who played the stock market that the economic dislocation which had been a lasting by-product of World War I had not yet done its worst. Soon it would gather the strength of a hurricane and sweep the financial structures of many nations before it. World trade was quietly out of balance in 1928, automobile sales were down, and gold was draining away, but it would have been next to impossible at the time to convince the manufacturers of America, or the bulk of the public, that stark disaster lay ahead.

The American press lavished its attention in the spring of 1928 on intrepid aviators who attempted long and exhausting flights. The timid and vicariously adventurous of the world rejoiced to see this evidence that space and time were taking a long overdue beating. The success of Al Jolson in the first "talking picture," *The Jazz Singer,* in 1927 had heralded the birth of a new medium of entertainment. Said westerner Ray Lyman Wilbur of the 21 national parks at the time, "No other people ever had or ever will have such a wealth of sylvan retreats or natural wonders." Visitors to the parks in the fifteen years before 1928 had climbed from 250,000 to 3,000,000. There were organized movements to prevent "billboard blight" on highways, to improve state capitols, to plan zoological gardens and city recreational areas, and to organize from scratch some better communities. Indeed, it was in 1928 that the American Civic Association, then twenty-four years old, was incorporated, and a Better Homes Movement grew from 760 participating communities in 1924 to 5,648 five years later.[11]

Americans tended to be self-satisfied when they were told, repeatedly, that more children were attending college than ever before. Over 350 cities were being serviced by air mail, and in the large cities the constant construction of skyscrapers was worth no more than passing comment.

Whatever faults of earlier years America retained in the late 1920s, it held its appeal to the ambitious of many nations. Nearly a third of a million persons entered as immigrants in 1928, half of them from Europe. While the immigrant torrent of earlier years had been legislated into an orderly stream (so that the six 12-month periods which had each brought more than a million immigrants lay over a decade behind), the bright hope of emigrating to the promised land remained embedded in foreign hearts. More persons were naturalized in 1928 than in any previous year, a figure not to be surpassed in the 1930s.[12]

The year 1928 seemed to men and women alike to be a peak year in the Jazz Age: the age of the golden glow. Americans in positions of leadership usually tolerated, ignored, or laughed at voices raised in pointed criticism. "The golden age men have dreamed of was almost realized," said Winston Churchill to an

[11] American Civic Annual, (Washington D. C., 1929), pp. 5-6, 40.

[12] U. S. Bureau of the Census, Historical Statistics of the United States (Washington, D. C., 1949), tables on pp. 33 and 37-38. The preparation of this key tabular grouping has made historical analyses far more easily accomplished. By gathering in one place many of the best tables from government and private publications, it scored a major breakthrough for the researcher. All the many subsequent references to it are to tabular pages.

American editor a few years later, "but somehow it slipped through your hands." [13]

II

The American businessman and manufacturer came close to being, in 1928, heroes of an admiring world. A scholarly observer has written, "In that year the prestige of businessmen was higher than that of any other class. . . ." [14] Even Sidney and Beatrice Webb departed long enough from their efforts to convert Great Britain into a socialist state to concede key premises that most leaders in the United States insisted were true. The Webbs said that modern Americans were descended from early settlers who had been "specially selected for energy, adventurousness, and relative emancipation from the old ruts of custom and convention." The later immigrants to America were conceded to be "distinctly superior in mental and physical strength to those who were left behind," while Americans—blessed with the possession of a vast continent—had developed a profusion of riches that staggered one's imagination. Wrote the humanitarian but decidedly collectivist-minded Webbs,

> And both the existence of so extensive a population and the production of so great an aggregate of wealth, have been made possible by the ability of the American inventors and the American employers, who have shown themselves not only equal to their continually expanding opportunities, but also (in assiduity, courage, and enterprise, and in open-minded readiness to apply new ideas and new processes) possessed of a peculiar genius for industrial development that has left the Old World amazed and admiring.[15]

Such hearty praise of the American businessman would go out of fashion shortly with the end of the prosperous times which had made such evaluations seem singularly inevitable.

[13] Writes William L. Chenery, longtime editor of Colliers, "The depression of the early 'Thirties was on and that gave him [Churchill] his text. He talked about the magnificent prosperity of the 'Twenties and the widespread distribution of the good things in life to nearly all classes of Americans." Then Chenery quoted him verbatim. *So It Seemed* (New York, 1952), p. 212.
[14] Ralph D. Casey, "Party Campaign Propaganda" *Annals,* 179, May, 1935, 104.
[15] Sidney and Beatrice Webb, "Labor," in *Whither Mankind?*, pp. 127-128.

That 1928 was prosperous when compared with many past years (and particularly with 1922) seemed undeniable to most contemporaries; yet the sunny day had clouds. It was assumed that increased production and improved distribution would, in time, eliminate most poverty, clean out the worst slums, and paint the shacks of worthy tenant farmers. Yet it was all too evident that there were still some without work and others poorly paid. There was enough poverty in the land, especially in cities and migrant labor camps, to shock reformers. Some Americans still worked long hours under unhealthful conditions. The humanitarian, the sensitive, and the observant of many generations in America had not forgotten the existence of these unfortunates.

But on the top of the heap there were some unthinking enough to assert that there was no suffering anywhere in the land. Overly self-righteous Henry Ford was quoted as saying that breadlines did not exist in the United States. He also erred when he tossed off the remark that if there was any unemployment it was because the unemployed did not *want* to work.[16] Yet for photographs of a breadline, contemporaries could glance at the popular *Literary Digest* for April 7, 1928, to see a long line of the "unemployable" [17] in New York City. And gifts of $67 million to community chests in 1928 showed the awareness in many American hearts that there was still human misery.

While there were serious blots on the total economic picture, particularly in the form of grossly overextended credit, most agreed in essence with the spirit of the observation that "nearly everywhere throughout the United States business and industry are prosperous," despite "readjustments." The fact was thought by the *Christian Science Monitor* "too completely established to require proof." [18] People looked forward to the better days which were assumed to be ahead. They also reflected that there had been noticeable improvement in the material well-being of Americans over a span of years. Secretary of Labor James J. Davis found that

[16] Henry Ford to newspapermen in England. *New York Times,* April 7, 1928.
[17] How these persons felt was brought out vividly by John B. Seymour through using quotations from writings of the once down-and-out. "The Unemployable" (Unpublished Master's thesis, Dept. of Economics, Stanford University, 1922).
[18] Editorial, *Christian Science Monitor,* May 14, 1928.

science had shortened the work day, lightened the burdens of the laboring man by giving him steam and electric power to replace his muscles, and freed him to enjoy life in a way unknown even to the kings of old. "Today nearly every laboring man in the United States has time to think, and he owes this mostly to science," he concluded.[19]

III

In the perspective of decades one would like to say something definitive on the true nature of *prosperity* in 1928. Hotly contested as a political issue by contemporaries, the ingredients of that prosperity do not reduce readily to accurate slogans. Still, in perspective, one can say with assurance that 1928 was more prosperous than the earlier 1920s and the subsequent 1930s. Of course, it was less prosperous than the air-conditioned and TV'd years after World War II. The general supremacy of 1928 compared with immediately preceding and following years is unassailable, however. It deserves to be better known.

That hours of work had decreased and the size of weekly pay checks had gone up was clear to contemporaries who could recall the turn of the century.[20] (The coal miners, workers in a sick industry, were a glaring exception. [21]) Southern wages lagged behind, and the income of farm workers was still below the highs of World War I. Textile and shoe workers also trailed.[22] Production workers in manufacturing earned an average of 56 cents an hour compared with 19 cents in 1909 and $1.02 in war-inflated 1945. Weekly earnings in 1928 were $24.97 (1909, $9.84; 1945, $44.39).[23] While the value of the dollar did peculiar things in this span of years, there is little serious questioning of the concept that real wages increased greatly, so that one's income bought more and more goods, in the first quarter of the twentieth cen-

[19] Address at Battle Creek, Michigan on "Science and the Worker." Read for him in his absence. *New York Times*, January 7, 1928.
[20] See various tables in *Historical Statistics*, pp. 67–71.
[21] *Ibid.*, p. 68, quoting the pioneering work of Paul Douglas on real wages.
[22] *Ibid.*, p. 70.
[23] *Ibid.*, p. 67, relying on Bureau of Labor Statistics, *Handbook of Labor Statistics*.

tury.[24] Hours of work per week dropped, meanwhile, from the 51-hour average of Taft and 45.6 of Harding to 44.4 in 1928.[25]

With the reality of greater purchasing power and decreasing hours of work, American workmen *on the average* had statistical grounds for optimism. On the other hand, the highest tenth of people receiving income got over a third of over-all earnings, while the lowest tenth got a mere 1.8 per cent. Here was maldistribution to be sure, although it had long been the nature of humankind that neither heredity factors, early environment, nor the will to succeed were distributed equally anywhere on the planet. The upper half of American wage earners got 77 per cent; the lower half 22 per cent.[26] Moreover, maldistribution of wealth was geographic by sections as well as structured vertically by classes. Per capita wealth was far higher in the predominantly urban Middle Atlantic States, for example, than in the rural South, the dollar figures for even Texas being far below those of California or Oregon. [27] There was variable awareness of this irregularity in the prosperity pattern.

Neither income nor wealth, impressive though they were in bare statistics when compared with lands overseas, sufficed to soothe the sensitivities of some who toiled at the time. An official of the National Women's Trade Union League reported in graphic terms on the holes she found in tenement prosperity:

> I wonder whether the time has not come for us to consider that our demands upon industry ought to be for a certain guaranteed number of weeks of employment. I do not see how we can go on in this disastrous way, never knowing what the next week

[24] National Industrial Conference Board Chart Service, No. 225, March, 1930; No. 227, April 1930, etc. "On the average, the workers of Europe can with their weekly wages purchase only 35 per cent of the comfort in food and housing accommodations which is at the command of workers in the United States." N.I.C.B., Economic Explanation, Chart 206, May, 1929, from I.L.O. figures. See also N.I.C.B. *Bulletin,* January 15, 1928, which states that the real wages of factory workers in 1927 were about 33 per cent above the prewar level.

[25] *Historical Statistics,* p. 67.

[26] *Ibid.,* p. 15, following 1929 approximations put together by the N. I. C. B. After nearly five years of the New Deal (1937), there had been but an insignificant shift to 78.4 and 21.2. The bottom tenth got 3.4 per cent in 1910, but only 1.0 in 1937. The top tenth, 33.6 per cent in 1934, had 34.4 in 1937. *Ibid.*

[27] National Industrial Conference Board Chart Service, No. 224, February, 1930. The writer greatly appreciated the courtesies extended by the N.I.C.B., which opened many files for my study in 1952.

will bring. . . . I think the time has come when we must demand that of industry, as a definite responsibility, and that is to
guarantee to the people in that industry some security, some
economic security, which there is not today.
. . . You may have a leisure wage or a cultural wage this week
and next week apply to the charity organization to pay your
rent. That is a very unhealthy condition. It is terrible to live on
the brink of something all the time, in a condition where you
don't know whether you can continue your child at school or
whether you can buy him the clothes he needs or any of the
other necessities that mean life today.[28]

Even so, the nation as a whole was fantastically rich in 1928 in
terms of the passage of centuries and the comparative wealth of
continents. Americans filed only 111,232 income tax returns in
1928, gross taxable income totaling $8,635,588,000. While all
income came to $78.7 billion,[29] there is little question that ex-
emption from paying income taxes brought no comfort to those
who suffered in urban sweatshops, or who counted and recounted
annual cash incomes of only a few hundred dollars on bleak farms
in remote, kerosene-lighted communities.

IV

Old men in the labor movement nevertheless brought long mem
ories to bear on the nature of present prosperity and rejoiced. The
president of the Bricklayers, Masons, and Plasterers Union in a
farewell speech to his union vividly recalled that in the early days
of the union "men worked, ate and slept, virtually slaves to their
hard and poorly paid tasks." The eight-hour day had arrived, and
a five-day week was on the way. "We have come forward by
leaps," he judged. "The speed of the last half century has been
phenomenal." He could hardly begin to describe what had happened in his lifetime.

[28] Rose Schneiderman to the convention of the N.W.T.U.L., Washington, D. C.,
May 8, 1929. Typed Proceedings, 1929, p. 173, N.W.T.U.L. Papers, Library of
Congress.

[29] U. S. Treasury reports, used by Leonard J. Calhoun, *How Much Social Security
Can We Afford?* (New York, 1950), p. 30.

Who among us went home to a piano or a phonograph at that time [1910]? These may indeed be called material things, but they are some of the material evidences of a growing betterment of life that goes far beyond the material. They are the material evidences of a growing freedom, a growing culture among men and women, a growing ability to possess the beautiful, the enriching, the ennobling, and above all a growing ability to order our own lives in the way that we believe best. Who among us but has not a better home today than then, and who among us but looks forward to a rising generation that shall enjoy far more than we enjoy or dream of enjoying?

He anticipated more prosperity and expected wages to continue spiraling ever higher.[30] The President of the Minnesota Federation of Labor predicted "a new dawning as far as relationships between employer and employee is concerned. There seems to be a realization on the part of the captains of industry that some of the things that organized labor has advocated have been just."[31]

American business called itself "prosperous" even though the statistics on which it relied when passing judgment were fragmentary by modern standards.[32] Many in responsible positions knew the textile and bituminous coal industries to be sick, however,[33] so that bitter assertions to this effect were not a surprise.[34]

The Democratic candidate for governor of New York in 1928, Franklin D. Roosevelt, chose his words with discrimination when evaluating prosperity. "I hope," he said, "that if the Democratic Party comes to power in Washington we will be able to have a better rounded-out prosperity—that we will have it all over the United States instead of just in spots." [35] As Charles A. Beard put it at the time, "One industry may be very prosperous while others

[30] President William J. Bowen on his retirement from office. Bricklayers, Masons and Plasterers *Proceedings, 1928,* 8-9.
[31] E. George Hall, August 21, 1928, quoted in a clipping in George Hall Papers, Box 5, Minnesota Historical Society.
[32] The N.I.C.B. admitted that "the statistical picture of business conditions, despite the enormous growth of business information, is still fragmentary and suggestive, rather than complete and definitive." *N.I.C.B. Bulletin,* January 15, 1928, 1.
[33] See James J. Davis' admission in *Trade Union News* (Philadelphia), October 7, 1926.
[34] See J. B. Dale, A. F. of L. general organizer, "Let Us be True to Ourselves," *Labor Clarion* (San Francisco), September 2, 1927, pp. 8-9.
[35] Address at Susquehanna, Penna., October 17, 1928. In Drafts and Reading Copies File, Speeches of F. D. R., 1921–1929, Roosevelt Papers, Hyde Park, N.Y.

are in a state of depression. Miners may be starving while railway conductors and engineers are living well and making large deposits in their union banks."[36] Common labor is grossly underpaid, lamented a union editor.[37]

Still, there was a vast flow of goods to consumers in those years,[38] and the value of the nation's assets climbed like the hero Lindbergh, high in the blue. Not for a decade after the stock market crash of 1929 would the total national wealth again reach the figure of $340.6 billions.[39] Valuation of the nation's telephone systems, railroads, pipelines, water works, electric light and power stations, and motor vehicles climbed ever higher in the 1920s.[40] Stocks of goods in the hands of merchants increased annually. Property values also rose, and there was much new construction. (Thus the value of the land and buildings on Manhattan Island soared from $3½ billion at the turn of the century to over $12½ billion in 1928.[41])

Many informed contemporaries admitted that the nation's farmers had not shared in the prosperity of the Coolidge years. Yet, even here, the mosaic was many-hued. The prices of cotton, potatoes, and many fruits declined in the late 1920s,[42] and the number of cattle was the lowest since 1913.[43] The value of farm horses was down. While cows gave far more milk than ever before in history, the beginning of mechanized farming caused economic heartaches as the value of each horse and mule dropped alarmingly. From less than a thousand tractors in the America of 1909, the total reached 782,000 in 1928. American farms had more chickens, turkeys, and eggs than ever before, but prices were shaky.[44] Farm indebtedness had hit new highs, 1921-1924, but the figure was down somewhat in 1928; farm bankruptcies were

[36] *The American Party Battle* (New York, 1929), p. 9.
[37] *Labor Clarion,* October 7, 1927.
[38] See decade by decade averages by Simon Kuznets, *National Product Since 1869* (New York, 1946), p. 119 and *Historical Statistics,* p. 15.
[39] *Ibid.,* p. 11.
[40] *Ibid.* But motor vehicle valuation and sales wavered in 1927 and 1928.
[41] *Ibid.*
[42] *Ibid.,* pp. 108-110.
[43] *Ibid.,* p. 101.
[44] *Ibid.* Generalizations based on tables, pp. 100-105.

also in decline.[45] Gross farm income, $13½ billion during the year 1928, would shoot down to half of that four years later.[46] While many farmers owned their homes, farm tenancy was increasingly common as the Presidential Election came into view. There was no question, however, that most tenants were young; tenants comprised nearly nine out of ten farmers below age 25, but only one out of five of the group aged 55–64. Illustrative of unevenness in the land of opportunity, however, tenancy among whites in the South was 47 per cent; for Negroes (six decades out of slavery) it was a discouraging 79 per cent.

The twenties were a decade of housing construction. Not until the years following World War II would the nation witness such a boom in family housing. (The 1925 total, indeed, stood unsurpassed until 1948.) The figure of 753,000 city-and-town housing units started in 1928 was a striking contrast to the low point of 93,000 in 1933.[47] (Moreover, all construction contract figures for 1928 dwarf those of the thirties.[48])

It is only in the full knowledge of such economic realities as these that one can understand the optimistic psychology of the late twenties and thereby give a properly sympathetic hearing to contemporary evaluations of prosperity as incontrovertible reality. Let us take "the attitude of assurance and confidence," said the National Industrial Conference Board on January 12, 1928, "viewing with skepticism prophecies of great change for the better or the worse, on the ground that our economic life today has too broad a base and too solid a foundation to warrant any expectation of either catastrophies or miracles." [49]

V

In view of undocumented charges of malnutrition, ill health, and wholesale death from "exploitation" leveled by the Communists of

[45] *Ibid.,* p. 11.
[46] *Ibid.,* pp. 99, 112.
[47] *Statistical Abstract of the United States* (Washington, D. C., 1950), p. 722.
[48] *Ibid.,* p. 723. Disregards expenditures by P.W.A., etc.
[49] "Survey of American Business Conditions in 1927," N.I.C.B. *Bulletin,* January 15, 1928, 101.

1928 as they surveyed the national welfare, one may examine *the record* with profit. Infant mortality, over 100 per 1,000 in two years of the World War, was down to 68.7 in 1928.[50] Longevity for whites was ten years greater than at the turn of the century,[51] modern medical practice, public health sanitation, and better nutrition probably being chiefly responsible. Statistics on basic food consumption per capita in that day offer no evidence for any allegations of undernourishment of Americans as a whole. The sheer volume of food produced had risen by 25 per cent in a quarter of a century, responding to population growth. People ate less meat, but canned fruits and vegetables were gaining in popularity. Citrus fruits gained new markets, and fresh vegetables appeared on tables as meat prices rose. The amount of fresh milk consumed per capita was similar to the quantity in 1941, and the people of 1928 disposed of more butter, eggs, and cheese. Taste for sugar and poultry was roughly similar in both years. Coffee, increasingly the beverage of leisure moments, gained steadily in popularity.[52] Deaths from t.b., diphtheria, and typhoid fever were lower than ever in 1928, while the increased age of the population and its urbanization were related to a rise in deaths due to heart disease and cancer.[53]

The 120 million Americans of 1928 were slightly more "urban" than "rural"—continuing the new balance first ascertained in the census of 1920.[54] Among the people of the forty-eight states were nearly 14 million foreign-born and 12 million Negroes. People lived closer to one another than in the days of John Adams or William McKinley, for the density of six persons per square mile in 1800 had become 25 in 1900 and 41 thirty years later.[55] The "citified" group had grown to become more than three times its rural rival.[56]

[50] *Historical Statistics*, p. 215.
[51] *Ibid.*, p. 45.
[52] *Ibid.*, pp. 52-54, from Dept. of Agriculture estimates. See also its *Consumption of Food in the United States, 1909–1948* (Washington, D. C., 1949), especially p. 123.
[53] *Historical Statistics*, p. 48.
[54] "Urban" means people in incorporated places of more than 2,500 inhabitants, in general.
[55] *Ibid.*, pp. 25-26.
[56] *Ibid.*, pp. 29. "Citified" here means nonfarm, thus includes "townsfolk."

While in metropolises it was notoriously a day of bootleg whis-
key, doubtful gin and bathtub beer, of flappers and flasks, and of
selected items in the only partially accurate stereotype of the Jazz
Age, the American family endured. The marriage rate of 9.8 per
thousand in 1928 was indistinguishable from the 9.6 of the Reconstruction era.[57] And the divorce rate of 1.7 was midway between
the 1867 figure of 0.3 and the 1945 total of 3.5. The trend of the
1920s in the creation of broken families was not markedly upward.
Mark Sullivan, a keen metropolitan newspaperman, observed cou-
rageously, "I think that at any time during the Twenties the essential standards, and the practices under them, were on the whole
rather more wholesome than in the past." [58]

Always a restless people, Americans continued in the twenties
their migratory habits, aided by Model T Fords or the equivalent,
and by newly paved highways or washboard roads. Still, the same
percentage of the native-born lived in their home states at the
close of the decade as had been the case in 1850.[59] But national
migration was no longer chiefly a Westward Movement. To be sure,
over five million eastern-born lived in the West. But a million and
a half western-born lived in the East. Nearly two million northern-
born were to be found in the South, while over three million from
Dixie resided in the North (nearly half of them Negroes).[60] America's human sectionalism was diluted.

VI

The precise extent of *unemployment* was an issue in 1928 among
labor leaders, politicians—and those affected. The A. F. of L.
began a pioneering unemployment survey in autumn, 1927, basing

[57] *Ibid.,* p. 49. From 1867 to 1945 the marriage rate never dropped below 8.0 or
rose above 13.2. The "Companionate" or experimental marriage was a figment of
the imaginations of a few hip-flasked and sardonic city commentators of the day.

[58] Mark Sullivan, *Our Times* (New York, 1935), VI, 396. The sober student of
the period tends to recoil from such superficial accounts of the era as that of Allen
Churchill, *The Year the World Went Mad* [*1927*] (New York, 1960), whose concluding chapter is "End of the Big Shriek." A good account is George H. Knoles
The Jazz Age Revisited (Stanford, 1955), which shows how British observers often
saw just what they wanted and told what would sell.

[59] *Historical Statistics,* p. 30. The percentage was 67.3.

[60] *Ibid.,* pp. 30-31.

it on reports from certain unions in twenty-three scattered cities. This "Survey of Business" showed noticeable percentages of unemployment among building trades workers (18 per cent), metal trades workers (7 per cent), and printing trades members (4 to 5 per cent).[61] Over-all, in 1928, the survey seemed to show variations by months and by areas (18 per cent in January to 10 per cent in November).[62] To some Republican businessmen, however, talk of *any* unemployment was called "a straw man." [63] Equally biased collectors of data urged, however, that "the nation must know that there is unemployment and its extent." [64] The National Industrial Conference Board, more interested in facts than propaganda, reported wryly at the time that nobody had any reliable facts on *how many* were unemployed. "The fact is that we have no adequate statistics available in this country for even estimating unemployment with a fair degree of accuracy." [65]

As of May 17, the public could take its choice of 1,874,050 (Secretary of Labor), more than 4,000,000 (Labor Bureau, Inc.), 5,796,920 (junior Senator from New York), more than 8,000,000 (senior Senator from Minnesota).[66] To one eager Democrat "the number of men out of work around here [Kansas City] is appalling."[67] Norman Thomas found discontent and unemployment in the Middle West.[68] But the A. F. of L. in August reported steady declines in unemployment.[69] And the Federation was by no means ready to request unemployment insurance, although some state federations did so. The Federation wanted to be convinced of the

---

[61] Philip Taft, *The A. F. of L. from the Death of Gompers to the Merger* (New York, 1959), pp. 29-30.
[62] A. F. of L. Circular Letter, December 31, 1928, A. F. of L. Papers.
[63] Advertisement, Patterson-Andress Co., *New York Herald-Tribune*, March 24, 1928. Sent to President Coolidge by the company. File 1917, Coolidge Papers, Library of Congress.
[64] Secretary, Labor College of Philadelphia, in a circular letter gathering data, March 21, 1928. In Socialist Party Papers, Duke University.
[65] Magnus W. Alexander, President, N.I.C.B., in *Twelfth Annual Report* (New York, 1928) pp. 1-2. See also editorial, *New York Times,* March 28, 1928.
[66] *Ibid., passim.*
[67] A newspaperman to Frank P. Walsh, October 12, 1928, Walsh Papers, New York Public Library.
[68] *New York Times,* August 27, 1928.
[69] *Ibid.,* The *Brotherhood of Locomotive Firemen and Enginemen's Magazine,* LXXXV (October, 1928), 310, found more re-employment and the hiring of new employees later in the year.

wisdom of such legislation "beyond peradventure of a doubt" before taking "so big and so important" a step. Still, unemployment was "the outstanding problem of modern life." [70]

The Republican administration view on the jobless was that two million reached working age each year; it took time for them to be placed; then there were temporary shutdowns, migration of several hundred thousand from farm to city, coal field problems, immigration, Florida hurricanes, and Mississippi floods.[71] There was no concession here. But the Democratic officials of New York City and State found sufficient persons drifting into their areas to make public works activity at least a possibility.[72] In retrospect, a leading economist has simply given an N.I.C.B. figure of 1.9 million unemployed and left the matter at that. [73] We must do substantially the same.

The 1928 American labor force (to shift now to the *employed*) was only 21 per cent agrarian. Women had grown from 16 per cent of the labor force in 1890 to 22 per cent.[74] There were 46,057,000 of the employed, or almost half the population over ten years of age. Thus the unemployed came to somewhat less than 4 per cent of gainful workers at the time.[75] While 28 per cent of the nation's laboring men were still unskilled, this was a decrease from the 36 per cent of 1910. During those same years the percentages of semi-skilled, skilled, foremen, clerical, and professional categories all increased substantially.[76]

Urban America found a need for a diversity of occupations which could scarcely have been said to exist in the middle of the nineteenth century. "The cult of beauty has spread like wildfire," reported the National Women's Trade Union League, "and thousands of young women have entered the trade. The young women

[70] William Green to Matthew Woll, May 22, 1928; Woll to Green, n.d. (received May 21); Woll to Green, May 29, 1928, A.F. of L. Papers, Wash., D.C.
[71] Secretary of Labor Davis, *New York Times*, March 27, 1928.
[72] *Ibid.*, February 8, 20, and March 6, 1928.
[73] George Soule, *Prosperity Decade, From War to Depression: 1917-1929* (New York, 1947), pp. 318-323. From 1926 to 1929 agricultural employment remained constant, coal mining decreased, manufacturing and steam railroads showed slight decreases, and electric light and power employment increased.
[74] *Historical Statistics*, pp. 63-64.
[75] N.I.C.B., *The Economic Almanac for 1946-1947*, pp. 263-264.
[76] *Historical Statistics*, computed from p. 65.

complain bitterly of long hours on aching feet, low pay, and few holidays or evenings off." [77] *Since 1870 the population had tripled.* But the number of electricians had increased 700 times; plumbers 21 times; barbers, beauticians, and manicurists 15 times, and janitors and sextons 105 times. Musicians and music teachers increased ten times; designers and draftsmen 77 times; and bookkeepers, accountants, and cashiers 24 times.[78] The 128,265 teachers of 1870 were dwarfed by the 1,044,016 counted by the census of 1930.

In such figures may be found much justification for even the most enthusiastic and laudatory words of praise mouthed by platform speakers of the day. The plain fact was that the people of the United States were more sanitary, more musical, and were getting more years of schooling than ever before. The gas lights had been going out and the electric lights going on. The telephone and the automobile had shortened the miles. The radio comforted the aged, children, and the disabled and homebound. It had been an amazing quarter century.

VII

In summary of industrial relations in 1928, the president of the Building Trades Department, A. F. of L., judged (after the election) that unions had achieved membership increases and financial successes during the year; there had been fewer strikes; wages had stabilized; and relations with employers had been friendly and cordial.[79] The number of strikes and persons engaged in strikes declined in the decade.[80] Prices remained relatively stable, 1923-1929, and real wages increased appreciably. Consumer goods like automobiles and radios took some of the increased income; so did

[77] N.W.T.U.L. of New York, looseleaf Convention Proceedings, 1926–1929. N.W.T.U.L. Papers.
[78] Computed from *Historical Statistics*, p. 66.
[79] William J. McSorley, A. F. of L. *Proceedings, 1928*, p. 41.
[80] Comparison of the periods 1916-1921, 1922-1925, and 1926-1930 shows: index number of strikes, 100, 37, 23; average number of workers involved, 1,798,809, 863,051, 244,949; average number of days strikes lasted, 29, 28, 23. H. M. Douty, "The Trend of Industrial Disputes, 1922-1930," *Journal of the American Statistical Association*, XXVII (June, 1932), 168-170.

housing and monthly bills for electric and telephone service. Installment-plan buying, ever more common, encouraged wage earners to live beyond their means. Thus workers had a stake in prosperity, and this is an important consideration in observing the nature of industrial inter-relationships.

Under the conditions described, the unions made little headway in organizing workingmen. A. F. of L. membership crept upward, 1926–1928 (by 92,097), but there was a gross decline, 1920–1928, from the postwar maximum of 5,047,800 to only 3,479,800. It brought scant comfort to union leaders to be able to say in exoneration that the prewar (1914) figure had been nearly a million less than 1928.[81] Still, similar declines were taking place in Great Britain at the time.[82]

Strikes were uncommon in 1928. To the president of the Minnesota Federation of Labor, this meant that "employers have met with employees or their representatives and differences have been adjusted in a truly peaceful way."[83] But early in the year, striking miners were suffering what A. F. of L. headquarters called "unspeakable misery and woe." [84] Statistically, the truth was that strikes ("work stoppages") during the year came to the smallest total in the twentieth century, for the 604 such events involved only 314,000 workers. What disputes there were arose from clashes over wages and hours (36 per cent), union organizing (36 per cent), and other reasons (28 per cent).[85] The modest strike figures are not surprising, since the fixed debts of workers normally climb during prosperity. In the days before possible eligibility for unemployment insurance and before the building of large union treasuries, a long strike could scarcely be afforded by individuals. Who will meet the installments? Thus the number, frequency, and effectiveness of strikes during periods of mature prosperity decline.[86] Nor was the A. F. of L. strike-minded. A general strike in

[81] Leo Wolman, *Ebb and Flow in Trade Unionism* (New York, 1936), p. 193.
[82] *Ibid.*, p. 239. On other countries, see his Table XII.
[83] Labor Day address of E. G. Hall, August 21, 1928. Clipping in Box 5, George Hall Papers, Minnesota State Historical Society.
[84] A. F. of L. Circular Letter, February 29, 1928, A. F. of L. Papers.
[85] *Historical Statistics*, p. 73.
[86] Thesis of Theodore Levitt, "Prosperity vs. Strikes," *Industrial and Labor Relations Review*, XI (January, 1953).

an American city was unthinkable. William Green wrote a union member, in those years,

> The American Federation of Labor is opposed to general strikes for any purpose. In 1911 it declared its disapproval of a general strike as proposed by the Confederation General du Travail which had submitted such a proposition to the International Secretariat. General or sympathetic strikes have never accomplished the purpose for which they are called. I hope, therefore, that you will not advocate any such proposal.[87]

Cooperation with employers and with the public was the union watchword.[88] Not for years, said a newspaper, had the relations between organized labor and the large employers been so satisfactory.[89] Thus an expert on the subject can summarize by saying that "between 1923 and 1929 the labor problem in the United States, regarded in terms of the subsidence of conflict, appeared to be on the road to peaceful solution." [90] Yet unions were far too weak to stick to their guns when hard pressed; while this could be praised as good citizenship, it was an inducement to some irresponsible employers to exploit tired workers and to place inordinate numbers of dollars into channels not well calculated to serve the best interests of wage earners. The day would come when such imbalances in industrial relations would be redressed, partly by union pressures, partly by government regulation, and partly by the "new" scientific management in industry; but in the twenties most employers and many union leaders thought that expansion of prosperity would, over a period of time, bring better things for all who labored.

Union leaders realized full well in 1928 that the unions were making little headway in total numbers, but they had other satisfactions which persuaded them that they were doing a good job. There was, for example, the coming of the forty-hour, five-day week in the garment industry. William Green predicted that a five-

---

[87] Green to George F. Crawford, Newark, N. Y. *(sic)*, April 19, 1926, A. F. of L. Papers.

[88] A Boston merchant wrote on "Cooperation" in the *American Federationist*, XXXV (July, 1928), 799.

[89] Editorial, *New York Times*, January 30, 1928.

[90] Leo Wolman, "Issues in American Industrial Relations," *Political Science Quarterly*, LII (January, 1937), 161.

day week would become general in the nation sooner than many thought, and he called it the Federation's chief ideal.[91] Some unions had been successful in business ventures and even in operating banks. In 1925 there had been 36 union banks, and the capital and surplus of the Federation Bank and Trust Company in New York rose from half a million in 1923 to more than forty times that in 1928.[92] There was, furthermore, the acceptance among some industrialists of the high-wage theories of Henry Ford—and of William Green. The A. F. of L. president said at Princeton University in 1926 that wages should not be kept low to save production costs; they should be high in order to increase purchasing power and create markets for increased production. In that case, lower costs would make the higher wages possible. The number of working hours would soon decrease. Green suggested that wages be based on production, not the cost of living. If production increased and wages failed to rise, who would buy?

> Among the masses of the American people there exists a potential buying power which can be made active. It is based upon the individual desire for the enjoyment of life and the realization of higher living standards. Working men and women desire better homes, comfortably furnished, suitable clothing and nourishing and substantial food. They also long for the enjoyment of educational advantages, music, art, literature and social advancement. They will satisfy these desires if their income will permit them to do so. They will buy, and buy freely, and thus increase the demand for manufactured goods.[93]

Cooperation, production, and "enlightened" union leadership were the paths to the better life, one judges from this and other expressions of contemporary opinion.

---

[91] *New York Times,* June 7, 1928.

[92] By 1931 there were but seven of these banks left, and three of those were being liquidated by 1935. Letter of Walter E. Spahr to *American Economic Review,* XXVI (March, 1936), 90.

[93] Published as a pamphlet, *Wage Theories* (Washington, 1926). Quotation from page 11. For a vigorous refutation of this interpretation, see Wilford I. King, "Wage Rates, Wage Costs, Employment, Wage Income and the General Welfare," *American Economic Review,* XXIX (March, 1939), 40. He wrote, "The whole high-wage, high purchasing-power theory seems to be based upon nothing more substantial than wishful thinking."

"Citadel of the Workers' Rights" (Drawn for *Labor* by John M. Baer)

VIII

To a leading Socialist of the day, the whole American union movement was then up against it, chiefly because it was "bending over backwards to convince big business and the labor exploiters of all kinds that it is one hundred per cent safe and conservative.

It lacks an ideal and a goal. . . ." [94] But the labor leaders had severe problems in the 1920s, and these have been insufficiently stressed by some critics. The problems of a union organizer in North Carolina, an experienced representative of the Textile Workers, graphically tell how great was the resistance of organized society to organized labor at the time. The few organizers worked all day but faced, said one, "tremendous odds." The organizer had real problems in the unorganized South. "He is followed wherever he goes; his hotel room is ransacked for papers; and if there is but one hotel in the town, the organizer will soon find that there is no longer a room for him in the establishment." Organizers from a single craft were helpless in the South in the absence of a strong state federation or of city centrals. The area needed help, for "our organizations are weak, our treasuries are small, and our enemies are many and powerful, and for that reason we need every bit of support that the American Federation of Labor and all international organizations can give." [95] The A. F. of L. soon sent this dismal report to the presidents of twenty-four major unions, stating that an organizer from headquarters would go to North Carolina in the spring, and that all addressees ought to emulate this.

There can be little doubt that the attitude of the public toward the present and the future in 1928 eased union leaders toward complacency and over-optimism. Their overemphasis on craft unionism was a fatal allegiance to tradition, especially in so far as organizing the automobile industry was concerned. Nevertheless, on August 1, 1928, the A. F. of L. Executive Council said it planned to organize the aviation industry. There were, over-all, major obstacles facing union leaders, most of them very impressive blocs to organization. The 1920s saw the spread of employer welfare capitalism. Stock-sharing plans, company pension programs, company magazines (700 in 1928) and some athletic programs were created in order to decrease employee discontent.

[94] James H. Maurer, president, Pennsylvania State Federation of Labor (just returned from Russia at the time) to Tom Mooney, March 22, 1928. Mooney Papers, Bancroft Library, University of California.
[95] Alfred Hoffman, "An Analysis of Problems Facing the American Labor Movement in North Carolina," quoted in a Circular Letter of May 7, 1928, A. F. of L. Papers.

These had their soothing effect on labor morale. Another factor in union distress was the spread of company unions. A well-financed and carefully organized open-shop drive also put the trade unions on the defensive. The ever-increasing consolidation of industry in the twentieth century and the intricate financial structure of American business in the years before the Crash made it difficult for union leaders to predict the success of any strike, for the ability of employers to absorb losses could not be estimated. William Green advised the Brotherhood of Sleeping Car Porters not to strike in 1928, despite his admission that they had ample provocation, because economic conditions were unfavorable; public opinion simply had not crystallized in support of their demands. [96]

Changing methods of manufacturing had destroyed many crafts and skills in the 1920s, so that many who had been skilled laborers were reduced to semiskilled or even manual labor status, whatever their daily wage rates might remain. Craft unionism thus became in part a victim of changing technological conditions, and this spelled doom to some craft union patterns. Migration of some industry from North to South and from East to West disturbed old patterns in still other ways.

It was in the mid-1920s that economic-determinist A. M. Simons, a keen observer, wrote that he and his wife were planning to write a book on "shifting of control in industry," saying,

> We think we see some tremendous movements carrying society along toward democratic, working-class control, that are operating with little regard to politics. . . . Consumer and employee ownership through stock distribution, employee management through unions and plant committees, leveling systems of taxation, more intelligent regulation, labor banking, and a host of similiar developments are really taking the control out of the hands of owners faster than any legislation has ever been able to do.[97]

This was scarcely a climate in which to expect labor leaders to stir up militant sentiments in the breasts of their followers. Secret instructions to A. F. of L. organizers in 1928 stated quite frankly

[96] *New York Times,* June 8, 1928.
[97] A. M. Simons to Charles Edward Russell, January 19, 1925, Simons Papers, Wisconsin State Historical Society.

that old appeals would not do in the new day. The organizer would have to be a *salesman*. Unions can do it better! Thus "insurance, savings, investments, leisure, study opportunities," *and* a chance to work would come through union membership. When "selling," organizers might take a lesson from the business world.[98]

Low-priced cars covered the highways in 1928, decreasing the old solidarity which union members sometimes shared socially when they lived closer together. Automobile registrations almost doubled from 1922 to 1928. As one union official put it,

> The Ford car has done an awful lot of harm to the unions here and everywhere else. As long as men have enough money to buy a second-hand Ford and tires and gasoline, they'll be out on the road and paying no attention to union meetings.

The predominantly square, black-painted cars cut across the plans of labor leaders. Wrote the A. F. of L. to all its units,

> It has been more than forty years since the first Labor Day was celebrated and these years have witnessed revolutions in industry and community life. Our celebration of the day should accept and utilize modern mechanisms and methods. The automobile and the raido probably have altered the habits of life of wage earners more than any other mechanical changes. It would be well to include specifically these two agencies in plans for a Labor Day celebration, for otherwise they may draw trade unionists away.[99]

The movies and the radio also weakened interest in unions by broadening the entertainment horizons of wage earners—whatever caustic criticism might be leveled at the quality of the offerings. Delighted with their new mobility and the ease of access to new forms of entertainment, large numbers of workingmen and their families had the resultant feeling that they were "getting ahead." If there was a tendency to ignore the appeals of radicals, there was an equal indifference to union organizers.[100]

An Australian took a sharp look at American trade unionism in 1928 and judged,

[98] A. F. of L., "Instructions to Organizers," (Washington, D. C., 1928), iii.
[99] Circular Letter, July 22, 1928, A. F. of L. Papers.
[100] Limited distribution of labor periodicals was also a handicap to unions. With higher dues, greater distribution of these magazines and newspapers would come in the 1930s and later.

With few exceptions, the workers in the mass-production industries have no industrial organizations comparable to the Australian trade-unions. They have no voice in determining wages,
hours, or conditions of labour. They have no protection against
the arbitrary will of the employers. . . . In the whole of North-
western America, Unionism—or rather, labour organization—
exists only by the tolerance of employers. So much free labour
is always available in the industrial cities that every job held by
a unionist could be filled a dozen times over.[101]

To a British observer, American unions sought to extend private
ownership and the capitalist system. By cooperation, the amount
of visible wealth would be increased and the division of wealth
would be just. To another visitor from overseas, the class war
simply did not exist in America.[102]

IX

As labor leaders contemplated the American economic and social landscape in the late 1920s, a spirit of optimism pervaded
their circles, showing itself in speeches, interviews by the daily
press, and articles in the labor press. The *Labor Clarion* of San
Francisco well summarized the current labor philosophy:

The program of the American Federation of Labor, the chief
labor body of this country, calls for education and calm consideration of every question that confronts the people, workers
and employers alike, and this plan of operation is the outgrowth
of long years of study and the experiences of people throughout
the world. We have the chance here to get whatever we desire
by appealing to the intelligence of the people and if, in any instance, we are unable to persuade them to our side of a question,
it is usually because we have not properly presented our case or
have, as rarely happens, gone off on unsound policies and tangled
purposes.[103]

Oriented in this way, *it was natural that, in general, the American
Federation of Labor did not usually look to government to solve*

[101] Hugh Grant Adam, *An Australian Looks at America* (London, 1928), pp. 80,
8. Written in 1927 for newspapers in Melbourne and Sidney.
[102] Paraphrased in Knoles, *op. cit.*, p. 85.
[103] "Mass Meeting Madness," (an editorial against radicalism and the use of
violence), *Labor Clarion*, August 12, 1927, p. 8.

its problems. Said William Green fervently, "We want the government to keep its hands off our throat. We do not want more of government, . . . we want less of government," Soviet Russia was a good example, he added, of what the Federation did *not* want.[104] The best thing government could do, it was felt, would be to give unions a chance to develop their economic strength. That meant that the court *injunction* against union activities, particularly during strikes —long a matter for bitter recriminations—would surely have to be the subject of restrictive legislation.

To grasp the significance of the injunction issue at the time and to show how it happened that the political activities of labor developed as they did in the Presidential Election of 1928, we will relive in summary, with organized labor, the political scene as it existed for them from William Jennings Bryan to Calvin Coolidge. This fascinating story will be the subject of the next chapter, which briefly traces through three decades the vicissitudes of the traditional path in labor politics.

First, however, in final delineation of the nature and mood of the twenties, it may be well to consider the conflicting opinions of several contemporaries. In a gloomy mood, the editor of the *Labor Clarion* wrote in 1927 that too many people were living in a fool's paradise, thinking only of automobiles, radios, player pianos, and other items purchased on the installment plan. "The serious things of life, just now at any rate, receive no attention, and things are allowed to drift without any direction." This was true to a large extent, he thought, in government, in trade unions, and in industrial affairs.[105] Not so, intimated Magnus W. Alexander, president of the National Industrial Conference Board. He spoke highly of the advantages of mechanization, saying,

> Our national prosperity and the diffusion of our wealth and income have been the "big news" in world affairs during recent years and a topic of conversation abroad in hut and palace alike. And this prosperity, as is now well understood abroad and at home, is identified with American industrial productivity—which is its foundation.[106]

[104] William Green, speech of reply to British labour delegates, A. F. of L. New Orleans convention, A. F. of L. *Proceedings, 1928,* 175–176.
[105] Editorial, *Labor Clarion,* July 29, 1927, p. 8.
[106] Twelfth Annual Report, N.I.C.B., *Mechanization (New York, 1928),* p. 3.

While the secretary-treasurer of the National Women's Trade
Union League charged that sweatshop conditions for women lived
on in such occupations as date picking, doll dress ruffle-making,
stockyard work, and among Negro women in cigar factories,[107]
the annual report of the Boston chapter reported in a more optimistic vein:

> Working conditions are better than they used to be, of course.
> The world does move. The long days of sweated exploitation,
> the inhumanly low wages, the unsanitary, unwholesome sur-
> roundings which were the lot of a generation ago have disap-
> peared under the combined attack of organized labor and of an
> aroused public opinion. The 48-hour week, the operations of the
> minimum wage, safety and health codes are now the order of
> the day.[108]

In just such differences of emphasis and choice of conflicting
economic and social facts when framing action, lay the seeds of
political disputation in the year 1928. There was disagreement on
how to measure the happiness of humanity. How was one to
guarantee the future of mankind? Candidates nominated for high
office disagreed on such fundamental matters. The wording of the
party platforms on which they would run reflected the lack of
consensus on means. Viewing America, those who spoke often relied on the particular to arrive at generalizations; others spoke in
generalities and overlooked particulars.

For many decades of self-government it had been like this in the
United States. There was a national heritage, to be sure; but in
evaluating its fundamental nature and its meaning for the present,
men of goodwill (and some who were largely self-seeking) often
failed to reach agreement. Particularly was this true in matters
concerned with earning a living, living the good life, and guaranteeing the future. Here was the heart of the economic basis for
American politics.

---

[107] Report of Secretary-Treasurer, N.W.T.U.L., 1926–1929. In looseleaf Convention Proceedings, 1929, N.W.T.U.L. Papers.
[108] Annual Report, 1928, p. 3. In *ibid.*, N.W.T.U.L. Papers.

Chapter 2

The Path of Traditional Labor Politics

BEFORE THERE COULD BE effective national political activity by organized laboring men in the United States, there first had to be enduring union organizations. Strong, stable labor unions in the nation have been a development of the twentieth century. It is not surprising, therefore, that it has been only in the comparatively recent past that the political desires of trade union leaders have received serious attention from platform makers and candidates for President.

To say this is not to deny that there existed a Workingmen's Party in the time of Andrew Jackson or to say that the National Labor Union from 1866 to 1872 had no political significance. Indeed, the Order of the Knights of Labor under the leadership of Terence V. Powderly had what one writer has called a broadly political and uplift program. Although the Knights of Labor had in theory hundreds of thousands of members, its rapid rise and even speedier fall reflected an overcentralized organization and inexperienced administration. The fact that the Knights and the craft unions could not reach a permanent understanding was important to its quick loss of influence after 1887.

I

The American Federation of Labor was founded in 1886 and soon assumed supremacy over the organized American labor movement. Established on craft rather than industrial lines and embracing a largely urban and Northeastern membership, the A. F. of L. soon had most of the union members in the United States. Under the strong leadership of the former cigarmaker, Samuel Gompers, it consistently avoided any temptation to form a political party of its own.

Gompers made it clear in several campaigns that he favored Bryan, but the support was personal on his part. And he said on several occasions that wealth and the bosses controlled government by controlling political parties. Socialist doctrines were consistently (although sometimes narrowly) rejected by A. F. of L. convention delegates, even though the formation of the Socialist Party of America in 1901 offered a unified and organized political alternative to the workers. Gompers repeatedly opposed third-party efforts, from whatever source they came. The formation of the I.W.W., the increased strength of American business, declines in membership, and the fact that no labor legislation of importance was passed in the years from 1900 to 1905 all served to make A. F. of L. leaders wonder in 1906 if the time had not come for them to try to gain more favorable consideration from government. Late in 1905 the trade unions in Great Britain succeeded in electing 52 labor members to Parliament, and the event had its effect in American trade union circles. Although it had not been thought when the Sherman Anti-Trust Act was passed in 1890 that it would apply to trade unions, the decision of the Supreme Court in the case of the Danbury Hatters showed that its provision saying "every contract, combination or conspiracy in restraint of trade is illegal" could cost the unions dearly. Other decisions aroused further resentment.

It seemed to Gompers by 1906 that there was nothing in the twenty-year tradition of the A. F. of L. that prevented an aggressive political policy during elections. Perhaps lobbying action against legislation was not really enough, any more. Yet endorsement of political parties remained anathema. Could there be a middle ground?

At a conference in Washington of the heads of the international unions belonging to the A. F. of L., a Bill of Grievances was prepared and presented on March 21, 1906, to the President and the Congress of the United States.[1] It asked action to remedy the defects in the eight-hour law, relief from excessive immigration and misuse of the injunction, and other matters. When little attention was paid to its demands, the A. F. of L. Executive Council issued on July 22, a "Campaign Programme" which stated that the first concern of all should be "the positive defeat of those who have been hostile or indifferent to the just demands of labor." Yet any "true friend to the rights of labor" should be supported.[2] Independent or "straight" labor candidates would be nominated wherever both parties ignored labor's demands. "If the British workmen, with their limited franchise, accomplished so much by their united action, what may we in the United States not do with universal suffrage?" it was asked. Principles were to be placed first; office, second. There was no intention of forming a political party, and "wherever possible, let labor elect its own men, but wisdom and foresight forbid the nomination of a labor man in a hopeless district, particularly when that action may result in the election of a man who is known to be a persistent opponent to the cause of labor, of justice and right."

Less than $10,000 was spent in 1906, but the Federation did succeed in obtaining much discussion of labor issues. It centered its fire on a Republican Congressman from Maine, Charles E. Littlefield, and succeeded in cutting down his margin of victory— even though such leading Republicans as Henry Cabot Lodge made speeches for him in his district. Lodge wrote Theodore Roosevelt afterwards:

> I spoke in Littlefield's district and I confess that I feel very anxious about the result. The question of whether there should be a Republican or a Democrat sinks into insignificance com-

[1] Printed in *Text Book of Labor's Political Demands* (Washington, A. F. of L., 1906), a pamphlet.
[2] Printed in *ibid.*, p. 36.

pared to the question whether Gompers shall dictate the choice
of Congressmen. . . . I . . . made my whole speech on the
question of the independence of Representatives and the perils
of dictation by non-political secret organizations. What I said
was very well received, but I know not what the effect really
was.[3]

Roosevelt agreed that it had been "more important to save Littlefield than almost anyone else who was up for Congress." [4] Later in
the campaign the President was at pains to point out that he had
taken "just as emphatically a position against the misdeeds of
labor as I ever have against the misdeeds of capital." [5]

Despite a sharp reduction in the majority held by the Republicans in the House of Representatives, the next two years saw no
improvement in the legal position of organized labor. In the election of 1908 Gompers led the A. F. of L. into open opposition to
the incumbent Republican Party. They "had set their hearts like
flint; they had no ears to hear," he wrote. Gompers disclaimed
being a Democrat, "that is, in the partisan sense." He then said the
words which would be repeated so often in following years.

> The American labor movement is not partisan to a political
> party; it is partisan to a principle, the principle of equal rights
> and human freedom.[6]

With variations, this sentiment would be repeated over and over
by orthodox trade unionists in following political campaigns. "Nonpartisanship" in this sense would be the watchword of labor in
politics. It was not the party; it was the individual candidate. It
was not really the candidate, either, it was only the principles—
the prolabor principles for which he stood. Here was labor's case.

Eugene V. Debs was a candidate for President in 1904 and ran
again in 1908 against Taft, but Gompers would have nothing to
do with the Socialist leader. "His past history," said the president
of A. F. of L., "is all in the direction of harming rather than helping the labor movement." Labor votes should not be wasted on

---

[3] Lodge to Roosevelt, September 10, 1906. *Selections from the Correspondence of
Theodore Roosevelt and Henry Cabot Lodge, 1884-1918* (New York, 1925), II, 230.
[4] Roosevelt to Lodge, September 12, 1906, *ibid.*, p. 231.
[5] Roosevelt to Lodge, October 16, 1906, *ibid.*, p. 247.
[6] This may or may not be the first utterance of the sentiment. President Gompers'
Report, A. F. of L. *Proceedings, 1908,* 34.

third parties, for the real battle was between the Republicans and the Democrats.[7] Not until 1924, when neither of the major parties was led by a candidate willing to make concessions to labor, would the Federation come obliquely to the aid of the presidential candidate of a new party in the political arena. Because in 1908 the Democratic Party was said to have made labor's contentions its own,[8] the American Federation of Labor would stand by its candidate for President and many of its other candidates. As they would on many later occasions, the labor leaders said they spoke "not only in our own interest, but in the interest of all the people of our country. . . ."[9] Organized labor would continue to insist that its voice was the voice of the people.

After the election of 1908 Gompers admitted to being somewhat disappointed with the results. Both "means" and "machinery" were necessary before real results could be expected.[10] An acute observer called the effort "a temporary makeshift thing" which had been forced on the labor leaders by a need for obtaining visible results for their followers quickly. He suggested a number of reasons why the results had been so meager.[11]

Late in the 1908 campaign President Roosevelt had come to the aid of Republican candidate William Howard Taft with an attack on the political activities of Gompers. That the President's typically vigorous words had been resented was apparent in the labor leader's postelection judgment of Roosevelt: "It is perhaps impossible to find in all our country another public man so intolerant, bitter, and relentless toward any man who happens to

[7] Editorial, *American Federationist*, XV (September, 1908), 736, 729–730. A general history of the Socialist Party is David A. Shannon, *The Socialist Party of America* (New York, 1955). (The present chapter was researched and written in virtually final form in 1950-1953.)

[8] *Ibid.* p. 727. See also "Protest to Congress," (1908) quoted in President Gompers' Report, A. F. of L. *Proceedings, 1908,* 33.

[9] Editorial, *American Federationist*, XV (August, 1908), 613.

[10] Editorial, *ibid.,* XV (December, 1908), 1064.

[11] Robert Hoxie, "President Gompers and the Labor Vote," *Journal of Political Economy,"* XVI (December, 1908), 693. Gompers wrote, however, that he believed that at least 80 per cent of the Federation had voted with its leaders. "I may add that I have had statements from some of the leaders of the political party which for the time being at least made our cause its own that the votes of the workers alone saved that party from utter, crushing oblivion." A. F. of L. *Proceedings, 1909,* 33.

be unable to agree with him."[12] When Roosevelt later sought office on a Progressive Party platform which offered virtually all that labor desired, there were personal as well as political reasons why the A. F. of L. leader did not come to his support.[13]

In 1910, the off-year elections resulted in a Democratic House of Representatives, and some union members were elected to Congress. The House by 1912 had passed a large number of bills greatly desired by the union leaders. The Democratic Party naturally received some credit for this from them, although some progressive Republicans had helped, too.[14] Since both the Progressive and Democratic Party platforms were considered infinitely superior to the Republican Party platform in 1912, the *American Federationist* ran praise for both platforms while heaping scorn on the G.O.P. Little was said about Roosevelt, however, and readers were often reminded of the past promises of the Democrats. The Executive Council contented itself with a reaffirmation of the political decisions reached in 1906 and did not endorse any Presidential candidate—*officially.* [15]

That the injunction can be traced as a major theme through American labor history goes without saying. Certainly the injunction was important to the A. F. of L. as early as 1891 when an antipicketing injunction hit Pennsylvania printers. The Federation thought the injunction a "weapon" restraining workmen from doing rightful and lawful things. By 1902 the injunction was to the unions second only to the eight-hour day for government employees, and it was claimed that personal freedom was at stake. A con-

---

[12] Editorial, *American Federationist,* XVI (January, 1909), 40.

[13] Gompers had other difficulties with Roosevelt in later years. See Samuel Gompers, *Seventy Years of Life and Labor* (New York, 1925) for his version of the incidents.

[14] For a proclamation of thanks, see *American Federationist,* XXIX (October, 1912), 814. A list of the measures appears in *ibid.,* XXIV (November, 1912), 889–890.

[15] Abstract of Executive Council Minutes, August 12-19, 1912. Printed in *ibid.,* pp. 851–857. Secondary works and the writings and speeches of labor leaders are in serious conflict on the question of whether the Executive Council of the A. F. of L. *endorsed* the Democratic candidate *officially* in 1908, 1912, 1916, and 1920. The present writer is prepared to say that it did not in any of those years. The strong leadership of Gompers in each campaign on behalf of Bryan, Wilson (especially in 1916) and Cox has obscured this point.

ference of 1908 called on Congress to do something about the injunction, and in 1912 Gompers urged President Wilson to do something about the problem.[16]

II

Samuel Gompers has told in his autobiography how he first viewed Woodrow Wilson with suspicion and later came almost to love him. There is little doubt that he was pleased with Wilson's success in 1912, and he gloated over the defeat of Taft, "the injunction judge," declaiming: ". . . it is not written in the history of the United States that ever a man who was a candidate for re-election to the Presidency of the United States was so utterly and humiliatingly defeated as Mr. Taft." [17]

With the Democratic Party in power in Washington after an absence of sixteen years, trade union leaders who had supported Bryan repeatedly, worked for a Democratic Congress in 1910, and read numerous promises of what would be forthcoming if the minority party ever obtained power, looked for their reward. They already had the office of Secretary of Labor, for Taft had reluctantly signed the bill creating the office at the very end of his term. Now they sought and found apparent relief from injunctions.

The Clayton Act of 1914 was thought to be the "Magna Charta of Labor." It said that the labor of a human being is not a commodity or an act of commerce. Whether the rest of the bill had been drafted in that spirit or not the labor leaders soon built up the act in many minds as the legal relief labor had been seeking.[18] Ex-President Taft grumbled that the new administration was "surrendering everything to Gompers. . . ." The Democratic Party, he alleged, had "boldly avowed its desire to make labor unions a favored class. . . ." [19] In 1915 came the Seamen's Act, and the

[16] Paragraph added in 1960 after reading Philip Taft's laboriously researched *The A. F. of L. in the Time of Gompers* (New York, 1957), pp. 289–300.

[17] Statement made by Gompers in convention debate. A. F. of L. *Proceedings, 1912*, p. 305.

[18] Lewis L. Lorwin, *The American Federation of Labor* (Washington, The Brookings Institution, 1933) contains a good survey of these events.

[19] Taft to Elihu Root, September 16, 1914. Quoted in Henry F. Pringle, *The Life and Times of William Howard Taft* (New York, 1939), II, 887.

name of its sponsor, Robert M. La Follette, was made a permanent jewel in labor's treasure chest.

It looked to A. F. of L. leaders as though the "nonpartisan" pressure tactics on behalf of friends and against enemies which the Federation had been pursuing had been the right ones. The evolution from mere partisanship on issues or bills had been achieved smoothly. The fight against the Socialists within the Federation was being carried on vigorously and successfully, moreover. The leaders of organized labor were quick to accept the greater share of the credit for the improvement which seemed to have come to American public life since the turn of the century. "We have tried to arouse public opinion," said Gompers as he defended his policies against Socialist Max S. Hayes and won a convention vote of 161 to 31 against the idea of a labor party.[20]

Time and again the president of the A. F. of L. lashed out at the Socialists. He insisted that he knew their doctrines as well as or better than they did but rejected them just the same. "The Old World is not our world," he wrote on his return from a tour of Europe. "Its social problems, its economic philosophies, its current political questions are not linked up with America." [21] But to Socialists like Victor Berger, Gompers was "an empty, self-complacent old fool." [22]

Unions were by no means accepted by the nation's industrialists, however. In a 1911 speech to the annual meeting of the National Association of Manufacturers its president said, "The American Federation of Labor is engaged in an open warfare against Jesus Christ and his cause." It was "a wicked conspiracy." Yet one observes in perspective that workingmen of that day were not so well off that they did not *need* unions. Young Walter Lippman wrote in 1914 a vigorous defense of unions and said that without them industrial democracy was unthinkable. Their failure would be a tragedy for civilization and force a class structure on the nation.

[20] A. F. of L. *Proceedings, 1912,* 304, 314–315.
[21] Samuel Gompers, *Labor in Europe and America* (New York, 1910), pp. 286–287. The sentiment was strikingly Jeffersonian. See many examples in Saul K. Padover, ed., *Thomas Jefferson on Democracy* (New York, 1939), 123–148; 151–2.
[22] Quoted in Taft *op. cit.,* p. 296. A documented book which takes a somewhat kindly view of the Socialist efforts to convert Gompers is Ira Kipnis, *The American Socialist Movement, 1897-1912* (New York, 1952).

Workingmen had not yet won a living wage, security of employment, respect from the government, or the right to be consulted about the conditions under which they worked.[23]

The Socialist Party polled nearly a million votes in 1912. It thus appeared to many, in and out of the labor movement, that the reforms which had come out of the Progressive Era and the legislation which had marked the first years of the Wilson administration were not enough. It was at this point that the outbreak of World War I changed the course of the Progressive Movement and with it the rate of progress of American Labor.

III

The American Federation of Labor rallied to the support of Woodrow Wilson in his campaign for re-election in 1916 against Charles Evans Hughes. In July, the Executive Council referred the matter of "the Political Campaign" to a Labor Representation Committee which was to confer with Wilson's Secretary of Labor, William B. Wilson, and get advice on how labor could help.[24] Soon, using Executive Council stationery—*but with the committee name as signatory*—Samuel Gompers, James O'Connell, and Frank Morrison sent all local unions a printed letter on politics.

> Never at any time within the last fifty years have the workers had more at stake in any political campaign than in the one that is to be decided in the election November 7th. . . . During the present administration the organized labor movement has been able to secure recognition for the rights of human beings and opportunity for all to participate in the affairs of the nation in a degree that has never before been accomplished.

The Chief Executive, when the world was involved in conflict, had managed the affairs of the nation in the interest of its citizens "without the horrors of war." Labor organizations had participated in national affairs "to a degree never before realized." It was impossible to list the remedial and protective legislation passed due

---

[23] Walter Lippman, *Drift and Mastery: An Attempt to Diagnose the Current Unrest* (New York, 1914), pp.81–82, 85–86.
[24] Executive Council Minutes, July 24–29, 1916, A. F. of L. Papers.

to Wilson's initiative. "It is as if the national thought and the national spirit had been humanized and had become more sensitive not only to injustice but to the rights and opportunities that ought to be accorded to all human beings." The labor leaders therefore urged that the issues in the election be considered at regular or special meeting of union locals. "Meet, discuss the great issues to be decided on Election Day, November 7th, and then go to the polls, cast your vote as your conscience directs for Labor, justice, freedom and humanity." [25]

The letter had not endorsed Woodrow Wilson by name, but its partisan character could scarcely have been plainer if his name had been emblazoned on the letterhead. Mixed reactions were naturally evoked. A local in Yeaden, Pennsylvania, said it would comply; one in Indiana said the letter had been cast in the waste basket, since the local "was not in politics"; a Socialist in Palestine, Texas, was critical; but a local of sixteen members in Worcester, Massachusetts, pledged that all would vote for Wilson. When a union man in New Hampshire asked whether the letter meant the Executive Council was advising all unions to vote for Wilson and the Democratic ticket, Morrison replied curtly, "The letter you received means exactly what it says." [26] In other words, despite the broad assertion later made by Morrison in a 1924 Executive Council meeting that the A. F. of L. in 1916 "named Wilson," the labor leaders did not make an official endorsement. But they did show real partisanship as Gompers wrote:

> It is up to the workers, the masses, of our liberty loving citizenship, to decide whether President Wilson, with his clear vision and courageous heart and mind, shall be supplanted by the reactionary candidate of predatory wealth—Mr. Hughes. [27]

How much influence Gompers had on this and other elections must remain obscured in doubt. It is interesting, as a sidelight, to read that one of the reasons Hughes lost California was a "labor scan-

[25] File, "Replies from Political Letter, 1916," A. F. of L. Papers.
[26] File, "Replies from Political Circular, 1916," A. F. of L. Papers.
[27] Editorial, "On Which Side are You?" *American Federationist*, XXIII (November, 1916), 1068.

dal" he set off around the San Francisco-Oakland area when he spoke at a luncheon served by "scab" waiters.[28]

It is not necessary here to trace the story of the A. F. of L.'s vicissitudes during the course of the war. When it seemed that the United States was about to get involved, in March, 1917, trade union leaders met in conference and issued a public statement on "Labor's Position in Peace or in War" which made it clear that organized labor would support the nation in a war against Germany. By asking the utmost cooperation of the government in working through them, union leaders naturally expected to gain in power and prestige, while still serving national interests. The next day a circular letter went to all union officers, pointing out the seriousness of the situation. There was "a great opportunity for wage-earners to participate in the formulation of national policies," it said, pointing out opportunities for service.[29] In reply, the Secretary of Labor congratulated the A. F. of L. on its point of view toward service to the war effort.

Nevertheless, the degree of labor's contribution to the war effort became controversial, in time, as critics found labor overly grasping, and labor found business overrepresented down in Washington.[30] Gompers and some former Socialist intellectuals united in the formation of the American Alliance for Labor and Democracy, an activity designed to uphold Americanism and to try to keep the unions separate in the public mind from the antiwar Socialists. For its part, the National Association of Manufacturers issued a poster in red, white, and blue, stating, "There should be no strikes during the war." Woodrow Wilson's name was affixed. Labor protested; but all efforts to make quick economic gains during a time of national stress did cause resentment in business (and some government) circles. The imprisonment of Eugene V. Debs and others disturbed many trade unionists, and the A. F. of L. protested mightily after the war against continuing such "political" acts.

[28] Frederick M. Davenport, "Did Hughes Snub Johnson? An Inside Story," *American Political Science Review*, XLIII (April, 1949), 321–332.

[29] In file 16/426, Labor Department Group 174, National Archives.

[30] D. Willard, Chairman, Advisory Commission, Council of National Defense to Secretary of Labor, June 15, 1917. Gompers to the Council, June 27, 1917. File cited above.

"Exitski" (Ball in the *Newark Ledger*)

IV

As the time for the election of 1920 arrived the atmosphere in America had changed considerably. Although Gompers could write with much justice that "labor in America threw its full strength without reserve into the great war for the overthrow of autocracy," and that it had kept its pledges,[31] the trade unions nevertheless suffered a loss of public esteem. Some thought—and said—that service to country, at home, compared unfavorably with service in the trenches of Europe. Others confused trade unionism with radicalism and worried over the loyalties and the intentions

[31] Editorial, *American Federationist*, XXVII (December, 1920), 1086.

of union members as much as over the posturings of the new radicals who urged or used violent methods. Yet the findings of the Lusk Committee in New York should have dispelled such worries. It reported after extensive investigation of subversive activities:

> Organized labor has made it extremely clear that it is absolutely opposed to revolutionary Socialism and Bolshevism. . . . It has increasingly set itself against the ideas and inroads of Socialism. . . . The Federation of Labor [A. F. of L.] founds itself solidly upon the continuation of the present industrial and political system and seeks for the reforms that it works to accomplish within the scope of the present situation [system].[32]

There was much third-party talk in 1920, and in some parts of the country labor parties or farmer-labor parties were created. A close observer wrote, "I have good reason to think that organized labor will cut far more of a figure in politics this year than it has ever cut before." [33] An American Labor Party in New York received some publicity for a time. But the A. F. of L.'s Committee on Reconstruction had already reported against organizing such a party,[34] and the close association of Gompers with the Wilson administration and his interest in the creation of the League of Nations inclined him once again toward a Democratic candidate for President. Gompers asserted, however, that it was not the intention of his organization to pledge itself in support of any political candidate "except as is done through the local union organizations." The labor record of candidates was to be the only basis for such local endorsements, he continued.[35]

Despite such protestations, however, the partisanship of the president of the A. F. of L. was displayed for all to see. The Republican Party was called in labor's official organ the "unqualified defender of the enemies of Labor." [36] Harding was said to be for going backward; Cox was for going forward. "Senator Harding

---

[32] New York State, Legislature, *Revolutionary Radicalism: Its History, Purpose and Tactics,* Joint Committee investigating seditious activities (Lusk Committee) (Albany, 1920), III, 2147–2148.
[33] Charles Edward Russell to A. M. Simons, January 2, 1920. Simons Papers, Wisconsin State Historical Association.
[34] See *Teamsters Magazine,* XVII (February, 1919), 11.
[35] *New York Times,* August 5, 1920.
[36] Editorial, *American Federationist,* XXVII (July 1920), 656.

does not use the word 'normal'; he speaks of 'normalcy.' The word is obsolete and so is the condition to which he would return," Gompers declared.[37] In retrospect, William Green said that Cox had "a labor record that was unsurpassed." Nothing Ohioan Green had ever sought had been denied by Cox. Yet, said President Green in 1928, the Executive Council of 1920 did not endorse Governor Cox, thinking it "unwise." [38]

The American Federation of Labor stayed aloof in 1920 from the effort to swing labor support behind the candidacy of former Presidential candidate, and then Federal prisoner, Eugene V. Debs, although both the I.L.G.W.U. and the Amalgamated Clothing Workers endorsed him.[39] The Socialists felt and said, as usual, that they spoke for the nation's workers, so they denounced the indifference of the Federation bitterly, saying that the A. F. of L. political policy in practice made it "an annex of the Democratic Party." [40] The Railroad Brotherhoods, meanwhile, opposed Harding vigorously, citing his vote on the Esch-Cummins Act (which had returned the railroads to private ownership after the war). They showed marked friendship for William G. McAdoo, Democratic son-in-law of Woodrow Wilson, who had administered the railroads during the war and supported the Adamson eight-hour law.

When Harding received the highest percentage of the vote a Republican Presidential candidate had ever received to that time, Gompers and the Federation were placed in a somewhat embarrassing position, even though official endorsements had not been made by the national hierarchy. A number of industrialists and newspapers contended, nevertheless, that the Democratic defeat was also a defeat for organized labor. The *New York Times* observed that the election showed that the trade unionist clearly would not vote as a trade unionist.[41] For his part, Gompers con-

[37] Editorial, " 'Normalcy' vs. Progress," *ibid.*, XXVII (October, 1920), 913.
[38] Executive Council Minutes, August, 1928, A. F. of L. Papers.
[39] New York *Call*, May 13–14, 1920. Cited in Virginia Ottini, "The Socialist Party in the Election of 1920" (Unpublished Master's thesis, Dept. of History, Stanford University, 1948).
[40] *A Political Guide for the Workers: Socialist Party Campaign Book,* 1920, (Chicago, 1920), p. 77.
[41] Editorial, "Mr. Gompers' Campaign," issue of November 8, 1920.

sidered "reaction in the saddle," but he claimed that fifty Congressmen who had been hostile to labor would not be back. With this in mind, he reasserted that "the American labor movement has long understood the fallacy and futility of political action through a separate and distinct third-party movement." [42]

Organized labor would get no consideration whatsoever from the next administration, wrote Democrat Daniel J. Tobin, already a power in the Teamsters, and he claimed that the great bulk of union men had voted Democratic—except perhaps in California. He declared philosophically:

> The election is all over, so . . . bear this in mind, that no matter what party is in power, this splendid country of ours is bound to go along after we have all passed away. The same political arguments will confront the generations that follow us.[43]

Gompers offered his services to the new administration and said hopefully that he knew Harding would be as much his President as anyone else's.[44]

The Secretary of the Republican National Committee said that he could not see a victory for labor in the returns. He pointed out that Senators Wadsworth, Cummins, Watson, and Brandegee had won despite strong labor opposition. Leaders of liberal-radical tendencies saw good portents in all this, however. Charles Edward Russell wrote A. M. Simons from the nation's capitol:

> If the reactionary program prepared by the Republicans is carried out we shall have a great tide running the other way in two years and then it may be possible to organize a radical progressive movement equipped to cut ice. What do you think?
> The pitiful figure made by the Socialist party in the recent election, when it had so much in its favor and cast a smaller percentage of votes than in 1912, shows that absolutely nothing can be hoped for there.[45]

By 1922, President Tobin of the Teamsters, strong supporter of Bryan and Wilson and convinced as early as 1920 that Alfred E.

---

[42] Editorial, "Reaction in the Saddle," *American Federationist,* XXVII (December, 1920), 1081.
[43] *Teamsters Magazine,* XVIII (December, 1920), 7, 5.
[44] *New York Times,* November 6, 1920.
[45] Russell to Simons, November 21, 1920, Simons Papers.

Smith was "the best friend labor ever had," [46] was beside himself with irritation at the way things were going. "Harding has surrounded himself with perhaps the most bigoted, anti-labor Republicans that can be found in this country," he wrote,[47] and many union leaders fully agreed.

The Clayton Act had proved a mirage for labor, as the Duplex Printing Company Case interpreted away the benefits labor thought it had won. The Hitchman Coal Case was another blow, and in 1922 Gompers wrote, "Scarcely a day passes that does not witness the issuance of an injunction against the workers somewhere in the country. . . . The injunction menace is growing rapidly, not solely because injunctions are being issued with greater frequency but because courts constantly are occupying new ground and constantly widening the scope of their orders so as to make them cover a very widening classification of acts." [48] The Harding appointment of Taft as Chief Justice of the Supreme Court infuriated Gompers. But within the Administration (internally seething) some voices passed happier judgment on President Harding. According to his Secretary of Labor, James J. Davis, Harding was fighting the twelve-hour day.

> Joe, I have been close to the President now for more than a year. I have talked to him about these things that mean so much to the American workmen and I know he is right and we will always find him a friend of those who toil. He has never yet turned me down and I am sure he never will. Of all the speeches he has made, I think the one in which he said of the American workman, "The workmen's lowest wage must be enough for comfort, enough to make his house a home, enough to insure that the struggle for existence shall not crowd out the things worth existing for," is the best.[49]

Most labor leaders would have been unimpressed. Yet on Harding's death an A. F. of L. conference framed a resolution and

---

[46] *Teamsters Magazine*, XVIII (December, 1920), 5.

[47] *Ibid.*, XX (December, 1922), 12.

[48] Document 65, Vote Book, February 8, 1922, A. F. of L. Papers. Quoted by Taft *op. cit.*, 403. The present writer wishes that at the time he wrote this chapter the orderly Taft book had existed. Several paragraphs and two or three pertinent quotations have been added as the result of reading Professor Taft's volume.

[49] Davis to J. A. Bowers, Amalgamated Association of Iron, Steel, and Tin Workers, May 26, 1922, File 163/127B, Labor Dept. Group 174, National Archives.

Gompers presented it to President Calvin Coolidge personally. Sorrow was felt, for "it is a characteristic of our people that, differ though we may among ourselves, over matters of policy and principle, we have an unfailing regard and respect for the president and the presidency." Moreover,

> Those who have sometimes opposed the president out of conviction feel no less deeply grieved today than do those who have been his consistent supporters. For ourselves, partisanship has never been a personal question. It has been and must always be a matter of conviction and principle—a matter of judgment in relation to issues, but not in relation to men. Our hope and effort is for humanity within our republic and for the perpetuity of its institutions. . . .
>
> As to the future the wisest are blind and we cannot see what lies ahead. But we profer to the new president our wholehearted consideration and co-operation in all that goes for the upbuilding of our country and for the welfare of our people.[50]

It was a wise and a moving document.

V

In the meantime, representatives of discontented labor and farmer groups had met in Chicago in February, 1922, to form a Conference for Progressive Political Action.[51] The depression of 1920–1921 with its high prices had left much discontent in its wake. When seven railroad shop crafts went on what has been called the "Shopmen's Strike" of 1922 and were forced to return to work finally under conditions which left them worse off than before, the Railroad Brotherhoods and the labor movement as a whole were greatly concerned and were ready to engage in more vigorous political methods. Yet the C.P.P.A. was not foreordained to independent political devices—a fact sometimes forgotten.

[50] Text in Gompers to Coolidge, August 6, 1923, File 142, Coolidge Papers, Library of Congress.
[51] Kenneth C. MacKay, *The Progressive Movement of 1924* (New York, 1947); and James Henry Shideler, "The Neo-Progressives: Reform Politics in the United States, 1920–25" (Unpublished doctoral dissertation, Dept. of History, University of California, 1945), and an article based on it, "The La Follette Progressive Campaign of 1924," *Wisconsin Magazine of History*, XXXIII (June, 1950), 444–457, are very useful on the rise and fall of this body.

As early as March 22, 1924, A. F. Whitney of the Trainmen and members of the Illinois branch of the C.P.P.A. endorsed McAdoo for the Democratic nomination.[52] It is often said that had the Democrats only nominated him rather than John W. Davis, there would have been no new Presidential ticket in the field in 1924.[53] The newspaper *Labor,* established in 1919 as a means of furthering the Plumb Plan, and the official organ of the Brotherhoods, ran pictures of McAdoo and Alfred E. Smith in the spring of 1924, in addition to praise for Robert M. La Follette. The railroad workers even had representatives lobbying in the Democratic convention for McAdoo.[54] Still, the lengthy balloting and inability to compromise which marked the Democratic convention gave the nomination to a corporation lawyer who was willing to run on a platform which, it was considered obvious, "ignored the hopes and ideals and demands of labor." [55]

Calvin Coolidge and the regulars of the Republican Party possessed even less attraction for labor leaders and discontented farmers. Surviving politicians and others who had bolted the G.O.P. in 1912 to support Theodore Roosevelt, and who had carried on the old antimonopoly traditions of Progressivism into a new era, looked longingly about them for new leadership. Moreover, the Socialist Party was willing to lend its organization to the cause of a new political movement which might develop into a new party, especially a "federation" that would leave its separate elements intact.[56]

It was under such circumstances, only briefly suggested here, that the Progressive Movement of 1924 came to select Robert M. La Follette and Burton K. Wheeler as its nominees. Would it gain the support of Samuel Gompers and the A. F. of L. in addition to

[52] Walter F. McCaleb, *Brotherhood of Railroad Trainmen* (New York, 1936), pp. 118–119.
[53] Morris Hillquit, *Loose Leaves From a Busy Life* (New York, 1934), p. 318; Paul H. Douglas, *The Coming of a New Party* (New York, 1932), p. 199; *Wall Street Journal*, November 4, 1924.
[54] Hillquit, *Loose Leaves From a Busy Life*, p. 318.
[55] American Federation of Labor *Proceedings, 1924*, 173.
[56] It would be a "federation" in which the constituent organizations would remain what they were and carry on their own work although supporting "labor candidates" in cities, states, and nation, wrote a Socialist leader. James Oneal, "Changing Fortunes of American Socialism," *Current History*, XX (April, 1924), 97.

the Railroad Brotherhood chiefs, the Socialist Party, a variety of farm groups, many 1912 Progressives, and discontented reformers?

VI

The Executive Council of the A. F. of L. was sorely tempted to give an official endorsement to La Follette and Wheeler. Recognizing this sentiment, Gompers spent three weeks preparing a carefully phrased document blistering the two major parties and praising the new candidates, saying "if it takes the last bit of energy I have to put it in the La Follette campaign and for La Follette. The situation is entirely different from the previous campaigns." [57] An effort by Daniel J. Tobin of the Teamsters to get the Executive Council to name La Follette and Wheeler as endorsed candidates could not gain unanimous consent, apparently because William Green and one other member opposed the idea. Tobin withdrew it, and Gompers hastened to say, regarding the rejected concept of "endorsement," that no other construction could be placed on what he had written than decided support for La Follette and Wheeler. But it was *not* an "endorsement," even though Green would call it one in the retrospect of only four years.[58]

Soon a leaflet over the names of Gompers and other leaders, organized as a National Nonpartisan Political Campaign Committee, urged, "Vote for your friends and defeat your enemies." The cause was that of progress, justice, freedom, and democracy. "The platform and records of the Hon. Robert M. La Follette and the Hon. Burton K. Wheeler, independent candidates for the Presidency and Vice-presidency, have been declared to more nearly than any other, conform to the needs and desires of the great masses of our people and the organized wage earners and farmers in particular." A. F. of L. units should therefore contribute money, organizers, speakers, and literature, for the struggle was against

[57] Executive Council Minutes, August 2, 1924, A. F. of L. Papers. (I cannot explain the slight differences in wording between my version and that of Professor Taft.)

[58] "I know it did not set very good when we endorsed La Follette, and if there was ever a man who should have been endorsed it was La Follette." Executive Council Minutes, August, 1928, A. F. of L. Papers.

"two powerful organizations which are defenders, advocates and apologists of special interests and privilege." [59]

The Progressives of 1924 were more or less hopeful of organizing a permanent political structure, but that was not the intent of A. F. of L. leaders as a whole. Over and over they warned that they were rewarding "friends" (that is, La Follette) and punishing "enemies" (the Presidential candidates of the major parties). They were *not* organizing a political party, they said. So far as Congressional races were concerned, organized labor was still pursuing the so-called "nonpartisan" political tactics which had brought good results in 1922. The Communists, meanwhile, failed utterly in an attempt to infiltrate the independent political movements of 1924. Frustrated, in part it seems by the alertness of an ailing Samuel Gompers,[60] they claimed that "the great fraud of the 1924 election is the 'Labor' endorsement of La Follette." They called him an enemy of labor![61]

One event behind the scenes, small in itself but illuminating to observers of labor politics, took place late in the election. The story is revealed in the photostats of two letters that found their way into Republican National Headquarters. It seems that La Follette partisan L. E. Sheppard, president of the Order of Conductors, wrote one Fred Stewart of division 364 of the union, Oakland, California, a letter criticizing him for organizing Coolidge Clubs. He began,

> You are no doubt aware that the General Legislative Committee of the Order by the authority vested therein endorsed Mr. La Follette and some of the money which members of the Order pay into the Protective Fund is being used to promote the Progressive cause and to pile up as large a vote as possible for Mr. La Follette. The Order does not attempt to say to any member how he shall vote but if proper ethics are observed a member of the Order will not openly work for Coolidge or accept money from any other political party. Therefore, a member of the Order cannot consistently go out and work for Coolidge.

[59] Copy in file 142, Coolidge Papers.
[60] Taft, *op. cit.,* pp. 482–483.
[61] Jay Lovestone, *La Follette—An Enemy of Labor: the Workers and La Follette* (Chicago, n.d., 1924), copy in A. F. of L. Library.

Expulsion might result, even though the Order's laws "as yet do not specifically provide that a man who works for another political party and accepts money to support other candidates than those endorsed by the Order has violated his obligation but the members of a Division of the Order are his brother's keeper as to his conduct and if one should prefer charges against you on account of your political activities at this time and your Division should convict you for violation of unbecoming conduct, you might lose your membership."

The accused conductor answered with spirit. He explained pointedly that the length of time elapsing before his answer was due to his activity as a member of the Republican State Central Committee organizing Coolidge-Dawes Clubs. He objected to the use of the Protective Fund for political purposes. "Your threat, by which you seek to coerce my vote and political activities, convinces me even more than ever that Samuel Gompers has been right all his life until now in keeping the Unions as organizations out of politics." Stewart contrasted the necessary unanimity of action in the trade union field with the diversity of action in the political field. "It will be fatal to Unionism if it ever undertakes by Union discipline to coerce the vote or political course of the individual member. . . . While Unions ought to be out of politics, Union men ought to be in politics." He would support Coolidge. "I propose to continue in active support of my political belief. I deny your right to threaten or discipline me as a Union man for anything but a Union offense." [62] While it cannot be presumed that the phrasing of this classic reply was independent of the best brains of Republican headquarters in California, the viewpoints expressed in the Sheppard-Stewart correspondence deserve to be better known, for they shed a flood of light on the total problem of trade union involvement in party politics.

When the campaign was over and the votes were counted, labor leaders naturally were disappointed that La Follette had not received more votes, but they rejoiced to think that they had done

[62] Quoted from photostats of L. E. Sheppard to Fred Stewart, October 6, 1924, and Stewart to Sheppard, October 27, 1924, file 1917, Coolidge Papers. The file also contains a pertinent exchange of telegrams among members of the Republican National Committee, who recognized its political value.

well in the Senate and House of Representatives. *A. F. of L. leaders absolutely refused to see in the five million votes received by La Follette the nucleus of a party that might develop into an American version of the British Labour Party.* They knew full well that the union leaders and the union rank and file had not supported La Follette as a unit. President Warren S. Stone informed the members of the Locomotive Engineers with his "usual bluntness" what he thought of this lack of labor unity:

> To those of you who either did not think enough of your franchise to register and vote (and more than one-half of you failed to register and vote), or else voted to return again the reactionary forces to power, we want to say that if the results of the next few years do not suit you, do not find fault with everyone else, but just remember you and you alone are to blame.[63]

Expenditures on behalf of the La Follette candidacy by labor had been modest in any event by later standards.[64]

VII

No new party resulted from the Progressive Movement of 1924. As early as November 8 in Cleveland the chief executives of the Brotherhoods and several related unions met and adopted a motion that they were not in favor of the establishment of a third party.[65] Gompers hoped that the remaining partisans of third-party action would see the light now that they had "the cold figures before them." In what would be about the last political advice he was ever to give his colleagues—indeed, an essay that comprised a political testament—Gompers wrote:

[63] "President's Page," *Locomotive Engineers Journal,* LVII (December, 1924), 889. See also *Teamsters Magazine,* XXVI (September, 1928), 16, for similar views in retrospect. President Coolidge was early informed of Stone's enmity toward him. See Ben E. Chapin to E. G. Clark (Coolidge's secretary), May 2, 1924, file 174, Coolidge Papers.

[64] See Louise Overacker, "Labor's Political Contributions," *Political Science Quarterly,* LIV (March, 1939), 56–68.

[65] *Brotherhood of Locomotive Firemen and Enginemen's Magazine,* LXXVIII (January, 1925), 12.

The results of the congressional elections have demonstrated again that which has been demonstrated over and over again. The non-partisan political policy of the American Federation of Labor is the only sound political policy for American workers and American farmers. There is no other policy that can possibly produce results in the form of political power.

The results of the presidential election prove the same thing, perhaps more strikingly. They prove that a labor political party would be a suicidal political venture. As a matter of democratic principle, American labor does not want a separate political party and as a matter of practical politics it is far too wise to indulge in any such futility.[66]

The political methods of the past, the elderly Gompers was advising, would be the best ones to follow in the future. In his last address before an A. F. of L. convention, Gompers reminded trade union leaders that guided by *voluntary* principles the Federation had grown from a weakling into "the strongest, best organized labor movement of all the world." [67] His elected successor, William Green, soon made it plain by words and actions that, in politics, what had been good enough for Samuel Gompers was good enough for him.

Immediately after the full election results were known, the Executive Council of the American Federation of Labor sent a circular letter to some newly elected members of Congress urging them to exercise great caution in making commitments before coming to Washington, "where you may possess yourself of full knowledge upon every subject laid before you for decision." Surely they would not want "unwittingly" to serve the cause of reaction! (The letter was not sent into states where it was believed machines controlled votes.) The permission of each Council member was obtained before affixing his signature to this letter of political counsel. The replies were polite.[68]

It soon became apparent that the C.P.P.A. experiment would not survive the year 1925. In June of that year both Warren S. Stone, an important builder of the C.P.P.A., and Robert M. La

[66] *American Federationist*, XXXI (December, 1924), 989–990.
[67] Reprinted in pamphlet form as *Samuel Gompers' Creed* (Washington, A. F. of L., 1934), quoted material from p. 7.
[68] A. F. of L. Circular Letter, November 8, 1924, A. F. of L. Papers.

Follette died. Both had been important to the movement. Stone, raised on a farm, had cherished the hope of uniting farmers and workers at the ballot box.[69] As for Wisconsin's La Follette, no man was so well suited to lead so diverse a group. His sponsorship of the Seamen's Act and other prolabor policies had won him the esteem of many union leaders. His support of government owner-ship of the railroads was the kind of action which the Socialist Party hoped to further, and his earlier opposition to America's entry into the war had brought down upon his head many of the epithets devoted to the Socialists at the time. La Follette had spoken in the old Populist tradition against "the interests." The California State Federation of Labor regretted the passing of "one of the greatest champions of justice in the affairs of government and a valiant fighter for the rights of oppressed people every-where." [70] William Allen White listed the causes for which La Fol-lette had fought, and wrote. "He has been the true, unflinching friend of the man who toils, either in the shop, in the office, or on the farm. . . . We shall not see his like again for a generation." [71] Eventually he would be named one of America's five great Sena-tors. Nevertheless, the diverse political movement he tried to lead failed to become a political party.

The loss of leadership was devastating to the independent party movement, of course, but the reasons why no permanent new party could be built transcended individuals. The American federal sys-tem was itself a major factor. The unions had worked in 1922 and in other years to try to build a "friendly" Congress and friendly legislatures. Incumbents were Democrats and Republicans. If labor should launch out into new party paths, all past gains might be lost. If the new party were to prove unable to organize effectively and quickly in each state, there would be a period, perhaps a lengthy one, in which labor would be at the mercy of resentful legislators. What of county and city governments—also filled with

[69] His death was the occasion for a full, page-one editorial "roughly dictated" by La Follette as one of his last acts. "Warren Stone, Master Builder for Democracy," *La Follette's Magazine,* XVII (June, 1925), 81. "In the campaign of 1924 no man contributed more than he to the establishment of an enduring Progressive movement."
[70] California State Federation of Labor *Proceedings,* 1925, 37.
[71] One of scores of tributes printed in *La Follette's Magazine,* XVII (July, 1925). Quotation on p. 98.

Democratic and Republican officeholders? There had been virtually no Progressive candidates for the multitude of lesser offices throughout the nation in 1924. C.P.P.A. standard-bearers won only a meager handful of races for county commissioner, mayor, councilman, or alderman. State and local government evaded its grasp. Government in the United States, subdivided and scattered, is more than the Presidential office alone. Somehow, this truth had been mislaid by the enthusiasts of the day. The postmortem of the C.P.P.A. showed that leaders had learned a valuable lesson. David B. Robertson, president of the Locomotive Firemen and Enginemen said:

> As for the Brotherhood of Locomotive Firemen and Enginemen it allied itself with a C.P.P.A. on a non-partisan political basis. We are made up of men of all political beliefs. Some, I guess, have none at all, like men in all walks of life. Some are dissatisfied, perhaps with the present situation. Some have never been satisfied with either old party, but we are not a political party. We are a band of workers working along non-political lines, and I leave it to some of you gentlemen and ladies who are advocating the third-party idea whether or not you would ask the chief executive of a band of workers of all political faiths, to assume the responsibility to speak for 120,000 members of your organization and try to affiliate them with a party, a political party.[72]

VIII

The Coolidge Administration did not turn out to be a total disaster for labor, as had been feared. The Coolidge philosophy was hardly an aggressive one, as can be sensed in the President's letter to one union leader. "The interdependence of capital and labor is universally recognized, and only as they are able to work in harmony through mutual understanding and agreement may we expect

---

[72] Typed Minutes of the Conference for Progressive Political Action, February 21, 1925, pp. 87–88, Library of Congress. The present writer's interpretation of the C.P.P.A. demise derives chiefly from an intensive seminar study conducted in 1948 under Edgar Eugene Robinson. The Hopkins Transportation Library, Stanford, contains all pertinent Railroad Brotherhood periodicals.

to have the most satisfactory business conditions," [73] Coolidge
wrote, clearly in the mainstream of the day. His secretary of labor
thought the economic situation, except for the mines, entirely satisfactory. "Day by day we are learning the wisdom of a true spirit
of cooperation in industry," he told the President.[74] Frank Kent, a
Democratic newspaperman of the time, waxed ironic on "Silent
Cal":

> More and more the man amazes me. He is so thin minded, so
> astonishingly small in his mental range and weak in his grasp,
> yet with a cunning, shrewdness and solemnity that enables him
> to keep perched on the very peak of popularity, with every busi-
> ness Babbitt in the country believing him of heroic size.[75]

In the off-year senatorial contests of 1926 the A. F. of L. sup-
ported Wilson over Vare (Pennsylvania), Wagner over Wadsworth
(New York), Walsh over Butler (Massachusetts), Barkley over
Ernst (Kentucky), and Hayden over Cameron (Arizona). Blaine
(Wisconsin) and Brookhart (Iowa) were supported and Willis
(Ohio) opposed. There was no general endorsement of candidates
for Congress, but a few letters went out from headquarters.[76]
There was some belated A. F. of L. liaison with the Railroad
Brotherhoods.[77] Early in the year the Los Angeles Central Labor
Council undertook to explain to President Green how it handled
political matters in what was then a normally Republican area.
Members were urged to register Republican; in that way, primaries
could be influenced. In state matters the Central had "a fairly well
defined policy" to accept in toto the recommendations of the California State Federation of Labor. In national politics it followed
the A. F. of L.[78] In reply, Green said:

[73] Calvin Coolidge to John T. Wood, President, Operative Potters, May 21, 1926,
File PPF 1512, Coolidge Papers.

[74] James J. Davis to Coolidge (Memo), November 6, 1925, Box 356, Coolidge
Papers. File 3393 contains correspondence on the Railway Mediation Law.

[75] Frank Kent, *Baltimore Sun,* to Franklin D. Roosevelt, October 9, 1925, Roosevelt
Papers.

[76] William Green to T. A. Rickert, November 13, 1926, A. F. of L. Papers.

[77] Green to Edward Keating, August 6, 1926; W. C. Roberts to Green, October 26,
1928, A. F. of L. Papers.

[78] Secretary L.A.C.L.C. to Green, January 26, 1926, A. F. of L. Papers.

No doubt each state federation of labor and city central body must adopt policies that are governed by local conditions. The principle that should not be forgotten is that whatever tactics are used they must all have one object and that is a careful carrying out of the non-partisan political policy of the American Federation of Labor.[79]

Early in 1927 an important New York labor official forwarded President Green a report that the National Association of Manufacturers was preparing a "platform of American industry" to present to the 1928 party conventions,

All of which means that you no doubt may want to start your preparation now and get the proper endorsement and authority put through at the [AFL] convention in October of this year, so that it will be all ready for the political conventions next year, and maybe organize a national campaign to bring the force and effect of the American Federation of Labor's requests upon the delegates to these national conventions from the various states through agitation by the various state federations, central bodies, local unions, and international unions.[80]

Green said he would take the matter up at the forthcoming Executive Council meeting. In an address a few weeks later he discussed "Labor and Injunctions," thus foreshadowing the issue that would be stressed the coming year.[81] When Hugh Frayne, an A. F. of L. organizer, defended the nonpartisan political policy of the Federation on the radio in July, Green praised the speech warmly, concluding, "It meets with my entire approval." [82]

The United Mine Workers Convention in 1927 debated seven resolutions calling for labor party formation. The resolutions committee substituted a resolution with a far different point of view. "We do not think the time opportune to directly affiliate ourselves with any political organization . . .;" the nonpartisan policy had

[79] Green to Secretary, L.A.C.L.C., February 10, 1926, A. F. of L. Papers. In 1927 a miniature boomlet of Green as Democratic candidate for U. S. President was attempted by a reporter for the Columbus, Ohio, *Dispatch* (issue of August 2, 1927), and the Ohio Federation secretary-treasurer was alarmed, thinking it a plot to show Green's long Democratic affiliation. Green said the reporter was just "over zealous." T. J. Donnelly to Green, August 5, 1927; Green to Donnelly, August 19, 1927, A. F. of L. Papers.

[80] Peter J. Brady to Green, May 3, 1927, A. F. of L. Papers.

[81] Copy in A. F. of L. Library.

[82] Green to Frayne, July 15, 1927, A. F. of L. Papers.

succeeded in various parts of the country. One Socialist delegate disagreed, saying, "We are being led by sheep without a leader. We march to the polls disorganized in every way. . . . There is in my opinion no hope outside of the political field." He wanted a labor party, but one free of Communist or even Socialist control. Another delegate argued,

> In the first place, we live in a nation where there are 42,000,000 working men and women, and there are not five million of those people organized industrially and economically. I feel that our biggest task is to organize the trade union movement before we are to organize a political party in America.[83]

The echoes of Debs, Stone, La Follette, Gompers—all gone—remained to be debated in the late 1920s.

IX

At the American Federation of Labor convention in Los Angeles in October, 1927, Socialist labor leader Max S. Hayes urged, as on innumerable past occasions, that labor travel down the path of independent political action. There should be an alliance like that of 1924, he told delegates. If the A. F. of L. could not get a decent hearing from the old parties at the conventions of 1928, a national conference should be called and "an independent stand" taken. This would "show the old line bosses that they do not own the workers of this country, body, soul and breeches, as they believe they do."

After other delegates had spoken, President Green arose to say that the Federations wanted relief from the injunction "now." The "non-political policy" *(sic)* had brought state and national legislation comparable to that of other countries. Workmen's compensation legislation had been passed in forty-three of the forty-eight states. The British unions, after all, had their Trade Union Act to complain over just as the A. F. of L. had the injunction. Various members of the United States Senate spoke for labor, Green said, mentioning the younger La Follette, Norris, and Shipstead. There were Congressmen there "who readily recognize and admit that

[83] United Mine Workers *Proceedings, 1927,* 199–209.

they owe their elections very largely to the support which labor
gives them in their respective districts." More were needed:

> We are not ready to have the great American labor movement
> isolate itself, to stand separate and apart from its friends and
> sympathizers, to withdraw its political support in co-operation
> with its friends from behind those who are for us and against
> those who are our enemies. . . .
> I look forward to a brighter and a better day. We are going
> to correct these evils; we are going to make an impression; we are
> going to elect our friends; we are going to defeat our enemies;
> and we are going to do it through the exercise of the sovereign
> rights conferred upon the working men and their families in
> this country. There is no wrong which we suffer that cannot be
> righted when the conscience of the people is sufficiently aroused
> so that public opinion will stand with us.[84]

Later in the convention debate a delegate interrupted to ask if it
were not true that the next Congress would have in it, *as the result
of the nonpartisan policy of the Federation,* a group of "progressive, forward-looking United States Senators" holding the balance
of power? "I think you are right on that," said Green.[85]

The political pattern to be followed in 1928 had already been
set. It would be the policy of 1908 and of 1920, in short, the policy
of Samuel Gompers which had first been clearly enunciated in
1906. It was not for nothing that the new president of the American Federation of Labor had said after his election to stewardship
on behalf of the labor movement in 1924, "It shall ever be my
steadfast purpose to adhere to those fundamental principles of
trade unionism so ably championed by Mr. Gompers and upon
which the superstructure of organized labor rests." [86] But greater
efforts in the political arena were in the wind. Conscious of its
past and hopeful for the future, the American trade union movement girded its loins on the eve of the Presidential Election of 1928
to utilize traditional political methods in pursuit of traditional
economic objectives.

[84] William Green to the A. F. of L. convention at Los Angeles, October 11, 1927,
A. F. of L. *Proceedings, 1927,* 304–305.
[85] *Ibid.,* p. 307. The Progressives would hold the balance of power in the new Congress, said an editorial after the 1926 elections. *La Follette's Magazine,* XXVIII
(November, 1926), 161.
[86] Quoted by Jacob Perlman, "Labor's New Head is Real Leader," *La Follette's
Magazine,* XVII (February, 1925), 21.

Chapter 3

Jockeying for Party Position

THE METICULOUS PLANNING in American Presidential Elections is conducted by small groups behind closed doors. Leaders make plans; strategies are born; and there is give-and-take which ultimately results in appeals to groups and individuals by the political party and its nominees. The names of possible candidates are advanced for discussion (with one eye on their reception in the press and by recognized groups). Candidates potentially weak in popular appeal are virtually eliminated. Few records of this hidden activity are kept, and it is years before the public hears what really happened—if, indeed, they ever know. There is at election time a choice among alternatives, but the nature and intensity of the alternatives is determined long before much public interest is aroused.

The planning for 1928 took place far in advance, in accordance with custom. On February 3, 1927, for example, the biographer Henry F. Pringle revealed to Franklin D. Roosevelt his intention to write a campaign biography of Alfred E. Smith. "Needless to say it will, on the whole, be friendly." It was his hope that the book would "enable the people of the country to get a clear picture of the real Smith. This should be of great benefit in the coming convention." [1]

[1] Pringle to Roosevelt, February 3, 1927, Roosevelt Papers.

Sometimes in memoirs the participants in the quiet game of "king-making" tell how it was done. James W. Gerard has described, for example, how in the winter of 1927–1928 a group of New York Democratic leaders met for dinner at the Vanderbilt Hotel at least every ten days to discuss ways and means of gaining the Democratic nomination for Governor Smith. The meetings were almost like conspiracies and cabals, he recalled years later. "The dinners were mysterious and secret; we went in by the side door of the hotel in cloak-and-dagger style." [2] While Smith did attain the nomination, the efforts of these enthusiastic "conspirators" were by no means solely responsible. Among other things, the Governor needed substantial support from the leaders of particular groups in the population. To gain that support he worked to place himself on the record in a favorable light on many matters of vital interest to them. On some aspects, of course, silence was thought a virtue. The same things could be said of the preconvention candidacy of Herbert C. Hoover and of other serious Presidential possibilities.

I

Organized labor was one group which even in pre-Wagner Act days was well worth cultivating; at the very least it was not to be antagonized needlessly. To appeal successfully to union men and their leaders it was first necessary to know what the leaders of the American Federation of Labor wanted most. What legislation would they want in 1928 from the Congress? What was the minimum to be expected of a "friendly" candidate for President? When and how would labor leaders make their desires known?

In considering these matters, one must believe that political bargaining is timeless and appropriate in a democracy. The publicly and privately expressed attitudes of the potential candidates and

[2] James W. Gerard, *My First Eighty-Three Years in America* (New York, 1951), p. 313. A pioneering article which stressed the importance of small groups of party leaders in American politics is Edgar E. Robinson, "Realities in Politics," *New Republic*, XXIV (November 3, 1920), 237-239. See also his "The Place of Party in the Political History of the United States" in *Proceedings of the Pacific Coast Branch of the American Historical Association*, 1928, pp. 11-36.

those of union leaders on labor issues are jointly important. We must try to see the jockeying for position that takes place in a democratic republic long before the national conventions convene. This will be the story of preconvention political bargaining between labor leaders and political parties in 1928.

As soon as the 1927 convention of the American Federation of Labor had adjourned, its Executive Council started planning pressure activities for the 1928 election.[3] President William Green stepped up his speechmaking, giving twenty-eight addresses from October 1, 1927 to January 17, 1928, and making twenty trips. (Another sixty-four invitations to speak were declined.) Correspondence in that short period came to 2,400 letters.[4] The most important work of the Council at its Miami meeting in January would be the building of a national organization capable of attracting attention to the demands of labor.[5] As Green put it, "Labor expects to exercise just as great, if not a greater, influence in the 1928 national political campaign as in any previous campaign, not excepting 1916." [6]

At the state level in 1927, the respective federations were already giving thought to 1928 politics. The president of the Illinois State Federation of Labor wrote a letter of inquiry to the group's chief counsel asking specific instructions on how to elect friendly precinct committeemen and what their duties were, etc. Did they play a role in influencing the appointment of judges? If so, because of the "injunction situation," this data would be useful. The reply said it should not be hard to get control of county committees of parties, since "people generally do not realize the importance of the office." [7] Commenting on the exchange of letters, one judge wrote, "You are on the right track at last." He suggested, "Impress upon the organization not to make so much noise about their work and plans. Real politicians always work quietly." And he urged work

[3] Report of the Executive Council November 19, 1928, in American Federation of Labor *Proceedings, 1928,* 75.
[4] Unsigned memorandum prepared for Executive Council Meeting, Miami, dated January 17, 1928, A. F. of L. Papers, Washington, D. C.
[5] Statement of President William Green, in *New York Times,* January 26, 1928.
[6] *New York Times,* January 25, 1928.
[7] John H. Walker to A. C. Lewis, December 26, 1927; Lewis to Walker, December 30, 1927, A. F. of L. Papers.

in both parties, for "there is nothing like having both ends of a rope." [8] (Election of union men, as such, was not a good idea, according to the Federation man.) In Milwaukee, meanwhile, the state leaders of the Wisconsin Federation discussed the election of a candidate for circuit court judge with the hope that a candidate could be produced who would "stand up for Labor." If only one such could be found, "we would be willing to support him." [9]

The A. F. of L. planned to have a Nonpartisan Political Campaign Committee direct its election activities. The presence on it of President Green, Vice President Matthew Woll, and Secretary Frank Morrison was something of a guarantee that the committee would act in practice as the alter ego of the Council itself.[10] Labor leaders plainly hoped by this early announcement of pressure plans to put the politicians of the United States on notice that the unions expected favorable consideration during the coming campaign. It was announced pointedly that the Federation would work in the primaries for friendly delegates to the party conventions and seek to elect "friends" of labor in both the primaries and the general election. So that politicians would understand what was involved, it was announced that the A. F. of L. consisted of 106 national and international unions with 3,500,000 members,[11] 48 state federations, four departments, and 749 city central bodies. (In January, 1928, the magazine *American Federationist* had 1071 subscribers, an increase of 100 in a year.) Candidates for all offices—national, state, and local—would be judged friendly or unfriendly on the basis of past records and the pledges they made to frown on offensive labor legislation. The Council announced that nonpartisan committees were already being formed by local, district, and state union bodies.[12]

[8] Louis Bernreuter (Third Judicial Circuit, Ill.) to Walker, January 2, 1928, A. F. of L. Papers.

[9] Minutes, Executive Board, January 7, 1928, Wisconsin State Federation of Labor Papers, Wisconsin State Historical Society.

[10] The other members were James E. O'Connell, head of the Metal Trades Department, and Martin F. Ryan.

[11] Detailed figures on union membership compiled from union sources by Professor Leo Wolman appear in *Ebb and Flow in Trade Unionism* (New York, 1936). His figures are a close approximation based on numerous factors.

[12] *New York Times*, January 25, 1928.

Rumors came out of the Miami meeting that the Federation would demand above all else a law to give relief from court injunctions. It was also said to want 2.75 per cent beer, action against child labor, continued immigration restrictions, relief for veterans, and "probably" farm relief. The direct primary must be retained, said the labor leaders. It was guessed that the action on beer had been urged by the National Brewery Workers.[13]

To kick off the pressure campaign of 1928, the officers of the A. F. of L. mailed a circular on February 11 "To All Organized Labor"—its affiliated unions, state federations, city centrals, and 35,000 local unions. They were urged to prepare for an active campaign, forming committees to work for the re-election of progressive congressmen if they had not already done so. "Support by your votes only those candidates who have proved the genuineness of their service, or desire for service, to the people and to labor," it said.[14] In the activity of A. F. of L. leaders at this time there was no sign of favoritism toward any party or Presidential candidate, only repeated warnings about the desirability of being a good friend to labor.

In March a number of letters were sent to local unions in Wisconsin, Illinois, Massachusetts, Pennsylvania, North Carolina, Ohio, Arkansas, Tennessee, Montana, and other states. These revealed the favorable attitude displayed by "progressive" members of Congress during the first session of the Seventieth Congress. The motto for the year would be "STAND FAITHFULLY BY OUR FRIENDS AND ELECT THEM, OPPOSE OUR ENEMIES AND DEFEAT THEM." All this activity was later said to have aroused "great interest" throughout the nation in labor's campaign," [15] although

[13] *Ibid.,* January 21, 1928.
[14] A. F. of L. Circular Letter of February 11, 1928, Book 6, A. F. of L. Papers; also Report of the Executive Council, A. F. of L. *Proceedings, 1928,* 75. For a detailed report on 32 years of pressure activity in a Southern state, see W. C. Birthright, "Tennessee Federation of Labor" *American Federationist,* (November, 1928), 1316, 1318. This enthusiastic account by the secretary of the state federation should be compared with the charges of low labor standards in Tennessee made by Addison T. Cutler of Fisk University in "Labor Legislation in Thirteen Southern States," *Southern Economic Journal,* VII (January, 1941), 297, 316. The labor official in effect compared the results after years of effort with what had been before; Professor Cutler compared what he found with what might be.
[15] Report of the Executive Council, A. F. of L. *Proceedings, 1928,* 76-77, 75.

this was an obvious exaggeration. On March 19, high officials of the Boilermakers, the Machinists, the Railroad Brotherhoods, and the A. F. of L. met in Washington to iron out existing political differences. The meeting was necessitated by a heritage of disagreement on the use of the Howell-Barkley Bill as a "record vote" for candidate endorsement purposes. The conferees agreed to use it,

"Neutral" (Knott in the *Dallas News*)

D. B. Robertson and E. J. Manion of the Railway Labor Executives Association expressing pleasure that fundamental agreement had been reached.[16]

The special efforts which the unions directed against the injunction received some attention at the time. An understanding of this anti-injunction agitation of 1928 is vital to any consideration of union pressure politics in the election and is fully deserving of our interest.

II

In the public New Year's Day greeting traditional to his office, President William Green appealed for cooperation between capital and labor. The burden rested squarely on employers. If they continued experiments with company unions and welfare plans in an effort to oppose the standard unions and continued to rely on injunctions to break strikes, said Green, the flame of industrial hate would be fanned. The *New York Times* replied that cooperation begets cooperation. Two weeks later Green returned to this theme before the Chicago Bar Association, calling the injunction "a real grievance against which labor emphatically complains, smarting under a deep sense of wrong and injustice." Labor was determined, he said, to seek legislative redress.[17]

To dilute the impression given by some overly ardent C.I.O. protagonists and even more recent accounts that A. F. of L. leadership of the twenties was totally asleep on social, legal, and political questions, one may consider what hitherto unused records show about the way President Green went about getting ready for the injunction fights of 1928. Circular letters were sent on January 3 to major union headquarters asking information on injunctions declared against them in the past two years. A similar letter and

[16] Various letters in file "Misc., 1928," A. F. of L. Papers.
[17] *New York Times*, January 2, 3, 14, 1928. Felix Frankfurter and Nathan Greene, *The Labor Injunction* (New York, 1930) is the classic work on the subject indicated by its title. See especially Chap. IV. Two valuable articles by Paul F. Brissenden are "The Campaign Against the Labor Injunction," *American Economic Review*, XXIII (March, 1933), 42-54, and "The Labor Injunction," *Political Science Quarterly*, XLVIII (September, 1933), 413-450. Harry A. Millis and Royal E. Montgomery, *Organized Labor* (New York, 1945), 629-651 summarize developments.

additional data were sent to national union leaders on January 21. The I.L.G.W.U. was revealed to have had a total of nine injunctions, 1926–1927, the Mine Workers 25 from 1924 to 1927, and the Teamsters five (1926–1927). Other bodies had been less affected. The central wording of 29 injunctions, most of them recent but some going back to 1913, was included. Typically, the injunctions enjoined unions from doing a wide variety of things, for example, picketing on public roads or "past, near, or in the vicinity" of a mine, singing songs of a threatening nature in the hearing of plaintiff's employees, annoying those seeking work with the plaintiff, inducing men to strike, and, of course, damaging property or engaging in violent acts.[18]

At the Council's Miami meeting Green expressed the hope that remedial action might be forthcoming from the current session of Congress. Denying that the Council had given up hope of this and was preparing its appeal instead for presentations to the national conventions of the parties in June, he informed reporters that 120 union representatives would soon assemble in Washington to discuss the injunction and see what could be done about it.

The measure on which labor pinned its hopes in the first session of the Seventieth Congress bore the name of Senator Shipstead, Farmer-Laborite from Minnesota. The bill was introduced on December 12, 1927, and was referred to the Committee on the Judiciary. It then went to a subcommittee composed of Senators Blaine of Wisconsin, Walsh of Montana, and Norris of Nebraska.[19] Because the bill bore the Shipstead name, a special effort was made as early as February to get labor in his state behind his re-election. The injunction was called, in the course of this effort, an abuse of the equity power.

> This power is absolute, irresponsible and personal. It deals with danger to property that is immediate and irreparable and is now made to supersede law. Many labor men feel that if it is allowed to continue in its present form it will ultimately destroy American institutions as well as nullify the efforts and work of organized labor.[20]

[18] File "Circular Letters," Book 6, A. F. of L. Papers.
[19] *Congressional Record*, 70th Congress, 1st Sess., p. 10,050.
[20] A. F. of L. Circular Letter to secretaries of centrals and locals in St. Paul, Duluth, and Minneapolis (221 in all), February 6, 1928, A. F. of L. Papers.

Hearings were held on the Shipstead bill from February 8 to March 22.

Testifying for the A. F. of L. were President Green; John P. Frey, author of a book on the injunction; Andrew Furuseth, writer of many anti-injunction articles; and Frank Morrison. Morris L. Ernst appeared for the American Civil Liberties Union. Representatives of the National Association of Manufacturers and the Association of Railway Executives led the opposition.[21] Although the original text of the bill had been only a single sentence limiting the jurisdiction of equity courts to matters concerning "tangible and transferable" property, the version that finally emerged from the subcommittee was more comprehensive and wordy and included a prohibition on "yellow-dog" contracts.[22]

In his testimony William Green told the committee, "we are suffering from a very serious grievance. All working men and women of America are conscious of this fact. They feel they must have legislative relief." [23] Over 600 injunctions had been issued in 1927 alone, he said, and he quoted with approval from an address of George Warton Pepper, in which, after describing the number and extent of injunctions, the noted legal authority who had succeeded to the Senate seat of Boies Penrose observed:

> Naturally enough, during the past two decades there have been bitter protests from the ranks of labor. To the striker it seems like tyranny to find such power exercised, not by a jury of one's neighbors, but by a single official who is not elected but appointed, and that for life, and whose commission comes from a distant and little-understood source.[24]

The president of the American Federation of Labor made it plain that the unions did not oppose in principle the use of injunctions to protect property; what he objected to was their "wrongful use." [25] In a concise remark which the newspapers quoted the next

[21] U. S. Congress, Senate, *Limiting Scope of Injunction in Labor Disputes.* Hearings before a subcommittee of the Committee on the Judiciary, 70th Congress, 1st Sess. (1928).

[22] For texts see *ibid.,* p. 1, and *Congressional Record,* 70th Congress, 1st Sess., pp. 20050-10051.

[23] *Limiting Scope of Injunctions in Labor Disputes,* p. 37.

[24] *Ibid.,* p. 38. Address before two bar associations in 1924.

[25] *Ibid.,* p. 41.

day he said, "If organized labor has the right to exist, it should be permitted to function. If it has no right to exist, it should be limited by legislation and not through the courts." [26] These comments were in line with an earlier remark of Senator Shipstead that government by injunction was government by men, not by law.[27]

III

During the late spring and summer of 1928, A. F. of L. leaders, hopeful of improving on the Shipstead Bill, began a quiet but intensified effort to pick the brains of leading legal thinkers. A new bill was drafted by Edwin E. Witte, Donald Richberg, Herman Oliphant, and Felix Frankfurter. Witte wrote Green that the bill had been "hastily put together"; the Shipstead Bill, like the Clayton Act, had been far too general, so *some* improvement had been made. Frankfurter thought the new bill satisfactory, while Richberg opined that "the bill, as drafted, would not prevent the use of injunctions in labor disputes." But evils would be cut very considerably, with the judiciary no longer being, as in the past, a strike-breaking agency.

President Green on July 6 sent the new bill proposal to twenty-nine authorities, among them Morris Hillquit, George Warton Pepper, Robert Wagner, Fiorello La Guardia, and Roscoe Pound. To each he wrote,

> The American Federation of Labor has a difficult problem in which I would much appreciate your help—that of getting relief from injunction abuse. Will you help us? We want very much the benefit of your judgment on the enclosed bill reported by the Sub-Committee of the Senate Committee on Judiciary to the full committee. The proposal is based upon a new approach to this problem which Labor has never considered before. In your opinion would this bill prevent the use of injunctions in labor disputes?

While no payment was offered, substantial answers were received. Pound said the Shipstead Bill would have achieved "nothing at

---

[26] *New York Times,* February 12, 1928.
[27] *Limiting Scope of Injunctions in Labor Disputes,* p. 10.

all." The new one was "exceptionally well drawn" and would achieve its object, so far as legislation could do it. Charles E. Clark of Yale Law School said, "I fear the bill will not succeed to any great extent in achieving its objects." It would in any event be declared unconstitutional. John A. Ryan, however, thought it offered the very best remedy for the evil "you can hope to get through Congress at the present time or in the near future." Several respondents thought it more important that labor prepare adequate briefs and contest cases properly than just seek remedies in legislation.[28] By the summer of 1929 Green would say on the matter of the Shipstead Bill, ". . . the more we think of it the more we think it is not what we want after all." [29]

While no remedial legislation passed in 1928, the hearings on the Shipstead Bill did help the cause of the labor leaders. They served in part to clarify the nature of the remedies organized labor would ask of Congress in later years, and of more immediate importance, they served as a good medium for publicity. They did not have the result of taking the injunction out of the election campaign. It was still a vital labor issue. The *injunction abuse* recurred over and over in 1928 as a favorite theme for speeches by labor leaders and for editorials in the labor press.[30]

Few hints of significant campaign expenditures by unions appear in 1928 issues of the *New York Times* or union journals. The day of big union money in national politics lay ahead.[31] When Hoover,

[28] For correspondence in this matter see the file "Attorneys-Injunction Bill, 1928," A. F. of L. Papers.

[29] Minutes, Executive Council, August 8-20, 1929, A. F. of L. Papers.

[30] For examples, see the lead editorial, "Labor's Petition for Redress," *American Federationist*, XXXV (March, 1928), 273-274, and reprints of speeches delivered at a Cooper Union anti-injunction rally by Dr. Worth Tippy of the Federal Council of Churches entitled "Injunction Abuse," and Rev. John A. Ryan of the National Catholic Welfare Council, "The Labor Injunction in the Light of Justice" in *ibid.*, pp. 287-288, 290-293. For later examples see the *American Federationist* for August, 1928, and *Official Magazine, International Brotherhood of Teamsters, Chauffeurs, Stablemen and Helpers of America*, XXV (November, 1928), 5-12, hereafter cited as *Teamsters Magazine*.

[31] James K. Pollock, Jr., does not mention labor union contributions in his survey, "Campaign Funds in 1928," *American Political Science Review*, XXIII (February, 1929), 59-69. This might be compared with Louise Overacker a decade later in "Labor's Political Contributions," *Political Science Quarterly*, LIV (March, 1939), 56-68, or with heavy union contributions in 1936. *Investigation of Campaign Expenditures in 1936*, Report of the special committee to investigate campaign expenditures . . . in 1936, *Congressional Record*, 75th Congress, 1st Sess., pp. 127-133.

Smith and others appeared before the special Senate committee investigating preconvention campaign funds, no questions about the role organized labor or its money might play in 1928 seem to have been raised.[32]

It was almost as though nobody cared what union leaders or union members might do politically in 1928. That this was not the case will appear shortly. Party leaders had not left the labor vote out of their calculations, especially since labor could on occasion lobby successfully in the Congress and in the states.[33]

IV

It is not easy to discover what labor leaders thought or did about the preconvention candidacies of Hoover and Smith, but what they said sometimes appears in the record. Union journals were guarded in the comments they ventured to make. The newspaper *Labor,* organ of the railroad brotherhoods, was alarmed at the thought of Charles G. Dawes at the head of the Republican ticket; its columns reveal the efforts of the railroad men in Ohio, Indiana, and elsewhere to defeat him in the primaries. Except for the noncommittal observation by William Green in March that Smith and Hoover seemed "the strongest men in their parties," [34] there is little evidence of public preconvention comment by union leaders on the Presidential race. Congress received much attention, perhaps because the nominations of the well-known Governor of New York and the Secretary of Commerce seemed probable in the spring of 1928,[35] while the nominees for seats in the Congress were far from certain.

One labor leader did not mind sticking his neck out on the Presidential race. Democrat Daniel J. Tobin had supported Wilson in 1916 and Cox in 1920, followed other union leaders by supporting

[32] *New York Times,* May 10 and 11, 1928, carried many columns on the investigation.
[33] Successful lobbying by the National Federation of Postal Employees in 1928 has been described in Morton Robert Godine, *The Labor Problem in the Federal Service* (Cambridge, Mass. 1951), pp. 200-2.
[34] *New York Times,* March 12, 1928.
[35] Note as a single example, "Smith-Hoover Contest Looming," *Literary Digest,* XCVII (May 5, 1928), 12.

La Follette in 1924, and made it a lifelong habit to comment on political matters in the journal of his union. He considered his post as editor of its magazine second only to that as union president. The magazine in those years was his personal organ, carrying no advertisements and little not written by Tobin personally. Indiana politics, national politics, New York politics—all politics was of interest to Tobin; for years the man who assumed the presidency of the Teamsters in 1907 wrote as he pleased.[36] The evolution of his 1928 political attitude is worth introducing here. To Tobin, then A. F. of L. treasurer, the Coolidge message of December 5, 1927 had been "long and tiresome." With other members of the Executive Council and John L. Lewis, Tobin had called on Coolidge in mid-November to ask that he say something about the serious abuse of the injunction. The group explained that workers suffered, and it made various requests, none of which had any effect on the Coolidge message in Congress. "President Coolidge is finishing up his administration without having done very much one way or the other. He will be leaving Washington in March, 1929, and in one or two years will be almost completely forgotten." So said Tobin, longing for the days of greats like T. Roosevelt and Wilson. Perhaps the fact that labor had been "rebuffed and kicked about" would arouse it to vote for friends and defeat enemies. He hoped so.

In January, Tobin discussed the candidates. *If no progressive could get the Republican nomination, Hoover would be the first choice of organized labor,* Tobin wrote. Of the Democrats, Smith would be by far the greatest friend labor could have as President.[37] In any event politicians were put on warning that organized labor could support the candidate and the party giving it the greatest consideration. Labor was becoming more intelligent and assertive all the time, he wrote (almost hopefully), and it would be "the prominent instrumentality in deciding the next election for President of the United States." [38]

[36] Entire paragraph based on close examination of the *Teamsters Magazine* from 1916 to 1928.

[37] *Teamsters Magazine*, (January, 1928) pp. 10-11, 13-14. Tobin had sought the nomination for Smith in 1920 and 1924 and could say nothing too strong in his favor.

[38] *Teamsters Magazine*, XXV (January, 1928), 14.

Tobin was sure by April that Hoover was a far better man than Dawes. "Hoover is not wanted by Wall Street," he informed the Teamsters, calling Hoover "too square" for the Republicans and too self-opinionated to be used. Hoover knew too much! He would be the best Republican for labor among the candidates mentioned to date. Hoover was "the man of brains, the man with ability, the man who has unselfishly done things, the man who has the courage to tell the truth, the man who has defied Wall Street, the man who for eight or ten years has been doing good things and helping our government." Such extravagant words of praise from a labor leader who would work for Smith in 1928—and later for Franklin D. Roosevelt in election after election—cannot be ignored. Tobin thought that Johnson, Borah, and Norris, "splendid, courageous, fearless and clear-thinking leaders in the Republican Party," would be for Hoover. Only the "gang" guilty of corruption would be trying to deprive "honest, fearless, able Hoover" of the nomination. While he would be the hardest man "to lick" on election day, he or Hiram Johnson or one or two others would "give us a square deal," wrote Tobin.[39] Yet Walsh and Smith and "even" McAdoo (a dry) would give "us" a square deal in the Presidency.

By late in May, Tobin was even more convinced about Hoover; he would be the best man for labor among the Republicans. He entitled an editorial "Why Mr. Dawes Won't Do," writing that as a blatant supporter of the "open shop" campaign and a man who had praised the Daugherty injunction, Dawes could not be considered suitable from the standpoint of labor. [40]

Tobin admitted that it would be "pretty hard" for labor to take sides against Hoover later in the campaign. It would be especially hard for the anti-Dawes Brotherhoods, since they had already supported Hoover in Indiana and Ohio. A great deal would depend on the nature of the Republican platform and other declarations binding the candidate. "If the declarations are reactionary and nonprogressive, then Labor will decide the best course to pursue in supporting the presidential candidate." He thought it fortunate that although the Republican machine did not want Hoover, a

[39] *Ibid.,* (April, 1928), 8-11.
[40] *Ibid.,* (June, 1928), 2.

man of opinions, courage, and nerve, it would take him anyway. It could not elect anyone else.[41] It looked as though there would be in both major parties in 1928 candidates "more human" than those of the recent past.

When he turned his attention to the Democrats, the president of the Teamsters wrote less as an outsider or merely an interested observer. He could scarcely have been more blunt in the warning he delivered. The union movement would not commit itself, Tobin explained, until it learned from the platforms and "other indications" just what the parties would pledge to do for labor if elected. He recalled that although the party out of office was usually the more generous, the Democratic Party in 1924 had been "just as reactionary as the Republican Party." Labor had been driven away.

> If the Democratic party in this convention makes the same mistake; if it believes it will get the labor vote anyway (as that party claims to represent the working people); if they refuse to insert any pledge in their platform because of their claim that the workers know what President Wilson did for the toilers during his eight years in office, then the Democratic party is going to find itself, after the election in November, on the outside trying to get in.[42]

The parties would be wise to remember, he wrote in conclusion, that the "toilers" had considerable influence. Labor should not be taken lightly. Many of the unorganized follow the lead of the organized. Many others could be expected to follow suit.

It cannot be said with assurance that either the facts or the conclusions of Daniel J. Tobin were typical of those held by A. F. of L. leaders in the preconvention period. A Catholic, and deeply interested as a teamster in regaining, through modification of prohibition, beer to be trucked around urban America, Tobin did say, "I am not a dry, nor am I a wet, as the term is usually known and understood." He wanted a "happy, conservative middle ground," i.e., beer! [43] Many union men no doubt thought as he did on the issues and the candidates; how many did is a problem.

[41] *Ibid.*, (June, 1928), 13.
[42] *Ibid.*, 13-14.
[43] *Ibid.*, (February, 1928), inside back cover.

V

Before the conventions Hoover and Smith played their cards carefully. When Hoover announced his candidacy for the nomination in a letter to an Ohio supporter in February, he stated that he would carry forward Republican principles and the Coolidge objectives, "all of which have brought to our country such a high degree of happiness, progress, and security." [44] He would return to this theme frequently in 1928. His appeal amounted to this: if the workingman of America wanted to know which party to support, Hoover intimated, he should look around him, compare what he saw with what had been but a short time before, and then project his imagination into the future. There he would see, if the Republican Party stayed in office, a land of happy people.

In June, William Randolph Hearst believed Hoover a strong candidate. He could carry the cities, wrote Hearst, because the elements of foreign descent in them had not forgotten his relief work in the World War. Hoover was termed "a conspicuously honest, able and popular candidate" who was not a demagogue.

> He makes no clap-trap appeal to public passion or prejudice. He has no tricks of expression or of attire to get himself in the newspapers. He depends on his public performances, on his acts, on his achievements, on his constructive program, on his belief that his fellow citizens have the same intelligence and understanding that he has, and will appreciate what he has done and what he plans to do in their service.[45]

Such a candidate might be what the average workingman would appreciate, he thought.

Since Hoover said he would continue the Coolidge policies, it is important to see how Coolidge spelled them out on the eve of the 1928 Republican convention. He had "rejoiced," he said, in keeping down the budget, reducing taxes, and paying off the national debt. "The influence of such action is felt in every home

---

[44] *New York Times,* February 13, 1928.

[45] His "conservatism" was called of the constructive rather than the reactionary type. Hearst newspapers would support him. Text in *San Diego Evening Tribune,* June 8, 1928. Hoover considered himself a *true* liberal, however. See the New York City speech, October 22, 1928, in Herbert Hoover, *The New Day* (Stanford University, 1928), pp. 162-163.

in the land." The result had been prosperity: more food, clothing, and shelter. It was not up to the government to furnish prosperity. By paying their debts, avoiding waste, and improving their credit, the people had earned their own reward. In 1921, said Coolidge, business and commerce had been at the bottom of the pit. Millions more had been unemployed then than in 1928. Since that time industry had improved, efficiency had increased, and in other ways security and stabilization had come from years of Republican administration. There had been four tax reductions since 1921 and millions of persons in the lower brackets no longer paid a tax. Coolidge thought state and local governments should reduce their expenditures. The rising cost of government was a menace to prosperity and held back new enterprise which could employ labor. Government extravagance was "about the worst enemy of the wage earner." A government affecting 120 million people should be conducted like .a business. A deficit would be unthinkable. While he thought that efficiency could be obtained only from adequately compensated employees, he was (rather quaintly) opposed to overcompensation.[46] The *New York Times* editors of that day thought that many of these points were good "homely virtues."

While President Coolidge dwelt on this contented portrait of the socioeconomic scene, his Secretary of Labor, James J. Davis, suggested to the Republican Party platform committee the incorporation of planks he thought labor would want. "One of the things in which labor is tremendously interested," he noted, "is to curb the application of the writ of injunction in labor disputes." Other items were the protective tariff, limited immigration, exclusion of child labor, the eight-hour day, an end to the seven-day week, prohibiting the shipment of the products of convict labor in interstate commerce, and "collective bargaining coupled with conciliation and arbitration." The advice Davis gave was substantially sound. Whether the Republican convention would pay any attention to the information he offered was another matter, for organized labor was only one of the groups the party leaders had to consider.

[46] *New York Times*, June 12, 1928.

VI

In his annual message to the opening session of the legislature in 1928, Governor Smith devoted 4½ out of 36 newspaper columns to the subject of the working man. He asked establishment, after due study, of a minimum wage board to recommend a living wage for women and children. There should be increases in the death benefits of widows and of workmen's compensation rates. New York, said Governor Smith, needed legislation to prohibit the granting of a temporary injunction in an industrial dispute until after a fact-finding hearing. And there should be the enactment into law of the principle that "the labor of a human being shall not be treated as a commodity or article of commerce." There should be mediation and conciliation around a conference table, for, as he put it, "the use of the big stick in the field of industrial relations is a thing of the past."

The annual message of Smith was widely regarded as the opening gun of his campaign for the nomination, and it received much publicity. In the closing paragraphs he wrote:

> The underlying theory of American democracy is that the government exists for the people [,] and the government which is closest to them and most responsive to the demands upon it, economically and efficiently managed, is the best form of government.

If people in other parts of the United States wanted to know what Governor Smith thought of his native state, they could find out in his final sentences:

> It means something to say "I live in New York." New York is the Empire State of this Union and as such has a responsibility in the league of States making up the Federal Government, to live up to the last degree of all that is expected of that civil division which claims leadership. We have adopted for our motto, "Excelsior," and we can go onward and to greater heights of leadership, lesson and example, only by uniting for the promotion of the ideals it is our bounden duty to maintain.[47]

[47] *The Governor's Message to the Legislature, January 4, 1928.* Legislative Document No. 3 (Albany 1928), pp. 65-70; 99.

The speech received favorable notice from union leaders in New York and apparently elsewhere.

The announcement that John J. Raskob, millionaire du Pont and General Motors executive, had been made chairman of the Democratic Party campaign was received with misgivings in union circles and with rejoicing by opportunist Socialist and Communist leaders. Many Democrats must have seen in the appointment a deterrent to their hope of presenting Smith to the country as a forward-looking friend of organized labor. Still, the party needed to strengthen its organization, and it badly needed adequate financing; the risk had to be taken. Raskob contributed $100,000 to the party in 1928 and must have been instrumental in attracting many thousands more. Possibly to alleviate doubts and misgivings, Raskob was soon quoted as saying that the time was coming when every workingman would have two days off each week.[48]

By early in May, Governor Smith was easily the leading Democratic candidate. He announced that the platform of the party should be built "by applying the fundamental principles of Jeffersonian democracy unflinchingly to each specific problem of the day." Issues needed to be met in the light of basic principles:

> The greatest degree of local self-government by the States, the minimum interference by the Federal governmnt or any State with the local habits and concerns of any other State, legislation for the interest of all, and not for any class or group, non-interference with the internal affairs of other nations, tolerance of conflicting opinion—these are our articles of faith.[49]

This did not mean that Smith would ignore the desires of groups like the American Federation of Labor, but it did mean that he would have no part of formulating a "working class" campaign against the businessman or making a villain of "Wall Street."

A few weeks later Smith was pictured standing beside a printing press just after receiving an honorary card in the Printing Pressmen's Union,[50] a body headed by Major George L. Berry, a leading candidate for the Democratic Vice-Presidential nomination in

---

[48] *New York Times,* March 13, 1928.
[49] *Ibid.,* May 4, 1928.
[50] Rotogravure picture section, *New York Times,* May 27, 1928.

1924. Such publicity would do Smith no harm among union members or leaders, especially as it was pointed out that the union card was merely "the latest of his collection." In June, the Governor was host to a group of important union and business leaders for lunch and a round of golf. The leaders of organized labor were not being ignored by Presidential candidate Smith.

VII

What can be said of the preconvention political bargaining in 1928 between major party leaders and union leaders? First, it should be emphasized that printed speculation about how labor might vote or what candidate or party it might support for the Presidency was conspicuously lacking from January to June, 1928. *The political eyes of the nation were on the farmer.* Its romantic eyes were on the daring aviators who filled the front pages week after week. The unions were not considered newsworthy in a time of little unrest and no general industrial strife. But the pressure politics of labor was very much alive. Union leaders made conscious efforts to reach agreement among themselves on programs to be presented to both major parties. Little was said about minor parties. *The chief item on labor's agenda was relief from injunctions.* It was felt that these court orders made it impossible to win strikes and thereby made questionable further gains in wages, hours, and union membership. An A. F. of L. circular letter of May 5, 1928, urged that secretaries of all local unions send in *detailed* information about every injunction ever issued against them—title of case, attorney's names, date of injunction, and the name of someone who knew what happened. A Legal Information Bureau would sift the data.[51] How many replies came in is not clear, but the effort was a sign of serious intention to seek redress.

Although a request would ultimately be made to the party conventions for legalization of beer with low alcoholic content, it was not prominently stressed as an item on the legislative program of the unions in 1928. The request was seldom mentioned in union

[51] A. F. of L. Circular Letters, Book 6, A. F. of L. Papers.

journals; yet issues like the injunction and immigration were often discussed in union conventions and union publications.

The preconvention candidacies of Smith and Hoover did not distress union leaders. *Labor feared neither.* Both were seen to have good points. While Hoover received support from the Railway Brotherhoods in the primaries, there were subtle signs that the New York State Federation and some important union officials were altogether likely to support Smith. The candidacies of Ritchie and Dawes were looked on with strong disfavor. In the preconvention conduct of Smith and Hoover there was absolutely nothing that could be adversely interpreted by labor leaders. Nor were their past records viewed with alarm. Governor Smith as a man in office put himself on record in his own state on many matters of importance to the state labor federation; silence was easier for Hoover in the preconvention period. The time for taking stands on vital labor issues like the injunction would come soon enough. The campaign was still young.

Chapter 4

The Socialists Organize
for Struggle

THE SOCIALIST PARTY of the United States called itself in
1928 the party of factory, farm, mine, and office workers: "the
producing classes." [1] It proclaimed that every great political struggle in American history had been a struggle for property interests,[2]
and it called politics a matter of class power.[3] The party led by
Norman Thomas had a goal toward which to work: the socialist
state. How did the leaders of this tiny party expect to attain that
goal in a democratic nation? Was its participation in the election
of 1928 in any sense a cloak for revolutionary plotting? Did the
party descended from Eugene V. Debs and inherited by Morris
Hillquit, Norman Thomas, and others really differ in any vital
sense from the Workers (Communist) Party? It is important to
know the form that Socialists hoped trade union political activity
would take in the United States. The basic change they intended
to make in the American two-party system needs to be analyzed
and weighed. This is an attempt to describe from public and various

---

[1] Platform of the Socialist Party, in *The Intelligent Voter's Guide. Official 1928
Campaign Handbook of the Socialist Party* (New York, 1928), p. 11.
[2] Editorial, "The Politics of Property and the Road to Power," *New Leader and
American Appeal*, September 15, 1928. This was the party newspaper. (Hereafter
cited *New Leader*, since the rest of the name was dropped in October, 1928.)
[3] Editorial, *ibid.*, September 29, 1928.

manuscript materials the fascinating activities of the Socialist Party in the Presidential campaign of 1928.

I

The Socialist Party held its convention in New York City from April 13 to 17, 1928.[4] By meeting early in the year its leaders sought to allow plenty of time for planning, organization, and fund raising. Problems would have to be solved despite limited resources. Leaflets would have to be printed and distributed, speeches scheduled in cities across the country, and party publicity organized and systematized. *Above all, the trade unions would have to be reached with the party message.* All of this could be accomplished, claimed a *New Leader* editorial, and it dramatically urged its readers: "Go forth to wrest power from the despoilers of the United States." [5] The "wresting," as will be seen, would be tried in the nation's voting booths.

The Socialist Party convention met twice daily, 3,000 persons attending the opening session.[6] At eleven o'clock at night various party leaders summarized the developments of the day over WEVD, the Debs Memorial Radio Station, and the more powerful WEAF. Both were thanked by official convention resolutions.[7] Present at the convention were 171 delegates from 39 states [8] representing a membership of between five and ten thousand; [9] dele-

---

[4] Other conventions about that time were: Czechoslovak Social-Democratic Party, Dutch Social-Democratic Party, Independent Labour Party of Great Britain. *Ibid.,* April 14, 1928.

[5] *Ibid.,* April 21, 1928. The "wresting" would be via the ballot, however.

[6] W. R. Snow to James O'Neill, June 6, 1928, Daniel W. Hoan Papers, Milwaukee.

[7] Letters of the executive secretary; Socialist Party Papers, Duke University.

[8] *New York Times,* April 14, 1928.

[9] The party announced a membership of 15,000 just before the campaign. *New York Times,* March 18, 1928. A 1932 memorandum for party officers gave the 1928 figures as 7,793. "Memoranda for the Baltimore Meeting of the National Executive Committee of the Socialist Party, December 9-11, 1932." Mimeographed, December 4, 1932. In file Socialist Party Campaign Material, Stanford University library. Figures for the larger states: New York, 1535; Wisconsin, 1272; Pennsylvania, 1097; Massachusetts, 1068; Illinois, 495; Ohio, 437; New Jersey, 348; and California, 252. Dues-paying membership figures are seriously inadequate as a gauge of the strength of a radical movement. The entire figures given here for Wisconsin and Pennsylvania could not have even elected the Socialist mayors of Milwaukee and Reading! Then how did the Socialists attain and maintain

gates were present from the Young Peoples Socialist League, and the Finnish, Italian, Jewish, Yugoslav, and Lithuanian federations.[10] The delegates seem to have arrived in a less than optimistic political mood, but the excitement of the convention turned their eyes toward the future with renewed hope. Again and again they were reminded that the old "battle call" was sounding and that it was their duty to the workers to respond.[11]

Morris Hillquit, writer, lawyer, and keen Socialist politician, delivered the keynote address in his usual well-organized style. The man that Upton Sinclair was to say had "made his mark, a deep wound in American capitalism," [12] told the delegates that the ultimate goal of the Socialist movement was the gradual transformation of natural wealth resources and basic industries to public ownership, "just as we own our post office[s], streets, and school-houses." The Socialist Party and the working man must be linked together. The ghost of unemployment walked among the miners and seasonal workers, he said, and "full stomach" prosperity could not last long. Workers must be free to strike. The judicial tyranny of the courts would have to stop. Injunctions would have to be completely abolished in labor disputes. Labor must fight for relief through political action; *that* was the road to progress. There must be old-age and sickness insurance, for the worker who could no longer be profitably employed did not belong on a "scrap heap" to beg, steal, or die.

The Socialist Party, said the keynoter, was always ready to cooperate in political action with "other" labor organizations, even to the point of self-obliteration. Yet the party had value in itself,

power in these cities? Through honest government and by practical compromises with abstract theory. Reading's utilities remained in private hands from 1928 to 1939 despite Socialist city administrations. The voters even defeated by a vote of about 17,000 to 10,000 in 1937 a proposal to float a bond issue to build a power plant and thus enter municipal ownership. Henry G. Stetler, *The Socialist Movement in Reading, Pennsylvania, 1899-1936* (Storrs, Conn., 1943), pp. 64-65, 68.

[10] *New Leader*, April 21, 1928.

[11] The banner headline over a historical survey of the party by James Oneal read, "TWENTY-EIGHT YEARS OF POLITICS FINDS SOCIALIST PARTY ONLY LASTING SPOKESMAN OF AMERICAN WORKERS." *New Leader*, April 14, 1928. "We are not a regional movement. Our movement embraces the whole country." *Ibid.*, May 12, 1928.

[12] Sinclair to Mrs. Hillquit, October 10, 1933, Hillquit Papers, Wisconsin State Historical Society.

because it served a good cause and possessed an "unshakable faith" in the ultimate victory.[13.] "I have never been more certain in my life that Socialism is inevitable," said a subsequent speaker.[14] Norman Thomas voiced early the classic cry, "We will be heard!" but he warned:

> The first question is not when shall we have that mighty labor party which is our heart's desire. The first question is how shall we work for that party. . . . It is to the answering of that question that we shall hopefully and courageously wage a campaign not only of protest but of *constructive building* in the Presidential year. We shall not let this issue be lost in political hokum.[15]

For a time the question of prohibition threatened to disrupt the convention. The Executive Council had been seriously split on the matter two years earlier.[16] Socialist Congressman Victor Berger of Wisconsin fought for a plank calling for the sale of light wine and beer under strict state supervision. When it was suggested that prominent party members would withdraw if such a program were adopted, Berger replied that Wisconsin might no longer be the backbone of American Socialism if it were not. Norman Thomas said he was of the opinion that prohibition was not a "political" or "party" issue, and he urged that the Socialists adopt no official attitude on the matter—a view with which a majority of the platform committee agreed.[17] So it was, ironically, that the party which would ridicule the major parties throughout the campaign for their straddles on water power, injunctions, and other issues would write a platform without a prohibition plank. It also issued a party handbook of 310 pages containing no discussion of prohibition, a matter on which it could reach no internal compromise.[18]

[13] Mimeographed prerelease text in Hillquit Papers; also printed in *New Leader,* April 14, 1928, and a lengthy summary appeared in *New York Times,* April 14, 1928.

[14] James H. Maurer, in *New Leader,* April 14, 1928.

[15] In *ibid.,* April 14, 1928.

[16] William H. Henry to Morris Hillquit, April 2, 1926, Hillquit Papers.

[17] *New York Times,* April 17, 1928.

[18] *The Intelligent Voter's Guide.* This booklet contained twenty-four articles. Among the writers were Thomas, Maurer, Harry W. Laidler, Victor Berger, Nathan Fine, Paul Blanshard, Harry Elmer Barnes, W. E. Woodward, Lewis Gannett, Edward Levinson, and James Oneal.

"How Can a Poor Fellow Pussyfoot?" (Harding in the *Brooklyn Eagle*)

Berger, defiant toward opponents and sincere in his convictions, sometimes thundering, sometimes expounding, delivered a report on his activities in Washington since the last Socialist convention.[19] What had this Socialist Party Congressman done while in office? One of his tasks, Berger reported, was to give consideration to the problems affecting his constituents. He proposed measures to the Congress for consideration which would afford relief from pressing evils. He sought publicity for his proposals in order that more people might learn what Socialists would do if they got in power in the United States. Berger added that he had opposed income tax reduction, since workers did not pay any tax. He had also opposed war debt settlements which he thought would help Wall Street and

---

[19] Adjectives used in describing Berger are those of Hillquit, delivered at Berger's funeral, August 10, 1929. The present writer is unable to evaluate charges that Berger adopted "a capitalist boss attitude" towards old associates in the Socialist movement. Ernest Unterman, Milwaukee *Leader* editorial writer, in letter of resignation sent to Berger, May 20, 1929. Socialist Party of Milwaukee Papers.

bolster non-Socialist governments abroad. He had offered legislation on aliens, miners, old-age pensions, and a forest reserve. And he had introduced bills to nationalize the railroads, the telephone and telegraph lines, and the food products "monopoly."

Every time he gave a speech in Congress, said the tensely earnest Wisconsin Socialist, he mailed advance copies and explanatory material to leading newspapers and press agencies. After delivery of an address he had copies printed at government expense and mailed them to such places. "I am glad to report," said Berger, "that considerable publicity has resulted from my efforts in this direction," adding, with eyes aflame, "I shall not attempt to do the spectacular, as Comrades have often suggested." Regardless of the consequences, he said would stand for what was right.[20] As Berger resumed his seat, Norman Thomas thanked him on behalf of the convention for his "magnificent fight" as the lone Congressional representative of the party.[21]

II

The time had come in the convention to choose the Socialist Party nominees for 1928. Who would have the task of trying to replace Eugene V. Debs? Party leaders were anxious to select a man not beyond middle age who would combine an ability to appeal with equal skill to laboring men and "intellectuals" alike. James H. Maurer, of Reading, Pennsylvania, a successful Socialist

[20] *New Leader,* April 21, 1928.
[21] *Ibid.,* April 21, 1928. Berger served in Congress 1911–1913, 1923–1924, and 1925–1929, but was excluded 1919–1923 despite regular re-election. Berger served on three committees in the House in 1928. The Republican floor leader told him on one occasion, he related, that he was helpful rather than obstructive in conducting the business of the House. (*Congressional Record,* 70th Congress, 1st Sess., p. 8208.) In the session from December 5, 1927, to May 29, 1928, Berger introduced one resolution, four joint resolutions, sixteen bills, and presented seven petitions for individuals and groups. He took the floor 29 times. At the beginning of a speech against militarism and imperialism, Berger said: "It is very hard for a Socialist to get over his point of view to an assemblage like this. You have a different psychology. I understand you very well, because I had it once upon a time, but you do not understand me. You still linger today where I was yesterday. Moreover, the average man . . . does not know the difference, between socialism, anarchism, nihilism, communism, and rheumatism. (Laughter) They are all fearful and wicked 'isms' to him." (*Ibid.,* pp. 4857-4858.)

politician, would reach his sixty-fourth birthday during the convention. He could not be expected to have many more years of energetic leadership ahead of him, whatever his skill at cutting through the debris of an argument.[22] He announced early in the proceedings that he would not be a candidate.[23] Other Presidential possibilities were said to be Mayor Daniel W. Hoan of Milwaukee,[24] Freda Hogan of Oklahoma, Cameron King of California, and Joseph W. Sharts of Ohio. Mrs. Victor Berger was mentioned for Vice President. These names and that of Norman Thomas were suggested in a *New Leader* item "not with any thought of influencing the decision of the convention" but merely as a matter of news.[25] Louis Waldman told the delegates what he considered to be the qualifications of a good candidate: first, he must be a loyal member of the party; second, he must be an excellent speaker; and finally, he must be a great and constructive Socialist statesman capable of following in the footsteps of Abraham Lincoln, Wendell Phillips, William Lloyd Garrison, and Eugene V. Debs.[26] There were problems in the analogy.

It was the opinion of Waldman as he nominated Norman Thomas that here was a man who met these qualifications admirably. Thomas had been in the thick of the fight on the side of the trade unions. He was termed an active leader in the "liberal" movement, serving as associate editor of *both* the liberal *Nation* and the Socialist *New Leader*.[27] When James H. Maurer agreed to accept the Vice Presidential nomination, the Socialist Party presumably had a strong ticket. In retrospect, Thomas would say,

[22] See the Labor College of Philadelphia *Workers-Student*, January, 1928, Socialist Papers, Duke University.
[23] The Maurer autobiography is *It Can Be Done* (New York, 1936).
[24] Hoan told his story in *City Government: The Record of the Milwaukee Experiment* (New York, 1936).
[25] *New Leader*, April 14, 1928.
[26] *Ibid.*, April 21, 1928.
[27] Lewis Gannett, the *Nation* associate editor, and Freda Kirchway, its managing editor, supported Thomas. Oswald Garrison Villard, its editor, did not. By November, another Thomas supporter, Paul Blanshard, was on the staff. A poll of its 25,000 subscribers during the campaign gave Smith 6,872; Thomas 2,830; Hoover 2,784; and Foster, the Communist candidate, 431. For an editorial praising Thomas and Hoan, see *Nation*, CXXVI (April 25, 1928), 475. The *Nation* advertised in the *New Leader* of October 6, 1928, and joint subscriptions to both could be obtained at reduced rates. *Ibid.*, January 5, 1929.

"I had to run for President in 1928. There wasn't anybody else. That was a sign of the weakness of the party." [28]

Norman Thomas told the convention in his acceptance speech that he did not claim to be a successor to Debs, but he promised to carry forward the fight for the cause Debs "so greatly loved, and for which he so greatly suffered." Thomas said he had no illusions about the condition of the party or the difficulties ahead. "We are not building for this election but for education and for the future." An "upheaval" was not the answer. The task was to bring into being a better world "without revolutionary and catastrophic woe." It would be just as easy to reach the goal by walking as in a single jump.[29] An enthusiastic Thomas supporter was quickly moved to write, "When we go riding out on the Great Adventure this year, we will have at our head as gallant a spirit as ever set lance against the three black horsemen, Cruelty, Greed, and Fear." Thomas was surely a flesh-and-blood human being who assayed pure gold in a world of "petty, scheming, grasping little grubs." [30]

That Socialist candidate Thomas was a dynamic crusader seemed obvious to most of his party at the time. The son of a minister who was also the son of a minister, Thomas was a graduate of Princeton and received his Bachelor of Divinity degree from Union Theological Seminary in 1911. In retrospect, Thomas would say, "I'm not a Christian in the sense I once was, and I am rather sorry. I was happier when I held the opinions that I held." [31] Before World War I, Thomas worked in a New York settlement house, carried on various welfare activities, and served as pastor of several Presbyterian churches. He had already toured the world once before 1914.[32]

[28] Thomas to Oral History Project, Columbia University, Spring, 1949, p. 43.
[29] New Leader, April 21, 1928; New York Times, April 17, 1928.
[30] New Leader, April 21, 1928.
[31] Thomas to Oral History Project (1949), p. 120.
[32] Sketches of the life of Thomas appear in reference works. The lengthy sketch in Current Biography (New York, 1944), pp. 688-691, was largely based on partisan articles prepared during the 1932 campaign.
See also W. E. Woodward, "This is Norman Thomas," in The Intelligent Voter's Guide, pp. 17-57. It was reprinted in the New Leader in weekly installments, August 18 to October 20, 1928. A convenient factual outline appeared in Ibid., April 21, 1928. The eulogistic Murray Seidler, Norman Thomas, Respectable Rebel (Syracuse, 1961), is silent on the events of 1928—when Thomas merely ran for President of the United States!

Thomas opposed the entry of the United States into World War I and later wrote a sympathetic book about the problem of the conscientious objector. He helped to organize the American Union Against Militarism, the Fellowship of Reconciliation, the National Civil Liberties Union (predecessor of the American Civil Liberties Union), and the League for Industrial Democracy. He served on the executive committee of the American Fund for Public Service (Garland Fund), an organization which spent hundreds of thousands of dollars to aid radical causes in the ·1920s.[33] He also founded the *World Tomorrow,* a magazine which merged into *Christian Century* some years later. A prolific writer, almost all of his literary output would be designed for many years directly or indirectly to further the Socialist cause he espoused publicly in 1918 by joining the party.

One of the clearest statements of the general point of view held by Thomas appears in a speech delivered at Princeton University before the campaigning of 1928 under the title, "Why I Am a Socialist." [34] In it Thomas showed that he believed Socialism and freedom of the individual fully compatible and even necessary to each other. Freedom, he said, is not the right to grab all you can and keep all you have grabbed. Instead, it is a guarantee of justice to the individual even from those not wishing to be just. It is the right "to know, to utter, and to argue freely according to conscience." Thomas called for a free press and for free speech, assemblage, and association. Yet the freedom of Daniel Boone was gone forever.

> The price of our freedom is *freedom in fellowship or in cooperation.* [Italics added.] Moreover it is true that there is a discipline which the struggle against tyranny requires which may sometimes compel a subordination of individual "rights" in the essential struggle to change the system.

[33] These included the Rand School in New York, the *New Leader,* the Mooney case, the *Daily Worker,* Brookwood Labor College, and the old Vanguard Press. See the *Reports* of the American Fund for Public Service, Inc. (New York, 1925-31). The fund made both loans and gifts. Stocks held by it increased vastly in value in the decade. Its intent, however, was to expend the principal. Many loans, especially to Communist causes, had to be written off.

[34] Printed in the April 6, 1928, edition of the Princeton student newspaper, the *New Leader,* May 5, 1928, and elsewhere.

Thomas added that he was a Socialist rather than a Communist because he believed that even in a transition period from capitalism to socialism, civil and religious liberty for the individual must be preserved. In an article on "Why Freedom Matters" he admitted that the pioneers had more freedom than modern man, but he claimed that they were enslaved to nature and to long hours of toil. Where was freedom in the modern world if a few men controlled most of the jobs? And what if only a few men controlled the radio, movies, newspapers, schools, and the "old line" political parties? Property, Thomas asserted, was better protected than liberty, and he urged voters to cast their votes to *increase* liberty.[35] The case was eloquent but arguable.

III

It is important to note the faith Norman Thomas has repeatedly expressed in political and evolutionary methods of getting results as opposed to extralegal and revolutionary methods. He was sure that socialism could come via the ballot. In a debate with Earl Browder on one occasion Thomas made these points forcefully, saying that he believed in "perfect democracy." [36] There could be no "perfect Socialism" without it. There must also be democracy within the party, for he could not trust rule from the top: the orders of a Third International acting for Moscow. Violence must be minimized. If there must be violence, let it come from those who would rather use it than give up their power. He told his Madison Square Garden audience that the "dictatorship of the proletariat" which the Communists supported was in reality the dictatorship of one party and not control by the working class.[37]

[35] Norman Thomas, "Why Freedom Matters," *New Leader,* July 28, 1928.

[36] An article on comparative uses of the word "democracy" is Murray S. Stedman, Jr., " 'Democracy' in American Communal and Socialist Literature," *Journal of the History of Ideas,* XII (January, 1951), 147-154.

[37] *Which Road For American Workers, Socialist or Communist?* Norman Thomas vs. Earl Browder, Madison Square Garden, N. Y., November 27, 1935. A debate. (New York, *Socialist Call,* 1936.)

This fact (as expressed in 1935) was one that even Lenin had granted his critics. [38]

More than any other party, claimed Thomas, the Socialist Party would be able to carry forward what was vital in the American tradition and to fulfill the Declaration of Independence in an age of power-driven machinery.[39] The American capitalists had cleverly retained their political control by deliberately cultivating among the masses a "blind, superstitious Constitution worship," he asserted. And the courts must not continue to act as bulwarks of private property and economic despotism.[40]

It is clear that the candidate of the Socialist Party, the apostle of an economic doctrine, was in revolt against the materialism of an increasingly industrialized America. "I ask you to face the most fascinating and most terrible task of our time," he told one audience, "—the task of controlling our modern science and our modern machinery so it will give us life and not death, a blessing and not a curse." [41] He liked to think that proper political action would suffice. "But if political action is utterly useless," he was to write, "what instruments shall we use to avert the war and destruction inherent in our blundering attempts to manage the age of chemistry, physics, and mechanical power under the law of the jungle?" [42] He deplored the fact that he saw in Marion, Ohio, a clear trend toward chain stores, chain ownership of the newspapers and their consolidation, and absentee ownership of industry. The city was coming into the stage of an "impersonal, rather irresponsible collectivist capitalism." The workers were helpless to meet the changes, since they lacked the protection of labor unions and their own political party.[43] Thomas thought he could see ahead a world wherein a fellowship of free men might live "in beauty and in peace." [44] It was, of course, an idealistic vision. But what, spe-

[38] For Lenin's defiant acceptance of the "dictatorship of one party," see quotes in Edward Hallett Carr, *A History of Soviet Russia*, Vol. I, *The Bolshevik Revolution, 1917–1923* (New York, 1951), p. 230.

[39] *Which Road for American Workers, Socialist or Communist?*

[40] *New York Times*, November 3, 1928.

[41] *New Leader*, October 27, 1928.

[42] Norman Thomas, "Why Not a New Party?" *North American Review*, CCXXVII (February, 1929), 150.

[43] *New Leader*, Oct. 20, 1928.

[44] Address delivered October 25, 1928. *Ibid.*, October 27, 1928.

cifically, did the Socialists plan to do to change the nation to match their hopes?

Before considering the provisions of the Socialist Party platform for 1928, it will be well to examine some of the separate resolutions which the delegates saw fit to pass. Resolutions supported antilynching legislation, opposed Jim Crow tendencies and peonage, and rejoiced in the organization of the Brotherhood of Sleeping Car Porters. A civil rights resolution asked restoration of citizenship for former political prisoners. Judges were not to deny citizenship because of economic or political opinions. Imperialism and militarism must go; the United States could not be a despotism abroad and a democracy at home, the platform said. Russia should be recognized, but such action need not mean approval of the Bolshevik regime. The Soviets were condemned for imprisoning Socialists and other dissidents for holding opinions contrary to "the ruling Communist Party." Soviet policy in this respect was termed "brutal" and "despotic" and constituted "organized terror." Italy, Hungary, and Rumania were called dictatorships engaged in destroying freedom.[45]

In an important resolution on political cooperation, the Socialists went on record as being ready and eager, as always, to cooperate in united political action with groups. Some vital provisos were that such groups be parties of the producing classes, that they believe in political and industrial democracy, and that they practice mutual confidence and respect. Claiming to be heir to the idealistic and working class aspirations which they said had animated the La Follette campaign, the Socialist Party appealed hopefully to the nearly five million dissident voters of 1924. The executive committee was instructed to cooperate with any local and regional groups devoted to the service of "those who labor by hand and brain." [46]

The resolution resulted in heated debate over whether it was an unwise attempt to form a labor party. Presidential nominee Thomas explained, however, that it was merely designed to attract the support of labor organizations and independent voters, and the

[45] Texts in *New Leader,* April 21, 1928.
[46] *Ibid.,* April 21, 1928.

resolution carried.[47] The year 1928 would be dedicated largely to rebuilding the Socialist Party. The idea of a great, class-conscious, mass party of the workers and farmers would not be forgotten,[48] but it would have to await Socialist regrouping and upheavals in the economy.

IV

It is well known that the platforms of political parties grow from the rubbing together of conflicting viewpoints. Nevertheless, leaders in the last analysis determine content. Such a leader was Mayor Daniel Hoan of Milwaukee. On the eve of the convention he wrote his viewpoints on a platform to Congressman Berger:

> I think our platform to be at all a practical document should be sufficiently brief and simple so that any child twelve years old reading it could understand it. If it is true that a large percentage of working people have minds of twelve-year-old children, it is high time our platform is written so that it can be understood by them. My humble opinion is that the platform should be no longer than the Milwaukee municipal platform, finally adopted, so that hundreds of thousands of them could be distributed as small hand bills. If the usual classical document is written it is more than useless to have them printed, except for a few copies to furnish to the parlor and literary variety of Socialist.[49]

In accepting the 1920 nomination for President, Eugene V. Debs had said, "Phrases do not make a revolution. I am glad that the platform has been written in clean American terms. The trouble with our platforms in the past is that we have not made ourselves understood." [50]

[47] New York Times, April 18, 1928.
[48] Appearing at the height of the campaign was Nathan Fine's volume, Labor and Farmer Parties in the United States, 1828-1928 (New York, Rand School, 1928) which reflected the conviction of its writer that despite the past failures of such parties, changing conditions might bring a "labor-farmer-progressive" party. "We go on and on because we have faith that the future belongs to us. And they who will follow will take up the fight where we left off." (p. 438.)
[49] Hoan to Berger, March 23, 1928, Hoan Papers.
[50] The Bulletin of the Socialist Party, June 1, 1920, in file "Society Publications, U.S.A., Socialist Party" in Hoover Library, Stanford University.

For whatever reason, the platform for 1928 turned out to be short, well organized, and written in relatively simple English. It opened with the bald announcement, "We Americans are told that we live in the most prosperous country in the world. . . . Yet poverty abounds." Prosperity was only in the stock market. Farm tenancy and unemployment were termed common. A third of the aged were said to depend on charity. Government had been used by the owning class to curtail the power of the workers, with exploitation of the many by the few the rule. Courts had been made "the instruments of class justice," and freedoms had been lost. Note, it said, the cases of Tom Mooney and of Sacco and Vanzetti! The sons of workers died in Nicaragua (in the Marines). The World War, alleged this economic interpretation, had been caused by trade and financial rivalries between nations.

Government must be made the servant of the people, continued the Socialist platform. Place no trust in political Messiahs leading major parties belonging to "landlords, bankers, oil speculators, coal and power barons." The capitalist class was called naturally corrupt. The platform summarized the Socialist cause in a rosy glow:

> As the only democratic labor party in the United States, we stand now as always, in America and in all lands, for the collective ownership of natural resources and basic industries and their democratic management for the use and benefit of all instead of the private profit of the privileged few.

The ten headings in the document were: public ownership and conservation, unemployment relief, labor legislation, taxation, civil liberties, "antilynching," political democracy, credit and banking, farm relief, and international relations. It is not necessary to reproduce the sentiments of each section, but certain highlights are revealing. Nationalization of the banking and currency systems would bring emancipation from the "money trust." Higher taxes on the rich and on corporations would provide money for social insurance, a step toward "social justice." The annual rental value of all land held for speculation should be appropriated through taxation. Citizens loaning money abroad should do so at their own risk. The war debts should be canceled if the debtor nations first canceled amounts due them and agreed to reduce their military budgets. The United States should enter the League of Nations and recognize Soviet Russia. War should be outlawed by treaty. The Philippines should be given independence, Porto Rico [*sic*] made autonomous, and the Virgin Islands ought to be given "civil government."

The Constitution of the United States should be modernized by a convention, said the platform, to bring direct election of the President, and changes like proportional representation, reduction of Congressional representation when voting equality had been withheld, and the abolition of judicial review. Injunctions in labor disputes were to be abolished. Civil rights were to be guaranteed by legislation. Jobs on public works or unemployment insurance were to be given the unemployed. *The party urged nationalization of coal mines, water sites, industrial power systems, railroads, and other means of transportation and communication "to recover the rightful heritage of the people."* There must be government operated health and accident insurance and old age pensions, for workers should be dependent on the "community" for such things rather than on employers. A shorter workday, a maximum five-day week, a child-labor amendment, and an end to convict labor were demanded. Detective agencies engaged in interstate business were to be abolished (presumably because they were sometimes used in breaking strikes).

In general consideration of the Socialist Party platform of 1928, it may be said that unlike that of the Communist Party the platform made proposals rather than demands. There were constant references to "our" country. The Marxist concept of the "few" and the "many" was ever-present. The tone was quiet, judicial, factual, and certain. Despite the calls for government ownership of the means of production, distribution, communication, and natural resources, the many proposed reforms, the general moderation of tone, and the trend of intervening events nearly persuade the reader that this economic radicalism was not so radical after all. Nevertheless it was—for that day. *Yet one notes the absence of any attempt to discuss in detail the path to be followed when converting resources and industries to government control and owner-*

ship. There is ample reason to believe that Socialist leaders in America felt no need in the 1920s to face that thorny (and presumably distant) problem. No less a person than Norman Thomas wrote formally a year later: "There is an immense and absorbingly interesting work to be done . . . especially in deciding where to begin the nationalizing process, how to acquire our natural monopolies, and how to administer them efficiently and democratically with due regard for both consumers and producers." [51] (This is a surprising admission by the leader of a movement nearly a century old in Europe and certainly no newcomer to America.) The platform was in no way antireligious nor was it excessively antipatriotic. It did not direct epithets against individual corporations or persons by name. The appeal was, above all, to the intellect rather than to the emotions. That it also called for reforms aplenty is evident. *That it called for socialism, however, is both clear and historically meaningful.*

Another significant result of the convention was the Socialist Party document entitled, "An Address to the Organized Workers." Surely the Socialists and the trade unionists could get along together, it stated hopefully. In every other modern country they had grown up together; elsewhere, the leading spirits in the two movements were the same. Socialist and trade unionist certainly sought to realize "fundamental democracy" in industry and society. Why should ancient grudges and misunderstandings live on in America when the Socialists had played such an important organizational role in the "sweated" needle trades and elsewhere? Who had raised nearly half of the steel strike funds in 1919? But the workers must not confuse the Communists with the Socialists. The former had nearly wrecked the few trade unions where they had gained a foothold, whereas the Socialists opposed the very idea of dictating to the organized working class. The Socialists said they wanted to see the unions grow until they covered all industries in the United States.

The "Address to the Organized Workers" stressed first and foremost the idea that *the road to self-improvement for the unions lay*

[51] Norman Thomas, "Why Not a New Party?" *North American Review* (February, 1929), 149.

in political action. The unions should not renounce government as an agency capable of furthering human welfare. Every other labor movement in the world already knew that the regulatory powers of the state could bring deliverance from evil. Because American unions had not demanded and gotten government relief, great corporations had been able to include welfare measures in their programs of company unionism, and this meant that workers got their accident and old age insurance as *favors* from the bosses rather than as *rights* from their own government. Who really believed that individual initiative had been alone in building the railroads or the merchant marine? Other groups and classes had used the government. The workers must do likewise.

Turning to the American Federation of Labor, the Address wondered how anyone could see successes in the "nonpartisan policy" the A. F. of L. had practiced since 1906. Were there any city councils or state legislatures composed of distinct labor groups? Could labor point to any political body and say, "They hold our mandate, are subject to our instructions, report to us on their work, and carry out our will"? The men labor considered "friends" owed their *first* allegiance to their parties and party leaders, not to the trade unions. The primaries had proved almost useless.[52]

V

The party convention left power over the forthcoming campaign in the hands of the National Executive Committee, a body which would meet in Baltimore, July 7-8, and Cleveland, September 22-23.[53] The group then discussed getting on the various state ballots, campaign plans, and organization work, attended a mass meeting Sunday afternoon, and enjoyed an evening banquet. Many details discussed were minute in the extreme. Berger of Wisconsin, Hillquit and Oneal of New York, James D. Graham of Montana,

[52] Text in *New Leader*, April 28, 1928. An editorial of five months before made similar points. "Independent Political Action," *ibid.*, December 3, 1927. Maurer and a colleague were named to "revise" this document for later use. (Minutes, National Executive Committee Meeting, May 19-20, 1928, Hoan Papers.)

[53] William H. Henry, executive secretary, to N.E.C., June 13, 1928, Minutes, N.E.C., both in Hoan Papers.

Joseph W. Sharts, Ohio, W. R. Snow, Illinois, and Dr. William D. Van Essen, Pennsylvania, comprised the group, with Hillquit International Secretary and Berger National Chairman. The New York headquarters of the party, directed by Julius and G. August Gerber, managed the over-all campaign, but the national headquarters remained in Chicago,[54] handling party organization, membership, and similar matters. Friction between the two was common, as will be seen.

A National Campaign Committee, consisting of the N.E.C. (ex officio), two delegates from state committees in Pennsylvania, New Jersey, and Connecticut, and the members of the Socialist Action Committee of New York, handled campaign details; its reports and those of the campaign manager were sent to various national officials. A National Campaign Council consisted of "the associate campaign representatives throughout the country." Decisions of both groups were subject to review by the N.E.C.[55]

The condition of the Socialist Party nationally was in the spring of 1928 an amalgam of problems in membership, leadership, and finances. William H. Henry, executive secretary, reported from Chicago on the first two matters to Julius Gerber late in May, saying that the use of two or three thousand dollars would have been a big help in organizational work earlier in the year.

In the South, reported Henry, the situation was blue. Scarcely any contact in Alabama; slight activity in Florida and Georgia; some hope in Mississippi and Kentucky—provided funds could be had; and in South Carolina, "the few votes we would get there would not be worth the time and expenditure." The same was true of Louisiana. Workmen's Circle branches were the chief Southern hope. In the West, an organizer would handle ballot problems in Oregon and Washington, while California would "take care of itself." A Colorado convention would nominate a ticket, and Idaho had a regular state organization with "a sprinkling of members."

In the Middle West, Wisconsin would need no attention from national bodies, while Illinois had held a state convention and Indiana was about to do so. In Iowa the necessary 500 signatures

---

[54] Henry to N.E.C. and state, district, and federal secretaries, June 13, 1928, Hoan Papers.
[55] Minutes, N.E.C., July 7–8, 1928, Hoan Papers.

were being gathered, and for $20 a week a comrade in Kansas was doing a good job. In the East, Connecticut, Massachusetts, New York, Pennsylvania, and New Jersey were taking care of themselves. All in all, the Chicago headquarters felt justified in regretting that the New York office had been given power formerly lodged in Chicago just when "the situation" was "in hand" and comrades were "looking to the National Office for direction." [56]

The financial affairs of the Socialist Party in 1928 are nearly as troublesome to the historian as to the worried Socialist leaders of that day. The party was virtually bankrupt in the spring; so much seems clear. It was behind in its payments to the International. Hillquit hoped that new spirit might make it possible "to pay all, or at least a very substantial part, of its arrears." [57] G. August Gerber gave $1,400 and August Claessens $1,000 in April, and the *Jewish Daily Forward* gave $1,000.[58] (The latter had been termed "the only wealthy Socialist institution in the United States" and the recipient of "substantial profits"; it had been generous in contributions to national and international party activities.[59]) The collection at the national convention came to only $1,700, a third of it from John T. Whilock of Chicago.[60] Meanwhile, the party could only pay $200 every 60–90 days on a thousand-dollar bank loan that fell due in 1928; to get it in the first place every member of the N.E.C. had to endorse it personally.[61] By midsummer the situation was so serious at national headquarters (with dues paid by 6,541 members the lowest figure in years) the national organization fell two months behind on payments of small sums (e.g., $20, $50) to state and local party offices.[62] N.E.C. meetings were only financed by holding special affairs concurrently in the host city; when at one point no city felt capable of performing this service the N.E.C. had to postpone its meeting.[63] A picnic staged by the Socialist state body in Wisconsin took in $4,880.73, to be

[56] Henry to Gerber, May 23, 1928, Hoan Papers.
[57] Hillquit to F. Adler, April 24, 1928, Hillquit Papers.
[58] Financial Report, April, 1928, Hoan Papers.
[59] Hillquit to Adler, September 22, 1926, Hillquit Papers.
[60] W. R. Snow to James Oneal, June 6, 1928, Hoan Papers.
[61] Henry to N.E.C., various letters, 1928, Hoan Papers.
[62] Henry to N.E.C., August 14, 1928, Hoan Papers.
[63] Henry to N.E.C., May 4, 1928, Hoan Papers.

sure, but expenses came to $3,197.72, with substantial sums being paid to rent tents and children's swings, $200 paid Norman Thomas to speak, and $611.99 going for raffle merchandise.[64] The State Federation of Labor in Wisconsin accepted $200 in cash and a note for $500 when $1,000 in bonds it held on the Social Democratic Publishing Company (Milwaukee *Leader*) fell due. Earlier, the union men had given $200 to the Socialist Lecture Fund.[65] Yet such measures as these fell far short of solving the problem of financing organizing work. How close the party ever came to reaching the $100,000 total for expenditure in all states [66] is difficult to say in view of all the committees and bodies involved. Certainly the recital just presented contains one sour note after another. One wonders how Morris Hillquit could have assured anyone in May, "I really feel that this campaign will witness the rebirth of the Socialist movement in the United States." [67]

So far as the Socialist Party was concerned, in any case, the time was at hand for recasting the nation into new patterns with new methods based on new ideas. Class consciousness was urged freely. "Be a farmer or a worker in politics as you are in your own organization," urged James Oneal, later party historian.[68] In a lead editorial on May Day, the Milwaukee *Leader* spoke noble words:

> While we Socialists continually work for the immediate interests of the common people, nevertheless, we always have our eyes on a farther goal. We are charged with being idealists. We admit the charge, and we are proud of it. We are not at all satisfied with the present everybody-for-himself social arrangements.

[64] Financial Report, January 1, 1929, File 22. Socialist Party of Milwaukee Collection, Milwaukee Court House.

[65] Financial Statement, January 1, 1927; Minutes of General Executive Board Meeting, January 4, 1929, and June 11, 1927, Wisconsin State Federation of Labor Papers, Wisconsin State Historical Society.

[66] Hillquit to Albert M. Todd, Kalamazoo, Michigan, May 23, 1928, Hillquit Papers.

[67] *Idem.* The present writer cannot grasp clearly what happened in Virginia, where it was alleged that the Socialist candidate for U. S. Senator withdrew when the Democrats allegedly paid $500 to the Socialist state chairman. It seems the party needed the money more than the votes, but the evidence is incomplete. "Summary of Findings and Decision of the N.E.C. [Socialist Party]," in File, Letters, 1931-1932, Norman Thomas Papers, New York Public Library.

[68] "Common Sense Politics," Milwaukee *Leader*, May 3, 1928.

Not competition but brotherly cooperation was the goal, wrote this leading Socialist newspaper, judging that competition leads to insanity, graft, and suicide. It contended that the "system" leads to poverty and unemployment. "We believe the time has come when it is possible for human beings to live together in peace, friendliness, and happiness. Therefore, it is our great object to change the capitalist system into the Socialist system." [69] On this challenging note the Socialist Party of the United States launched its crusade to achieve a political mandate to remake the nation's economic structure and party system.

[69] "May Day Thoughts," *ibid.*, May 1, 1928.

Chapter 5

The Communists Organize For Battle

THE POLITICAL CAMPAIGN OF 1928 had neither a beginning nor an ending for the Communist Party. The nominating convention in May was not its beginning. The counting of the votes in November settled nothing with finality. To a certain extent this is true of all parties; yet with the Communists the situation differed considerably. As William Z. Foster announced in his speech accepting the nomination for President:

> We are not going into the national election campaign solely for the purpose of getting votes. . . . We also have other bigger objectives. . . . Our aim must be to arouse the class-consciousness of the masses in a political sense and to mobilize them for struggle on all fronts. Vote-getting is only one aspect of this general mobilization of the workers.[1]

[1] *Acceptance Speeches . . . of the Workers (Communist) Party* (New York National Election Campaign Committee, 1928), p. 11. This chapter and chapter X together comprise the story of the Communist Party in the Presidential Election. In earlier drafts, they appeared in the author's doctoral dissertation, "Labor and Politics in 1928," Stanford University, 1951, and as "The Communist Party in the Presidential Election of 1928," *Western Political Quarterly,* XI (September, 1958), 514–538. The story told, in the context of other political appeals, is the manner in which this group in American life offered itself to the citizenry during a regularly scheduled election. Leaders are quoted from official party sources which are authentic beyond question. Those interested in minute maneuverings among the Communists in the 1920s will want to read the volumes of Theodore Draper on this subject. David J. Saposs, *Communism in American Politics* (Washington, D.C.,

Foster refrained from announcing what party leaders knew, that its method of participation in the campaign had been determined by direct orders from the Third International (Comintern)—a fact openly admitted after the election.[2]

The Communist press began to take notice early in 1928 of the rumors that Herbert C. Hoover would be the nominee of the Republicans and Alfred E. Smith the candidate of the Democrats. Both were quickly subjected to thorough and imaginative character assassination in the pages of the *Communist* and the *Daily Worker*. Nor did Socialist party leader Norman Thomas escape vilification. Hoover was venemously attacked as a man who allegedly made fabulous profits out of relief work in World War I. Smith, Tammany Hall, and Democratic leaders were cartooned repeatedly as grafters and thieves. Thomas was termed the "arch betrayer" of the working class. An article on Hoover in the January issue of the *Communist* used typical invective:

> The election of Hoover in 1928 means that for the next four years there will head the government an unscrupulous adept at utilizing misery and devastation for imperialist purposes. There is no infamous act he has not been guilty of against defenseless people.

His hands were alleged to be "dripping with the blood" of the European workers.[3] Against these candidates of the hated capitalists, the Communists would present, they said, a truly proletarian ticket.

The tone of the campaign was set in a *Daily Worker* editorial on May Day. The Soviet Union was exalted as "the Socialist fatherland" of all who toiled "in every nation of the world." The

1960), deals with party activities in later years, and his *Communism in American Unions* (New York, 1959) is another interesting account; both appeared after the present account was brought to completion.

[2] "Carrying out the decisions of the Ninth Plenum of the Comintern, the American Communist Party entered the campaign as an *independent force* . . . ." J. Louis Engdahl, "The Victors in the American Elections," *International Press Correspondence*, VIII (Vienna, November 16, 1928), p. 1500. Italics in the original. Engdahl was an important official in the American party writing in the interparty house organ of the Third International.

[3] H. M. Wicks, "Herbert Hoover," *Communist*, VII (January, 1928), 73–74. See also J. Louis Engdahl, "The Presidential Elections in the United States," *International Press Correspondence*, VIII (Vienna, June 28, 1928), 641–42, an article subtitled "Herbert Hoover—Wall Street's Agent."

Red Army of the Soviet Union was said to be "at the disposal of the working class and of the exploited peoples of all nations," for here was "the army of the Revolution."

> working class that none of its demands and needs of life can be secured except through class struggle under the leadership of the revolutionary Communist Party and the Communist International. . . . The Union of Socialist Soviet Republics is the stronghold of the revolution.
>
> The World revolutionary movement is the Communist movement. Its leadership is the Communist International. The world revolution casts up accounts today and finds itself stronger than ever for the stormy times which will usher in the Union of Socialist Soviet Republics of the World.
>
> In all imperialist countries the developing events show the

Readers of the *Daily Worker* were therefore urged to "Join the Workers (Communist) Party of America, section of the Communist International." [4] The American party's chief English-language organ had set the tone for the coming political fray, and the nine foreign-language newspapers followed suit.

I

The Communists held their party nominating convention in New York City from May 25 to 27, 1928. The message of greetings sent the group by the Political Secretariat of the Third International hoped that the coming "fight" would develop the "class struggle." [5] The convention quickly replied with enthusiasm:

> The National Convention pledges itself to be worthy of the confidence of the Communist International, and solemnly promises to enter into the election struggle—which will be a struggle against the corrupt bureaucracy of the American Federation of Labor and the renegade Socialist Party—with the true platform of the class struggle, as a champion of the working class, working farmers, and oppressed Negro race and as an organizer of the struggle against United States imperialism.[6]

[4] "Revolutionary Greetings," *Daily Worker*, May 1, 1928.
[5] *Daily Worker*, May 25, 1928.
[6] *Ibid.*, May 28, 1928.

The nearly three hundred convention delegates [7] represented thirty-nine states and the District of Columbia,[8] although the method of their choosing is shrouded in doubt. The size of a state's delegation was proportional to the "strength" of its party organization and its "industrial importance" as a state. New York had 48, Pennsylvania 32, Illinois 25, Massachusetts and Michigan 20 each, and Ohio 19.[9] The credentials committee reported with outspoken pride that 60 per cent of the party's delegates had been jailed at least once because of their devotion to the cause.[10]

Two thousand people gathered in the Central Opera House at Sixty-seventh Street and Third Avenue to hear the acceptance speeches of William Z. Foster and Benjamin Gitlow. Over their heads hung banners proclaiming: "HAIL THE WORLD REVOLUTION," "HAIL THE COMMUNIST INTERNATIONAL," "USE THE CAMPAIGN TO SPREAD COMMUNISM," and "THE STRUGGLE OF THE CHINESE WORKERS AND PEASANTS IS OUR STRUGGLE." [11] Delegates from coal mines in Ohio, Pennsylvania, West Virginia, and Illinois reported their versions of life in company towns. Representatives were present from New Bedford textile mills, Bethlehem steel mills, Detroit automobile factories, and Akron rubber factories.[12] Anita C. Whitney, a California "militant" of some standing, told the audience: "The California delegation has come across the continent to give tangible proof that this convention has roots in working men and women, not only in New York and in the East, but also in the states of the Pacific Coast." [13]

The committee chairmen have a special interest in the perspective of years, since three would leave party ranks before the 1932 campaign. James P. Cannon of the resolutions committee would go into the Trotskyite opposition to found and become by mid-century the "grand old man" of the Socialist Workers party. Bertram D. Wolfe of the campaign and propaganda committee would

[7] *New York Times*, May 28, 1928, gives 267; a party pamphlet gives 296 "regular" and 150 "fraternal."
[8] *Acceptance Speeches*, "Foreword," p. 5
[9] *Daily Worker*, May 12, 1928.
[10] *New York Times*, May 27, 1928.
[11] *Ibid.*, May 26, 1928; *Daily Worker*, May 28, 1928.
[12] *Daily Worker*, May 28, 1928.
[13] *Ibid.*

carve out a more conservative and constructive career as a writer on the Russian Revolution, and Jay Lovestone of the platform committee would found and then abandon a group of "Lovestonites," joining the staff of a conventional trade-union in New York City instead. The other committee chairmen of 1928 were Alexander Bittleman, press; Alexander Trachtenburg, ways and means; and Jack Stachel, credentials.[14]

Robert Minor presented the report of the committee on nominations, noting that agreement had been reached "without any dissenting vote or dissenting thought, without the proposal of any other names." In the light of this political unanimity, an experienced observer clearly used the right word in later years when he said that the Communist convention of May, 1928 had been designed for the "ratification" of its candidates,[15] rather than for selecting them. The assembled delegates certainly had little chance to do more than applaud the renominated candidates of 1924 when they were presented from the platform. There were no nominations from the floor.

The rest of this committee report tells modern readers much about the nature of the party in 1928. "The purpose of the Communist Party in making nominations is utterly different from the purpose of the Republican Party, the Democratic Party, or the so-called Socialist Party. . . ." Communist candidates were not being selected for their probable capacity to administer the machinery of the capitalist state. Instead, they were being chosen to mobilize the working class against the present form of society, and to bring about the "overthrow of the present form of society." Foster and Gitlow were being nominated as a step toward the establishment of a revolutionary state, Minor's report told the convention. These purposes were obviously "utterly antagonistic to the purposes for which the American democracy, so-called, was formed." The party's candidates would be busy in coming months

---

[14] *Ibid.* Stachel was in the first group of Communist leaders convicted by the government in the 1950s; Bittleman and Trachtenburg were in the second group. Foster was thought too ill to stand trial.

[15] U. S. Congress, House of Representatives, *Investigation of Communist Propaganda,* Hearings before special committee to investigate Communist activities in the United States, *Congressional Record,* 71st Congress, 2nd Sess. (1930), Part III, Vol. I, 214.

supporting various strikes, fighting the old enemy the labor bureaucracy, and building the Red trade-union movement, said the
report—all in connection with an election campaign.

Was it wrong for the Communist candidates for various offices
in a capitalist country to take office and serve if elected? Minor
asked. His answer was a ringing "No," and he cited Lenin's reputed endorsement of the action of a Communist chief of police
in Berlin who had used his post to good advantage by passing out
arms to the workers in that city. Minor asked delegates to remember one fact: "We are putting up candidates to mobilize the workers for the class struggle. In reality it is not individuals, but our
Party itself, which is the candidate." Its candidates would campaign
"under the discipline of the Party and subject to the iron command
to carry out the will and the program of our Party." [16]

When presidential candidate William Z. Foster rose to begin
his acceptance speech, he had to wait a full twenty minutes for a
noisy demonstration to die down. With radio microphones before
him,[17] he began with the orthodox politician's expressions of gratitude for the honor he had just received and expressed the hope
that he might be found worthy in the years of work in the class
struggle which lay ahead. He observed that wonderful fighting
spirit had been shown by his audience of "militants"—representative elements in the American proletariat. Foster reviewed the
recent past with some approval but warned that basic tasks lay
ahead. The workers must be induced to vote for the party candidates, taught to accept party leadership, and "drawn" into membership in the party. He then answered a basic question: Why
would the Communists participate in this capitalist election?

> We are not going into the national election campaign solely for
> the purpose of getting votes. It is of course important that we
> register the extent of our Party's support in the working class by
> mobilizing the maximum number to vote for our candidates. It
> is also important, should the possibility present itself in any of
> the state or local elections, to elect Communist candidates, so
> that they can utilize the legislative bodies as a forum wherefrom

[16] *Acceptance Speeches*, p. 8.
[17] *New York Times*, May 27, 1928.

to acquaint the workers with the iniquities of capitalism and the necessity of the Communist program.[18]

There must be no illusions that the workers could vote their way to emancipation—as taught by the Socialist Party. The workers must understand, said Foster, that the capitalist class would never permit them to take over control of the state peacefully; instead, it would fight violently to retain control. The Communist objective was stated clearly: a new state, a new government of workers and farmers; in short, "the Soviet Government of the United States."

William Z. Foster (left), Communist candidate for President, and Benjamin Gitlow (right) his running mate.

[18] *Acceptance Speeches*, p. 11. The *Daily Worker's* editorials at the time were fully cognizant of this theme. Before the convention it was explained editorially that "brother" Communist Parties abroad had only recently made fine records in the "sham elections" in Europe. Comrades in the United States would do likewise, "not with illusions in regard to capitalist elections, but to utilize the election campaigns for the mobilization and development of the American workers revolutionary movement." (*Daily Worker,* May 25, 1928.) A later editorial concluded with this sentiment: "And our candidates will make clear to the workers in this campaign that these sham 'democratic' elections cannot be the means of freedom for our class—that only the working class revolution can liberate them from the growing exploitation and repression." (*Ibid.,* May 28, 1928.)

Foster turned to the concrete demands of the platform and explained why they had been made. The demands would be stressed because revolutionary slogans would not suffice. Yet relying solely on such demands would only lead into the blind alley of simple "reformism." The energetic speaker drove home his point: *"Our Party is a revolutionary Party. It aims not simply to ease conditions a bit under capitalism for the workers but to abolish capitalism altogether."* [19] Demands for immediate changes in details of the existing order could be used to develop class-consciousness, organize the masses, and begin their mobilization for the eventual overthrow of capitalism. The coming election was a chance to further *all* the party tasks. The comrades would want to bear in mind that even a small party might accomplish big tasks.

As he neared the climax of his long oration, Foster visualized for his audience a happy day when the Communist Party would be "the only political party in the United States." When that time should come, the Communist Party would be in truth the party of the victorious proletarian revolution! In closing, the Communist candidate for President of the United States urged:

> Let us make our Party a worthy brother of the Communist Parties of the Soviet Union, Germany, France, England, Czechoslovakia, China, and other countries, which under the leadership of the Communist International, are gradually mobilizing the working masses of the world for the overthrow of world imperialism and the establishment of the International Socialist Republic.[20]

A period of cheering and singing followed, accompanied by a noisy demonstration.[21]

Presidential nominee Foster was 47 years of age in 1928, the product of a fabulously varied career. Few men have seen more places, earned a living in more different ways, or belonged to more organizations of a protest nature. Son of a railroad car washer, he was raised in the slums. "I have probably seen some of the worst

[19] *Acceptance Speeches*, pp. 12-13.
[20] *Ibid.*, p. 31
[21] *New York Times*, May 28, 1928. Foster's acceptance speech was run serially in the *Daily Worker* months later and appeared also as a pamphlet. Many of its sentiments appeared in other party materials of the day.

sides of life," he has said. He joined the Socialist Party in 1900, abandoned the Catholic religion, and became a "conscious atheist." Expelled by the Socialists in 1909, he became an I. W. W. and then a Syndicalist. In 1918 a Federal judge found him "particularly intelligent, honorable, moderate, tactful and fair." Active in the Chicago Federation of Labor, Foster soon turned up as a leader in the postwar steel strikes of 1919. In 1921 he spent three and a half months in Moscow and declared himself (behind the scenes) a Communist. Until 1924 he labored on behalf of a front group, the Trade Union Educational League, and in January, 1924 was elected chairman of the central executive committee of the Workers Party. In July he was elected a member of the Executive Committee of the Communist International in Moscow, and in the autumn he was the Workers Party, that is, the Communist, candidate for President of the United States.

His comrades described him as a "tallish thin Yankee with scanty hair, a slightly bulging forehead, a narrow chin, and mobile mouth," one combining the characteristics of a church elder and a typical Western railroader. Mild mannered and a hard fighter, zealous, a vegetarian and nondrinker, he looked the part of an intellectual and appreciated good music, possessing a library of socialist and literary classics. At the time of his nomination in 1928, William Z. Foster was to his comrades and to a tiny handful of the general American public the symbol and, so far as could be ascertained, the reality of top leadership in the American section of the Communist Party.

One characteristic of the acceptance address of Foster in 1928 was its call for the eventual creation of a labor party. This new party would embrace trade unions "and other labor organizations." Although such a mass labor party could be expected to turn weakly to "reformist" tendencies (trying to improve the lot of the worker under capitalism), its creation was called a step in the direction of one important goal: *the masses must be broken from their party allegiances*. The labor party would be well worth the building.[22]

---

[22] The party's Sub-District of Wisconsin had sought similar unity on a local level six months earlier, appealing to the Socialist leaders of Milwaukee to unite with them and with trade unions in order to win the local elections in the spring of 1928. Petty details could be ironed out in committees. Revolution and the

A *Daily Worker* editorial synthesized such reasoning the next day: "no labor party can lead the working class to victory. Only the Communist Party can do that." [23] Four years after 1924, therefore, the memory of the vigorously anti-Communist La Follette-led Conference for Progressive Political Action with its amalgamation of Progressives, orthodox trade unionists, and Socialists (from which Communists had been excluded) had not been erased. Even as early as 1921 the Executive Committee of the Comintern had complained: "The chief indictment of the Gompers' trade unions should be the fact that they refuse to participate in the establishment of a united front of the workers against the capitalists. . . ." [24] Seven years of failure to convert trade union leaders were galling.

II

When the platform of the Communist Party appeared in pamphlet form, its eighteen divisions covered sixty-four pages. Few of its points, it may be surmised, were new to faithful readers of the *Daily Worker*, the *Communist*, or the numerous foreign-language publications of the Communists, for the way had been long prepared. In a real sense, the important Communist literature of 1928 was uniform in language, attitude, and reasoning regardless of author, length, or form of publication. The party line having been established, party writers and speakers stuck to it. Such uniformity deadens the modern reader's senses, and he often gets the feeling that he has previously read material he is really seeing for

International were not mentioned in the two-page, single-spaced letter of the Communists. "Were it possible for all working-class organizations to unite upon a common platform and a joint slate of candidates in the forthcoming municipal election campaign, we have no doubt but that Labor in the city of Milwaukee would be able to register considerable gains in political influence and this in turn would stimulate the movement for the improvement of economic conditions through a stronger trade union organization." The letter concluded "with Fraternal Greeting." B. Sklar, Secretary, Sub-District of Wisconsin, Workers (Communist) Party of Wisconsin, to Milwaukee County Central Committee, Socialist Party, December 2, 1927, in Socialist Party of Milwaukee Papers, File 22, Milwaukee County Historical Society.

[23] *Daily Worker*, May 30, 1928.

[24] "Theses on the United Front," December 28, 1921, in *International Press Correspondence*, January 10, 1922, pp. 17-19.

the very first time. The Communist of the 1920s does not seem to have written anything without a party purpose. Originality was not regarded as a virtue. Foster's speech and the platform of his party were out of a single mold—the same one that shaped the contemporary editorial comment in the *Daily Worker*.

The Communist platform's first section, "America Today," described a land of great resources, huge capital, and immense wealth—all concentrated in the hands of a few millionaires. The rich were getting richer and the poor poorer. "The overwhelming majority of the people work on starvation wages," it baldly asserted.[25] Capitalist decency and morality were equated by the Communist platform with "almshouses, brothels, slums, and bootleg saloons."

The capitalists were charged with prostituting science, literature, and art to the level of the prostitution of women, and "capitalist justice" was described in terms of "frame-ups" and the third degree.

The other political parties of the United States were beyond all hope, the platform charged. The Republican Party might once have been the party of "revolutionary capitalism" when opposed to chattel slavery, but had it not come to foster the perpetuation of wage slavery? The Democratic Party was no more than the party of Negro peonage in the South! The struggle between them was a "staged fight, a mock struggle." Yet it was admitted that some small differences of opinion existed within each party.

The Communist platform observed acidly in passing that the surviving Progressives of 1924 were enemies of the workers and farmers even more dangerous than the hated spokesmen of big business. These reformers were said to hide their capitalist faces,

[25] Average weekly earnings in 1928 for production workers in manufacturing were $24.97, for a payroll index number of 109 (1939=100). Common labor in Southern steel mills, it was true, received only 28 cents an hour compared with 45 cents paid for similar work in Pittsburgh. *Historical Statistics of the United States, 1789-1945,* 67, 69. The top 1 per cent of the population actually received only 15 per cent of the total national income, while the top 5 per cent received 27 per cent. (In 1938, after the New Deal had almost run its course, the 95 per cent of the people lowest in earnings received 77 per cent of all income—a figure not too different from the 73.2 per cent of 1928. *Historical Statistics,* p. 15, following Kuznets. Strict immigration laws had proved necessary in the 1920s to stop the tide of Europeans and Asians seeking to "starve" in America.)

thus creating illusions in the minds of the masses. Serving chiefly to prop up capitalist society, reformers would have to be combatted at all costs.

The Socialist Party of Norman Thomas came in for its share of abuse. It was charged with having lost its militancy and to have cast aside its working-class composition in favor of a lower-middle-class membership. It was sneered at as a foe of revolution. Norman Thomas was called "the worst kind of pacifist, a typical preacher." [26] It was small wonder that in a reminiscent mood in later years Mr. Thomas said of the Communists, "They were really incredible people in many ways." [27]

Yet the position of Norman Thomas on pacifism in those years was not quite absolute. In May, 1928, he wrote his fellow-Socialist, Mayor Hoan of Milwaukee, "I am especially glad that you are going to officiate at the launching of the cruiser Milwaukee." [28] In 1932, he wrote, "We are not, of course, absolute pacifists. We are not democrats first and socialists afterwards." [29] On Communism, however, his position was unequivocal. The Socialist and Communist parties differ sharply on the question of tactics, he wrote a questioner in 1932.

> The Communists believe that catastrophe, probably new World War, is inevitable; that catastrophe will bring the revolutionary movement; that our transition from a capitalist society to a socialist society can only be brought about by a stern dictatorship of the proletariat; and that in working for this end anything goes.
>
> We socialists believe, on the contrary, that at least in America with our tradition, it is better to try to improve democracy than to scrap it and that we ought to make socialism the alternative to disaster rather than its doubtful consequence. We want to get a hold in the unions by methods consistent with ordinary fair play.[30]

The cleavage between Socialist Thomas and Communist Foster was, in 1928 as later, quite substantial. Nor had the situation four

[26] *The Platform of the Class Struggle*, 5–16.
[27] Interview of Norman Thomas by Oral History Project, Columbia University, Spring, 1949, p. 62, Manuscript in Columbia University Library.
[28] Thomas to Daniel Hoan, May 8, 1928, Daniel Hoan Papers, Milwaukee County Historical Society.
[29] Thomas to the Editor, *Nebraska State Journal*, June 1, 1932.
[30] Thomas to Charles A. Emerson, April 18, 1932. Thomas Papers.

years earlier been different. Eugene V. Debs had made a real effort in the early 1920s to reconcile the unreconcilable, as an able biographer has shown,[31] but the principles involved were too big for goodwill or the ties of friendship to bridge. His brother, Theodore Debs, summed up the years 1919 to 1925 in bitter words:

> If the socialists have hate and rancor the communists are responsible for it. When they left the Socialist party they declared they would at once organize the real revolutionary party. After six years they have organized nothing but disruption and destruction.[32]

In this spirit of unreconcilable conflict the two largest of the Marxist parties in the United States waged the Presidential campaign of 1928. The Socialist Labor Party was described by the Communist platform as wholly "fossilized." Throughout the campaign, the Marxist enspirited rivals of the Communists—the Socialist Party, the Socialist Labor Party, and the moribund Proletarian party—were venomously attacked by those allied with the Third International. They were adjudged betrayers of the working class.[33]

The initial blast by the Communist platform against the status quo was followed by more detailed sections containing what Robert Minor and William Z. Foster had characterized as the immediate "demands" of the party. It will be recalled that these were intended only as a means of converting workers to full class-consciousness and of interesting them in joining the Communist Party. They were preliminary steps toward the revolution. It is only in this realistic light that the party's "demands" may be understood. They were not framed with any hope of practical results or for any intrinsic virtues they had in themselves. The last thing the party wanted was to persuade capitalistic legislatures to pass reform legislation which might alleviate suffering or serve to reduce unrest. If that were to happen, the revolution might have to be postponed indefinitely. A few examples will serve to illustrate the point.

---

[31] Ray Ginger, *The Bending Cross,* Rutgers University Press, New Brunswick, 1949.
[32] Theodore Debs to David F. Karsner, March 11, 1925. In David Karsner Papers, New York Public Library.
[33] For a good example of a thoroughgoing diatribe against the Socialist Party see the *Daily Worker,* October 1, 1928.

Chapter II of the platform discussed the problem of unemployment in capitalistic countries but stated, in italics, *"There is no cure for unemployment under capitalism."* Neither a shorter work day, increased wages, nor public works would help. In spite of this hopeless picture the platform proceeded to demand a general forty-hour, five-day week without overtime, and extensive public works. There should also be employer-financed unemployment insurance, but its administration "should be in the hands of the workers" [34]—representatives of trade unions, organizations of the unemployed, and factory committees. This qualification is the vital one.

Such calls for ersatz reforms were transparent steps toward ultimate goals. If read out of context, each demand might appear to be in the American tradition of humanitarian concern for the underdog. If viewed in such a half-light, the Communist leaders of 1928 would appear to be no more than well-intentioned but rudely outspoken representatives of a reformist political party. This was hardly the case. Because the Communists then and since have called for free speech, a free press, civil rights, and other components of American democratic belief, they have sometimes led the unwary toward a false and quite limited view of their ultimate goals. The Communists of 1928 feared the possibility that many of the evils still existing in capitalist countries might be corrected. One of their most frequent complaints against the Socialists was that here was a group willing to step forward when capitalism might be sick, thus thwarting the necessary revolution.

Under a variety of headings the Communist platform discussed the real or imagined woes of the American "proletariat." The "bosses" were condemned and the miners praised. United States "imperialism" in Latin America and the Far East was contrasted with an alleged reduction by the Soviet Union of its military forces. American democratic capitalism was pictured as the oppressor of the Negroes, the foreign born, women in industry, and working children. The Communists called for an end to *all* taxes touching wage earners, and they demanded other changes in taxes and the

[34] *Platform of the Class Struggle*, p. 42.

tariff which were aimed at destroying the middle class as well as the hated rich.

Prohibition was considered an outstanding example of capitalist corruption and hypocrisy, and three pages of the platform made much of the evils of lawlessness which had accompanied it. The party regretted that it had become a political issue, for it made more difficult the clarification of "real major class issues." The platform managed to get on all sides of this question before finally demanding repeal of the Eighteenth Amendment. Prohibition was introduced, the platform said, at the behest of the manufacturers in order to increase worker efficiency. Its enforcement hit the poor more than the rich. It was an invasion of the private life of the workers. Yet those wanting repeal were the "powerful alcohol capital." Prohibition had created a government machine of spies, prosecutors, provocateurs, and courts—all adjuncts of the government's strike-breaking apparatus. Nevertheless, the government was damned for not enforcing prohibition, since bootleggers, "an underground capitalist world," operated, frequently against the labor movement. Alcoholism, a "terrible social disease," would be cured by the attainment of a Communist society. The platform demanded repeal of prohibition, dissolution of the enforcement apparatus, and propaganda against alcoholism.

The platform called for the formation of a labor party, much as Presidential candidate Foster did in his acceptance speech. The invitation was not news to trade-union organizations. On opening their mail the second week of January, 1927, several groups—the Executive Council of the A. F. of L., the secretary of the Socialist Party, someone acting for the tired IWW, and officials of "Labor Organizations Not Affiliated with the A. F. of L."—had discovered an invitation to form a united front with the Communists. Three pages of single-spaced prose ripped into United States policies in Nicaragua, China, and Mexico, with the immediate object of persuading all labor and farmer organizations to unite with the Reds.[35] The 1928 platform cry for a labor party was an old story to union leaders and to radical agitators of long experience.

[35] Central Committee, Workers (Communist) Party to Addressees, January 8, 1927. Socialist Party Papers, Duke University.

After considerable repetition of phrases, the Communist Party platform concluded in a forest of exclamation points: "Forward by means of relentless class struggle!" "Down with capitalist rule!" And finally, "Forward to a Workers' and Farmers' Government!" [36] Readers of the platform were reminded on an inside cover of the pamphlet that they could now purchase from the party at the reduced price of fifty cents the vitally important publication, *Report of the Fifteenth Congress of the Communist Party of the Soviet Union.*

As he brought the convention to a close, Jay Lovestone told the delegates that they had "the best Communist platform" that the party had ever seen. They had chosen "sterling, model revolutionists, sterling model standard-bearers" as their candidates.[37] As the delegates applauded, Lovestone assured them that communism could grow and certainly would grow in the United States. The convention of the Communist Party was over. The party was organized for battle.

[36] *Platform of the Class Struggle,* p. 64.
[37] *Acceptance Speeches,* pp. 41–42.

Chapter 6

The A. F. of L. in Convention Cities

MEMBERS OF the American Federation of Labor Nonpartisan Political Campaign Committee attended the conventions of both political parties. They talked privately with political figures, and they no doubt heard reassuring promises, off the record. Of these things contemporaries knew little. Labor delegations appeared before the resolutions committee of both parties on behalf of the planks they wanted to see placed in the platforms. What they asked and what they received is easily told. The rest can now be more or less pieced together.

I

Several weeks before William Green left for the Republican Party convention in Kansas City, he released a statement explaining what was meant by a "nonpartisan" political policy in the eyes of the American Federation of Labor. *It meant that principle would be placed above party.* Organized labor would support the candidates favoring its proposals, for these persons were on the side of "the people" rather than "the interests." Reactionary and unfriendly candidates would be opposed. *Green announced that the A. F. of L. would not lend itself in 1928 to an independent or third party movement. To do so would render impossible the advancement of the economic, industrial, and political welfare of the Federation.* No one should get the idea, however, that labor was abstaining from political action. Dawes and Ritchie would be opposed, and an active and aggressive part would be played in the political campaign.[1] Ever since the 1927 convention of the A. F. of L., close political observers had known that a policy along these lines would obtain the next year. The "federation" in the news in the spring of 1928 was not the A. F. of L. but the American Farm Bureau Federation.[2] The big question in national political circles was "what will the farmers do?" Labor's political views were of slight interest in newspaper circles.

After checking in at Kansas City's Ambassador Hotel, two to a room, the leaders of the A. F. of L. transmitted to Republican Party leaders the legislative program decided on at a May 2 Executive Council meeting in Washington.[3] The suggestions and recommendations were advanced as the "matured judgment" of the Executive Council and were thereby claimed to be representative of "the wishes and hopes" of millions of working men and women.

The Resolutions Committee of the Republican Party gave the A. F. of L. group (Green, Morrison, Woll, Ryan, O'Connell) what it later called "the widest opportunity to present its Platform Proposals." The five-minute rule was overlooked as James J. Davis shepherded them about. A full hour passed, Morrison reading and Green arguing each in turn. *The proposal for injunction relief legislation was stressed above all else.*[4] The two labor leaders suggested as a model plank this wording:

[1] *New York Times,* June 9, 1928.

[2] Note the *Literary Digest,* May-June, 1928, and *New York Times,* June 10, 1928. On the pressure activities of the farmers, see Gilbert C. Fite, "The Agricultural Issue in the Presidential Campaign of 1928," *Mississippi Valley Historical Review,* XXXVII (March, 1951), 653–672.

[3] Formal letter from the Nonpartisan Political Campaign Committee to the Resolutions Committee, *New York Times,* June 11, 1928.

[4] Minutes, Executive Council, A. F. of L., in A. F. of L. Papers.

We believe that injunctions in labor disputes should be granted
only to protect physical property when there is no adequate
remedy at law.

When a person is cited for contempt for violation of an injunction in labor disputes, except when such contempt was
committed in the presence of the court or so near thereto as to
interfere with the proper administration of justice, he should be
granted the right of trial by jury.

The idea of submitting a model wording had come from the Republicans.[5]

The injunction plank was not the only proposal of the labor
leaders. The Federation called for amendment of the Sherman
Anti-Trust Act to exempt labor (and agriculture) from prosecution under its provisions. "The very existence of organized labor"
was said to have been jeopardized by a law framed to protect the

"How Much Farther Will the Injunction Go?" From *United Mine Workers
Journal*

[5] *Ibid.*

people from extortion and oppression. A remedy for the injunction evil must be found, since "the people" were discontented, dissatisfied, and determined. The workers must be given the right to organize so they could cope with modern industrial conditions.

Immigration should, of course, continue to be rigidly controlled. The use of child labor must cease, and the shipment of the products of convict labor in interstate commerce should be prohibited. The coal industry, "demoralized," needed constructive legislation. Government public works should be used to attack unemployment, but not in times of general employment—at least until a scientific study could be made. The vital principles of freedom of speech, press, and assembly should not be abridged. Several suggestions were made on behalf of government employees. The high wage theory of the Federation was urged as a general principle, and the five-day week was advocated. The group endorsed graduated income, estate, and inheritance taxes, but the sales tax and similar taxes were opposed. The union consensus on prohibition was expressed briefly in a request that 2.75 per cent beer be legalized. It was slyly presumed that this would not violate the spirit or intent of the Eighteenth Amendment.

In an editorial reaction to all this, the *New York Times* found above all that the labor leaders had not supported the farmers in their current complaints; the 1924 marriage of convenience was at an end. Labor was saying that other economic groups could look out for themselves! Labor was bringing pressure on "nervous local statesmen," that is, on candidates for Congress as individuals, said the editorial. In a close election such "nonpartisan" tactics could be extremely effective.[6]

How would the Republican convention react to the requests from the trade unions—a major group in the American population? Could organized labor be given all it asked without at the same time antagonizing industrial, business, commercial, or farm interests?

[6] Editorial, "Labor Planks," *New York Times,* June 12, 1928.

II

Prospective nominee Herbert Hoover was not present at the Kansas City convention. One speculates on what would have been his attitude toward the demands of pressure groups as they sought to incorporate their desires into the language of the party platform. Suppose Hoover had been a member of the committee which had to combine conflicting views into a platform of reasonable length and clarity; did he believe in political compromises?

In a letter Hoover had sent to friends back in 1920 he said that convention compromises were proof that the nation would not succumb to multiparty formation. An effort should be made to bring extreme views "to realization" within the party organization. Elaborating, he continued:

> Nothing could be more disastrous than the development of several party organizations representing the complexion of every group in the country. With the legislative and executive functions more widely separated than in any democracy, the whole process of constructive government will come to an end if we have more than two dominant parties. If we should come to this position there will be no possibility of the American people securing the will of the majority, and we shall be entirely ruled by log-rolling minorities or sterile political coalitions.[7]

Hoover showed himself in this letter a believer in a party system in which each of two parties would include elements of all important groups in the population. Such parties would not be separated by an ideological gulf. The parties should be similar in their general philosophy, yet they would be different because when in power, "by actual administration," they would take on a different complexion. The Hoover position in 1928 seemed unchanged. It is interesting to note the comment of Franklin D. Roosevelt that he was sorry in 1928 to see the evolution of Hoover (a favorite of his in 1919–1920) into a "rather ordinary politician" who straddled the issues.[8] Here one finds the "compromise" of Hoover called a "straddle" by Roosevelt.

[7] *Ibid.*, June 19, 1920.
[8] *Ibid.*, September 27, 1928.

The only way such parties as these could endure very long as units would be to remain representative of many diverse groups and elements in the population. The primary problem of the platform makers at Kansas City and at Houston was to assay the relative voting strengths of groups whose desires were known, to decide whether requests made to them were really considered vital by the rank and file of the groups, and to determine the extent to which persons said to be group members would vote with their leaders at the polls. Were union members trade unionists first? Did they agree, with their leaders, that the injunction was the paramount issue of the campaign? Did they even grasp the importance of the problem? Perhaps the ordinary workingman would vote with the party that promised to preserve immigration barriers or with the party that promised to hold high tariff walls to preserve American jobs. Here was the dilemma.

How complex the problem could be may be seen in these propositions: Suppose the American Federation of Labor were to be given all it sought in Kansas City, including a binding promise to regulate the injunction. How many citizen voters did not like strikes or strikers and would hold responsible the party that facilitated them? How many votes from stockholders, the retired and widows on pensions, employers, and businessmen would turn against any party that strengthened organized labor in its struggle for a larger share of industrial profits? And how much campaign money which the party could normally count on from businessmen and financiers would flee elsewhere? Would the unions plug the financial gap? Politicians in the Republican Party thought they knew the answer to some of these questions and particularly the last one. Unions were not about to help finance, directly or indirectly, a Hoover campaign in 1928.

It can be seen that platform makers have a difficult time trying to reconcile what may in truth be unreconcilable. The platform which came out of Kansas City did not (and could not by the nature of things) give the labor group very much that it asked. The Republican platform began in the normal way; it viewed the status quo with satisfaction:

> Under this Administration a high level of wages and living
> has been established and maintained. The door of opportunity
> has been opened wide to all. It has given to our people greater
> comfort and leisure, and the mutual profit has been evident in
> the increasingly harmonious relations between employers and
> employees, and the steady rise by promotion of men in the shops
> to places at the council tables of the industries.

The tariff, it said, had raised the well-being of the people and
brought higher wages and increased industrial productivity. In
certain industries "American labor" might expect still higher tariff
aid. It was "inconceivable" that labor would ever consent to any
abolition of protection that would bring with it a decline to European levels of living. Farmers were reminded in passing that they
were dependent on the purchasing power of labor.

The platform supported the idea of "freedom in wage contracts"
and the concept of collective bargaining by voluntary agreement,
but it did not elaborate. *Injunctions,* the Party said briefly, *"have
in some instances been abused and have given rise to a serious
question for legislation."* [9] One editorial ironically called this generalized observation "an epoch-making discovery." [10] Certainly the
Federation's proposed wording was wholly missing. Labor leaders
who sought to know what improvements in labor legislation might
be anticipated from another Republican administration would find
scant comfort in a sentence which appeared earlier in the platform:
"The record of the present Administration is a guaranty of what
may be expected of the next. Our words have been made deeds.
We offer not promises but accomplishments." [11] The Federation
leaders had kept in touch with the Resolutions Committee throughout the session, and their seats for convention sessions were good.
But accomplishments had been few.

III

As he studied the situation after Kansas City, President Tobin
of the Teamsters felt that the Democrats could not possibly do less

[9] Republican Party Platform, in *Official Report of the Proceedings of the Nineteenth Republican National Convention* (New York, 1928), pp. 113–131.
[10] Editorial, *New York Times,* June 15, 1928.
[11] Republican Party Platform, in *Republican Convention Proceedings,* 114.

for labor than had the Republicans. What was the trouble? Why
was labor failing to get its point of view across?

> My opinion is, Labor should expect but very little from poli-
> ticians until it is fully organized or more thoroughly organized
> than at present. . . . Until we can prove to the political party
> managing the affairs of our nation that we have the power to
> dethrone them we can never hope to get anywhere.

A labor organization weak, divided, or cursed in part with selfish
leaders, said Tobin, could never "strike terror" into the hearts of
politicians. Labor must act as a body on election days.[12]

If Matthew Woll, William L. Hutcheson, or John L. Lewis, Republicans in the labor movement, made any public protests over
what was left undone at Kansas City, the public record is silent.
William Green, too, had nothing to say. A reporter for the *New
York Times* editorialized a bit in a signed news column devoted to
the platform, saying, "There are no planks with a progressive
trend, and no advocacy of social changes—just promises that the
Republican Party will endeavor to go forward on the traditions of
the past with as little interference with business as possible." [13]

A. F. of L. leaders seem to have hoped that Herbert Hoover
would advance well beyond the bare language of the platform in
his acceptance speech and later campaign utterances. After all,
John L. McNab of California in his nominating speech said that
Hoover always had shown sympathy for the laboring man, once
worked with his hands, and was a person who would understand
the toiler's problems. Hoover was termed humanitarian, statesman,
administrator, and "wholesome human being." [14] Perhaps he would
have much to say on labor issues when the time came. The labor
leaders would just have to wait. In the meantime, there was a trip
to be made to Houston, Texas, for the convention of the Democratic Party.

When interviewed enroute to Houston, William Green stated that
labor would seek there a modification of the Volstead Act to per-

---

[12] Editorial, *Teamsters Magazine*, XXV (July, 1928), 9. Written in June, between the conventions.
[13] Charles R. Michael in *New York Times*, June 15, 1928. The *Times* pinned
its hopes on Governor Smith in 1928, but its news column remained free of bias
for the most part.
[14] Text in *Republican Convention Proceedings*, pp. 177–185.

mit the sale of 2.75 per cent beer, clauses on better wages and working conditions for Federal employees, and relief from injunctions. Shortly after his arrival it became known that the labor group was pressing the Smith leaders to accord Major George L. Berry of Tennessee, president of the Printing Pressmen, the Vice Presidential nomination. "Of course the Smith people could give us no assurances," said Green, "but we came away with the distinct impression that our man would be favorably considered." Perhaps 250 to 400 votes might be obtained from the Middle West and South for the former vice commander of the American Legion, he thought.[15] Berry had been urged for the post as early as April by the president of the Colorado State Federation of Labor, and Hearst wrote at the time that Berry was very popular with both the union men and the publishers of America; the Democrats should take notice of him. Nothing came of this boomlet, however, for the big problem of 1928 seemed to be the farmer. Vice Presidential nominees Charles Curtis and Joseph T. Robinson were tailored by their parties to meet the alleged needs of the day. The campaign manager for Senator Alben W. Barkley of Kentucky asserted (correctly) that his man had the support of labor, especially the Brotherhoods, for the office, but to no avail. Berry's own explanation of his failure reads lamely. Senator Caraway, he said, had lined up Senators for Robinson, largely to get him out of the way in Arkansas politics! Berry said that he was at least second choice for the post, anyway.[16]

While there is no need to discuss here in any detail the Houston convention of the Democratic Party, a few items unknown to more than a handful of contemporaries may be mentioned briefly. Two speeches were noteworthy. One was the keynote speech of Claude G. Bowers, biographer and later ambassador; the other was Franklin D. Roosevelt's speech nominating Governor Smith. The two speeches had a certain kinship. Back in 1925, Bowers had discussed in a letter to Roosevelt his new book, *Jefferson and Hamilton*. "I wrote the book really to recall the party of Jefferson to the

[15] *New York Times*, June 24, 27, 1928. Other acceptable candidates: Robinson, Barkley, or Congressman Rainey of Illinois. Executive Council Minutes, August 1928, A. F. of L. Papers.
[16] Berry to Green, July 9, 1928, A. F. of L. Papers.

real meaning of Jeffersonian Democracy," he said,[17] obviously thrilled at Roosevelt's *New York World* review, which had applauded, "I feel like saying 'at last' as I read Mr. Claude G. Bowers' thrilling *Jefferson and Hamilton*." A few weeks after his first letter Bower added, "I am delighted because I really feel that the book is of political value." [18]

It was early in 1928 when Roosevelt, possibly recalling this interchange, asked that Bowers be named to a special committee on Preconvention Campaign Work "so that we may avail ourselves of his wonderful knowledge of the historic traditions of our Party in preparing material." [19] Bowers was selected to make the keynote speech and did so. Roosevelt's private reaction was, "I doubt if . . . he made many Republican or independent converts." Roosevelt said that in his *own* speech he took the other tack, since "it is my belief that the Democratic Party can never win until it converts about four million people who have usually voted the other way." [20]

Roosevelt nominated Smith from a manuscript posted on cardboard sheets and marked carefully for emphasis. "Heavy" and "low" appear. The speech was polished from half a dozen drafts, with the last paragraph written, changed, and rewritten repeatedly.[21] All this was "deliberately prepared" for "the benefit of the radio audience and the newspapers rather than for any oratorical effect it might have on the Convention itself," according to him.[22] "Smith had the votes anyway and it seemed to me more important to reach out for the Republicans and independents throughout the country." [23]

What did the visiting national labor leaders think of the Roosevelt emergence from years of partial paralysis? One can only guess. Al Smith wired, "HEARD YOUR SPLENDID SPEECH ON RADIO. MY DEEPEST THANKS AND APPRECIATION." [24] Among a thousand let-

[17] Bowers to Roosevelt, December 2, 1925, Roosevelt Papers.
[18] Bowers to Roosevelt, January 19, 1925, Roosevelt Papers.
[19] Roosevelt to Clem Shaver, January 7, 1928 (a preliminary draft; mailed?), Roosevelt Papers.
[20] Roosevelt to George Foster Peabody, August 7, 1928, Roosevelt Papers.
[21] Drafts in Roosevelt Papers.
[22] Roosevelt to C. I. Burch, August 22, 1928, Roosevelt Papers.
[23] Roosevelt to Walter Lippmann, August 6, 1928, Roosevelt Papers.
[24] Smith (at Albany) to Roosevelt, June 28, 1928, Roosevelt Papers.

ters and telegrams attracted by the speech [25] was Hamilton Holt's friendly appraisal that it was "the best I have heard from anyone, anywhere, since the death of Woodrow Wilson.[26] The immediate future for the man nominating Smith lay in the party nomination for Governor of New York State, and one must surmise that the Houston convention speech played a part in this outcome. As for the Bowers book and speech, they laid some of the groundwork for the "people" versus property rights issue which Roosevelt would make his own in the years ahead, applauded by many—including most leaders of labor.

IV

The A. F. of L. delegates at Houston had what they called the "widest possible opportunity" to present their viewpoints; theirs was a "respectful hearing." One and a half hours were occupied by the matter. (The request on the injunction was identical with that of Kansas City. [27])

The Democratic Party platform was vigorously criticized by the *New York Times,* which said editorially, "The interminable and wordy assertions and charges and pledges represent the resultant of many conflicting views and divergent hopes urged upon the Committee on Resolutions." [28] Like the Republican platform, it was a mass of compromises which tried to reconcile extreme views into positions that all might support. Its judgment on the worth of the political administrations since Wilson left office was the cry, "Turn the rascals out." To a business-minded nation it offered the idea that the Democratic Party stood for "businesslike reorganization" of the government; the party would use "businesslike methods." Moreover, "honest business, no matter what its size, need have no fears of a Democratic administration." Yet the government should "preserve equal opportunity," since prosperity should not be confined to a favored few. The platform found "agriculture prostrate, industry depressed, American shipping destroyed, work-

[25] Roosevelt to G. A. Rogers, Esq., August 6, 1928, Roosevelt Papers.
[26] Holt to Roosevelt, August 14, 1928, Roosevelt Papers.
[27] Executive Council Minutes, August, 1928, A. F. of L. Papers.
[28] *New York Times,* June 30, 1928.

men without employment, everywhere disgust and suspicion and corruption unpunished and unafraid." Although the tariff had been "monopolistic and extortionate" under the Republicans, the Democrats would manage to base it on rates sufficient to maintain legitimate business and a high standard of wages. The American laborer was promised adequate safeguards. Aid was promised the farmer in a lengthy section on agriculture. Some compromises tended to make the platform look somewhat ridiculous. Armaments would be reduced but national defense maintained adequately. The nation would cooperate with other nations, yet at the same time "stand as a unit." While the Republicans had not financed many important government agencies adequately, the Democratic platform thought taxes should be reduced.

The labor plank of the Democratic Party favored collective bargaining in principle and asserted that organized labor should choose its own representatives without coercion or interference. Labor was not a commodity and should therefore be exempt from the antitrust laws. If machinery were displacing men, something should be done about it, the platform said vaguely. There were sympathetic words for government employees, women in industry, and the coal industry. Immigration limitations should be preserved. It was thought that public works should be used to relieve unemployment once a study had been made.

The injunction plank was carefully phrased. The Democratic Party recognized that investigations showed that there had been "grave abuse" in the issuance of injunctions in labor disputes. Yet the party did not promise to do anything about it, even though a quick reading of the plank might give that impression.

> No injunctions should be granted in labor disputes except upon proof of threatened irreparable injury and after notice and hearing and the injunction should be confined to those acts which do directly threaten irreparable injury. The expressed purpose of representatives of capital, labor and the bar to devise a plan for the elimination of the present evils with respect to injunctions must be supported and legislation designed to accomplish these ends formulated and passed.[29]

[29] Democratic Party Platform, in *Proceedings of the Democratic National Convention* (Indianapolis, 1928), pp. 186–200.

What might constitute "irreparable injury"? Was there any "expressed purpose" of capital and labor to devise a plan satisfactory to both? The plank did not resemble labor's model in wording.

A tiny labor pressure group other than A. F. of L. with an interest in events in Kansas City and Houston was the National Women's Trade Union League (N.W.T.U.L.). A representative was sent to Kansas City, where she gave a four-minute speech to the Resolutions Committee (getting "splendid" local publicity but no national notice). No delegate went to Houston, inasmuch as Mrs. Franklin D. Roosevelt and several others who were called "exceptionally good friends" were to be present.[30] The group's secretary-treasurer, Elisabeth Christman, wrote a candid letter, however, to the chairman of the Democratic Party Resolutions Committee. She said that the group was "more than ordinarily interested in the coming national election" and therefore in the Democratic convention.

> There is no denying that our economic and political interests are closely related. In fact, they are interdependent. So it follows quite naturally that the eight and one-half million women in industry look to the Government to take a leading part in the establishing and upholding of industrial standards and safeguards.
>
> These working women have a responsibility and therefore a stake in our Government, so that the coming national convention of the Democratic Party holds for them a real significance with respect to principles and policies which shape the platform of the party especially as these policies affect the conditions of the workaday lives of these millions of women.

Legislation was to this executive the "supplementary arm" of unions. She wanted some limitation on issuance of injunctions.[31] "We have no way of judging just how effective our efforts were," wrote a N.W.T.U.L. official shortly, "but we do know, as you also know from the Democratic platform that [it] . . . contains much that suits our views." [32]

It probably was true, as Senator Key Pittman, chairman of the Committee on Platform and Resolutions told the convention, that

[30] Gail Wilson to Executive Board, N..W.T.U.L., July 31, 1928, N.W.T.U.L. Papers, Library of Congress.
[31] Letter of June 23, 1928, N.W.T.U.L. Papers.
[32] Wilson to Executive Board, July 31, 1928, N.W.T.U.L. Papers.

every group desiring to express itself had been given all the time it needed. He said that they "aided materially" in framing the planks. Labor had not been snubbed; yet the Democrat's injunction plank was not the one that American Federation of Labor leaders had hoped to see written in Houston.

"Which?"' (Drawn for *Labor* by John M. Baer)

V

A. F. of L. reaction to the Republican and Democratic platforms and candidates in 1928, as expressed behind the scenes, was unfavorable. Meeting behind closed doors, the Executive Council of the A. F. of L. found the Republican platform plank on injunctions "merely declaratory." It contained "no suggested specific remedy." The Council declared that the Democratic platform "failed to be specific" and was "susceptible of numerous interpretations." The labor leaders saw no value in the reference to a possible conference with capital and "the bar" and called such a step out of the question [33] (although the A. F. of L. *was* consulting lawyers and jurists by mail in summer, 1928). William Green explained the trying situation to the membership in a later issue of *American Federationist.* "The paramount legislative problem of Labor is relief from abuses of the injunction process," he declared. Neither major party had made "a satisfactory reply." [34] Thus even though Smith was to labor's friend Robert M. La Follette, Jr., "the most appealing and most progressive candidate offered by the Democratic Party in a national election since the World War," [35] and the *New York Times* said, "all those who cherish the fine American tradition of opportunity knocking at the door of the lowliest must find renewal of their faith and hope," [36] the leaders of labor would have to reach a consensus at their Atlantic City meeting before they could do what most wanted: endorse Al Smith.

From July 31 to August 7 the Executive Council met and argued. Matthew Woll had previously visited Hoover to try to get prolabor statements into his speech of acceptance. As someone put it casually, this would "give the Fat Boys a chance to support the Republican ticket." [37] The Nonpartisan Political Campaign Committee was puzzled. They asked William Green to gather

[33] Minutes, Executive Council, August, 1928, A. F. of L. Papers.
[34] "Injunction Planks Need Clarifications," *American Federationist*, XXV (August, 1928), 916.
[35] *La Follette's Magazine*, XXI (February, 1929), 18.
[36] Editorial, *New York Times*, June 29, 1928.
[37] A small scrap of torn Ogden L. Mills letterhead dated July 20, 1928, in the Walsh Papers, New York Public Library; writer unknown.

further data. The inside story of what happened next is fascinating. Said Green to his colleagues,

> I called upon Mr. Hoover, nominee on the Republican ticket and upon Governor Smith, nominee on the Democratic ticket. I explained to each of them that the platform declarations had not come up to our expectations. I told Mr. Hoover, however, that the Democratic committee had given us far more recognition than the Republican committee and had incorporated far more proposals of ours than the Republican. I said that the injunction plan was very unsatisfactory to the committee. They did not refer to the yellow dog contract. I mentioned the injunctions based on that issue against the Stone Cutters, Miners, and Textile Workers. I asked them to set forth what they thought about injunctions in their addresses of acceptance.

In response to Green's plea, Hoover said he recognized that the injunction abuse existed and said he expected to say in some definite way something about what he felt on the problem. Smith told Green that he thought the plank in the Democratic platform would be satisfactory to labor, since he had the impression from what someone had told him that it would be satisfactory before it was ever adopted! President Green quickly disabused Smith of this idea.

> I went into it and said the first paragraph was all right. I stated however that the statement that no injunction should be issued except to protect property was not satisfactory because that is what they are doing now, that the courts put a broad interpretation upon the term property.

Governor Smith was apparently much disturbed at this news and asked for a written memorandum on all this from Green; he also wanted much other material. Naturally, he got what he wanted. More than that, the head of the A. F. of L. hopefully sent him a section on the injunction "to be used in his address of acceptance." This statement concluded, "The preservation of American institutions and the perpetuation of the Republic require that Labor must be both economically and politically free." [38]

Meanwhile, the Executive Council was confronted by a resolution by Daniel Tobin of the Teamsters to the effect that the Council

---

[38] Minutes, Executive Council, August, 1928, A. F. of L. Papers. Mr. Green could remember little of all this when interviewed by the present writer in 1952.

endorse the Democratic platform and candidates for President and Vice President. The motion was duly seconded by a "wet" from the headquarters city of the Teamsters. In support of his motion Tobin intimated that the Executive Council in the days of Gompers had endorsed Bryan and later Wilson, saying he "understood" that to have been the case. Hoover, said Tobin, was brilliant and able.

> Perhaps he is sympathetic to labor, but as far as I know Hoover has never made a clean-cut declaration in favor of organized labor. He has talked about the consideration that labor is entitled to, has expressed himself in favor of the workers, but to my knowledge has never come out with a clean-cut statement for organized labor. I may not be fully informed. Hoover has taken the careful position of the technical engineer, recognizing the rights of all men, that they are entitled to a just living, hours of leisure and so on. On the other hand the candidate of the Democratic Party has not only fully expressed himself open and above board, but has gone from one end of the state to the other, and in all of his public utterances has spoken in unmistakable language as to the rights of organized labor.[39]

These were not quite the same sentiments to be found in the *Teamsters Magazine* in spring, 1928, but it was easy to recognize the Tobin touch.

Little of this was known to the public at the time. There was ample speculation in the papers, where it was made clear from the outset that there would be *no* third-party movement like 1924 in 1928. President Green had already said so publicly, and perhaps significantly, in Wisconsin.[40] Examination of numerous newspapers shows little speculation on the matter at the time. When the Executive Council met, however, it was rumored that there was a political division in its ranks.[41] And there were rumors that several Railroad Brotherhood leaders would support Hoover.

Some of the union leaders wanted to adjourn and meet again after the acceptance speeches had put the candidates more clearly on the record. The injunction picture might be changed. "With possibly two exceptions," wrote a reporter, "the members of the

[39] By "the state" Tobin meant New York State.
[40] *New York Times,* July 20, 1928.
[41] *Ibid.,* July 27, 1928.

Executive Council are personally in favor of Governor Smith." [42]
Two days later the count was said to be two for Hoover, two for
Smith, and the rest not known.[43] One group was said to be too
disappointed in the injunction planks of both platforms to be willing to come to the aid of either nominee. By August 6 the Council
was still undecided, but it was said that the partisans of Smith
were battling for him and that no effort was any longer being made
for Hoover.[44]

The leader of the pro-Smith forces was, as has been revealed
above, Daniel J. Tobin. Reporters identified him as having been
long an admirer of the Governor's policies on labor and welfare
matters. He had come to know Smith when the latter was president
of the United States Trucking Corporation. Tobin delivered long
arguments in favor of his position. He made a motion to endorse
Smith and got a second.[45] Then, according to him, the motion
was "side-tracked by a substitute which in the judgment of the
maker of the motion was entirely illegal." [46]

Reporters did the best they could to find out about the argument
that was going on behind closed doors, but they were forced to
rely on stray comments dropped accidentally or judiciously between sessions. Thus one Smith partisan said, "The majority was
against us today. They were not for Hoover, but simply because
they feel we should center our fight on Congress and not commit
ourselves on the Presidency they would not endorse Smith. We
will make another effort tomorrow." Tempers became frayed.
Green simply commented, "We had a discussion of labor's nonpartisan policy and reached no decision." Others said, "We won't
reach an agreement in a week," and "It looks tough." [47] What was
really going on behind those doors?

Debate on the Tobin motion calling for a Smith endorsement
was acrimonious. Several Council members said, in effect, "What

[42] *Ibid.*, August 2, 1928. There were eleven men on the Executive Council.
[43] *Ibid.*, August 4, 1928.
[44] *Ibid.*, August 7, 1928.
[45] Jacob Fisher of Indianapolis, president of the Barbers, said to be a "wet."
The Teamsters' headquarters was in that city, it should be noted.
[46] New York State Federation *Proceedings, 1928,* p. 140. An observation made
in public in an address before the Federation convention, August 29, 1928.
[47] *New York Times,* August 7, 1928.

if we endorse a candidate and in his acceptance speech he is un-satisfactory on the injunction or something else vital to our in-terests?" These opposed endorsement. Ryan added that to endorse might actually *hurt* the man endorsed. We should leave it up to the members or we will be challenged as to our *right* to intervene in private affairs. Do not endorse! Noonan agreed, saying that the case of La Follette in 1924 was exceptional. "Members of our af-filiated organizations do not surrender the right to vote as they please when they join the American Federation of Labor," he said. O'Connell's argument amounted to "wait."

Matthew Woll judged that it would be "fatal" to endorse the *platforms,* in the first place, because then labor would be standing squarely in back of their wording. Another member inquired of no one in particular at this point: What would be done about union officers and members who had already declared for Hoover? Sev-eral other Council members spoke up for nonpartisanship on the Presidential campaign. Then it was William Green's turn.

President of the A. F. of L. a scant three years at the time, Green began as follows: "My opinion is the fact must be recog-nized that most of the members here are friendly and sympathetic towards Governor Smith." Their feelings were clearly to adopt Brother Tobin's motion. Yet what of *solidarity* in the labor move-ment? "I feel at this time if we made the endorsement the fight would be transferred from the political to the economic field, and we cannot afford that."

Secretary-treasurer Morrison hoped that the Tobin endorsement motion would be withdrawn, he said, for special circumstances had dictated actions of this kind in the past. It was true that Taft had been opposed on his injunction record in 1912. Wilson had been supported in 1916 because of his wonderful legislative record as President. In the latter's case, however, it would be recalled that the Labor Representation Committee's report to the Executive Council was submitted *to the full Convention.* It had been the Convention that directed that every honorable effort be made to elect Woodrow Wilson. The result of these words was more dis-cussion, and so ended the day. No doubt the Council members walked the Boardwalk, took a dip in the ocean, or visited the famous Steel Pier—evading questions of reporters all the while. Late at night the argument continued in various hotel rooms.

President Green opened the next day's session by saying that he judged the consensus to be that *no endorsement* be given. He paid reference to the continuing existence of the Tobin motion calling for a Smith endorsement and said he had a substitute "proposal" for that of Tobin. Ryan, who had expressed doubts previously, seconded Green's substitute amendment for the Tobin motion, saying, however, "I do not think there is any member here who is not friendly to Governor Smith." Green then proceeded to defend what he had done—that is, *by a parliamentary maneuver turn a Smith endorsement motion into a nonpartisan policy statement.* It was not a matter of "fear," he said. To endorse anyone at all just was not in the interests of the labor movement. If the Executive Council had voted down the Tobin proposal the step could have been interpreted in some circles as an act favorable to Hoover! "That is not true." Then why force a vote on the clear-cut matter? "There is a difference between a man going out and supporting a candidate, and committing the American Federation of Labor to a political party through the official action of this Council," said Green. To endorse a *candidate* means to endorse a *platform*— and to endorse a *party*. ". . . The fight would be intense in our ranks. We are an economic organization," Green reminded fellow leaders of the American Federation of Labor.

A parliamentary fight of much heat ensued, with Tobin claiming that his motion was on the floor, so that another was out of order, and Green contending (correctly) that he had been within his rights in offering an amendment to an existing motion, even though the step had the effect of negating or changing its purpose. Tobin appealed the matter but lost by a six-to-one hand vote (some abstaining). As a result, the Green nonpartisan amendment was tacked on and the original motion passed as amended without any dissents—all reference to Smith having been excised!

Tobin was incensed. Angrily he said that because of this parliamentary maneuvering and its results he would not "from today on" serve as a member of the Executive Council. He would not be a party to this "railroading." The official Executive Council min-

utes then read, cryptically, "Members of the Council endeavored
to dissuade Treasurer Tobin but he retired from the Council room
upon concluding his statement." [48] In this atmosphere of hard feelings the leaders of American organized labor concluded their latest
foray into the arena of official candidate endorsement.

The amended motion (minus the whole story just told, of
course) was quickly given to reporters. "We will await with great
interest the expression of each of the candidates, reserving to ourselves a final decision regarding our future policy during the remainder of the campaign," it said. This was a rather transparent
warning.[49] The Federation had found through experience, it continued, that the best interests of the membership were protected
through a nonpartisan political policy. Nevertheless, Tobin was
convinced that this policy ought to mean across-the-board support
for friends and opposition for enemies. He would say later in the
summer that nonpartisanship does not require neutrality. Smith
was a "friend" and should therefore be supported. Said Tobin, "Let
me say in espousing his [Smith's] cause I feel honestly that I am
carrying out the policies of the Federation of Labor and the Executive Council in helping to elect to office the friends of labor." [50]
Others knew better. Obviously disappointed at the failure of the
A. F. of L. to endorse Al Smith, the *New York Times* called the
action in the light of 1924 a case of "the burnt child dreading the
fire." But then "neutrality certainly does not mean hostility," it
said hopefully, suggesting that maybe a tacit understanding would
prove as strong as a formal endorsement.[51]

Where did the events at Atlantic City, "the convention city,"
leave the official position of the A. F. of L. in the election of
1928? Labor would continue to engage in pressure politics at national, state, and local levels. Full information about platforms
and candidates would be made available to the individual members
of organized labor. They would know what to do! The Executive

[48] Minutes, Executive Council, August, 1928, A. F. of L. Papers.
[49] *New York Times*, August 8, 1928. See also *Christian Science Monitor*, August 9, 1928.
[50] *N.Y.S. Fed. Proceedings, 1928*, p. 141.
[51] Editorial, "Organized Labor and Parties," *New York Times*, August 8, 1928.
See also, "Labor's Neutral Strategy," *Literary Digest*, XCVIII (August 25, 1928),
15.

Council would report later that after all, the labor movement was made up of men and women of differing political opinions who had not been required to identify themselves with a political party when they joined the union. Working people were perfectly free to vote the dictates of their consciences.[52]

When, as in 1928, organized labor is confronted with two Presidential candidates, neither one of them recognizable as an "enemy," the policy of rewarding "friends" cannot operate effectively. If neither party is prepared to make a strong bid for union support as such, union leaders can hardly expect to make the rank and file see the necessity of voting for either ticket. Only as between black and white can labor leaders agree fully on white. This seems to be an important lesson of 1928. Even as late as August—after the party nominees had been selected and the platforms written—labor found it impossible at the national level to agree on which Presidential candidate and which party would best serve the needs and interests of the unions.

As one result of this decision for indecision at the top, the union membership, the local union officials, the leaders of city centrals and state federations, and those who controlled the national and international unions would have to choose between Hoover and Smith without reference to advisory or partially authoritative decisions from above. One of the many that did just that was the New York State Federation of Labor, a top official of which would tell why Al Smith had been endorsed officially in spite of the national nonpartisan declaration.

The Democratic Convention [in New York State] very clearly and definitely pledged itself to the support and enactment of our bill to change the procedure in the issuance of injunctions. . . . The Democratic platform also included a number of our other proposals. The Republican Convention [in our state] did not respond at all to our injunction proposal and gave a very indefinite pledge on improvements in the labor laws. The Socialist Party adopted our program as presented.[53]

[52] Quoted in Report of the Executive Council, A. F. of L. *Proceedings, 1928*, pp. 75–76. The Council judged with vast overoptimism that labor "invariably" supported the political friends of the A. F. of L.

[53] John M. O'Hanlon to William Green, October 23, 1928, A. F. of L. Papers.

Labor at the *state* level, he seemed to be saying, could make the difficult choice on candidates for *national* office, basing the decision on the line-up of men and issues within the state. How many other labor bodies would follow this or related reasoning in 1928? The answer would depend on many things, but among them would surely be the postures assumed in the months before election day by Hoover, Smith, Thomas, and Foster—candidates appealing nationally for votes. It is to the framework of these strikingly different appeals that we will now turn, for a spectrum may be seen.

Chapter 7

Hoover Appeals To The Laboring Man

ONE CAN HARDLY ACCOUNT for the nomination and election of Republican candidate Herbert C. Hoover in 1928 on the basis of the antagonistic and partisan treatment he has often received in accounts written since that time. We are told, "Leaders like Herbert Hoover had not, by their personal life, been attuned to the wants of inconspicuous people. . . ." Here was "a member of the managerial class" unacquainted with the "daily yearnings of ordinary humankind." [1] Another volume found little good to say about the man elected overwhelmingly in 1928, except that he was a rich and successful man, a good organizer, and a friend of business with a passion for facts.[2] Yet another book, on the other hand, found him to be a man with "a vivid record as a humanitarian" who actually "assumed office amid the warm plaudits of his countrymen who hailed him as a brilliant liberal who had earned his position by his distinguished humanitarian and administrative services for over fifteen years." [3] Can this be the same person? It is admitted

[1] Ray Allen Billington, Bert James Loewenberg, and Samuel Hugh Brockunier, *The United States: American Democracy in World Perspective* (New York, 1947), p. 648.
[2] Oscar Theodore Barck, Jr., and Nelson Manfred Blake, *Since 1900: A History of the United States in Our Times* (New York, 1947), p. 427.
[3] Harvey Wish, *Contemporary America: The National Scene Since 1900* (New York, 1945), p. 411–412.

in at least one textbook—and ought to be better known—that Mr. Hoover "was not regarded with approval by the old-line Republican politicians." [4] Indeed, the favorable portrait of Hoover painted by the Beards in their final "historical judgment which we have reached after more than forty years" has been ignored by some historians who pay qualified tribute to Charles A. and Mary E. Beard in matters of politics and economics. To them, Hoover was in 1928 "widely known as a philanthropist and a man of avowed social sympathies." [5] Thinly veiled contempt for Hoover as evidenced in books, articles, and book reviews written since his Presidential years has made it nearly impossible for two decades to get a sympathetic hearing in historical circles for plain facts about his career—facts which would be admitted instantly if they were to be presented about a public figure of an earlier generation. The fact is that Candidate Hoover was no enemy of labor in 1928; he was not, and he could not have been factually portrayed at the time in any such light.

I

The Republican candidate, who avoided ghost writers and prepared his own speeches, has written in retrospect that from the very beginning of political activity in 1928 he felt that victory was certain. Had Smith been a Protestant, Mr. Hoover claimed, the margin of his own victory might have been even greater! [6] The worst plague on the campaign, Hoover judges, was the religious issue, but it had "no weight on the final results." As for the famous prohibition issue, it was "forced into the campaign by Governor Smith," but it "did not do him any good." [7] One need not be in agreement with these opinions to sense that Mr. Hoover has felt

[4] Frank Lawrence Owsley, Oliver Perry Chitwood, and H. C. Nixon, *A Short History of the American People,* Vol. II (New York, 1948), 597.

[5] *A Basic History of the United States* (Philadelphia, 1944), pp. 443–444. A survey of books published for college textbook use in the 1960s might (or might not) show some improvements over those quoted here.

[6] *The Memoirs of Herbert Hoover: The Cabinet and the Presidency, 1920–1933* (New York, 1952), pp. 199, 198, 208.

[7] *Ibid.,* pp. 200, 202, 207, 209.

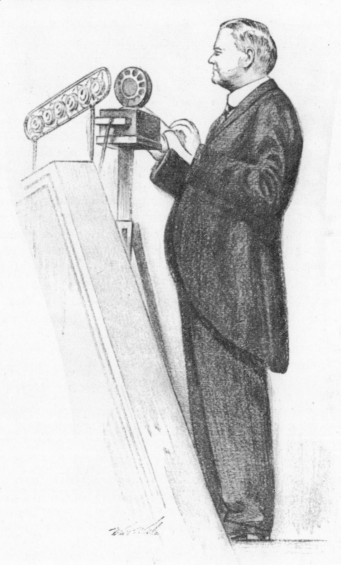

Herbert Clark Hoover, Republican candidate for President

that his attraction for the ordinary citizen was a broad one, transcending the sensational issues of the day.

While the appeal which Hoover and his Party made for labor support in the election of 1928 will be described here in detail, there can be no question that the major efforts of the Republican Party were devoted to other matters. "As a matter of fact," the Assistant Director of Publicity for the party in 1928 has written in retrospect, "I think so far as the Republican campaign leaders were concerned, we were much more troubled about the attitude of the farm vote than we were about the attitude of the labor group." After all, "There were no such close political-labor alliances as exist today." Still, the tariff and immigration issues were among the items of economic controversy emphasized by the Republican National Committee.[8] The laboring men of America were not out of the minds of Candidate Hoover and the party lieutenants.

The Republican Party organization called Hoover a leader without peer. This was a view facilitated by the well-known facts of his career to that time. The Party reprinted in booklet form a standard biographical sketch from an encyclopedia, whose subheadings read, "earned own living early," "courage, ability, honesty," "began relief work in 1914," "solved Belgian problems." Then followed "how Hoover fed a nation" while "others followed his lead." His "services [were] claimed by U.S." so that he "saved Europe's starving." In all, "23 countries [were] fed by U.S.A." and he even "fought famine in Russia." Thus, "new tasks [were] given Hoover" so that at length he "holds many high honors." [9] In a pamphlet, "Herbert Hoover: A Product of America" [10] the Republican organization promised that Hoover would "carry out his plans and ideas which will insure a greater country and more prosperity for all." *What had been so psychologically oversold would one day fall in psychological ruins.* Hoover's own speeches,

---

[8] Alfred H. Kirchhofer to the writer, February 23, 1952. Republican Party pamphlets cited here were loaned by this helpful journalist.

[9] "Biographical Sketch of Herbert Hoover," reprinted from the *National Cyclopedia of American Biography*, Washington, D. C., 1928. See also the reprinted article by Charlotte Kellogg reprinted from *Commonweal*, "Herbert Hoover as Women See Him," Washington, D. C., 1928.

[10] Washington, D. C., 1928.

unified around the theme of "The New Day," promised far less than this, indicated problem areas, and stressed the idea that progress depended in part on the necessity of cooperative leadership in the government. "I can only succeed in my part by the cooperation and unity of spirit of all leaders of opinion and action for the common service of our country," he said.[11] As has been so well put, "President Hoover's New Day was to end before sunrise." [12]

Herbert Clark Hoover delivered his acceptance address at Palo Alto, California, on August 11, 1928, thus taking responsibility for party leadership. He stressed in his speech the progress which America had made in the eight years of Republican administration, and he predicted, with the lack of omniscience that affected nearly all contemporaries, that the future would see a happy and prosperous nation. The recent past, judged Hoover more correctly, had seen increases in income, production, consumption, and home ownership. Electricity, telephones, and radios had come into more homes. It was an automobile age, with splendid roads linking the countryside together. Cities had grown magnificent with "beautiful buildings, parks, and playgrounds." The speaker's eyes were fixed on the broad facts of accomplishment, not on the sins of omission.

Electricity had reduced manual labor, Hoover observed with approval. The purchasing power of wages was up; hours of work were down. Job security was on the increase, and "unemployment in the sense of distress" was on the downgrade. Savings deposits and life insurance had almost doubled, and gifts to charity had risen. "We in America today," said the Republican nominee confidently, "are nearer to the final triumph over poverty than ever before in the history of any land." And, indeed, so it seemed to most hearers. Hoover paid tribute to the value of the protective tariff and immigration restriction. *To reduce the tariff,* he said, *would be to injure every home, fill the streets with idle workers, and destroy the income of the farmers.*

[11] Concluding sentence of statement on election day, November 7, 1928, *The New Day,* p. 217.

[12] Edgar Eugene Robinson, *The Roosevelt Leadership, 1933–1945,* (Philadelphia, 1955), p. 37.

Trade unions in America have been staunch supporters of American individualism and American institutions, Hoover told his nationwide radio audience over a 107-station network. Unions had steadfastly opposed "subversive doctrines" from abroad. They usually welcomed basic improvements in industrial methods, and their effort to get higher wages was proper. Employers realized that the "highest practicable wage" was the road to increased consumption and prosperity. Thus machines, effort, and production would together bring higher wages. *After endorsing collective bargaining in principle, he limited himself to a paraphrase of the Republican platform on the injunction, observing simply, "We stand also pledged to the curtailment of excessive use of the injunction in labor disputes."*

Hoover stressed the supreme importance of equality of opportunity, calling it a fundamental national principle against which all policies should be tested. "The success or failure of this principle is the test of our government." Individualism based upon equal opportunity to every citizen was the "negation of socialism." Therefore:

> Conservative, progressive, and liberal thought and action have their only real test in whether they contribute to equal opportunity, whether they hold open the door of opportunity. If they do not they are false in their promise no matter what their name may be.[13]

The speeches of Hoover in 1928 were marked by a special effort to delineate the relationship that should obtain between government and business. In general, government should regulate business, not compete with it, but regulation should be avoided so long as equal opportunity for all citizens had not been invaded or public rights violated. Yet it was the duty of business "to conduct itself so that government regulation or government competition" would not be necessary. "Our whole business system would break down in a day if there was not a high sense of moral responsibility in our business world." Hoover condemned socialism, anarchy, and despotism. He praised the American way of life for "with

[13] Text in *New York Times*, August 12, 1928, pp. 2–3 or Herbert Hoover, *The New Day* (Stanford University, 1928). pp. 9–44.

impressive proof on all sides of magnificent progress, no one can rightly deny the fundamental correctness of our economic system."

There was no appeal in Hoover's acceptance address to union leaders or union members as such. There was no class or group appeal. In effect, Hoover denied that there were stabilized classes or that Presidential candidates should recognize or sponsor interest groups, as such, in America.

The acceptance address, widely heard through earphones and loudspeakers, would have a strong appeal over a far-flung nation which believed itself prosperous and thought of its past with pride. Hoover's audience in August, 1928 seemed unaware of the coming economic collapse, preferring instead to believe in continued national progress toward an inevitably happy future.

The themes stressed by the Republican candidate in his acceptance speech appeared elsewhere in party circles in the summer and fall of 1928. The acceptance speech of Charles Curtis, the Vice Presidential nominee, reflected his agrarian interests and ignored organized labor. Senator Smoot found tariff and immigration bars great Republican gifts to labor. A national committeeman from Connecticut said he considered the reference Hoover had made to a job for every man likely to prove one of his most effective statements. The Republican National Committee predicted that Smith, if elected, would probably follow a low tariff policy which would dump the low-priced products of Asia and Europe on American markets, so that homes and wages of American workingmen would be adversely affected.[14]

The Republican National Committee issued a booklet entitled "Hoover's Record as a Friend of Labor." [15] The candidate's 1908 book, *Principles of Mining,* was quoted:

> Given a union with leaders who can control the members, and who are disposed to approach differences in a business spirit, there are few sounder positions for employers, for agreements, honorably carried out, dismiss the constant harassments of possible strikes. Such unions exist in dozens of trades in this country, and they are entitled to greater recognition. The time when the

[14] *New York Times,* August 19, 16, 27, and September 1, 1928.
[15] Wasington, D. C., 1928.

employer could ride roughshod over his labor is disappearing with the doctrine of laissez faire, on which it was founded.

Another quote was from a Hoover address of August 27, 1925.

It is my opinion that our Nation is very fortunate in having the American Federation of Labor. It has exercised a powerful influence in stabilizing industry and in maintaining an American standard of citizenship. Those forces of the Old World that would destroy our institutions and our civilization have been met in the front-line trenches by the Federation of Labor and routed at every turn.

Another campaign booklet, "Hoover and Labor," had on its cover a quote attributed to the candidate, "The Highest Practicable Wage is the Road to Increased Consumption and Prosperity." Within appeared the judgment, "He has been a worker and is still a worker." [16] The campaign textbook of the Republican Party contended that while credit was due organized labor for maintenance of high wage levels, the satisfactory levels of the day were the result of industrial prosperity—not its cause. From the tenor of these partisan publications, it is clear that the Republican Party framed its appeal to laboring men as such, rather than to trade union organizations or their leaders.

II

In West Branch, Iowa, on August 21, Hoover applied himself to the question of farm relief, and on September 17 in Newark, N. J., he devoted his major address to industrial America. The Newark speech contained statistics designed to show the progress of the nation to date, how little unemployment and distress actually existed in America, and the bright hope for "social peace and contentment" which was presumed to lie ahead. The problem of adjusting the economic system to the social ideals of the nation was thought to be well on the road to solution; yet much admittedly remained to be done. Hoover reiterated that his party stood in "positive support of collective bargaining." It was necessary,

[16] See also "Hoover on Human Relations in Industry," (Washington, D. C., 1928), a Labor Council publication.

moreover, "to impose restrictions on the excessive use of injunctions." Still, no particular legislative action in these areas was promised.

Hoover said that full and stable employment was essential and a strong and balanced economic system absolutely necessary. Restriction of immigration, the protective tariff, and the work of the Department of Commerce were said to have played important roles in furthering prosperity.

What Hoover stressed at Newark was the identity of interest which he felt had come to exist between employer and employee in America. Each group had largely come to accept high wage theories, the virtues of efficiency and mechanization, and the advantages of "full personal effort." Here he found the pathway to cheaper costs, lower prices, wider consumption, and larger production. Neither employers nor employees any longer thought that labor was "an economic commodity"; both realized that increased efficiency ought to bring a reward in either higher wages or lower prices. Employers and employees had joined in repelling "socialism and other subversive movements." He said it would be idle to argue that the two groups no longer had any conflicts of interest between them, but he felt that prosperous times and sound governmental policies would see an increase in their areas of agreement.

In concluding this address in an industrial community of the East, the Republican nominee paid tribute to the virtues of *leadership*. How might leaders be developed in the "great American experiment"? Not through birth or money, selection by divine right, class advantages, or "bureaucracy." Rather, said Hoover, in paragraphs widely approved and quoted by the press:

> Our leadership can be found and it will be sympathetic to our ideals if we maintain the decency and dignity of family life through a stable economic system; if we maintain free and universal education and thus provide them the open stair to leadership; if we maintain for every individual an equality of opportunity to attain that position in the community to which his character and his ability entitle him. Then our supply of leadership will stream forward of its own impulse. It is in this insistence upon an equal chance and a free road to rise in leadership that our great American experiment has departed from those of his-

tory. It is our sure guarantee of the future. In its vast possibilities is the hope of every mother for her boys and girls.

Under such leadership, replenished constantly from the great mass of our people, we can aspire to a democracy which will express a common purpose for the common good. We can build a civilization where national conscience is alert to protect the rights of all, curtail selfish economic power, and hold to the ideals of distributed contentment among the whole people.[17]

No one will ever know what thoughts passed through the minds of millions of radio listeners as they heard this spirited rejection of the idea that America was a land of classes into which children were born and from which they could not escape, except by death. Were Americans of the twenties attracted by this vision of a government and an economic system which would not handicap the ambitious and intelligent? We know that a few persons felt like replying that they were "proletarians crushed by the capitalist system." These believed that neither they nor their children could rise to positions of leadership until the "system" came to be changed fundamentally. Some readers of labor union periodicals, moreover, preferred to analyze the position of Hoover on the injunction or other "labor issues" and voted against him on these matters. But how many men and women in 1928 thought in such terms? Did leading radicals and union leaders of the day expect too much technical and legal understanding from their rank and file when they talked in such terms? Under the heading "Mr. Hoover's Economic Essay," the *New York Times* found his comments on American inventiveness and self-reliance "sound and just" and his views of leadership praiseworthy. Was it not probable, the editorial asked, that people might go into "a kind of rapture" over his dry statistics and declare that he was just the man needed to head "the greatest business government in the world"? [18]

[17] Address at Newark, New Jersey, September 17, 1928, *The New Day*, p. 86. Printed at the time in pamphlet form as "Herbert Hoover Champions Labor."

[18] Editorial, *New York Times*, September 18, 1929. The irrepressible Will Rogers wrote that "Herbert" had come into Newark marked " 'Exhibit A.' " (*Ibid.*, October 4, 1928.) A Socialist Party spokesman found the speech a mixture of "shameless Prussianism" and "statistical sleight-of-hand designed to bulldoze the American worker into voting the Republican ticket through abject fear of unemployment." (*Ibid.*, September 20, 1928.)

Speaking in New York City toward the close of the campaign, the engineer in politics described for his fellow countrymen his vision of the future:

> My conception of America is a land where men and women may walk in ordered freedom in the independent conduct of their occupations; where they may enjoy the advantages of wealth, not concentrated in the hands of the few but spread through the lives of all, where they build and safeguard their homes and give to their children the fullest advantages and opportunities of American life; where every man shall be respected in the faith that his conscience and his heart direct him to follow; where a contented and happy people, secure in their liberties, free from poverty and fear, shall have the leisure and impulse to seek a fuller life.[19]

To Republican partisan Charles Evans Hughes, Herbert Hoover was without a doubt "labor's best friend." [20]

Various party leaders, meanwhile, framed appeals designed to woo the "labor vote." Ray Lyman Wilbur told a Norfolk, Virginia, audience that the Democratic tariff plan meant "distress and disaster to the American laborer and farmer." Charles Curtis campaigned in Indiana on the importance of continuing prosperity, and Secretary of the Treasury Mellon concurred with this theme, saying that the word "prosperity" translated into automobiles, bank deposits, foreign trade, reduced taxes, and reduced public debt. Another speaker claimed that over seven billion dollars had gone to workmen through the efforts of Secretary of Commerce Hoover to maintain wage scales and to keep employment at high levels [21]—a claim not readily subject to proof or disproof.

[19] Address in New York City, October 22, 1928, *The New Day*, p. 176.
[20] *New York Times*, October 25, 1928.
[21] *Ibid.*, October 5, 6, 12, 14, 1928.

III

The Republican Party had within it in 1928 the Progressives [22]
—a group favoring alternative appeals on many major matters. At
the Kansas City convention they had agrarian-oriented allies
among the delegates who shared their convictions on agriculture,
and urban allies who agreed with their stand for a modification
of the Volstead Act. But true-blue Progressives were the ones who
supported the minority platform which was presented on the floor
of the convention by young Robert M. La Follette, Jr. (who spoke
on behalf of a "Progressive Republican delegation" from Wisconsin) on behalf of delegates from seven other Midwestern states
who signed his platform. La Follette told the convention that similar dissenting platforms had been presented at every convention of
the party since 1908 and that thirty-two of the "thirty-five or
more" propositions thus advanced had been written into law. The
delegates applauded, some wryly and some with enthusiasm, at this
reminder that the G.O.P. had not in the past rushed to espouse
ideas from Wisconsin.

The labor plank of the minority platform was far different from
that of the majority document. Its single paragraph was devoted
largely to the injunction. On this matter, which so greatly concerned labor leaders in 1928, it said:

> Government by injunction is repugnant to American institu-
> tions and traditions. The use of injunctions in labor disputes
> threatens to destroy the effectiveness of labor organizations. We
> uphold the right of labor to organize and to bargain collectively
> through representatives of their own choosing. We urge the
> passage by Congress of legislation to restrict the issuance of in-
> junctions in labor disputes and to guarantee jury trial in contempt
> cases.[23]

[22] A capital "P" will be used here to indicate that faction in the Republican
Party, largely in the Middle West, that rallied behind the minority plank presented to the convention in 1928 or who shared its general viewpoints. When the
word appeared with a capital letter in 1924 it indicated supporters of the C.P.P.A.,
many of them Democrats. Earlier, it meant followers of the 1912 Bull Moose
movement.

[23] *Proceedings of the Republican National Convention, 1928* (New York, 1928),
p. 139. The minority platform appears on p. 133 to 142.

The paragraph embodied the major desires of trade union leaders. It was to be rejected, together with the platform containing it.

After the close of the Republican convention, the themes of the abortive Progressive platform formed the chief subject-matter of *La Follette's Magazine,* organ of Progressivism. Although the problems of organized labor had not been a primary concern of the magazine from January to June, 1928, it had carried in March an article by A. F. of L. leader Andrew Furuseth directed against the abuse of injunctions. The "reactionary platform adopted at Kansas City" was condemned during the summer and fall, for among other things, it had failed to meet the issue of injunctions (a matter said to be threatening the very existence of labor organizations). The Progressives thought that the Republican convention had been controlled by "the great bankers and industrialists of the East." [24] Populism was not dead! When a Progressive Republican Platform for Wisconsin came to be written, it contained the same strong anti-injunction plank as this rejected national platform.[25] On Labor Day La Follette spoke in Milwaukee on the labor legislation pending before Congress. He quoted William Green with approval, saying that the "wrongful use" of injunctions was undermining free institutions.[26]

Thus the road taken by the majority at Kansas City was not the only road open to the Republican Party. While there had been a far more conservative path—with Dawes, there also had been the path of Progressivism, offering in its labor proposals a forthright appeal for the support of union leaders.

The general theme of the Progressives was the existence of a battle between what was called "the principle of equality" and "privilege." The words "equal" and "equality" were almost the punctuation of the minority platform, for in the first six sentences they were used seven times. Yet the emphasis on equality rather than opportunity was more apparent than real. Over the years many Americans had come to believe that freedom of opportunity had given ground to privilege, monopoly, and the very negation

[24] Editorial, "The Opportunity for Progressives in 1928," *La Follette's Magazine,* XX (July, 1928), 97.
[25] Text in *ibid.,* XX (August, 1928), 123.
[26] Text in *ibid.,* XX (September, 1928), 140–141.

of opportunity. By fighting monopoly, Progressives felt that they
fought the battle for opportunity. By "equality" they did not have
in mind state-enforced equalitarian doctrines preached by the
Communist Party. While in their advocacy of government activity
in the power field they were socialistic, it was not an across-the-
board socialism that they urged. Thus it was far removed from the
Socialist Party platform of the day.[27] Nor was the Progressive
program aimed at the general destruction of property rights.

The point being made here about Progressivism in the late 1920s
is that it was a repository in the Republican Party of a desire to
redress substantially the balance between employers and working
men in the direction of the latter. Perhaps if the Progressive point
of view on the injunction had been accepted by the leaders of the
Republican Party in 1928, it would have increased support by
union leadership for Hoover and his party.

Informed advisors urged Democrats to bid for Progressive support. One veteran of the C.P.P.A. campaign of 1924 wrote:

> If you want to see Smith elected I urge you not to fail to
> present this situation to him as strongly as possible. I am afraid
> that Smith's New York advisors do not realize the importance of
> his securing the active and wholehearted support of the Western
> Progressives. He can have this support with the right sort of a
> platform and the right sort of campaign.[28]

After the election Franklin D. Roosevelt, in an effort to rebuild
the Democratic Party, wrote the son of an old political associate
(then in Wisconsin), "I was hopeful that the La Follette crowd
would help us some, but quite the reverse seems to have been the
case." In reply he was told

> I believe you are quite wrong. The help was not as strong as
> one would wish, but so far as I know, no Progressive of promi-
> nence publicly supported Hoover and very few voted for him,
> while as you well know, many Progressives, from Senator Blaine
> and William T. Evjue (editor of the leading Progressive paper)
> down, actively campaigned for Smith. Indeed, I would go so

---

[27] The present writer examined *La Follette's Magazine* from 1925 to 1929. So
far as could be determined, neither the Socialist Party nor Norman Thomas as
an individual or candidate was mentioned—even in the election year of 1928.

[28] Basil M. Manley to Frank P. Walsh, June 13, 1928, Walsh Papers, New York
Public Library.

far as to say that the only effective campaigning outside Milwaukee and the adjacent German area was done by Progressives and thru the Progressive organization.

Roosevelt replied, "I hope you are right about the Progressives. Do you think we can keep any of them in line?" [29]

The feelings of A. F. of L. leaders toward the Progressives were friendly. To a correspondent who suggested that labor actively oppose La Follette in Wisconsin, President William Green wrote:

> For many years the late Senator La Follette, and since his death his son, supported all remedial legislation urged by the American Federation of Labor. The present Senator La Follette has on many occasions gone out of his way to be helpful to labor. He is ever ready and willing to discuss the cause of labor before committees or on the floor of the Senate.

All union men and friends of labor would certainly be urged to vote for him.[30]

While Herbert Hoover was not one of the Progressives, he clearly considered himself dedicated to progress. Desiring to conserve what he felt to be finest in the past of America, that is, freedom of the individual and full equality of opportunity, he was conservative—resisting fundamental institutional change. Standing in opposition to the government actively engaging in business or indulging in unnecessary regulation of industry or the individual, Hoover was not free of traditional laissez faire sentiments. He was quite sure he was a *true liberal*. In his New York speech of October 22 he dwelt on the semantics and political philosophy of the point:

> It is false liberalism that interprets itself into the government operation of commercial business. Every step of bureaucratizing the business of our country poisons the very roots of liberalism— that is, political equality, free speech, free press, and equality of opportunity. It is the road not to more liberty, but to less liberty. Liberalism should be found not in striving to spread bureaucracy but in striving to set bounds to it. True liberalism seeks all legitimate freedom, fired in the confident belief that without such freedom the pursuit of all other blessings and bene-

---

[29] William Gorham Rice, Jr., Wisconsin Law School, to Franklin D. Roosevelt, December 26, 1928, and Roosevelt to Rice, December 21, 1928, and January 6, 1929, Roosevelt Papers.
[30] Green to F. C. Erdmann, August 27, 1928, A. F. of L. Papers.

fits is vain. That belief is the foundation of all American progress, political as well as economic. Liberalism is a force truly of the spirit, a force proceeding from the deep realization that economic freedom cannot be sacrificed if political freedom is to be preserved.[31]

In a sense, Hoover might be termed a "radical," for few in 1928 were more determined on improving the material well-being of fellow Americans. The status quo would *never* do.

On November 3, the Republican candidate summarized in Pueblo, Colorado, the case for believing *his* program progressive. Although America was set in a changing world, he observed, "the fundamental principles of ordered liberty and freedom" must be preserved. "If we guide our country aright we shall go forward to a nobler America and we shall carry the whole of humanity forward by our example and influence." [32] This was a "filter-up" theory, one that A. F. of L. and Railroad Brotherhood leaders followed in their own daily work. They thought that whatever strengthened the union vanguard ought to make *all* workers rejoice. As William Green put it, "The organized workers have been the flying wedge that has raised wages and incomes for the unorganized as well as union workers." [33]

The desirability of material progress was perfectly understandable to labor audiences in 1928. When Secretary of Labor Davis told the A. F. of L. convention delegates that he hoped to live long enough to see every working man and woman in the United States own at least one automobile, he was cheered to the echo.[34] William Green said of the radio, "Working men and women and their families derive great pleasure and satisfaction from radio, and radio receivers may be found in a very large percentage of the homes of the working people." [35] The union men worried, of

[31] *The New Day,* pp. 162–163.
[32] *New York Times,* November 4, 1928.
[33] William Green, *A Great American Institution* [the A. F. of L.] (Washington, A. F. of L., 1930).
[34] *New York Times,* November 24, 1928.
[35] *Ibid.,* April 30, 1928. Compare this with the stereotype of the evils of the radio as propagated by the more cosmopolitan: ". . . I can't recall more than thirty occasions when I have got anything remotely describable as civilized entertainment. The height of comedy on the air is reached by the dialogues of Amos and Andy. . . . [*sic*] Music, if it be instrumental, is supplied mainly by

course, over the threat machinery seemed to make to their jobs. Kaleidoscopic changes in industry were creating perplexing problems. A labor official sounded awed and proud as he said:

> We, today, are living in the most marvelous age in the history of civilization. There seems to be no end to the inventive genius of man. Science, as never before in the history of mankind, is revealing the hidden secrets of nature.[36]

The representatives of radical parties who came before the American people in 1928 with denials of the comparative *value* as well as the *fact* of material progress in the United States were out of step with the spirit of the times.

A large Republican advertisement which appeared toward election day summarized the party's economic case. "A vote for the Democratic Party would be a vote for *uncertainty* and *experiment* at the high hour of American power and affluence." It would risk "lower tariff, *lower* wages, *lower* dividends, *relaxed* immigration and prohibition laws, and a general withdrawal of investment funds.[37] At the close of the campaign as at its beginning, the party clung to a staunch defense of the protective tariff, claiming that it did so on behalf of the American laboring man. Here is a theme worth pursuing.

IV

Disputation over the tariff has long been part of the American political scene. Critics usually suggest, and with some justification, that what many politicians seek to protect is the industrialist— not the workingman. However this may be, one cannot assume that high tariffs have been supported in the past contrary to the desires of union leaders and the workingman. What positions did union leaders actually take toward the tariff in the late 1920s?

gangs of union men sawing dismally away in the dining rooms of second-rate hotels . . . . [*sic*]" H. L. Mencken, ca. 1928, quoted in William Manchester, *Disturber of the Peace: the Life of H. L. Mencken* (New York, 1950), p. 229.

[36] Robert T. McCoy, editor, *International Molders Journal*, in the Convention Number (November, 1928), 112.

[37] In *New York Times*, November 1, 1928.

In the spring of 1928, an American Wage Earners Protective Conference was created in New York City.[38] Although not formally launched until the November meeting of the American Federation of Labor in New Orleans, it cannot be considered apart from the issues of the 1928 election despite its initial declaration that it would avoid "partisan politics," and the fact that it avoided endorsing any candidate or party. It declared its purpose to be *the organization of labor leaders and unions in favor of high tariffs.*[39] The first meeting was attended by delegates from the photoengravers, wallpaper crafts, glass bottle blowers, and potters. Twenty organizations were represented after a few months.[40]

The position of A. F. of L. headquarters toward the tariff had long been one of overt neutrality. Occasionally a member union had asked the Executive Council to support its efforts to get higher duties on an article of special importance. When requested to do so, the Council lent such legislative assistance as it could. It did so, however, in such a way as to avoid taking a generalized protection or free trade position,[41] for the tariff was regarded as a dangerous issue, something that might divide the ranks of organized labor if not well handled.

In the 1920s signs began to multiply that more than a few unions in the Federation favored increased tariff rates on imports which competed with items produced by workers in America. In 1917 at Buffalo a resolution in favor of protection had been passed. In

[38] Sometimes called a League. The word American was not always used; sometimes it was spelled America's and sometimes the word Earners appeared as Earners' or as Earner's.

[39] Economic aspects of the Conference are discussed by Lyle W. Cooper in "The Tariff and Organized Labor," *American Economic Review*, XX (June, 1930), 210–225.

[40] Cigar Makers; Pattern Makers; Upholsterers; Iron, Steel, and Tin Workers; Bookbinders; Flint Glass Workers; Molders; Brick and Clay Workers; Hatters; Stereotypers and Electrotypers; Paper Makers; Plate Printers and Die Stampers; Neckware Makers; Cloth Hat, Cap and Millinery Workers; Boot and Shoe Workers. The Lithographers belonged but sent no representative. The Painters and Textile Workers were absent; they wanted lower duties on linseed oil and raw wool respectively. The organizations involved had a combined membership of 250,000, nearly a tenth of the total A. F. of L. membership. *Ibid.*, pp. 210–211.

[41] Some references to tariff discussions in union literature appear in Lloyd G. Reynolds and Charles C. Killingsworth, *Trade Union Publications*, III (Baltimore, 1945), pp. 793–795. See also Margaret Hardy, *The Influence of Organized Labor in the Foreign Policy of the United States* (Liége, Belgium, 1926), pp. 195-204; a University of Geneva dissertation.

1921 the names of John L. Lewis, William Green, and Philip Murray, officials of the United Mine Workers, and William L. Hutcheson of the Carpenters, appeared on a request to the Federation to support higher, even embargo, rates on crude oil and by-products from Mexico.[42]

Party leaders were much interested in labor's attitude on the tariff. In 1923, Thomas O. Marvin, chairman of the Tariff Commission, successfully alerted the forces for protection within the A. F. of L., thereby preventing a possible policy change. "This will have considerable bearing upon the campaign of 1924," he rejoiced in a letter to President Coolidge, "and will make it impossible for the Democratic National Committee to claim that the American Federation of Labor had repudiated protection as it had hoped to be able to." [43] Coolidge thought the result "most satisfactory." [44]

In 1925, the Painters, the Textile Workers, and the Metal Trades Department of the Federation all asked higher duties on items affecting them. In 1928 the Boot and Shoe Workers and the Printers asked protection. The reasoning of the union men was not greatly different from that of employers, for the plea of the general manager of a brick works against importing Belgian brick could have been seconded by his employees:

> These bricks were made by workmen whose wages averaged less than one dollar a day. The cost of manufacturing brick is chiefly in labor cost and for that reason domestic manufacturers cannot compete with foreign manufacturers paying only twenty per cent of the wages paid here.[45]

That Franklin D. Roosevelt (recipient of the letter) and his party appreciated the importance of such reasoning was evident in private correspondence if not in platform addresses. Roosevelt wrote one businessman,

[42] American Federation of Labor *Proceedings*, 1921, 403–404.
[43] Marvin to Coolidge, October 17, 1923, Coolidge Papers, Library of Congress.
[44] Coolidge to Marvin, October 18, 1923.
[45] D. J. Strickland, Denning Paint Brick Works, Beacon, N. Y., to Franklin D. Roosevelt at the Houston convention, June 25, 1928, Roosevelt Papers.

It seems to me that no businessman need worry about the effect which a Democratic administration would have on business. The day has gone by when people could be fooled into believing that the Democratic party would immediately put in free trade or anything like it.[46]

Shortly thereafter, in a bantering but worried tone, Louis Howe wrote his absent chief,

We at Democratic headquarters are at present desperately trying to convince the Republican converts who are still on the fence because they are afraid of tariff reduction that never, never, never would we touch a sacred item. In fact, this is being played up so hard by the people at Headquarters that I expect fully to see a speech by Smith announcing that he will appoint a special commission to jack up the duties before they get through.[47]

That union leaders were among those who worried about tariff reduction at the time is clearly apparent. To men thinking as producers rather than consumers, and charged with the well-being of the men in their own unions rather than that of the national trade balance or maintaining the purchasing power of some foreign country, the tariff was a shield against adversity. The argument that the tariff had been designed solely to protect the fortunes of great industrialists would have made these realists laugh.

The Wage Earners Protective Conference, it is certain, was formed primarily to pressure for higher tariffs. A contemporary suggested that it was also intended to keep the unions from going en masse to the support of Smith and the Democrats.[48] Its own disclaimer must be discounted. Matthew Woll, a Federation vice president—conservative, Catholic, and Republican—was the head of the Conference. He was a respected leader in the National Civic Federation, a group consisting largely of businessmen. In 1924 he was considered one logical successor to Samuel Gompers. A native of prewar Russia, Woll was an outspoken foe of the Communist regime in the Soviet Union, and a bitter enemy of the Communists

[46] Roosevelt to Joseph O'Neill, Joseph O'Neill Wire Works, Inc., Port Chester, N. Y., August 22, 1928, Roosevelt Papers.
[47] Howe to Roosevelt at Warm Springs, September 21, 1928, Roosevelt Papers.
[48] Cooper, "Organized Labor and the Tariff," p. 222; *New York Times*, November 26, 1928.

in America. In 1928 he was the enthusiastic president of the Union Labor Life Insurance Company. As a leader in the typographical union, Woll shared the concern of the printing trades over the importation of inexpensive books. So far as can be determined from his speeches, however, he stood clear of partisan public political comments in 1928. Did his religion play a role in Woll's failure to oppose Smith? On such personal matters speculation is absolutely fruitless, even though Carlyle has written that "a man's religion is the chief fact with regard to him." [49]

Was the Wage Earners Protective Conference intended to be Woll's contribution to the Republican cause in 1928? Was it thought that if the tariff could be given enough favorable publicity in union circles the unions might be enticed into the Republican fold to stay? During the 1920s the President of the United States had come to have the real power to manipulate tariff rates, since he acted upon the recommendations of tariff commissions appointed by himself.[50] If unions became wedded to high tariffs they might have to be wedded at the same time to high tariff candidates for President of the United States. This idea must be pursued, even though conclusive proof is lacking.

The reasoning of the protectionist labor leaders was simple. Matthew Woll revealed part of it in a Labor Day address when he said that American industrial profits were being spent abroad, largely to build factories to compete with American workmen. The products of those factories were returning to America in successful competition with domestic manufactures. The result had been some unemployment and would soon be lowered wages. A crash would surely follow. Then where would the workingman be? [51] In this

[49] The quotation appears on the title page of the *American Catholic Who's Who* (Grosse Pointe, Michigan, 1946–1947), in which appears a sketch of Matthew Woll on page 461 and one of Teamster president Daniel J. Tobin on page 434. The importance of religion to many men of affairs in 1928 has been amply demonstrated by Edmund A. Moore, *A Catholic Runs for President: Alfred E. Smith* (New York, 1956) and Roy V. Peel and Thomas C. Donnelly, *The 1928 Campaign, an Analysis* (New York, 1931).

[50] E. Pendleton Herring, "The Political Context of the Tariff Commission," *Political Science Quarterly,* XLIX (September, 1934), 428, 430.

[51] *New York Times,* September 2, 1928. This analysis of 1928 was being heard again in the 1960s.

light it was a strong appeal that Dr. Hubert Work, chairman of the Republican National Committee, made when he said:

> Protection of the great American payroll, which is greater than the payroll of the rest of the world together—there's an issue. The Republican Party has stood for the protective tariff, which protects the wages of the workmen in mill, mine, and factory, who in turn have money to buy the products of the American farmer.[52]

In an election campaign notorious for the irrelevance of some issues, it is important to note his positive, midsummer proclamation, *"The campaign will be waged on the protective tariff and its benefits."* [53]

Some may say that the tariff issue of 1928 was buried under the prohibition and religious issues and therefore played a role of little significance. Yet only a year after the election it was said seriously that the 1928 vote in industrial areas showed signs that wage earners voted their protective tariff sentiments.[54] The tariff debate of 1929–1930 would cause one strongly Democratic union journal to comment:

> The tariff seems to be occupying most of the space of the front pages of our news dailies for the last few months, and few of us give it any consideration, but if everything was on the free list it would not be long before we would begin to feel it adversely. . . . Just watch and see how your congressman votes on the tariff bill and all of its amendments. It pays each one to look out for himself in this day of big business, schemers, politicians, mergers, and efficiency experts.[55]

The important point is not whether the labor leaders who wanted higher tariff rates were in economic error in their day. If one should accept the validity of later assertions by opponents of pro-

---

[51] *New York Times,* September 2, 1928. This analysis of 1928 was being heard again in the 1960s.

[52] *Ibid.,* July 4, 1928.

[53] *Ibid.,* July 7, 1928. "Your Job Versus the Spectre of Idleness and Ruin," an essay on the tariff, was issued in pamphlet form by the Republican National Committee (Washington, D. C., 1928).

[54] Cooper, "The Tariff and Organized Labor," p. 224.

[55] *Teamsters Magazine,* XXVI (November, 1929), 16.

tection as correct in abstract theory,[56] it would not change the plain self-interest of high tariff sentiment in the labor unions of the late 1920s. *If there was any agitation at all for low tariffs in labor circles at the time, no sign of it appeared in a single one of the fourscore union periodicals examined by the present writer,* nor was the Wage Earners Protective Conference criticized by A. F. of L. or Brotherhood periodicals.

Politicians writing the platforms of the day must have noted this well-publicized high tariff sentiment in union circles. The Conference had a publicity budget of $12,000 for the period June to November. Its activities were reported briefly in the *New York Times* on several occasions, and it even drew postelection criticism from the newspaper of the Socialist Party.[57] That Herbert Hoover was aware of labor's vocally protectionist sentiment may be presumed.

V

The *immigration issue* was of deep interest to labor leaders and the workingmen of America. While many recent arrivals longed for the entrance of close relatives from abroad, most union leaders took a different view. The Republicans were correct in pointing out that with labor-saving machinery seeming to create employment problems, increased immigration might add to those problems.[58] However prospective immigrants might seem to yesterday's immigrants—and certainly many (and in a sense, all) Americans were in that category—to union leaders they were new faces seeking jobs that paid any wage.

In early October, Candidate Hoover spoke on this issue. Accompanied by eleven camera men and thirty correspondents, he

[56] For such an argument, see Francis B. Sayre, "Does American Labor Stand to Win or Lose by Trade Agreements?" *Political Science Quarterly,* LIV (June, 1929), 186. Labor, he said, was "definitely injured" by embargo tariffs. "The overwhelming majority of the workers in this country unquestionably stand to gain from a policy of tariff moderation which, by fostering healthy trade, promotes the sound prosperity of the entire nation." Would this argument sway a potter who watched foreign pottery eliminate his job?

[57] *New Leader,* December 1, 1928.

[58] See "Governor Smith *Wrong* on Immigration," Republican National Committee, 1928.

journeyed to Elizabethtown, Tennessee, where he stated, "I do not favor any increase in immigration. Restriction protects the American home from widespread unemployment. At the same time we must humanize the laws, but only within the present quota." [59] The Hoover pronouncement on immigration was the most encouraging to reach William Green since the opening of the campaign, for as he put it, "apprehension and deep concern" had been felt on this in labor circles. Hoover had "struck the right note," announced Green, and the A. F. of L. Information and Publicity Service promptly released his full remarks, adding the following appraisal:

> Mr. Hoover's statement regarding immigration is in accord with the declared policy of the American Federation of Labor. His announced opposition to any change in the quota and restrictive provisions of existing immigration legislation is most welcome indeed. Mr. Hoover's announcement upon this subject will create a most favorable impression among the vast majority of working people everywhere. [60]

While a favorable Smith pronouncement on immigration quickly ensued from Louisville, so that the Federation was more pleased than ever, the Republicans had already seized on the Green remarks as a sign that Hoover had gained in favor. The allegiance of John L. Lewis to the Hoover cause was announced on October 11, and a possible Republican trend in union circles was loosely suggested in the press. Major Berry, labor adviser to the Democrats, quickly telephoned his fears to Secretary-Treasurer Frank Morrison at A. F. of L. Headquarters, and in a forceful letter to President Green on October 10 he foresaw dire consequences to the Smith candidacy from the Green immigration statement. It was "unfair" and "out of line with the so-called nonpartisan, neutral position of the Executive Council," he charged. Green defended himself within a week, assuring Berry that his quoted remarks

[59] *The New Day,* p. 104.

[60] Release of October 8, 1928. The balance of the immigration story given here has been pieced together from material in file "Miscellaneous 1926–1928," A. F. of L. Papers.

could not be considered an endorsement of Mr. Hoover's candidacy. The remark was termed his own, not the Council's.

But clever political brains at Democratic labor committee headquarters, in the meantime, had been at work on a new matter—Hoover as "enemy" of labor. In his October 10 letter, Major Berry warned President Green that in 1920 Hoover had told the Senate Educational and Labor Committee, "The principle of individual freedom requires the open shop." Berry cited the *New York Times,* May 15, 1920, p. 21. On October 17, surmising that his "bombshell" had failed to explode, Berry wrote identical letters to Green and Morrison, placing the offensive Hoover words in solid black capital letters; he called for an outright endorsement of Alfred E. Smith.

While President Green endorsed his copy "no answer," Secretary Morrison asked W. C. Robert, Federation legislative expert, to ascertain the facts. Roberts went to much effort and reported back in detail. The offending statement was genuine enough, he said, but Hoover's enemies would have to take care! For Hoover had also rejected (a) legal repression by injunction, (b) compulsory arbitration, and (c) industrial courts (such as that in Kansas—detested by union leaders). Thus, wrote Roberts, "If too much is said about what Hoover said about the open shop his friends can come back with the statement that at the same hearing he was against the injunction in labor disputes, compulsory arbitration, and industrial courts." [61] Berry nevertheless set the propaganda wheels in motion. The Democratic National Committee released a printed circular letter, "To the Officers and Members of the American Labor Movement," repeating the earlier Berry half-truths. Green endorsed his copy "No reply." Berry saw to it that a copy of an irritated telegram he sent a Chicagoan was routed to Green. So far as he knew, Berry boasted, the only top A. F. of L. leader supporting Hoover was John L. Lewis.[62]

President Green was not to be smoked out of official neutrality by this end-of-campaign tactic. He wrote Berry on October 25,

[61] Roberts cited the *Washington Post* and *Baltimore Sun* of May 15, 1920, the *Washington Star* of May 14, 1920.
[62] Berry to Emmet F. Flood, October 24, 1928, A. F. of L. Papers.

"The information you gave Mr. Flood is correct. By no stretch of the imagination could any statement I have made during the campaign be considered as an endorsement of the Republican platform." [63] The incident was closed, chiefly, it is clear, because Herbert Hoover had not been proven, and even by extreme partisans could not be proven, an "enemy" of organized labor.

VI

A behind-the-scenes meeting of enduring interest took place when, on October 26, the president and the secretary-treasurer of the National Women's Trade Union League obtained an interview with the Republican candidate. ". . . He certainly left no doubt in my mind as to his position regarding industrial legislation for women," Elizabeth Christman enthused later. "Before this you will have seen his very splendid statement on this subject, one which does not permit of the slightest misconstruction." [64] The Hoover statement forwarded with such approval read

> I am absolutely with you in your efforts to get adequate labor legislation for women. Such legislation establishes standards for industry, which although they already exist by voluntary agreement between many employers and the organized workers, must be written into law to bring up the laggards of industry.
>
> On this subject I have not altered my opinion as expressed in 1920. If women in industrial occupations are to be protected equally with men, they must have safeguards additional to those provided for men. I favor especially the laws limiting hours of labor, with progressively higher standards in accordance with the purposes of organized working women. I should greatly deplore any weakening of the existing regulations, or any interference with their extension.

All local leagues and committees of the National Women's Trade Union League were soon advised officially by headquarters of the group that Hoover had made "one of the finest statements ever given us favoring industrial legislation for women." [65]

[63] William Green to G. L. Berry, October 25, 1928, A. F. of L. Papers.
[64] Secretary-Treasurer, N.W.T.U.L., to Executive Board, November 7, 1928, N.W.T.U.L. Papers, Library of Congress.
[65] Elisabeth Christman to Addressees, November 14, 1928, N.W.T.U.L. Papers, Library of Congress.

VII

It can be seen, in summary, that the appeal Herbert Hoover and the Republican Party directed to the workingmen and women of America in 1928 had in it very substantial and appealing elements. As phrased by Mr. Hoover and paraphrased by various party leaders, the appeal made sense to many a person working for wages at the time. The contemporary slogan, "Hoover and Happier Homes" (one which would be politically jarring in the retrospect of depression years), had real meaning in earlier days. Although the support of union leaders and union members had not been singled out for courtship except insofar as these persons were members of the working force of the nation, neither had the special concerns expressed by union leaders been passed over in silence.[66] Immigration bars would clearly remain in place in the event of a Republican victory—and labor thought this desirable. Collective bargaining, not a central theme in the election, had been recognized as a worthwhile method of settling industrial disputes. The strong stand of the Republican Party on behalf of the protective tariff would actually help it in trade union circles in the late 1920s. But the party's attitude and that of Hoover on the injunction did not satisfy union leaders.

In the well-organized and clearly expressed thought of Herbert Hoover on the American society and economy in 1928 the Republican Party had an important asset. The speeches of Hoover were read clearly from carefully prepared manuscripts to an audience quite entranced with the magic of political campaigning by radio. The present writer ventures to take exception to the vigorous general and specific criticisms of the Hoover rhetoric made by a student of speech.[67] Laboring men and their wives shared at the

[66] It is not correct, in my view of the matter, to say that the Hoover appeal was general in nature—a view expressed by Ralph D. Casey in "Party Campaign Propaganda," *Annals*, 179 (May, 1935), 104.

[67] Howard William Runkel, "Hoover's Speeches During His Presidency" (Unpublished Doctoral dissertation, Stanford University; 1950). "Certainly the radio was an ideal medium for Mr. Hoover in communicating with millions of Americans who were independent in their politics or not completely bound by habit to any particular political party. His nonpartisan approach to great national issues appealed to them." *The Memoirs of Ray Lyman Wilbur, 1875–1949*. (Edgar Eugene Robinson and Paul Carroll Edwards, eds.; Stanford, 1960), p. 401.

time the Hoover optimism at the material progress of America. They joined in his expressed hope that a prosperous future lay ahead, one that would touch all citizens. That the handful of unemployed concurred in such hopes may be assumed; that they rejoiced over the economic progress of that day and time is extremely far-fetched.

Union leaders would have been greatly cheered if the injunction plank of the Progressives had only become Republican policy in 1928, but their rank and file knew little of this. They were obviously more attracted by the Republican candidate's determination that opportunity for each person to rise to the heights ought never be curtailed in America. Each union member's wife had hope for her children, and the America of Hoover's vision sounded like a good world in which they might grow up, especially when the memories of rigid class structure in the Old World, and its lack of opportunity, were freshly in mind.

The American people had been taught in their grade schools that their nation had in years past been a land of opportunity. This they believed.[68] As voters in 1928 they were not prepared to reject a candidate for President who was fully identified with the idea that *freedom of opportunity for every individual* was something to be preserved at all costs. "Security" had not yet become a common word in the American vocabulary. Herbert Hoover as candidate for office was identified with the qualities most admired in that day by his voting fellow citizens, most of whom were to be numbered somewhere within the working force—or its family circles. What Hoover *was,* as well as what he *said,* convinced the electorate that here was a man neither to be hated nor feared.

Above all, Hoover was no "enemy" of labor in fact or contemporary portrait—except those painted by a handful of Democratic and radical partisans. His expressed convictions on the tariff, immigration, women's rights, and child labor were at one with those of union leaders at the time. He believed in collective bargaining

[68] See Mark Sullivan, *Our Times,* Vol. II (New York, 1927), Chapters 1 to 4, where the education received by the adults of the late 1920s when they were youths, ca. 1880 to 1910, is clearly sketched. This *belief* in opportunity was a reality, whatever the degree of fact—which some historians have been chipping away at to some extent. See William Miller, "American Historians and the Business Elite," *Journal of Economic History,* IX (November, 1949), 184–208.

and was no defender of an unbridled injunction. It is noteworthy that union leaders who came to the support of Smith in the campaign seldom, if ever, attacked Hoover.

In concluding, one must weigh heavily the judgment of lifelong Democratic Party partisan Daniel J. Tobin, Teamster president and ardent Alfred E. Smith supporter in the campaign. "Hoover is not wanted by Wall Street," he informed fellow Teamsters. Hoover was called "too square" for the Republicans, and the best candidate they could name. He was the "man of brains, the man with ability, the man who has unselfishly done things, the man who has the courage to tell the truth, the man who had defied Wall Street, the man who for eight or ten years has been doing good things and helping our government." Furthermore, "honest, fearless, able Hoover" would be a hard man to lick on election day, but he would "give us a square deal." [69] In summary, deep-eyed Democrat Dan Tobin suggested to the truck drivers and other laboring men in his union

> Hoover may change his attitude towards Labor upon becoming President, but we hardly think at the age of fifty-six he will change and become different from what he has been in the past, because a man of his age who has always insisted on a square deal for the downtrodden surely cannot, on becoming robed in the regalia of the presidency, change his nature and his attitude.[70]

Here in summarized form was the fundamental Hoover appeal to labor in 1928. These attractive features—too long omitted from many schoolbooks—were unquestionably important factors leading to his overwhelming success at the polls in the Presidential Election of 1928.[71]

[69] *Teamsters Magazine*, XXV (April, 1928), 8–11.

[70] *Ibid.*, XXV (June, 1928), 2.

[71] A handful of high school and grade school textbooks leafed through by the writer wasted few adjectives on Hoover in their haste to lavish attention on his successor in Presidential office. Even the dubious concept that a twelve-year President deserves three times the space of a four-year President does not justify the current indifference to the Hoover of the 1920s. See *The Memoirs of Ray Lyman Wilbur*, chapter 31, *et passim*, and the Hoover *Memoirs* for facts that have gained little hearing in competition with political attacks of the 1930s that brainwashed a nation.

Chapter 8

Smith Appeals to Union Organizations

DEMOCRATIC PARTY LEADERS hoped mightily that under the leadership of Alfred E. Smith the "labor vote" might be brought into the fold en masse in 1928. "We are going to do everything short of breaking our necks to elect Al Smith," said one leader.[1] A Labor Committee was formally created under the leadership of Major George L. Berry in late July, and by early September it was expanding rapidly.[2] Berry announced on behalf of the committee that the Democratic Party was fortunate in its candidates, since it was a time when capital and labor could join hands upon the political field. He saw in both Smith and Robinson "business capacities"; yet both had "proved their friendship for organized labor." As a partisan-type in a partisan job, Berry proclaimed, "It is my judgment that the workers of America, organized or unorganized, will enter into the campaign enthusiastically and will give the ticket the strongest support ever registered in the national campaign." [3]

[1] Frank P. Walsh to Max Levand, Wichita, Kansas, July 27, 1928, Walsh Papers, New York Public Library.
[2] Ralph Casey, "Party Campaign Propaganda," *Annals,* 179 (May, 1935), 97.
[3] *New York Times,* July 27, 1928.

I

It is apparent that Democratic Party leaders considered the so-called "labor vote" to be more than union members plus nonunion industrial workers. The labor vote was considered an amalgam of many large and small groups including union and nonunion personnel, Negroes, immigrants, the Irish, the Jews, and others. The groups were not mutually exclusive. Approaches to them would vary.

In an attempt to attract some Negro votes in Northern cities the party spent only $125,000 out of its total of $5,342,349.89.[4] A Negro was nominated for Congress in the 12th Missouri District, however, and some young Harlem Negro leaders worked for the Democrats. When the Republicans charged Smith with having a Negro stenographer and putting Negroes on the New York State payroll, Democratic headquarters promptly denied it, saying that under his administration jobs in the state had been given Negroes exactly as in the South; that is, to "porters, charwomen, etc." [5] Such a comment is (to modern ears) an odd way to attract Negro support, but the South had to be pacified.

There were signs, however, that the Democratic Party was making progress with the Northern Negro. The influential Chicago *Defender* expressed dissatisfaction with the Republican ticket and thought Negroes should vote against the party of the dead Lincoln. Eight years of Republican administration, it thought, had brought little progress to the race. "If we have outlived our usefulness to the Republican Party, there is a possibility that we can be of the same service to the opposite party. At any rate, this is the only political means which we have not tried." As emotions came to be aroused over the Catholic faith of Smith, the National Association for the Advancement of Colored People became alarmed at an accompanying prejudice against the Negro which its spokesmen thought to be greater than in any election year since the Civil War.

---

[4] Campaign figures from James K. Pollock, Jr., "Campaign Funds in 1928," *American Political Science Review,* XXIII (February, 1929), 66, 63. The Republicans spent a total of $3,814,815.45. These are National Committee figures. On the Missouri candidacy, see *New York Times,* September 4, 1928.

[5] *Ibid.,* August 5 and September 9, 1928.

The Baltimore *Afro-American Weekly* came to the aid of Smith, because it considered that the Republicans had invited Ku Klux Klan support in the South. It was the first time it had ever supported a Democratic Presidential candidate.[6]

The Democrats also went to some effort to gain the support of persons of relatively recent immigrant status. Democratic headquarters included the following linguistic/national divisions. Porto Rican, Hungarian, Rumanian, Slovanic, French, Italian, Polish, Jugo-Slav, Greek, Carpatho-Ruthenian, Ukrainian, Danish, Jewish, Slovak, Czech, and Spanish. Five persons were assigned to relations with the foreign language press.[7] The struggle over the so-called "foreign" vote was accompanied by pronouncements from the editors of the foreign language press and statistics of dubious value. Some interest was shown in the effect that prohibition might play in swaying those who had long considered wine on the table or beer in the cellar a normal part of living. Some feared that the still famous relief work of Hoover might be an important factor among recent immigrants and those with relatives in Europe. The evidence on such matters is utterly inconclusive.[8]

Democratic Party leaders were well aware of the extent of the Jewish population of New York City, and they hoped that it might somehow be brought to the support of their candidates in the state and mobilized for Smith as well.[9] An experienced New York politician judged, "There *is* a Jewish vote, just as there is an Irish, a German, and Italian vote, which has been recognized by the manner in which nominations have been made by both parties for time out of memory."[10] The Jewish press was divided, however,

<hr/>

[6] Quoted in *New York Times*, October 20, 26, 1928.

[7] Casey, "Party Campaign Propaganda," p. 98.

[8] It was announced that 14 Hungarian language newspapers in New Jersey were for Hoover. Although all but 27 of 220 German language newspapers were said to be nonpolitical, of the 27, 17 were pro-Smith, 7 pro-Hoover, and 3 pro-Thomas. Of 160 Italian language papers, 18 were pro-Smith, 15 pro-Hoover, 2 supported Thomas, and 2 William Z. Foster. The Czech and Slovak press was 19 to 2 in favor of Smith; the Scandinavian press, 26 to 2 in favor of Hoover. While 57 non-English papers had supported radical parties in 1924, only 46 did so in 1928. *New York Times*, September 7, October 25, 27, November 5, 1928.

[9] In 1926 there were 1,728,000 Jews in New York City—30 per cent of the total population. Survey by the Bureau of Jewish Social Research, 1926, made public in 1928. *World Almanac*, 1929, p. 504.

[10] Party of a lengthy discussion of the subject. Robert Darn, Asst. Dist. Atty., New York City, to Franklin D. Roosevelt, October 3, 1928, Roosevelt Papers.

and it certainly is not known how Jews voted. They were almost as heterogeneous as other parts of the population, being of many national stocks, length of time in the country, financial conditions, and occupations.[11] It is recorded that twenty-six Jewish trade unions in Chicago with a membership of 75,000 endorsed Smith.[12] At the Democratic National Convention in Houston, Franklin D. Roosevelt arranged for a rabbi to give the invocation on the first night, Herbert Lehman having asked Henry Morgenthau to ask Roosevelt to do so. F.D.R. asked Joseph Robinson, who forgot about it. Just as a Baptist was about to fill in, police and firemen produced a rabbi.[13] In the New York State gubernatorial campaign the Jewish vote situation was taken very seriously, in view of the religion of Lehman, Roosevelt's running mate, and Ottinger, Republican candidate opposing F.D.R. for governor. Rumor had it that some "bigoted" gentiles would split their tickets, supporting Roosevelt and the Protestant Republican candidate for lieutenant-governor; some "bigoted" Jews, it was said, would do just the opposite.[14] A Democratic memorandum on the "Jewish situation" worried that Ottinger would inevitably take the Jewish vote, otherwise "in the next twenty years neither one of the parties would nominate in city or state, any Jewish candidate for high political office. . . ."[15] It is utterly impossible to interpret or pass judgment on all these predictions or evaluations of the day, except to note that Roosevelt and Lehman won—and Ottinger did not.

II

Alfred E. Smith has long been an appealing figure for many Americans—even for many who did not support him in 1928 or

[11] Jews would vote for Hoover in gratitude for the relief work of Hoover, said the publisher of the *Jewish Daily Press*, Chicago. *New York Times*, October 11, 1928. They would vote for Smith, said the editor of the *Jewish Morning Journal*, New York City. *Ibid.*, October 12, 1928. Herman Bernstein, a former Jewish newspaper editor, said that while he was for Hoover, he thought the Jewish vote would divide. *Ibid.*, October 22, 1928.

[12] *Ibid.*, October 14, 1928.

[13] Lehman to Roosevelt, July 5, 1928; Roosevelt to Morgenthau, July 7, 1928, Roosevelt Papers.

[14] Letter from a New York City lawyer to Roosevelt, October 8, 1928, Roosevelt

[15] Letter to Roosevelt, October 15, 1928, Roosevelt Papers.

deplored his break with F.D.R. in the 1930s. *Up from the City Streets* was the inspirational title of the 1929 autobiography of the man Charles Michelson once described in musical prose:

> Alfred E. Smith, the ingenuous child of the New York sidewalks, simple beyond belief, but with that simplicity is combined a knowledge beyond that given in books; a demigod to whom all the complexities of government are clear as day; a paragon of wisdom, gentleness and righteousness, whose facile mind fathoms automatically every depth of economics and politics.[16]

Smith inspired loyalty. To New Yorkers he was "really something." Frank P. Walsh wrote his emotional hopes in private:

> We are all going to do everything short of breaking our necks to elect Al Smith. I am wondering if you think, confidentially, that he has a chance. It is hard to come to a conclusion as yet, but Smith has made such a wonderful record as Governor of New York, and has such a keen sense of politics himself, that I cannot but feel that he has a first-class chance. In any event, he will give the opposition a nut to crack every few days during the campaign.[17]

Governor Smith delivered his acceptance address on August 22 in Albany, New York, eleven days after Hoover's and about three weeks after the adjournment of the A. F. of L. Executive Council meeting in Atlantic City. On a rainy day which held down the size of his immediate audience but may have increased the size of a radio audience which "listened in" on 111 stations, Smith began by saying:

> Upon the steps of this Capitol, where twenty-five years ago I first came into the service of the State, I receive my party's summons to lead it in the nation. Within this building, I learned the principles, the purposes and the functions of government and to know that the greatest privilege that can come to any man is to give himself to a nation which has reared him and raised him from obscurity to be a contender for the highest office in the gift of its people.

[16] In the *New York World*, July 1, 1928 (as quoted by Casey, "Party Campaign Propaganda," p. 103). A biography that treats Smith with understanding is Oscar Handlin, *Al Smith and His America* (New York, 1958).

[17] Walsh to Max Leonard, Wichita, Kansas, July 27, 1928, Walsh Papers.

The Governor of New York said he stood for the "people" rather than "material things." He was for "progressive measures," for honesty in office, and against the idea of government by and for a "benevolent oligarchy." His party stood for the maintenance of "legitimate business" and for a high standard of wages. These were thought consistent objectives.

Smith wanted the tariff taken out of the realm of politics and treated on a strictly business basis. The Democratic tariff would be "honest," would "play no favorites," and would do "justice to every element in the nation." There would be no "sudden or drastic revolution" in its provisions. Thus spoke the candidate of the historic low-tariff party.

There was much in the Smith address to attract groups of various persuasions. There were a plea for the conversation of natural resources, kind words for veterans, promises of aid to the farmers, and a courageous statement on prohibition which went beyond the party platform and was called in urban editorials an honest appraisal of what had become a very trying national scandal.

It is very important to record the Smith denial of any reality in Republican claims of full employment and of distributed prosperity. His denials were neither as strong as those of the Socialist candidate nor sarcastic and violent like those of the Communist candidate, but they were aimed at the very basis of the Republican Party position in 1928. He insisted that there were four million unemployed. He said that 40 per cent of the 430,000 corporations in the country had lost money in 1926, while one-fourth of one per cent of them had earned two-thirds of all corporation profits. "Specific industries are wholly prostrate and there is widespread business difficulty and discontent among the individual businessmen of the country." Furthermore,

> Prosperity to the extent that we have it is unduly concentrated and has not equitably touched the lives of the farmer, the wage earner and the individual business man. The claim of governmental economy is as baseless as the claims that general business prosperity exists and that it can exist only under Republican administration.

Alfred Emanuel Smith in a series of informal poses

In short, "The Republican Party builds its case upon a myth." [18]
Each voter would have to decide the correctness of this attempt
to contradict what Hoover, the Republicans, the daily press, and
many leaders of opinion claimed as irrefutable fact.

When he turned to labor topics in this formal address, Governor
Smith said he stood for labor's "reasonable contentment." He
praised the labor legislation of the Wilson administration and
favored collective bargaining. He repeated, as he had so often
while campaigning in New York, that labor was not a commodity.
Then he gave the injunction three full paragraphs.

Dissatisfaction and social unrest had grown from the injunction
abuse, said Smith. "Undoubtedly legislation must be framed to
meet just causes for complaint in regard to the unwarranted issuance of injunctions." Unlike Hoover, he took cognizance of the
recent Senate hearings on the matter, saying:

> The Judiciary Committee of the United States has already in
> progress a careful study of this situation. I promise full coopera-
> tion to the end that a definite remedy by law be brought forth
> to end the existing evils and preserve the constitutional guaran-
> tees of individual liberty, free assemblage and speech and the
> rights of peaceful persuasion.

In these words Governor Smith reiterated what he had been accustomed to saying in his native state. Not only did he take the
side of the union leaders on the injunction; he proceeded to argue
their cause.

> Chief Justice Taft in 1919 stated that government of the rela-
> tions between capital and labor by injunction was an absurdity.
> Justice Holmes and Justice Brandeis of the United States Su-
> preme Court unite in an opinion which describes the restraints
> on labor imposed by a Federal injunction as a reminder of in-
> voluntary servitude.

The statement might have been written by William Green himself.
Union leaders would be pleased. On immigration, Smith thought
some adjustments should be made to reunite families and avoid
discrimination against particular nationalities.

[18] Text in *New York Times*, August 23, 1928.

Smith granted that the United States had a government of laws and not of men, but he pointed out the laws did not "execute themselves." He would therefore appoint men and women to office regardless of whether they were rich or poor, wet or dry, from one part of the country or another, or of a particular religion. (The Democratic candidate did not mention race or color.) Integrity and the ability to give devoted service would be touchstones for appointees. In conclusion, Smith said with what must have seemed to radio listeners the greatest sincerity:

> Victory, simply for the sake of achieving it, is empty. I am entirely satisfied of our success in November because I am sure we are right and therefore sure that our victory means progress for our nation. I pledge a complete devotion to the welfare of our country and our people. I place that welfare above every other consideration and I am satisfied that our party is in a position to promote it. To that end I here and now declare to my fellow countrymen from one end of the United States to the other, that I will dedicate myself with all the power and energy that I possess to the service of our great Republic.

III

Union speakers and union publications generally preserved silence on the prohibition and religious issues in 1928. If there were Catholics in the unions, there were also Protestants. If there were those who "liked their good, wholesome beer" and others who were used to wine on the table in the "old country" there were also believers in temperance and long-suffering wives who were glad to see the passing of the saloon. It would be surprising if, under the circumstances, a labor organization like the A. F. of L., one to which belonged millions of Americans of diverse occupations and interests, could have agreed on such issues. For all practical purposes, none of the union speakers or union publications cared to discuss Catholicism in public in 1928. This is understandable. A few of the journals of the railroad brotherhoods did take strong stands on prohibition, however, and this, too, is no surprise. A brief review of A. F. of L. sentiment needs to be given at this point in connection with the Smith appeal on the "wet" issue.

The A. F. of L., numbering in its membership bottle blowers, teamsters, bartenders, and other affected trades, viewed the Volstead Act with ill-concealed distaste. An Executive Council appeal on the matter was issued in 1922 and approved by the convention in 1923. While no further convention action was taken through 1928,[19] the labor body was active in an Association Against the Prohibition Amendment and a Joint Legislative Committee . . . for Modifying the National Prohibition Act. Green explained that "the A. F. of L. has not asked for the repeal of the Eighteenth Amendment. It has asked for the modification of the Volstead Act." [20] What the Federation wanted, Green wrote President Coolidge in 1925, was the return of a national beverage—wholesome beer. He explained in one letter the philosophy under which he acted when he had testified on Prohibition before Congressional Committees:

> I realize that individual members of the American Federation of Labor may differ very widely and sharply upon the subject of Prohibition and the proposed amendments to the Volstead Act. Individuals have the right to exercise their own opinions upon matters of this kind but I am sure you will distinguish between the opinions of individual members of the American Federation of Labor and the decisions of Conventions of the American Federation of Labor. You could present your individual view and opinion to the Senate Committee but in my official capacity I am called upon to submit the decision of the American Federation of Labor in convention assembled.[21]

One need not bother to count laboriously the number of resolutions against strict Volstead Act enforcement passed by state federations of labor [22] and city centrals to believe that the Smith position on prohibition was well calculated to attract the automatic support of many union leaders.

What the Democratic nominee had to say on the *injunction* gained little attention from the press. What he said about state

[19] William Green to Albert Porter, November 3, 1926, A. F. of L. Papers.
[20] Green to D. M. Jarnagin, February 20, 1926, A. F. of L. Papers.
[21] Green to Joseph Oliver, Scranton, Pa., April 23, 1926, A. F. of L. Papers.
[22] For example, Louisiana State Federation in April, 1926. File "Prohibition," in A. F. of L. Papers.

option on prohibition—with its clear threat to the Volstead Act—
made headlines. His position on the tariff, unusual in a Democrat,
also drew much comment.[23] It was hardly necessary for Raskob
to state soothingly that the business element in New York had the
utmost confidence in Smith and knew that no legitimate industry
would suffer by his election.[24] Labor leaders were plainly satisfied
with the emphasis Smith placed on the injunction. They had long
said it was to be the principal issue for them in 1928. But would
the rank and file understand the meaning of the three Smith paragraphs? Or would they be diverted by the rather poor radio delivery
and the New York accent of the Governor of the Empire State?
Smith said that he was for "the people," but he had not made an
outright class appeal or excoriated the wealthy in dramatic or
demogogic terms. Was this a clear-cut, emotional type of leadership
that lower income families in the forty-eight states would follow?

It is apparent that the Democratic candidate intended to appeal
to *union leaders* through the injunction and other labor issues,
taking a stand on the tariff which would be considered "reasonable" by both high tariff union men and some industrialists. Smith's
advisors sensed that his labor record in New York would speak
for itself. His stand on prohibition might turn out to be attractive
to many urban and rural Americans. The "wetness" of the ticket
was to be made less offensive to drys by stressing that only Congress could amend the law; until that might happen, the Democratic
President would try to enforce the law on the books—only better
than ever. Republican prosperity was to be made to seem mythical
by constantly reiterating that it was spotty in distribution.

Could the Democratic Party, with or without the help of labor
leaders, possibly explain such qualified stands to the country? It
is never easy to keep issues grey rather than black or white. Could
the fact that Alfred E. Smith was a Catholic and a product of the
largest city in the United States be minimized in the eyes of all but

---

[23] The *Pittsburgh Post-Gazette* (Ind. Dem.) thought both labor and business
would be reassured by his comments on the tariff and on injunctions. The Topeka,
Kansas Daily Capital (Rep.) said that on the tariff he had shown himself "as
good a protectionist as any Republican." The American Tariff League was dissatisfied and thought it saw an end to prosperity in the Democratic tariff proposals. *New York Times*, August 25, 1928.

[24] *Ibid.*, August 28, 1928.

"You're Going to Need It" (Hanny in the *Philadelphia Inquirer*)

Catholic and city voters? Could his lack of higher education be built into an asset, his accent be forgiven, his derby hat kept in the realm of friendly good humor, and his Tammany connections

—however free from scandal—be subordinated? Meanwhile, the Republicans would do all they could to persuade the public that the Smith states rights attitude on prohibition was in reality an advocacy of the return of the saloon. Such matters might prove the crucial ones in the campaign.

The reaction of labor leaders to the program and person of Alfred E. Smith would come in the form of wholesale endorsements by individuals, city centrals, state federations, and major unions. Leaders who were silent or took contrary positions had their reasons, but they certainly did not condemn the stand the Democratic candidate had taken on the injunction; they could not say enough in praise of his labor record in New York.

IV

It was the assigned task of Senator Joseph T. Robinson to appeal to the farmers, and he did so in his acceptance address. He ignored industrial workers for the most part. He was scheduled to deliver an address on the labor record of Governor Smith and the position of the party toward labor a few days later at Dallas, Texas, but most of the prepared address was not delivered at this time. Instead, he broke away from the manuscript suddenly to deliver a vigorous attack on those who were dragging the religion of Governor Smith into the campaign. He denied that Smith as a Catholic in the Presidency would conduct a government " 'of the priest, by the priest, and for the priest' "—as had been alleged by someone. And it was false that Smith was a drunkard! Thus far had the whispers gone in a few short months. By late July, Roosevelt could write to a friend, "I am a bit disturbed by reports from certain sections of the South and West, but on the whole I think the campaign is starting off pretty well and I hope that the religious and prohibition issues will not remain at the front in the South and West much longer." But such hopes were in vain. A constituent of Senator Neely of West Virginia wrote the stark prejudices of many when he said, "I am afraid of a Roman Catholic, with their dark bloody record of some sixty-five million dead martyrs, and would much sooner and with far more honor vote straight for Satan than such a man as Smith, or anyone who bows to him." [26]

By late summer it became apparent to Democratic Party leaders that the South and much of rural America might vote *against* a candidate in 1928, not *for* one. The unpleasant religious and prohibition issues placed the injunction issue, the tariff issue, the prosperity issue, the immigration issue, and the other economic and social issues in subordinate perspective. The address Candidate Robinson had once intended to deliver (see above) was scheduled to stress economic differences between the parties and would have continued the Jefferson vs. Hamilton approach inaugurated by Claude G. Bowers in his Democratic convention keynote speech. On that occasion Bowers had said, "Mythical prosperity, mythical economy, mythical facts, mythical figures, and mythical men, the last eight years may well be treated by the historian of the far future as the mythical age of American history." The 1920s to Bowers had been "putrid beyond precedent." It was hardly a fair or even a particularly decent view, but bad as it was, a campaign waged along such lines would have been better than the one that developed and is well known to students of the era.

After an address devoted to the farm issue at Omaha on September 18, Smith spoke publicly of the campaign of slander being waged against him. At Oklahoma City he lashed out against his accusers, reciting his own record in New York in some detail, reading favorable things that had been said about him in past years, and defying the purveyors of bigotry to do their worst. No Catholic should vote for him, he said, simply because he was a Catholic.[27]

---

[26] A letter dated August 18, 1928, forwarded to Roosevelt by Neely after the campaign.

[27] Full text in *New York Times,* September 21, 1928, beginning, "Oklahoma City, Okla.—The verbatim speech of Governor Smith tonight was as follows: . . . "It cannot be said too strongly that the alleged texts of the campaign speeches of Smith as published later in book form are defective to the point of outright fraud on the reader. See *Campaign Addresses of Governor Alfred E. Smith* (Washington, D. C., Democratic National Committee, 1929). While the acceptance speech is reproduced almost exactly, the Oklahoma speech and the Newark speech (discussed below) are scarcely rough approximations of the stenographic accounts. Paragraphs are added, deleted, altered in meaning, and changed in language. Introductions are eliminated, and conclusions are substituted. The present writer cannot account for this travesty of fact. It certainly is not excused by the Foreword of Smith which describes the addresses as being "substantially as delivered."

The religious issue was officially out in the open. In May, a Virginian had predicted confidently (and brashly) that an attempt to hold his religion against Smith would "practically insure his triumphant election, or else I greatly misjudge the character and intelligence of the American people." [28] By late summer conditions had changed to so great an extent that speakers often explained that their support of Hoover had nothing to do with the religion of Smith.[29] An editor of a Protestant magazine put it succinctly:

> Every intelligent person knows that religion is already perhaps the principal factor in the discussion of the people throughout the country, outranking prohibition, farm relief and any other question that the press attempts to keep foremost.[30]

V

The leaders of the Democratic Party tried desperately to keep the mind of the nation on less emotional matters. Raskob tried to identify the needs of farmers and workers by stressing tariff protection for agriculture, saying that it would result successively in more farm income, higher wages and greater purchasing power for farm labor, increased production to meet the new demand, and consequently more employment and higher wages among industrial working people. From time to time leading Democrats denied that the party intended to lower the bars that kept immigrants from depressing wages. There was "not the slightest difference" between the platforms on the issue, said Senator Robinson.[31] *Such economic and social matters were more difficult for many voters of the day to understand than the alleged threat of an emissary of the Pope in the White House or the possible return of the saloon.*

The Democrats faced a hard fight as they tried to sell their views on more sophisticated issues to the public. Governor Smith toured the West in an eleven-car train, accompanied by eighty

---

[28] Letter to the editor from Tazewell, Virginia, in *New York Times*, May 11, 1928.

[29] For example, W. J. Abbot, editor of the *Christian Science Monitor*, to a conference on the press at Charlottesville, Virginia, *New York Times*, August 17, 1928.

persons, half of them members of the press. There were typists, telegraph and mimeograph operators, and motion picture operators, in addition to male and female public relations experts. The Smith message was Jeffersonian democracy, farm relief, benefits to labor, proper use of public power, and honest administration. But increasingly Smith had to defend his good name—hitherto one that had been unassailable on his home grounds. Because the Democratic platform and his own views on the issues had to be qualified carefully in order to please groups with conflicting interests, his speeches soon turned out to be full of explanations, repetitions, refutations, and denials. They ceased to dwell on the elements of a clear-cut, constructive, or organized program. Yet what Smith did was not a total loss. Even Norman Thomas, a persistent critic, said that Smith seemed to him to be making a harder appeal for "progressiveness" than Hoover. Still, he predicted the Governor's defeat.[33]

Smith attempted to speak from notes rather than from manuscript. Improvising as the inspiration struck him and seldom ignoring comments shouted from the audience, he was vastly more effective in person than on the radio. In spite of his fine record of public service, his great assets as a man, and the fact that he ran on his record as re-elected governor of a great state, it became increasingly apparent that, for reasons beyond his control, he was in trouble with much of the American electorate.

Derby-hatted Smith, cigar in mouth, had a voice that made many of his countrymen shudder. While some radio listeners thought that what he had to say was just "fine," [34] others shared the belief of a Minnesotian, who said he would support Smith, but "after hearing Governor Smith over the radio several times, I believe that if he were recalled to New York and men of the type of John W. Davis sent out on his behalf, Governor Smith could still be

[30] Dr. Albert C. Dieffenbach, Unitarian minister and editor of *The Christian Register*, Boston, quoted in *New York Times,* August 17, 1928.
[31] *Ibid.*, September 6, 14, and November 1, 1928.
[32] Based on Casey, "Party Campaign Propaganda," pp. 99–100, who tells the story in rounded detail.
[33] *New York Times,* October 10, 1928.
[34] A Hernando, Mississippi, supporter, October 20, 1928, Roosevelt Papers.

"Al" Smith, Democratic candidate for President

elected." [35] From Detroit a man commented, "A friend of mine asked me the other day if I had heard Governor Smith's notification speech and called attention to his murderous accent, or mis-

[35] An M.D. to Roosevelt, October 20, 1928, Roosevelt Papers.

pronunciation, in the use of the English language." [36] The present writer hazards a guess that personal characteristics of this type hurt Smith terribly in the election of 1928, but the guess is only comprised of projections from such letters as these.

Democratic orators naturally tried to sell to industrial areas the image of Al Smith, friend of labor, a man largely responsible for the passage of welfare legislation in New York State.[37] There was truth in the vision, but by election day such matters were beside the point. The fact was that Smith had come to represent the forces of evil to some myopic Americans, while to others he was a strange and even a humorous figure up from the city streets. Here was provincialism, plus an ill-considered and suspicious anti-Catholicism, from persons who, meaning no profound harm, nevertheless dishonored the spirit of fair play. In retrospect, the slurs slung at Alfred E. Smith in 1928 make the historian pity—not Smith—but the little ones who reviled him.

If Alfred E. Smith had been a Middle Western Protestant and prohibition enforcement had not been an issue in 1928, it is theoretically possible that the man who had befriended working people in New York and sought the confidence of labor leaders might have looked to the nation more like the democratic friend of a more distributed prosperity for little people. His words might have received a hearing on their merits. Even so, he might not have won. At least in such an event he could not have been disregarded or crucified both in backward areas and in some of the nation's parlors as a mixture of antichrist, John Barleycorn, and Charlie Chaplin.

VI

The major labor address of the Democratic Presidential candidate was made toward the close of the campaign at Newark, New Jersey. The October 31 address was ostensibly directed to working people in general, but there were more than a few thoughts in it

---

[36] Undated letter, summer, 1928, Roosevelt Papers.

[37] Note the effort of William B. Wilson, Secretary of Labor under President Wilson, before Maryland miners. *New York Times,* October 25, 1928.

which seem to have been made with union leaders and members in mind. The *New York Times* headlined the next morning "SMITH PLEDGES PROTECTION TO LABOR" and said the audience of over 12,000 had thundered approval. The candidate had been forced to warn his audience repeatedly that its cheers used up valuable "raddio" time.

Smith observed at Newark that his Republican friends expressed great love for and devotion to the American workingman when elections rolled around; yet in office they had not matched the accomplishments of the Wilson administration. Wages had climbed during the war years, not during ensuing Republican years. There was much unemployment in 1928; it must be remedied, where present, by public works.

Nothing would be done to the tariff by the Democrats that would take a five-cent piece out of a worker's pocket, said Smith. Did not he, himself, come from the ranks of labor? Surely workingmen would not swallow the "meaningless, senseless" injunction plank of the Republicans. The Governor of New York said the people would know to whom to turn on election day. "I have the greatest possible confidence in the intelligence, the common sense, and the sound judgment of the rank and file of the American people." [38]

Norman Thomas followed Governor Smith into Newark the following night. Smith, he said, had been "evasive, inadequate, and indefinite." He should have espoused government-operated employment offices, unemployment insurance, and the five-day week. Had not judges appointed by the Governor always granted injunctions just like other judges? he asked. Take a look at businessmen supporting the Democratic Party to see why its candidate equivocated on such matters. [39]

The tariff issue bothered Democratic spokesmen. The protectionist sentiment in many unions in 1928 helps to explain how the Democratic Party under the managership of John J. Raskob, a party then operating with funds obtained chiefly from businessmen, could rally around the tariff with relative impunity. The president of the New York State Federation of Labor, a strong

[38] Stenographic text in *New York Times,* November 1, 1928.
[39] *Ibid.,* November 2, 1928.

Smith supporter who visited the Governor frequently, was himself an advocate of higher tariff rates on shoes in 1928.[40] Early in April, A. F. of L. local officials in Brooklyn had called a meeting to condemn the practice of buying foreign-made products.[41] Democratic politicians might well ask themselves whether it was worthwhile to continue the fight for lower tariffs just to woo the farm vote, free-trade economists, and a few others. Why not just place the farmer under the wing of Federal legislation, too?

James W. Gerard, treasurer of the Democratic National Committee, is said to have caused "old-time Democrats" to gasp when he stated just before the opening session of the Houston convention, "It is time that this tariff obsession should be dropped." To change the tariff might injure business and labor alike. "American labor must be protected against foreign labor." Gerard saw industrial prosperity and full employment in "protection without robbery schedules." [42] Although Cordell Hull thought such ideas would destroy the party, some of the supporters of Smith were quick to claim that their favorite was not a low tariff man.

Thus, some political policies of old no longer seemed sacred, and certain issues were not readily discussed. (When Smith was sent a cable in July asking where he stood on chain stores and trusts, he sent it to Roosevelt, who had the writer looked up in Bradstreet in vain. Louis Howe penciled a note to Roosevelt, his personal hero, saying that since Smith was the addressee, and an answer was not mandatory, "why should we burn our fingers with so awkward a communication?" [43])

VII

The Democratic Party appeal to union leaders in 1928 was intended to be a strong one. But its strength was in the addresses of the candidate more than in the party platform. Smith tried to

[40] *New York Times*, November 21, 1928. Note also the August 30 resolution introduced by the Boot and Shoe Workers asking higher tariffs. New York State Federation *Proceedings, 1928,* 166.
[41] *New York Times*, April 3, 1928.
[42] *New York Times*, June 24, 1928.
[43] J. H. R. Grant to Alfred E. Smith, July 23, 1928, plus attached note. Roosevelt Papers.

strike at the roots of the Republican position by denying the general distribution of prosperity. He stressed the unemployed rather than the employed. Neither the tariff nor immigration laws would be changed at his hands in such a way as to harm the workingman, he intimated. Because his position on each issue was not clear-cut, however, Republican speakers found it easy to distort and obscure his position.

Governor Smith realized the importance of a strong posture on the injunction. He devoted more attention to it than did Hoover, and he was far more specific—hoping to gain tangible help from union leaders. In the Smith addresses union leaders obtained their primary desires. The impression that had been made on the union rank and file and on nonunion wage earners would appear, it was hoped, when the votes were counted. Unfortunately for Alfred E. Smith, an able and self-made man of the people, the workingmen and women of America had their eyes on collateral matters in 1928—not on the intricacies of his well-meant appeal to their economic self-interest.

Chapter 9

Thomas Appeals to "Workers" and "Progressives"

THE SOCIALISTS came out of their 1928 convention rejuvenated in spirit. A column written during the convention by one leader radiated confidence. Workingmen and women might be giving lip service to the prosperity god, wrote McAlister Coleman, but in their hearts they knew they were worshipping false images. He claimed that the Socialists spoke as "the sole interpreters and spokesmen for the great masses of America's workers." They therefore considered themselves to be, in the words of H. G. Wells, "watchers and guardians of the order of the world." The coming political campaign would be one more engagement in the long battle for human freedom and happiness.[1] The Convention had been enough "to make you hold up your head and stick out your chest and be all-fired proud of the fact that you are a Socialist." [2]

The editor of the *New Leader* was certain that the old party spirit had returned, and he quoted a delegate as saying, "We are coming back with a bang." [3] In retrospect, however, Mayor Hoan

[1] "The Political Prospects of 1928," *New Leader*, April 14, 1928.
[2] "We Go Riding Out," *ibid.*, April 21, 1928.
[3] James Oneal, in *ibid.*, April 21, 1928.

189

of Milwaukee recalled that "the party was completely bankrupt, financially." [4] At the time, the leaders of the Socialist Party talked as though the major parties had been placed on the defensive. The Democratic and Republican national committees, candidates, and spokesmen chose to ignore the challenge issued by the successor of Debs—Norman Thomas.

An unusually vivid picture of the Socialist candidate was painted by Hoan from his practical political viewpoint a few years after the 1928 campaign. He wrote Oneal as follows:

> I have always recognized that Norman Thomas is inclined to work too hard and gets fagged out, that he is impulsive and inclined to lean too strongly towards the college groups. I have personally forgiven all this for the reason that I do not know where else we can look for a candidate for President who would be willing to go through all the agonies of crusading for the Socialist Party. Only the old-time campaigners, like yourself, can understand that this is a thankless, tiresome and disheartening job and one that will wreck a man in body and mind as it did to Debs, if long continued.[5]

It was a keen comment, no less pertinent in the 1920s than at the time it was written. Representing an impoverished party, it was up to Thomas to breathe life into doctrines and points of view of little interest at the time.

I

In later years Norman Thomas asserted that both in 1924 and 1928 several of the close political friends of Alfred E. Smith came to him and urged him not to attack the governor too severely. They claimed that Smith stood for many of the things that Socialists and other progressive workers wanted. [6] Whatever effect this may have had on Thomas, neither his speeches and writings in 1928 nor those of other Socialists bristle with personal denunciations of either Smith or Hoover.

---

[4] Hoan to Oneal, August 7, 1934, Hoan Papers.
[5] Hoan to Oneal, June 30, 1933, Hoan Papers.
[6] Norman Thomas, *Is the New Deal Socialism?* (Chicago, 1936), p. 4.

To Thomas, both men were "able" and better qualified by experience and by administrative ability than any major party candidates since 1916.[7] His rivals were *not* to be considered "the white-haired boys of the most reactionary—and stupid—employers."[8] Smith was undeniably an able administrator thoroughly conversant with state affairs and "a pungent speaker with a gift of making the state's business interesting to the electorate.[9] Thomas called his acceptance speech a "clever and emotionally sincere appeal to liberals" that would require attention.[10] Hoover *at the time* was termed "a benevolent bureaucrat devoted to an outworn economic philosophy." The Hoover acceptance speech need not be analyzed at length. In the perspective of years, Thomas thought better of Hoover (having gotten to know him personally and therefore to appreciate his better qualities).[11]

Morris Hillquit called Hoover "a typical representative of American capitalism" who would be bitterly opposed by farmers and workers alike.[12] Although Victor Berger used a familiar expression of the day in calling the candidates of the old parties the "Gold Dust Twins," it was hardly defamation to allege in this way a similarity in the leading Democrat and Republican. The article on Hoover in the Socialist handbook, "Hoover, the Incompetent," was more condescending than insulting; it even admitted that he was "a very worthy opponent."[13] A Socialist writer warned voters, "You'll pretty soon, if you have not already done so, wake up to the cold, hard fact that your boasted 'individual independence and initiative' don't amount to a hill of beans."[14]

It was Governor Smith that the Socialists considered their chief competitor. The party literature spent hundreds of thousands of

[7] Norman Thomas, "Timely Topics," *New Leader,* July 7, 1928, a weekly column distributed to 130 labor and liberal publications.

[8] *Ibid.,* August 4, 1928.

[9] Review of *Progressive Democracy: Speeches and State Papers of Alfred E. Smith* (New York, 1928), in *ibid.,* June 23, 1928.

[10] *Ibid.,* September 1, 1928.

[11] Thomas to Oral History Project (1949).

[12] *New York Times,* June 17, 1928.

[13] Freda Kirchwey, "Hoover, the Incompetent," in *The Intelligent Voter's Guide,* p. 86.

[14] Oscar Ameringer, *Milwaukee Leader,* May 1, 1928.

words and dozens of cartoons trying to make Smith and Tammany
Hall seem one and the same. The political rise of Smith in New
York State was examined in minute detail. Stressed repeatedly was
the idea that no matter what Smith might want to do personally,
big business interests behind his party would unite with a conservative South to keep down liberalism and progressivism. The Socialists rejoiced at the appointment of John J. Raskob as Democratic campaign manager, and they tried to identify the Democratic
Party with him and with the conservative South.[15] Smith is no
friend of labor, said Socialist leaders, and a party booklet warned:

> If you want a Democratic replica of Republican kowtowing
> to the bosses, then Smith is your man. But don't make the mis-
> take of voting for him on the ground that he is a liberal or a
> friend of labor, or anything of the sort. And forget the idea that
> with Smith in the White House the hitherto submerged city
> workers are coming into some sort of utopia, where they will
> enjoy freedom from injunctions, the benefits of social legislation,
> and a general era of good feeling.[16]

II

The Socialists were keenly alive to the value of local issues,
seldom failing to expose errors of omission and sins of commission
when they thought they had discovered them. The National Executive Committee chose a panel of forty-seven speakers in May, six
of whom may have been women. This initial group was drawn
from states with large populations.[17] Louis Waldman, Socialist
gubernatorial candidate in New York, has told in his autobiography
how speakers were to stress the corruption issue and other issues
during the campaign in that State. The power of organized crime
and its alliance with politics, the need for public rather than private
control of water power, and the role of the injunction in thwarting
the organization of labor would get major attention.[18] The *New
Leader* made much of these. It also discussed the need for unioni-

---

[15] By accepting the aid of Raskob and other "financial and industrial magnates,"
Smith had made workers question his friendship for labor, said the Socialist
campaign manager. *New York Times,* September 3, 1928.
[16] Quoted in *ibid.,* August 7, 1928.
[17] Minutes, N.E.C., May 19–20, 1928, Hoan Papers.
[18] Louis Waldman, *Labor Lawyer* (New York, 1944), p. 182.

zation of the Southern textile industry and did not ignore the farm issue. When it seemed that WEVD, "the Socialist radio station," [19] might lose its license, the party had a ready-made issue in its hands and decried the discrimination in numerous articles.

For certain states and local Socialist units the Presidential race was only one of several races of importance. In the Milwaukee city election, Hoan and his colleagues said the party would provide maximum achievement, continue the merit system, "make courtesy and service our motto," employ the best standards in municipal finance, advance city planning and zoning, and develop harbors and deep water projects. Transportation would be promoted, workers would be assisted "in their struggle for betterment," and the fight for "a better, bigger, and brighter city" would continue.[20] The situation in Milwaukee was helped by "left-handed support" lent by some opposition candidates jealous of each other, according to Hoan. Moreover, the party was said to gain support because it exercised "some discipline over its officials" and had a program for managing city affairs.[21] Such reasons as these do not seem related in any way to socialism as doctrine. Nor were they.

In Reading, Pennsylvania, for example, Socialists in power had praiseworthy, yet routine, accomplishments to their credit. As the locally powerful James H. Maurer analyzed the situation in his autobiography:

> All this sort of thing is not Socialism—perhaps not even a first installment. But it is part of a necessary preparation for Socialism. So long as people think that politics is in its nature corrupt, they are not likely to understand what Socialism means. Only clean political action can usher in the new social order.
>
> Of course, Socialists in control of a single city cannot establish Socialism there while the rest of the state and the nation remain capitalist. They cannot do much more than give a clean, honest, efficient, humane administration, free from graft, thereby proving that workers are not all hands and no brains, as exploiters of labor would have the world believe. To do that is worth while.[22]

[19] One of its policies was to broadcast news and features regarding "the aspirations of the American labor movement. . . ." *New Leader,* December 3, 1927. Note the call letters of the station: *Eugene Victor Debs.*
[20] *Milwaukee Leader,* February 27, 1928.
[21] Hoan to Berger, March 23, 1928, Hoan Papers.
[22] James H. Maurer, *It Can Be Done* (New York, 1938), pp. 303, 305.

One must leave to the students of Milwaukee, Reading and Bridge-port affairs the question of what balance existed in each city between socialism and reformism, returning now to the larger story of 1928.

Above all other national issues the Socialist Party stressed the alleged similarities between the old parties. The cartoons of Art Young stressed the identity theme over and over, and Norman Thomas seemed to get special delight from his often repeated "Tweedledum and Tweedledee" interpretation of American party politics. As he put it,

> The exigencies of our parties will compel Smith and Hoover to talk as nearly as possible like each other so as not to antagonize important factions of their own parties. Both will continue their policy of saying nothing if they can help it. Men will vote for or against them on personal likes and dislikes of the men or their religion.[23]

William Karlin, Socialist candidate for Attorney General of New York, claimed the old parties stood for the same thing: "protection of property rights against the rights of the individual." Victor Berger said, "All I can say is that there is absolutely no difference of principles, methods, or aims between the two old parties now. They are both ultraconservative and even reactionary." The Socialist Party, obviously, did not approve of a two-party system in which the parties differed only slightly. Then what did they propose?

The entire Socialist Party campaign in 1928 was unified around one particular theme—the hope that the party might come to be the nucleus of a new mass party composed of trade unionists, Socialists, and such others as might wish to lend their support. Socialism would furnish the party doctrine and Socialists most of the party leadership.

The Conference for Progressive Political Action of 1924 had been, over-all, a great disappointment to Socialists. [24] Indeed, the whole failure of the American Socialists to sway trade unionists toward unity in the manner of the European Social Democratic

---

[23] Speech, Framingham, Mass., *New York Times,* June 25, 1928.
[24] Note Morris Hillquit, *Loose Leaves from a Busy Life* (New York, 1934).

movements and the British Labour Party had long been a matter for soul-searching concern. As Morris Hillquit put it, "A Socialist movement without the support of the workers is a sort of disembodied spirit, in fact a spook. Socialism must remain the political and spiritual guide of the working class, but it must reorganize and re-educate the working class." [25] The plea along these lines that Thomas made at the convention of the International Ladies Garment Workers Union in Boston was eloquent though tactful. Thomas called the step necessary "for the sake of your class, and for the sake of mankind, for the sake of the present and the future. . . ." [26] He wrote in the New Leader just before election day under the headline, "VOTE THE SOCIALIST TICKET! THE GREAT ISSUE—TO REBUILD A PARTY" that the one political task that mattered was to build the new party: "the party of workers with hand and brain. . . ." [27]

Sometimes the Socialists told themselves that their task was already well along. They could say on occasion that Thomas and Maurer "are the Labor candidates," and that they were "nominated by a Labor Party." [28] They would even proclaim, *"The Socialist Party is the Labor Party."* [29] In more sober moments, however, party leaders admitted that while the times ought to be ripe for a new party, the day for its creation lay ahead. Thomas admitted in August, "There is, as yet, no spontaneous mass movement"; yet he thought he could see "widespread interest." [30]

Socialist Party leaders knew that there were already Socialists in the trade union movement. Socialist Vice-Presidential candidate Maurer was no less than *president* of the Pennsylvania State Federation of Labor! Self-styled "representatives" of 31 unions had pledged support to a committee of one thousand which Hillquit formed in 1928 to work for the party among union mem-

[25] *The Immediate Issue* (inside title: *The Socialist Task and Outlook*) (New York, 1920?), p. 8. Or see Ralph Korngold, *Are There Classes in America?* (Chicago, Socialist Party, 1914), p. 9, "If the workers rise, they will rise together."
[26] I.L.G.W.U. *Proceedings*, 1928, p. 101.
[27] *New Leader*, November 3, 1928.
[28] Editorial, "A Fruitless Political Policy," *ibid.*, May 5, 1928.
[29] Editorial, "The Politics of Prosperity and the Road to Power," *ibid.*, September 15, 1928.
[30] *Ibid.*, August 25, 1928.

bers.[31] Minor officials in the unions would on occasion take the platform on behalf of the party.[32] The needle trades in New York City contained numerous Socialists and sympathizers,[33] and I.L.G.W.U. resolution 123 called for aid to the Young People's Socialist League in order to increase Socialist influence.[34]

Yet the truth was that nearly all the member unions of the A. F. of L. were led in 1928 by men opposed personally both to Socialism and to third-party action. [35] The Gompers tradition in political action lived on.[36] Labor leaders of the day felt themselves among the beneficiaries, not the victims, of capitalism. Such sentiments as these were common:

> Labels matter least in the struggle for higher civilization. No labor union will move one inch further because it may be classed as radical. The test of progressive trade unionism is its vitality and effectiveness. Only organizations which move ahead count.[37]

III

Socialist leaders were in an embarrassing position with regard to leaders of the unions. They wanted to condemn them for their failure to accept the doctrine that separate political action is the only true light. Repeatedly they stressed their love for unionism, that is, industrial as opposed to craft unionism. Somehow they must stay on speaking terms with union leaders in the event that

[31] *New York Times,* March 29, 1928.

[32] A. I. Shiplacoff, president of the International Leather Goods Workers Union, spoke at a Socialist meeting, for example. *Ibid.,* September 6, 1928.

[33] Note tributes to Debs, to Sacco and Vanzetti, and to "an all-inclusive labor party" as a *future* goal, by the officers of the Amalgamated Clothing Workers in *Report of the General Executive Board* (New York, 1928), p. 85. Sidney Hillman was then its president. See also Joel Seidman, *The Needle Trades* (New York, 1942), p. 230, and Benjamin Stolberg, *Tailor's Progress* (New York, 1944), p. 318.

[34] *I.L.G.W.U. Proceedings,* 1928, 153.

[35] Based on extensive examination of A. F. of L. and state federation proceedings and union journals. The newspaper of the railroad brotherhoods, *Labor* (Washington, D. C.), shows the same disinterest in Socialism and third-party action in 1928.

[36] This fact was especially irksome to Communists. See J. Louis Engdahl, "Sam Gompers is Not Dead," *Workers Monthly,* V (November, 1925), 10–14. (This periodical later merged with two other magazines to form *The Communist.)*

[37] From the journal of the Amalgamated Clothing Workers, the *Advance,* quoted in an editorial of the *New York Times,* January 3, 1928.

circumstances might change. Thus temperance in language was essential. Suppose the labor leaders should change their minds and decide on independent party action? Personal attacks were seldom made at the time, therefore, although ridicule for specific *actions* of leaders like William Green or Matthew Woll was common. An editorial in the *New Leader* deplored the political division of labor and laughed at A. F. of L. political activities, but it warned, nevertheless, that labor leaders only reflected the lack of initiative among the rank and file. *The leaders need not be denounced.*[38] "As a political organization we have no right to interfere in the internal affairs of the trade-unions as they have no right to interfere in ours." [39]

A lengthy and featured Socialist analysis of A. F. of L. political activities by Louis Stanley in 1928 tried to make at least ten specific points against going policy; he did not deal in personalities. "Where is there the politician who worries about the vote of organized labor?" he asked. "The plain fact is that the trade union official has no way of delivering the vote of his fellow union members.[40] Although Stanley charged that the old parties had given as little as they could, he admitted that the years had brought an increasing humanization and liberalization of legislation. To most trade union leaders in 1928, this was sheer gain and one thing that made Socialism unnecessary. Many a trade union leader of the day would have endorsed the tart warning of former Socialist writer John Spargo as he gazed on his ex-comrades:

[38] *New Leader*, May 5, 1928.
[39] *Ibid.*, April 21, 1928.
[40] Louis Stanley, "A. F. of L. Policy on Politics Breaks Down," in *New Leader*, August 18, 1928. His points: Labor officials support political friends for personal favors. Local political machines are not all of one party, so labor must be divided on the local level to be effective. Yet labor leaders cannot "deliver" votes, so politicians do not fear them. Workers vote from habit, race or religion—not as ordered. State labor federations lack organization and influence with member unions, lack contact with the rank and file, and must please city centrals located in both Republican and Democratic areas. The nonpartisan policy of the A. F. of L. creates apathy rather than giving the thrill to the worker of building up a better world. Where was labor (class) solidarity? Too few workers were organized. Nonpartisanship as a policy gained only a few "sops." The adherence of organized labor to the Socialist Party would "electrify" the wage earners. A labor party must be created.

While you go on preaching the old doctrines of class war and irreconcilable conflict, the leaders of organized capital and the leaders of organized labor are quietly but steadily and surely working out plans of harmonious cooperation in the realization of genuine industrial commonwealth. You gabble; they work.[41]

IV

The Socialist Party hoped to gain the support of workers of the mind as well as workers with the hand. Socialist Party leaders considered the appeal to progressives and liberals almost as important as the appeal to organized labor. "I hope that progressives will soon muster enough courage," said Victor Berger in Congress, "to stand by their guns and become a nucleus for a new and larger [political] movement." He found it shameful the way they had put patronage above principles after 1924.[42]

Although that appeal to Progressive politicians would go unheeded, the Socialist appeal to teachers, ministers, artists, and writers for support had more success. Several committees were formed from white collar groups and these gained publicity for the ticket, even though they represented only a small minority of their fellows. One thing that helped recruit these articulate leaders in the 1920s was the activity conducted on college campuses by the League for Industrial Democracy.[43] Another was the scope of the personal contacts Norman Thomas had built up through his years in the ministry as an opponent of war and as a writer on behalf of various causes. There was some appeal in such pamphlets as Harry W. Laidler's *An Appeal to White Collar Workers and the Professions,* which stressed the benefits educators and creative thinkers might gain under a Socialist state.[44] The appeal to altruism was well developed, and scorn was heaped on the "ma-

[41] *Ibid.,* September 8, 1928. (A response to a *New Leader* challenge.)

[42] *Congressional Record,* Seventieth Congress, 1st Sess., May 9, 1928, p. 8209.

[43] Its officers in April, 1928 were: President, Robert Morss Lovett, professor of English literature at the University of Chicago; treasurer, Stuart Chase; executive directors, Norman Thomas, Harry W. Laidler; field secretary, Paul Blanshard; among the vice presidents were Maurer and Rev. John Haynes Holmes. *New Leader,* April 14, 1928.

[44] New York, Socialist Party, n.d. The appeal to teachers was almost entirely to their self-interest.

terialistic" joy America seemed to be getting out of the radio, the automobile, the lodges and civic clubs, and generally improved living conditions.[45]

The Socialists of 1928 were by no means a unit or a close-knit team. It was for them a trying period of East-West backbiting and organizational controversy, most of which can be ignored here. There was the quarrel over adoption of a new Constitution for the party. Was it antidemocratic? Was it calculated to turn the party over to newcomers or to New Yorkers? There was the fuss over moving the campaign management from Chicago to New York City. Such matters would not be settled in 1928. Indeed, in 1933, Hoan could write Oneal from Milwaukee

> A political party that does not have its roots well grounded in the West cannot amount to anything in this country. One thing is certain and I except you from what I have to say, that most residents of New York get a sectional psychology that is entirely foreign to the usual psychology which prevails throughout the U.S.[46]

Wisconsin socialism and New York socialism might come from identical books and advocates might even share similar national origins and religious beliefs (although this is open to much doubt indeed), but they did not see eye-to-eye on which element should control the party machinery.

The bitterness of certain Chicago officials as power moved East is understandable. Henry's irritation has already been noted. The state secretary of Illinois, W. R. Snow, was more outspoken. The campaign in June looked like a farce; "the folks at the forks of the road don't like things as they are running," he wrote Hoan.[47] To Oneal he was blunt. Oneal, a son of the Wabash, was writing like a "native-born New Yorker," and he wondered if it ever occurred to any New Yorker that "other parts of the country might have somewhat different economic, political, and psychological problems to deal with." Eastern Socialists he called "The Commisars of Legal Technicalities," and other names. If Chicago was

---

[45] Socialists were not alone in this. A popular book of the day which ridiculed America was Charles Merz, *The Great American Bandwagon* (New York, 1928).
[46] Letter of June 30, 1933, Hoan Papers.
[47] Letter of June 6, 1928, Hoan Papers.

no longer to be head of the movement, the new heads should at least "remain in touch with the American people." The list of speakers had 19 from New York, one from Illinois. Did this reflect importance? Too many New Yorkers spoke at the national convention. Pamphlets were being censored by New Yorkers, but editing Congressman Berger and George H. Kirkpatrick was like a hick poet editing Shakespeare.[48] Norman Thomas was thoroughly in sympathy with the New York group. To Berger he wrote that while the Chicago group had "admirable qualities," they were not the proper persons in whom to center authority. Comrade Henry "simply cannot conduct a proper campaign" whatever his personal speaking ability.[49] Meanwhile, the Women's Campaign Committee came to consist of seven Easterners.[50] Immediately after the close of the campaign, Thomas would urge that the National office be moved from Chicago to New York.[51] Letters in the negative on this idea were on hand from Kansas, Wyoming, Idaho, Montana, Indiana, and Minnesota. Thomas said the move would result in (1) more people being available to work at different tasks, (2) more volunteers, and (3) more financial sponsors. The presence in New York of the Rand School and the *New Leader* would mean a lot, Thomas said. Discussion on the matter was heated. Clearly, the Socialist Party campaign in 1928 suffered from the effort to shift control eastward. Yet one must say that from that shift came great increases in liaison with "intellectuals."

V

While the "old guard" was none too happy about the "college crowd" that was prominent in the Socialist Party in 1928, they could not deny the importance of some persons who lent Norman Thomas their support. Some of these were clergymen who looked on life on this perspective:

[48] Letter of June 6, 1928, copy in Hoan Papers.
[49] Thomas to Berger, June 14, 1928, copy in Hoan Papers.
[50] N.E.C. Minutes, Newark, N. J., May 19–20, 1928, Hoan Papers.
[51] N.E.C. Minutes, New York City, November 24–25, 1928, Hoan Papers.

> I say to you that the church is awakening to the great issues
> between capital and labor, the reorganization of society, and we
> are coming to a time when the church, through some of its most
> potent organizations, is not afraid to espouse the cause of labor
> in its great fight for emancipation.[52]

Some ministers had zealously aided the investigation of the great
steel strike of 1919.[53] In the magazine *World Tomorrow,* this
growing social consciousness of some sections of the church found
ideas to its liking.[54] Morris Hillquit explained to someone overseas

> The *World Tomorrow* is a magazine of somewhat limited circu-
> lation. . . . It is entirely friendly to the Socialist Movement but
> has a distinct pacifist background. There could be no possible
> objection to your writing for that magazine on the part of the
> Socialist Party.[55]

As it happened, the editor of the magazine in 1928, Kirby Page,
was like Thomas a former minister and a peace advocate and was
hopeful of a realignment in the parties. Perhaps progressives and
radicals would "buckle down to the long and laborious task of
creating a new party based on economic realities" if Thomas received a large vote.[56] A professor in the department of religion at
Smith College found the Socialist Party platform "nearer to the
New Testament ideal" than any other he had ever seen.[57] By
October the Ministers Committee for Thomas and Maurer had 73
names on its list.[58] When ministers read the *New Leader* in 1928
they found little arid discussion of the theory of Socialism, and
they might take pleasure in the idealistic expressions of its writers,
so long as they could overlook such references as "stock-gambling
Episcopal preachers" and "Catholic priest politicians." More

---

[52] *Can the Church be Radical? Debate . . . February 12, 1922, [Between] John
Haynes Holmes [and] Scott Nearing* (New York, Hanford Press, 1922), p. 27.

[53] The Interchurch World Movement put out several volumes on the strike during its short existence.

[54] Not all written by Socialists necessarily. There had been, said one writer, "a
commercializing and materializing of everything which once was sacred, lofty, and
sublime." Paul Arthur Schilpp, "Is Western Civilization Worth Saving?" *World
Tomorrow,* XI (September, 1928), 369–371. He was a professor of philosophy
at the time.

[55] Hillquit to Friedrich Adler, December 5, 1924, Hillquit Papers.

[56] Kirby Page, "Why I Shall Vote for Norman Thomas," *World Tomorrow,* XI
(November, 1928), 452.

[57] S. Ralph Harlow to Harry W. Laidler, in *New Leader,* June 23, 1928.

[58] *Ibid.,* October 6, 1928.

pleasant was this: "I suppose most of us are Socialists because we do take the Christian ideal of brotherly love to heart. . . . We possess in heart and faith the one excuse for Christianity's existence. Love for humanity," wrote S. A. de Witt in the *New Leader* of October 20, 1928.

When W. E. Woodward, the author, invited seven hundred writers and artists to join the Writers, Artists, and Publicists Committee for Thomas and Maurer he announced, "I am a Socialist of the deepest dye," but he asked only "support" for his cause. "I am not asking you to become a Socialist," he wrote.

> A vote for Thomas and Maurer . . . will help to make American politics more realistic. It will give increased prominence to important industrial and international issues stressed by the Socialist Party. . . . It will help lay the foundation for a powerful party of progress and social justice.[59]

Among those answering his plea were W. E. B. Du Bois, Fola La Follette, Robert Morss Lovett, Upton Sinclair, and Paul Blanshard.[60] Du Bois was particularly anxious to break up the old party alignment, but he saw in the one-party South a death blow to any new party hopes.

Famous names in education and intellectual pursuits lent their prestige to the cause of the Socialist Party in 1928. Harold Underwood Faulkner, Jerome Davis, Granville Hicks, and Maynard C. Kruegar;[61] Charles Edward Russell, an old-time Socialist,[62] and others supported the ticket, some of them identified actively with the Educators Committee for Thomas and Maurer. The committee called Hoover and Smith "men of personal honor" backed by "sterile and corrupt groups." To them, the Socialist Party had shown what they called the desire and capacity to deal with unemployment and world peace.[63]

An open appeal to "Progressives" to support the ticket was signed by 36 persons, only four of whom were Socialists! There was a

---

[59] Form letter of the committee, n.d. In file "Socialist Party Campaign Material," Stanford University Library.
[60] *New Leader*, October 6, 1928.
[61] *Ibid.*
[62] *Ibid.*, October 20, 1928.
[63] *New York Times*, August 25, 1928.

sociologist, a historian, two educators, five in philosophy or religion, three economists, two mathematicians, three English teachers, and a scientist.[64] While Gilbert E. Roe, chairman in 1924 of the Eastern division of the Progressive campaign, was no Socialist, he supported Thomas in 1928.[65] Frederick Vanderbilt Field, an heir to the family fortune, inaugurated his radical career by turning Socialist on the heels of his Harvard graduation. His lengthy reasons made tiresome reading in the *New Leader,* which busily published numerous pleas to progressives and liberals.[66] Other party appeals appeared in the *New York Times.*[67] The editors of the *World Tomorrow* said elections should be based on "genuine issues"; a new party should be built; a negative answer should be given to the editorial's question, "Shall We Vote for Al?" [68]

While Arthur Garfield Hays, the liberal- lawyer author of *Let Freedom Ring,* and supporter of the cause of Tom Mooney,[69] was eagerly courted, he choose to engage in public debates against the idea of deserting Alfred E. Smith. In a debate against Hillquit he said:

> However able an administrator, however liberal an individual, whatever be the principles he espouses, you Socialists will not play with him unless he joins your party. . . . Your socialism has become a religion. You have a pattern. Economics must fit into that pattern. You have a philosophy. You have a dogma. You have a religion. . . . You forget that any system of society is a means, not an end.[70]

The Socialist Party candidate did win an articulate supporter in Paul H. Douglas, then professor of industrial relations at the University of Chicago and later Democratic Senator from Illinois. In an essay, "Why I Am for Norman Thomas," Douglas told readers of the *New Republic* and *New Leader* that the Socialist Party had dispensed with "economic theology" and was rooted in "reali-

---

[64] *New Leader,* September 1, 1928.
[65] *Ibid.,* October 27, 1928.
[66] *Ibid.,* June 23, 1928, September 29, 1928.
[67] September 17, 18; October 15, 23, 1928.
[68] *World Tomorrow* (August, 1928).
[69] See letters in Mooney Papers, Bancroft Library, University of Calif.
[70] Reported in *New Leader,* November 3, 1928. McAlister Coleman dedicated his 1930 biography of Debs to Hays!

ties." [71] The way he saw it, a new party should be built around clear-cut names, much as the Labour Party of Great Britain had been built. The "brilliant maturity" of the latter was praised. Collective economic measures should be the basis for the new party, of which the Socialist Party would be the "evangel." A party should be founded on the solid economic interests of those who would benefit from change, he thought; if only the unskilled and semiskilled could be unionized, their natural desire for protection would probably force the A. F. of L. to support a labor party. By contrast with this vista, Douglas called the Republican Party the representative of "property" and the Democratic Party "that hodge-podge of the reactionary South and the boss-ridden Irish Catholic machines of the North." Paul Douglas was to survive this phrase, carrying the Democratic label of later years successfully in many elections.[72] Despite such views as those of Douglas, vast numbers of reformers in 1928 did not intend to overlook Socialist doctrine in any haste to change or to rearrange the American party system, build strong unions, or improve civil liberties.

VI

Appealing to union men, "workers of the mind," and students, there was one group to which the party of Norman Thomas refused to appeal in 1928. Socialists liked to say that the Communists were too insignificant to require notice,[73] but it is evident that they resented the extremities of Communist attacks on them, and they replied in kind, using less violence in epithets. Socialists did not consider themselves "fascists" or "enemies of the working class." The Socialist campaign manager said wryly, "One might think we were the party in power from the way this element concentrates its activity against us." [74] *Daily Worker* violence of expression was

[71] *Ibid.*, October 27, 1928.
[72] See Cabell Phillips, "Paul Douglas—'Instinctive Liberal,'" *New York Times Magazine*, June 24, 1951, for a rounded career portrayal. "In answer to your question, I was not a member of the Socialist Party in 1928, and never was." Senator Douglas to present writer, April 16, 1962.
[73] *New Leader*, May 26, 1928.
[74] *New York Times*, October 28, 1928.

enough to bring out bitter resentment.[75] The Socialists termed such attacks "garbage" and said (hopefully) that Communism was dying all over the world. The working class would be better off for its death.[76] Humorous but keen was this comment:

> The mandarins in Moscow supply the brains and all that the boys here are required to do is to wiggle. Of course the gents who do the thinking in Moscow for the boys in the United States have a right to command [,] as they pay for the American wiggle.[77]

The editor of the *New Leader* could admire the enthusiasm and earnestness of the Communists—nothing more. His party would never form cells in unions and try to steal leadership. The Socialists would "educate." He claimed they favored the utmost democracy within the trade unions and in other institutions of society as well. They could not approve of venomous assaults on the character and motives of mankind.[78] Indeed, as far back as 1924 the "Declaration of Principles of the Socialist Party" had stated, "The Socialist Party seeks to attain its end[s] by orderly methods, and it depends upon education and organization of the masses." [79] Hillquit was to indicate the gap between Socialists and Communists a few years later when he rebuffed an advocate of closer relations with the Soviets in these words:

> I am not overcritical of the Soviet regime in Russia, but I utterly reject the opinion that such a regime is applicable to the United States or any other country of western civilization. I must confess I cannot see how we can "get into closer relationship" with the administration of Stalin, since the Soviet government and the Third International consistently repel all attempted social democratic approaches.[80]

The gulf separating the leading Marxist parties in the United States, the Socialists and the Communists, in 1928, was far more than a matter of obscure doctrine. It was one of *method*. The di-

[75] For examples, see *Daily Worker,* June 1, 1928, on Thomas, and October 1, 1928, on the party.

[76] *New Leader,* September 8, 1928.

[77] Editorial, "Nuclei vs. Nuclei," *ibid.,* May 12, 1928.

[78] *Ibid.,* November 17, 1928.

[79] *A.B.C. of Socialism: Declaration of Principles of the Socialist Party, July, 1924* (Chicago, Socialist Party, 192?), a leaflet.

[80] Morris Hillquit to W. W. Passage, July 25, 1932, Hillquit Papers.

vision between Socialists and dedicated craft union labor leaders was one of political methods and social goals. The ideological chasm between reformers and Socialist Party members was one of doctrine—whatever the apparent similarities in immediate criticisms of the status quo. Moreover, the geographical and personal divisions within the party itself were all too real.

Much that the Socialist Party stood for in the 1920s would one day be enacted into law after prosperity faded and a new spirit in economics came into vogue. But one must not forget that the central plea—for *government ownership* of the means of production —was a reality in 1928. The Party's commendable rejection of revolutionary force, violence, and conspiracy as paths to power in a democracy cannot obliterate that. To intimate that the Socialists really meant the words they devoted to reforms but did not stand behind what they so plainly said on government ownership (which would then and since have been economic idiocy in America) is to do them a disservice. Of their plans to destroy the two-party political system by building a giant Labor Party more will be said subsequently. At this point it need only be observed that the appeal to "Workers" and "Progressives" in 1928 was a naive but enthusiastic mixture of the realistic and the unrealistic; the idealistic and the opportunistic; the enduring—and the ephemeral.

Chapter 10

Foster Appeals to The "Proletariat"

THE PRESIDENTIAL CAMPAIGN of the Communist Party can be fully comprehended only by those who understand the threat it offered the American trade-union movement. To A. F. of L. leaders of the day this was obvious. To an undercover agent of the United States Department of Labor in the Far West the matter was equally plain. Reporting secretly, he wrote,

> The communists here [state of Washington] that are members of the various unions are pretty well known but proving that they are actually members of the party seems to be and is a very difficult task. All of them will sidestep a direct question as to their membership and in that they differ from the average I. W. W., the latter proud of his membership, hating the A. F. of L. and wanting the wide world to know it. Without access to the membership rolls it is well-nigh impossible to bring proof of membership, without which it seems impossible to suspend or expel them from their respective local or international unions.[1]

Five days later from the nation's capitol across the continent the high command of the A. F. of L. sent a sharp warning to international unions about the Communist menace.

[1] E. A. Marsh, Seattle Division of Conciliation, to Hugh L. Kerwin, Director of Conciliation, February 10, 1928, File 20/580B, Group 157, Dept. of Labor Files, National Archives.

Quoting extensively from the 1927 strictures of the Executive
Council against Communism, the warning referred anew to "the
persistency and subtlety with which the adherents of the Communist Party spread their pernicious propaganda to catch the unwary
and unthinking. . . ." Only unceasing, repeated, and reiterated
warnings and constant vigilance would prevent the growth of
"such destructive doctrines." [2]

I

To one union in particular the Communist danger was an ever-
present fact of life. The Amalgamated Clothing Workers had seen
Local Number 5 captured by William Z. Foster's Trade Union
Educational League in the mid-1920s, a triumph followed by the
temporary seizure of the union's New York Joint Board.[3] Vigorous
countering action had checked the Communists by 1926, so that
Sidney Hillman was able to admonish his union's convention: "As
to political parties, you can have as many as you like; you can
disagree in the union as much as you want; but we will not allow
an outside organization to run our affairs." A year later Hillman
wrote a similar conciliatory message which became official union
policy in 1928:

> To those individuals who are carried away by their enthusiasm
> to attempt the impossible, the union must be tolerant; it must
> give them time to rid themselves of their mistaken notions and
> to learn through experience that the labor movement is con-
> fronted at all times with real, everyday problems which must be
> made the best of, under prevailing conditions. . . . It was only
> when the so-called left wing opposition attempted to corrupt the
> morale of our organizations, sacrifice the interest of the organiza-
> tion to their own ends, and break up the unity within the move-
> ment that we were forced to call a halt to their activities.[4]

[2] A. F. of L. Circular Letter to all Presidents, February 15, 1928, in Circular
Letter Book 6, A. F. of L. Papers.

[3] Mathew Josephson, *Sidney Hillman: Statesman of American Labor* (New
York, 1952), pp. 275–276.

[4] General Executive Board Report, in Amalgamated Clothing Workers *Proceedings*, 1928, 78–79, quoting a Hillman editorial in *Advance*, October 28, 1927.

Yet such fatherly patience was not characteristic of senior A. F. of L. leadership in those years; indeed, the spirit of opposition among city central and state federation leaders was more nearly expressed in the words of a labor newspaper on the West Coast:

> There is no point on which the trade unionist and the Bolshey can agree. One believes in an expanding democracy; the other is committed to rulership from above. One believes in making every day a better day for wage workers; the other scorns these efforts and considers strikers but pawns for this revolution [ary] purpose. . . . The man who talks of mutuality of interests between trade unionists and Communists is either a knave or a sentimentalist. . . . The trade union should be held to its purpose. It should not be a hatchery for revolution. It should not be a haven for wild men who whine for free speech as an excuse to bore from within.[5]

On July 14, 1928, Communist Vice-Presidential candidate Benjamin Gitlow announced that henceforth the Communists would augment their old boring-from-within tactics with the formation of new rival trade unions. [6] Dual unionism, whether Communist or not, was a language orthodox trade union men understood full well. And it was something to be crushed at all costs. The A. F. of L. Executive Council soon reiterated that the unions had no intention of giving up in the battle against Communism. In the New Bedford strikes, the Council said pointedly, it was a tragedy that the Communists had come in, for they had played into the hands of the mill owners by appealing to the passions of the mob—solely for their own purposes. The needle trades, mine unions, and railroad brotherhoods were also menaced, said the announcement.

A few days later a Communist candidate told a New Jersey party rally that that state was dedicated to the open shop because it was a corporation state made up of powerful interests. The solu-

---

[5] "Communists Can't 'Fit In,' " *Labor Clarion* (San Francisco, A. F. of L.) February 4, 1927.

[6] *New York Times*, July 14, 1928. This was in line with the provisions of the "Resolution on the Trade Union Question," February 25, 1928, of the Ninth Plenum of the Executive Committee of the International which had ruled, "In the United States . . . the Communist Party must on its own accord recognize trade unions in those branches of industry where workers are not organized at all or very inadequately organized (the steel, automobile, rubber, boot and textile industries, water-transport service, etc.)." *International Press Correspondence*, VIII (Vienna, March 15, 1928), 320.

tion? Workers should join the Communist Party. William Green
quickly announced that any member union of the A. F. of L. would
have the support of the parent body in a fight against Communism.
A. F. of L. vice president Matthew Woll boasted that the Federation's vigorous countermeasures against the Communists had been
responsible for their shift in tactics. He predicted that employers
would inevitably be faced with the necessity of choosing between
American and revolutionary unions.[7]

Meanwhile, some of the Communist leaders had gone to the
meeting of the Sixth Congress of the Third International in Moscow.[8] Soon a leading party official bragged, "At the Sixth World
Congress of the Communist International, the American Communist Party participated actively in the formulation of policies aiming
to mobilize more effectively the workers for the destruction of
imperialism, for the wiping out of capitalism, for the victory of the
working class, [and] for the establishment of Communism." [9] The
American Communist of 1928 cannot be convicted of trying to
minimize his international connections, activities, and obligations.
The record shows, moreover, that the party's leaders were more
concerned from August to October, 1928, with which of them
would attain the highest favor with the Soviet leaders of the Third
International than they were with how well their various election
efforts might succeed.[10]

Labor Day gave American Federation of Labor leaders a chance
to repeat their strictures against the Communists. Hugh Frayne,
the Federation's general organizer in New York, said that there
must be no compromise with Communism, "this menace to human
welfare and progress." The Federation, he said, stood for loyalty
to the government and its institutions. Peter J. Brady, president of
the Federation Bank and Trust Company (A. F. of L.) and an
important financial figure in the labor movement, described how his
bank had proved a means of bringing unions, employers, public

[7] *New York Times,* August 3, 6–7, 20, 1928.
[8] *Christian Science Monitor,* August 9, 1928.
[9] *Daily Worker,* October 1, 1928.
[10] *I Confess,* the memoir of Benjamin Gitlow, shows this quite clearly, while
Stalin himself stressed the point vehemently. See *Stalin's Speeches on the American Communist Party* (May 6 and 14, 1929) (New York [?], Central Committee,
Communist Party, U.S.A., 1930 [?]).

officials, and other groups into pleasant contact. Labor had established its right to respect in the business field in more than one way,
he observed.[11]

It was small wonder that many labor leaders in 1928, deeply
involved in the capitalist world, vigorously resented the Communist
challenge to their way of life and to their personal livelihood.
Loftier motives for opposition were offered, however, in the nationally noticed Labor Day address of William Green in Cleveland:

> The American Federation of Labor is endeavoring to exercise
> a strong moral and economic influence in the political, social,
> and industrial life of the nation. It is a constructive movement.
> It seeks to promote and advance the material, moral, and spirit-
> ual welfare of the masses of the people. In formulating its poli-
> cies and pursuing a practical course it will oppose employers
> of labor and employing interests which seek to place working
> men and women in a condition of involuntary servitude.
> It will also oppose those destructive elements which appeal to
> the passions and feelings of men and which seek to substitute
> for the policy of the American Federation of Labor their own
> destructive policy, which if adopted would reduce working men
> and women to a condition of demoralization and degradation.
> Our greatest movement is endeavoring to translate the ideals,
> hopes, and aspirations of working men and women into practical
> realities. We ask all friends who believe in us and in our policies
> to give us their loyal and valuable support.[12]

Individual union conventions listened to similar sentiments.
President William J. Bowen of the Bricklayers, after a lifetime
spent in union leadership, bade farewell to his union on September
10. He said that he knew as well as any man of burning injustices
in the industrial and political order, and felt sick at heart at times
over the inequalities that existed. But in his lifetime great progress
had been made. Communism was no savior. "The pitiful and de-
luded band that stands to one side, snapping and snarling under
the banner of red destruction, is as futile as it is wrong." The
Bricklayers were committed to democracy, said Bowen, and "if
the Communists in their misguided frenzy stand for any one thing
above another it is for destruction of that democracy and substitu-

[11] *New York Times,* September 3, 1928.
[12] *Ibid.,* September 4, 1928.

tion of dictatorship. . . ." There could be no compromise.[13] The union's committee on officers' reports heartily endorsed these forthright sentiments.[14]

Soon the October issue of the *American Federationist,* the offiicial magazine of the A. F. of L., appeared with an editorial by President Green castigating Communism. The Reds sought to destroy the present order along with trade unionism, Green believed. Party activities were expensive, but who knew where their funds came from? It was "incredible" that they got them merely from supporters. The unions would have to keep an eye on these "mischievous busy bodies." [15] The Communists had invited, and they had quickly obtained, vigorous denunciation from the leaders of the American trade union movement.

With its leaders back from their trip to the Moscow meeting of the Comintern,[16] Communists ranks in America- were even more the scene of internal bickering. It began to appear probable that there would be important resignations from the movement before many months had passed. The grounds for such extreme factionalism, couched at the time in the party dialectic, amount to little more than a simple struggle for power and prestige in the group.[17]

II

The Comintern dominated its national "sections" closely in 1928. One instance of the effectiveness of this control appears in the *Daily Worker* of October 3, 1928, at a time when Presidential Election news filled the "capitalist" press. The Communist Party organ printed four documents in sequence. The first consisted of

[13] *Bricklayers' Proceedings,* 1928, 8, 10. The speech was reprinted at length in the Communist-hating *United Mine Workers Journal,* XXXIX (October 1, 1928).
[14] *Bricklayers' Proceedings,* 1928, 127.
[15] William Green, "No Compromise With Communism," *American Federationist,* XXXV (October, 1928), 1172.
[16] Highly biased Communist Party accounts of this conference are: A. Rothestein, "Sixth Congress, 1928, Moscow," *Labour Monthly,* X (December, 1928). 728–737; and Jay Lovestone, "The Sixth World Congress of the Communist International," *Communist,* VII (November, 1928), 659–675.
[17] Speeches made by Americans at the World Congress in the summer of 1928 tell part of the story. Texts in *International Press Correspondence,* Vol. VIII (1928).

paragraph 49 of the Sixth Comintern Congress' blueprint for the future, "Theses on the International Situation and the Tasks of the Communist International." This paragraph mixed praise for the Communist Party of America with aggressive criticism of what was called its "right" mistakes.[10] The American comrades had not been vigorous enough against the Socialist Party. They were charged with lethargy in pushing work among the Negroes. They had organized only a pitifully weak fight against the "predatory policy" of the United States in Latin America, continued the Comintern, and it sternly laid down the future line on the controversial matter of a labor party. Such a party was to be created through work in the trade union field and among the unorganized. Finally, the Third International called for an end to factionalism in the American Communist group. The second document was a supplementary ruling of the Politico-Secretariat of the Comintern supporting and clarifying the first. The third document was a very brief and mild statement of opposition opinion, something rarely seen in Communist literature after a question has been decided.[19]

The final document was a long and abject official response to the International by the central executive committee of the Communist Party of America. It conceded in its very first sentence the group's "complete acceptance and full endorsement" of Comintern criticisms. "We pledge ourselves," wrote the leaders humbly, "to execute these decisions energetically and without the slightest reservation." To make absolutely certain that the officials of the Third International got the point, they again proclaimed publicly for all readers to see, with election day only a month away, "The

[18] Since the Communists consider themselves on the "left," they use the words "right" and "rightist" as insulting epithets to indicate errors of doctrine. "Centrist" is almost as bad. "Opportunist" and "deviationist" are other opprobrious terms. "Fascist" supplanted these somewhat in the next decade.

[19] Prepared by James P. Cannon and two other Americans, it contained their opinion that the degree of "rightness" which the Comintern had found among the ruling faction in the American section was greater than had been charged. The three dissidents were saying that the International should have found more serious crimes among the American party majority. Before long, after this and similar heresies, Cannon had been driven out of the Communist Party and had become a rallying point for American Trotskyites.

Central Executive Committee will carry out the decisions of the Sixth World Congress of the Communist International." [20]

Of course they would. Only a month earlier, *Pravda,* the official Communist Party newspaper of the Soviet Union, had stated what all the comrades throughout the world knew already: "the program of the Communist international is obligatory on all its sections." [21] Here was a group professing to be an American political party. It had been ordered to participate in an American Presidential Election by an international body. At the height of the campaign it received explicit orders on the nature of party activities and program from a body of which it was but a single small "section." It publicly promised to do, moreover, all that it was ordered to do.[22]

Communist Party plans made in the spring had called for the division of the country into election districts. In each one a com-

[20] "The Comintern Decision on the American Question," *Daily Worker,* October 3, 1928.

[21] "The Revolutionary Compass," *Pravda,* September 9, 1928. The context in which this observation appeared is worth quoting here:

> The worldwide nature of our program is not mere talk but an all-embracing and blood-soaked reality. It cannot be otherwise. . . . Our ultimate aim is world communism, our fighting preparations are for world revolution, for the conquest of power on a worldwide scale, and the establishment of a world proletarian dictatorship. Therefore, *the program of the Communist International is obligatory on all its sections* [Italics added. "Section": American section, Chinese section, etc.].
>
> It is the guide to the *fighting of the millions of the oppressors,* in the fighting of the proletarian masses and the fight of the toilers generally—white, yellow, and black. [Italics in the original.]
>
> In the fights in the Tropics and in the fights in the most distant places of our planet; in the fights in factories and on plantations; in the forests and in the deserts, on the railways and in the mines—everywhere where the class war must take place. . . . Our program openly throws down the deadly challenge to all the bourgeois world.
>
> The Communists have no reason to hide their aims. Our ultimate aims and the means of their achievement, our strategy and our tactics, are clearly elucidated in the program.

Paragraphing that of the original translator. Translation closely verified by the writer with the aid of Nicholas John Rokitiansky, then at the Hoover Library. See also *Investigation of Communist Propaganda,* Part III, IV, 258–259.

[22] In this treatment of the foreign domination of the Communist Party of the United States in 1928 the immediate senior authority is seen to be the Comintern—the Communist International. Many writers tend to ignore this stage and state simply that Communist "sections" of the 1920s and 1930s were dominated by "the government of the U.S.S.R." by "Soviet leaders," or simply by "Moscow." The short cut is understandable and perhaps satisfactory for practical purposes, since there can be no doubt of the iron grip which Russian authorities exercised over the Comintern. A succinct summary statement by a scholar and close student

mittee of Communists was supposed to charter an automobile, a "Red Special," in order to carry on propaganda.[23] It would be hard to say how extensively these plans were carried out—if at all.

The party had candidates for congressional and other offices in some states, but in others it had neither candidates nor electors on the ballot. In New York the party offered thirty-four electors, only eight of them from upstate. In sixteen states the party offered some candidates other than electors for the presidential ticket. In Minnesota, the party ran Vincent R. Dunne for the Senate, offered J. O. Bentall for governor, and had congressional candidates in the Third, Fourth, Fifth, and Eighth districts.[24]

Like the major parties, the Communist Party opened its New York State campaign in late September. It held a rally on September 28 in New York City at which the speakers were Robert Minor, candidate for the United States Senate; Bertram D. Wolfe, candidate for Congress in the Tenth Congressional District; and Richard B. Moore, Negro organizer of the American Negro Labor Congress, a Communist-front organization. The New York State ticket had been nominated at a state convention in June.

Meanwhile, the party was experiencing trouble in getting on the ballot in the state of Washington and elsewhere.[25] Benjamin Gitlow made much of this alleged travesty of democracy in a speech he

of the subject is that of Harold Fisher: "And the Comintern was dependent on and subject to the Soviet Communist Party." *The Communist Revolution: An Outline of Strategy and Tactics* (Stanford University Press, 1955), p. 20. On the supremacy of the Soviet Communist Party within the Soviet state there can be —then and since—no debate.

[23] *Daily Worker*, May 29, 1928. The train Socialist candidate Debs used in campaigning for President in 1908 had been called the "Red Special," it will be recalled.

[24] Typed document entitled "Communist Party Candidates—November 6, 1928," compiled by Charles Kettleborough, Director, Indiana Legislative Bureau, for Harry B. Dynes, Conciliator of Labor, File 20/580, Group 174, Department of Labor Papers, National Archives.

[25] For facts gathered from contemporary Communist publications and reprinted, see the *Open Forum*, Vol. V (October 20, 1928), publication of the Southern California Branch of the American Civil Liberties Union. Roger Baldwin and others saw the issue as an infringement of free speech (*ibid.*, December 1, 1928 and June 9, 1928).

gave in Tacoma.[26] Such electoral troubles have been common obstacles to third-party efforts in America, and the resentment of the Communists was similar in kind to that felt four years earlier by the Progressives. The third party that would operate nationally faces political hazards in the American federal system itself, regardless of what its program may be, but a base of support among the electorate is helpful. The Communists lacked this.

The Communist candidate for governor of New Jersey was the lecturer, writer, and economist, Scott Nearing. Something of the party's attitude toward the election is revealed by the fact that he spent the first two weeks of October campaigning—not in New Jersey, but in Pennsylvania, West Virginia, and eastern Ohio. He spoke at least once a day.[27] Apparently the party felt that the immediate objectives of the campaign were conquest of the A. F. of L., increased class consciousness, and augmented party membership; therefore its candidates did not need to appeal to their own particular electorates.

The A. F. of L. was not ignorant of this Communist campaigning technique. When a subordinate labor official sent a Communist handbill to the Washington headquarters with a request for guidance on the Communist Party, Federation officials wrote:

> Its leaders declare they do not expect to elect any candidates but it gives them an opportunity to spread their propaganda in favor of a revolutionary movement to overturn the government of the United States and establish a soviet government on the ruins. The circular . . . will not have any influence on loyal Americans.[28]

[26] *Daily Worker,* October 2, 1928. (A party, after all, needs *some* support to be eligible to get on a statewide ballot.) Gitlow had been released from prison in 1925 when pardoned by Governor Alfred E. Smith. The Detroit *Free Press* intimated in 1928, when Gitlow was speaking harsh words about Smith in that city, that gratitude must be dead. To this the *Daily Worker* replied editorially that the pardon had undoubtedly come because the "capitalists" felt that granting it would further the interests of the capitalist state. Fortunately, it said, the Communist leadership was composed of seasoned class fighters who did not let their personal actions be influenced by any considerations of "personal comfort, safety and freedom from prison." The party accepted favors "only from the working class, and expresses 'gratitude to no capitalist hangman [i.e., Smith] of the working class'." *Ibid.,* November 9, 1928.

[27] *Ibid.,* October 2, 1928.

[28] William Green to an A. F. of L. Organizer, Sioux City, Iowa, September 25, 1928. The rough draft was prepared by W. C. Roberts, File Misc. 1928, A. F. of L. Papers.

III

Communist candidates kept on the move in 1928, and some went into the South to see what could be done about the Negro. It had been asserted early in the year that party workers would fight lynching in the heart of Dixie. Much was published in the party press about the problems of the Negro in America. There is no reason to believe, however, that they made any progress among the Negroes either in the cities or on the farms of the South.[29]

Plans for the campaign were, on paper, most impressive. On the same day that the Central Executive Committee promised to mend its way to meet the criticisms of the International, it also wrote a full page open letter in the *Daily Worker* addressed to district, city, and section committees. The grandiose plans announced by the Committee were, it is almost certain, the result of the accusations of lethargy and deviationism made against it by the International.

There was to be a house-to-house canvass throughout the United States, the Committee announced, but it was admitted in an obscure paragraph that this would have to be done within the limits of the party's small membership. Millions of leaflets and pamphlets would be distributed. A million copies of a special edition of the *Daily Worker* were to be given free distribution. The four Sundays until election day were to be designated "Red Election Sundays," and reserved for intensified work. "It is obligatory that every Party member shall consider it a matter of Party discipline to participate in these Red Election Sundays." Before mobilizing the workers, the Committee admitted wryly, it would be necessary "to mobilize

[29] Gitlow wrote later that his group made very little headway among them. *I Confess*, p. 482. Robert W. Dunn charged in a speech before the Sixth World Congress in Moscow on July 24, 1928, that the Americans had been "very badly lacking." No serious work had been done among the Negroes for two-and-a-half years, he said. The speech was aimed at a rival faction in the party. *International Press Correspondence*, VIII (Vienna, August 3, 1928), 781. The Fish Committee in 1930 could uncover little evidence of progress by the Communists among the Negroes. *See Investigation of Communist Propaganda, passim,* especially the hearings in Atlanta, Georgia. Two detailed books on this subject have been examined in a brief article by the present writer, "Historical Scholarship, Communism, and the Negro," *Journal of Negro History,* XXXVII (July, 1952).

first the Communists themselves." Far greater effort would have to be exerted if real success were to be achieved.[30]

That leading candidates of the party kept busy during the campaign is quite evident; that they said they found much enthusiasm in party ranks and among their audiences is not surprising. Foster commented toward the end:

> The workers I have spoken to throughout the country have listened eagerly to the message of class struggle our Party has brought to them. Our meetings have in the main been splendidly attended, and our election campaign literature has reached larger numbers of workers who never before came in contact with Communist propaganda.[31]

Space does not permit much discussion of the election activities of the Young Communist League or its junior partner, the Young Pioneers of America—both adjuncts of the Communist Party. Nearly a thousand youngsters, supposedly under 14 years of age, attended a meeting of the Young Pioneers on October 28, 1928 in New York City. As the gathering opened, the children raised their right hands and recited the pledge of allegiance of the Young Pioneers: "I pledge allegiance to the workers' red flag and to the cause for which it stands; one aim throughout our lives—freedom for the working class." Speeches and songs followed. Among the slogans displayed were the group's usual twin sentiments: "Fight the Boy Scouts" and "Fight Anti-Labor Propaganda in the Schools." The sixteen-year-old chairman of the meeting delivered an address attacking American school teachers as "tools of the bosses" who worked in schools controlled by the bosses. The meeting seems to have been, by Communist standards, a fine success.[32] The Boy Scouts of the day, according to the *Young Pioneer* of April, 1929, were nothing but "a tool in the hands of the bosses to prepare good willing slaves for the bosses' wars." [33]

[30] *Daily Worker,* October 3, 1928.

[31] *Ibid.,* November 2, 1928.

[32] *New York Times,* October 29, 1928. For other activities of the Young Pioneers, copies of their publications, etc., see *Investigation of Communist Propaganda*, Part III, Vol. V, 15 and *passim.*

[33] The fact that the Boy Scouts used much World War I surplus clothing and camping equipment in the 1920s and were probably led, by and large, by veterans of the war, may have been related in some way to these vicious attacks.

One of the Posters in the Election Campaign of the Workers (Communist) Party of America in 1928. From *The Communist* (Oct., 1928).

IV

The Communist election effort of 1928 was brought to a close with a rally at Madison Square Garden. Absent were the American flags and the thousands of yards of red, white, and blue bunting normally present there near Election Day. Instead, red flags and placards congratulated Soviet Russia and predicted the creation of similar revolutionary governments elsewhere.[34] About a thousand Young Pioneers wearing red scarves were among the 12,000 present.[35] Cheers greeted the appearance of Foster and Gitlow but ceased as Foster raised his hand for silence. The crowd rose and sang "The Internationale."

Foster then delivered a speech attacking the major parties as enemies of Communism, and the Socialist Party as the arch-betrayer of labor. Another world war was imminent, he predicted. In every country the Communists would use the war to bring on revolutions and establish Soviet governments in accordance with the strategy of Lenin. [36] As for court injunctions, the workers should simply disobey them. Some day a "jury of class conscious workers" would make the capitalist who were guilty of the executions of Sacco and Vanzetti pay for this judicial crime! Candidates Benjamin Gitlow's speech chiefly interested an outsider in the audience because of its request for 1000 "Red Guards" to watch the polling places on Election Day. Ten floats depicting the class struggle were carried around the auditorium. [37] The Communist Party was ready to hear the will of the "capitalist" American electorate.

Even before the votes had been cast, the executive secretary of the party, Jay Lovestone, stated in the *Daily Worker* that because of the campaign of 1928 great party gains had been made. He fore-

[34] *New York Times*, November 5, 1928.

[35] The *Daily Worker* ridiculed this figure and claimed twice as many. It published a front-page photograph which purported to be of a capacity audience in Madison Square Garden standing and cheering the Communist candidates. Foster and Gitlow stand dominating the foreground. They are out of perspective, and many of the rows of alleged cheerers stand with their backs to the candidates. The photograph is clearly faked—the result of superimposing cutouts of the candidates over a typical convention crowd picture and then rephotographing the result. *Daily Worker*, November 6, 1928.

[36] The prediction has a morbid fascination in perspective.

[37] *New York Times*, November 5, 1928.

stalled possible disappointment in the ranks by saying, "None of our Communist candidates will be elected today—we did not expect any such results." [38] Regardless of the extent of the party vote, Communist leaders were obviously preparing to proclaim a glorious victory.

Such a "victory" was soon arranged. The party press chose to ignore or to distort the true meaning of the 36,408,162 votes cast for Hoover and Smith and the 350,000 votes cast for other non-Communist candidates. It was actually unaware of the exact amount of its own insignificant 43,917 total.[39] Communist leaders deplored the fact that more people had voted than in any previous American election. As one put it, "This means greater illusions, and more widespread belief in fake democracy." [40]

In its analysis of the vote, the Communist Party was at some pains to compare its totals with those of the Socialist and the Socialist Labor parties rather than with those of the Democratic and Republican parties. The faithful were even advised not to be unduly concerned over the millions of non-Communist votes, the *Daily Worker* suggesting, "large as the vote *for capitalist* reaction is in this election, *there is on record a larger vote—against capitalism*." It referred, astonishingly, to the "vote" of the adults among the 160 millions of the U.S.S.R.[41]

To ensure its superiority, vote totals were given only for such areas as had shown some partiality to the Communist cause. Thus the New York City vote was publicized with special emphasis on results from certain precincts in the Bronx. Such widely dispersed areas as Powhatan, Ohio; Luzerne County and Ambridge, Pennsylvania; Perth Amboy, New Jersey; Chelsea, Massachusetts; Denver, Colorado; and Alameda County, California, were given prominent attention in the *Daily Worker*.[42] Local leaders were urged to telegraph the party's totals to New York headquarters, prepaid, as soon as the figures should become known. In the 112th precinct of

---

[38] *Daily Worker*, November 6, 1928.

[39] See footnotes 42 and 47, below.

[40] Jay Lovestone, "The 1928 Elections," *Communists*, VII (December, 1928), 743.

[41] *Daily Worker*, November 9, 1928. Here was a concept of "the electorate" for political scientists to conjure with.

[42] *Daily Worker*, November 8, 9, 13, 1928.

the Sixth Assembly District in the Bronx ("two blocks just east of Bronx Park from Mace to Arnow [sic] streets") the vote was:[43]

	President		Governor	
Communist	Foster	386	Dunn	385
Democratic	Smith	55	Roosevelt	70
Republican	Hoover	6	Ottinger	14
Socialist	Thomas	14	Waldman	10
Socialist Labor	Reynolds	1	Corrigan	2

The failure of the Socialist Party to match its Debs vote of 1920 was cause for special rejoicing in Communist circles, even though the final totals for New York State showed the Socialists with 107,332 to 10,876 for the Communists. The Socialist Labor Party total in the state had been outdistanced—something the Communists had not been able to do in 1924.[44] The Communists had appeared on the ballot in twice as many states as in 1924 and received nearly 44,000 votes in all.[45] This was nearly five time its probable dues-paying membership.[46]

The actual vote polled by the Communist Party was not revealed at the time to party leaders, their opponents, or the public, since in its apparent insignificance it was not "news." Neither secretaries of state, local election clerks, nor the press bothered to total it in many states until weeks after the election. The party had appeared on state ballots under a variety of names, Workers (Communist)

[43] *New York Times,* November 27, 1928.
[44] The New York State vote:

	In 1924	In 1928
Communist Party	8,244	10,876
Socialist Labor Party	9,928	4,211

Edgar Eugene Robinson, *The Presidential Vote,* 1896–1932 (Stanford: University Press, 1947, first issued 1934), p. 390. These definitive figures are from the official printed manuscript returns of the states and often do not agree with early press or later almanac totals. They supplant all other compilations.

[45] Professor Robinson's official total is 29 states; the *American Labor Year Book,* 1929, p. 115, says 32; the Communists claimed to have been on the ballot in 33 states. See the astonishing J. Louis Engdahl, "The Capitulation of the Petty-Bourgeoise in the American (U.S.A.) Election Campaign," *International Press Correspondence,* VIII (Vienna, November 2, 1928), 1431.

[46] Lovestone had reported the paid-up membership of the party as of September, 1927, as 9,642. *American Labor Year Book,* 1929, p. 154. The usual figure used by the party spokesmen at the Sixth World Congress was 15,000.

Party being the usual designation. [47] It polled more votes, in general, in the more populous states,[48] although on a percentage of the total vote basis states like New York dropped toward the bottom of the list. In some states its vote was slightly higher than in 1924;[49] in others the party lost ground.[50] Its best percentage of the vote came in Florida, nearly 1.5 per cent; its poorest, where it was on the ballot, was in Connecticut, .013 per cent.[51]

V

In commenting on the meaning of votes cast for the Communist Party in American elections, William Z. Foster has explained that persons voting with the party in excess of its membership are to be construed only as "sympathetic enough" to *vote* for it. Asked if these sympathetic voters actually *believed* in the party's principles and aims, Foster pointed out that the party raised many collateral questions in an election campaign which might attract votes at the polls.[52] Persons who merely voted for Communist candidates, in other words, could by no means be considered party members.

With the results announced, political news connected with the election disappeared rapidly from most of the "capitalist" press of the nation. Yet readers of the *Daily Worker* noticed little change in their favorite proletarian journal. In its pages the capitalist world was still the great villain. Hoover's projected goodwill trip to South

---

[47] The party used the name Workers Party in 1924, Communist Party in 1932. The year 1928 was a transitional year, the word "Workers" disappearing from the title early in the campaign. The party did not appear on the ballot under any name in Alabama, Idaho, Louisiana, Maine, Mississippi, Nebraska, Nevada, North Carolina, Oklahoma, South Carolina, Vermont, and Wyoming. The name Independent Party was used in Arkansas, Kansas, and Oregon; Independent Workers Party in Wisconsin. In Pennsylvania, Foster and Gitlow ran on two tickets, the extra one being called the Labor Party. Excluding all of these except Wisconsin, which did include the word "Workers," the party polled 43,917 votes in 33 states.

[48] New York, 10,876; Minnesota, 4,853; Florida, 3,704; Illinois, 3,581; Michigan, 2,881; Ohio, 2,836; Massachusetts, 2,461; Pennsylvania, 2,039; Washington, 1,541; Wisconsin, 1,528; and New Jersey, 1,240.

[49] New York, Minnesota, Illinois, for example.

[50] Massachusetts, Pennsylvania, Wisconsin, New Jersey.

[51] All computations have been made from data in Robinson, *op. cit.*

[52] Testimony before the Fish Committee in 1930, *Investigation of Communist Propaganda*, Part I, Vol. IV, p. 386.

"The Missionary" (Knott in the *Dallas News*)

America was featured as conclusive evidence of capitalist imperialism in action. Communist news columns were still carrying stories designed to create the illusion that capitalism, the "great oppressor," was soon to fall of its own misdeeds. The elaborate money-raising activities of the party continued in the usual vein, although it was no longer possible after election day to ask contributions for the "Election Drive Anti-Terror Emergency Fund."

If the election campaign had not been a total success from a party standpoint, Communist literature of the day does not reflect the fact. Lovestone assured the comrades of the world movement, "Never before did there appear in an election campaign in the United States a party so openly revolutionary, so thoroughly communist." [53] To all *outward* appearances, the Communists were content with the results of the election of 1928. They were prepared to keep working toward their ultimate goals.

The leaders of the American Federation of Labor were aware of this continuity of purpose among their sworn opponents. In his speech to the annual convention of the Federation in New Orleans on November 19, William Green took exception to a charge heard at a recent meeting of manufacturers that the A. F. of L. was "a menace to American institutions." He struck back at the industrialists. Only a short time before, he said, the Communists had hung in effigy—not the manufacturers—but the leaders of the A. F. of L. as their great enemies. "Oh, my friends," exclaimed Green, "we have the two extremes attacking us—the manufacturers and the Communists. We must be pretty respectable to invite antagonism from these two extremes." Lest his hearers might think him complacent in his respectability, the president of the largest labor organization in America promised that the A. F. of L. "would never permit a human scrap heap to be created in America." [54] The labor movement would press on in its own time to get what benefits it could from the capitalist system. When later in the convention the degree of radicalism existing at Brookwood Labor College became a matter of sharp floor debate, the delegates acted to sever the

[53] Lovestone, "The 1928 Elections," p. 750.
[54] *New York Times,* November 20, 1928. Great enthusiasm greeted these words.

relations of the Federation with the school [55] (although the *Daily Worker* ridiculed the idea of Communist influence there [56]).

On December 22, President Green and Vice-President Woll praised the United Hebrew Trades organization on its 40th anniversary for its long and successful fight against the "fanatical" Communists. The American Federation of Labor would not relax its anti-Communist vigil simply because the campaign of 1928 was over. The labor leaders knew that their Communist enemies would carry on their unremitting program against them.

Communist post-mortems were optimistic in tone. Jay Lovestone wrote that the size of the Communist vote in the elections "apparently" did not reflect the real influence of the party. "Sharpening class struggles are in sight. Increasing opportunities for development of our Communist Party into a mass Bolshevik party are at hand," he judged.[57]

J. Louis Engdahl, an important Communist official, unabashedly called his comrades "the victors in the American elections" in an article written for the party leaders in other lands. He gave seven tortuous reasons why. Perhaps the most meaningful was the success the party had allegedly experienced in carrying its *"parliamentary campaign"* to the workers in *"the shops and factories, mills, and mines."* Nothing was said of the electorate, of mere voters. The everyday struggles of the workers had been linked up, he said, with the parliamentary campaign. It had been possible to give the imperialist war danger against the Soviet Union much publicity. The Socialist and Farmer-Labor parties had been attacked frontally, he thought, as "third parties of capitalism." The Communist

---

[55] *Ibid.*, November 29, 1928. The dispute can be followed in the A. F. of L. *Proceedings,* and in the Socialist newspaper, the *New Leader.* For a list of individuals and journals opposing the A. F. of L. stand, see box "1926, 1927, 1928," Socialist Party Papers, Duke University.

[56] A short list of books used at Brookwood then included Communist Scott Nearing's *Where is Civilization Going?,* which was "heartily recommended" and Anthony Bimba's *History of the American Working Class,* called "the most comprehensive book for popular reading" at a time when the worthwhile non-Communist Mary Beard and Selig Perlman surveys were available. "Books Used in Courses at Brookwood Labor College . . . , March 13, 1928." Socialist Party Papers, Duke University. Socialist A. M. Simons' book *Social Forces in American History,* it predicted, would "open the eyes of those who have been brought up on bunk about our past."

[57] Lovestone, "The 1928 Elections," pp. 751, 755.

Party was better prepared than ever, claimed Engdahl, to take advantage of the contradictions within the capitalist system that were leading it to inevitable "defeat and decay." [58] This leading spokesman of the American section of the Third International predicted confidently, a week after the election, "From this victory the Communist Party marches forward to great and even greater triumphs." [59] The fight of the Communists against the capitalist world, in election years and between them, would continue.

VI

That the alternative to the American party system which the Communists offered in 1928 was rejected by union leaders and by the American people, with the exception of a tiny minority, is not surprising. The Communists indicated that only struggle, conflict, or revolution—seldom defined—would bring them to power. Their openly expressed attitude toward democratic institutions—courts, legislatures, existing laws, and electoral processes—was intensely antagonistic.

During the campaign, unquestionably, the nation's Communists were operating as part of the Third International. They obeyed its orders and accepted its slurs. The purposes of the Communist Party in the American presidential campaign of 1928, in their own words, were to mobilize the working class, to develop increased class consciousness, to abolish capitalism, to build the party, and to bring about the "overthrow" of the "present form" of society. Both candidates and party literature stressed defiantly that the workers could never obtain their own emancipation through use of the ballot. Close examination of the party platform shows that demands of the party which look superficially like reformism were nothing of the kind; they were designed to further the ultimate ends. Reformism and reformers were held beneath contempt.

However a "political party" may be defined, one assumption normally made in a republic is that a party exists to seek the power to govern by having its candidates elected to public office. The

---

[58] J. Louis Engdahl, "The Victors in the American Elections," p. 1500. Italics added.

electoral process in a true democratic republic is not a "sham" or an irrelevant game one plays as a temporary means to destructive ends. While the Communists indicated that their candidates would accept office if they should happen to win, they had no intention of permitting office-holders to waste their time in mere administration of governmental offices.

The Communists planned to create a one-party state once they were securely in power. "Bourgeois elections" (*i.e.,* a choice from alternatives at the polls) would not be needed. For the 1928 campaign period this organized conspiracy found the election machinery created by constitutions and laws a useful tool for publicity purposes and the achievement of divisionary results. In the light of the plain facts of the matter, openly declared and scarcely subject to dispute, one need not feel the slightest hesitancy in concluding that the American section of the Communist International was *not a political party*. It did not operate within the framework of the American political system, and it was not in the tradition of self-government laboriously (and painfully) built through centuries of Western civilization.

Chapter 11

The Pattern of Labor's Party Allegiance

WHILE CONTEMPORARIES knew full well that the American Federation of Labor, as a national body, did not endorse a presidential candidate or political party in the election of 1928, it can now be shown (by assembling bits and scraps of data) [1] that meaningful choosing of sides at lower levels did take place. Of course, the Executive Council of the A. F. of L. did not choose between Alfred E. Smith or Herbert C. Hoover, and it officially ignored the candidacies of Norman Thomas and William Z. Foster. But the formal "nonpartisan" attitude adopted after much debate by the Council and lived up to by President William Green by no means meant that many individual labor leaders, local unions, city centrals, some state federations, and a few international unions would refrain from outright partisanship. Cumulatively, their expressions of support are sufficient to provide a conclusion seldom given in general accounts of the election: substantial elements in the American trade union movement supported in 1928 the candidate of one party—the Democratic Party—well before the New Deal and its Wagner Act, the rise of the C. I. O., and the birth of

[1] To discover how the complex hierarchy of American organized labor divided in a past election campaign proved no simple matter. The degree of effort required to succeed in this for the 1928 campaign proved a distinct surprise, and may indicate why similar analyses for other campaigns have been long delayed.

229

personalized labor partisanship for President Franklin D. Roosevelt. That some bodies and leaders preserved neutrality in the emotionalized election of 1928 is nevertheless of interest in itself. The result indicates clearly that the "nonpartisan" attitude of the Gompers and early Green years certainly did not imply "nonpolitical." One must make such detailed investigations of the extent of union partisanship in Presidential, congressional, and state election campaigns if perspective on labor politics is to be clarified. Generalizations on the political attitude of trade unions in an election year in the United States must not rest solely on the mere presence or absence of a national Executive Council or convention endorsement of a candidate or party in the Presidential race. The truth of these observations will, it is hoped, become evident as the facts are revealed.

I

The American Federation of Labor and the Railroad Brotherhood leaders of the 1920s were far from indifferent to the passing political scene. But action was not easy. In spite of the network of telephone and telegraph lines connecting the states and cities, however, they could not yet centralize national political policymaking and activities in Washington, D. C. The road from political decision to blanket distribution of that decision to the rank and file was then a long one. While many union officials were very anxious to support "friends" and defeat "enemies," as Gompers had urged, they lacked the knowledge, the money, and the machinery to be effective. They were babes in the political woods.

The year 1928 was in a real sense a year of experiment, education, and transition in pressure tactics. The independent party experiment of 1924, with its Conference for Progressive Political Action and support for Robert M. LaFollette, was dead and gone. In an editorial in the *American Federationist* in 1928, President William Green of the A. F. of L., then three years in office, explained why no endorsements would be made at the top level in the Presidential election. "Our nonpartisan policy enables our economic movement to avoid the danger of splitting into groups over partisan political issues," he wrote, stressing that it would be unwise and impossible for American labor to try to act as a political unit. *He was at pains to point out that wage earners belong to many different churches.* The Federation, he wrote, would avoid declarations on matters which were *personal* in nature.

One gathers on reading Green's reasoning that the differences between the candidates in 1928 had not proven sufficient to show that one was an "enemy" and the other a "friend." Nevertheless, the Federation headquarters would try to make information available about candidates and issues so that labor's rank and file might make up their own minds.[2] Outsiders, quaintly enough, would not be furnished data on "record votes" of congressional candidates! "We never give out a list of our friends for publication as we have found that certain interests would become active in their districts in an effort to defeat them," he wrote.[3]

In an address on Labor Day President Green (himself a former Democratic senator in the Ohio Legislature—1910-1913) shared the speakers platform with the Republican candidate for governor of Ohio.[3] The A. F. of L. leader stressed the benefits of a high wage economy, urged the five-day week as a weapon against unemployment, and lashed out against company unions and the misuse of the injunction. Labor should vote for its political and economic interests. Since the Federation was an economic organization composed of men and women of differing political opinions, the Council had thought it unwise to follow a partisan political policy in "this campaign." Yet information would be disseminated so that labor's friends might be supported and its enemies opposed. After all, "Labor possesses a potential power in the political and economic fields. If this power can be made active and can be centralized, I am sure that the balance of power upon such decisions as may be made can be exercised by labor." [4]

In other speeches made in the early autumn, chiefly before conventions of international unions, Green dwelt on similar themes. He

[2] "Labor's Non-Partisan Political Policy," *American Federationist*, XXXV (September, 1928), 1042–1043.
[3] William Green to Paul D. Hasbrouck, October 25, 1928. A. F. of L. Papers. Federation Headquarters.
[4] *New York Times*, September 4, 1928.

claimed that both major parties had promised to relieve labor on the injunction and said the A. F. of L. would hold them to their promises. This confident posture was assumed for political effect, for the Republican Party platform and its candidate had made no such precise public promise. Green told one union that the non-partisan decision at Atlantic City had been taken "in order to maintain tranquility and internal peace." [5] (These vital words were spoken at the high tide of national disputation on the prohibition and religion issues, it may be noted.)

Just before election day Green praised a Hoover statement on immigration. Some jumped to the conclusion that his views had changed—in the direction of Hoover. Telegrams of inquiry came to A. F. of L. headquarters from several union leaders. Plainly irritated, Green telegraphed:

> By no stretch of the imagination could any statement I have made be construed as an endorsement of any candidate for president or political party. I have strictly adhered to the nonpartisan political policy adopted by the Executive Council PERIOD. The Statement which you explain as appearing in the press [on endorsement of Hoover] is a misrepresentation of my position.[6]

Frank Morrison, Secretary of the A. F. of L., claimed in his Labor Day speech that labor had planted the seed of nonpartisanship in America and was watching it grow. "Today," he boasted, "party spirit has disappeared as far as the great mass of workers is concerned." This was, to say the least, something of an exaggeration, as will now appear.

The American Federation of Labor headquarters tried with severely limited financial resources to bring influence to bear on Senatorial and Congressional races in 1928. Little active cooperation was received from subordinate units. Although the nation was linked from coast to coast by telephone, telegraph, and airmail, neither time nor distance were conquered by the men at the Washington headquarters who used letters where moderns would use the telephone. Limited information on candidates running against incumbents proved a severe handicap, and inability to define a

---

[5] Address to Brotherhood of Maintenance of Way Employees in their *Journal*, XXXVII (October, 1928), 18.

[6] Green to Neal J. Ferry, Hazelton, Pa., November 1, 1928. A. F. of L. Papers.

"friend" hurt severely. In the recent off-year elections, state federations and city centrals had complained that A. F. of L. Washington headquarters was not providing enough "record votes." In the spring of the Presidential year this problem continued. Without record votes on the injunction or similar legislation, how could one tell whom to support? "No record votes have been made during this term of Congress," wrote President William Green in April, "on questions of interest to labor. We are in hopes that the convict labor bill will come up for passage." [7]

Yet mimeographed endorsement letters would be prepared. These urged support of favorites in the primaries and general elections.[8] At least forty special letters were sent out to locals, state federations, and international unions in response to requests for political guidance. *None of these headquarters letters took a stand on the controversial Presidential race.* After the major party conventions in Kansas City and Houston, 50,000 copies of a pamphlet were mailed. Between 200 to 500 copies went to each of the larger city centrals, 10 copies went to other city bodies, and each of 35,000 local unions in the United States at the time received a single copy.[9] Political slogans were urged on the rank and file:

(1) No loyal citizen of the United States should vote for a candidate who will not support legislation prohibiting the abuse of the use of injunctions in labor disputes. (2) No child-loving citizen will vote for a candidate for a state legislature who is not in favor of protecting the nation's children from industrial exploitation. (3) No wage earner should vote for a candidate who has opposed remedial legislation urged by labor. (4) No loyal citizen of our country will vote for other than those candidates who have proved that the interests of all the people are above the selfish demands of the few.

Simpler wording would appear in labor pronouncements of later years! Local labor groups were urged to prepare records of local candidates for office and to have them read at each regular meeting. How much attention was paid to this advice would be hard to say.

[7] Green to President, Illinois State Federation, April 12, 1928. A. F. of L. Papers.
[8] Copies in A. F. of L. Papers.
[9] Report of the Executive Council, A. F. of L. *Proceedings*, 1928, 76.

A. F. of L. headquarters had a particularly difficult time exerting effective pressure in Congressional races. By September 17 labor officials in Washington were desperate, and President Green sent telegrams to state federations asking them whom they were opposing for Congress! The California Federation replied on the 24th, but many state leaders took even longer than this.[10] City centrals were then asked how they handled political problems. Some, like the San Francisco Labor Council, replied promptly, receiving letters of appreciation from President Green. The Los Angeles Central Labor Council said it was carrying front-page articles in its paper on how to get registered; it used a 25,000 name mailing list to circulate sample ballots and recommendations on the eve of election day, and tried to bring its message to civic organizations.

Correspondence that passed between Morrison and Secretary Arthur Huggins of the 4,000-member Paper Makers shows how logistics problems blocked labor's political pressure tactics. Huggins wrote from New York, September 12, asking for labor records of Senatorial and Congressional candidates in *nine* states. He hoped to print a summary in the October issue of his union's journal. Morrison sent all the names he had: Illinois and Minnesota. "The difficulty," wrote Morrison, "has been in obtaining the names of the nominees who were successful in the various primaries." Anyway, the 143 voting records requested would fill 100 pages of the *Paper Makers Journal*. Did he want so many? (Tabular presentation must not have occurred to the 69-year-old Morrison.) When Huggins replied on the 25th that he planned a condensation, Morrison sent on October 4 the records he sought for seven states. It was too late for the Huggins deadline. But he would try to circularize his locals in some other way, he said.

While this laborious by-play was going on, the A. F. of L. was trying to reach some basis for agreement with the Railroad Brotherhoods on what votes to use for "record votes." In 1926 the Federation had agreed with the Brotherhood position that votes on the Cummins-Esch, Howell-Barkley, and Watson-Parker bills ought to be a basis for endorsement. A. F. of L. leaders had protested but

[10] Green to State Federations, September 17, 1928. File "Calif., 1928," A. F. of L. Papers.

had gone along. After an unpleasant dispute over Brotherhood endorsement of a Kentucky gubernatorial candidate, the Federation men were suspicious. Charging that two of the three Brotherhood-proposed votes were "dead letters" and that the nation's *railroads* had also urged the passage of the Watson-Parker bill, all three votes were virtually eliminated from A. F. of L. record vote consideration in 1928.[11] Yet the Federation and the Brotherhoods maintained formal liaison on politics in the autumn of 1928, most of it by word of mouth.[12]

II

October brought increased political efforts to the understaffed national and state union headquarters offices. One of the Washington executives wrote privately, "I will be glad when the campaign is over as we are just worked to death." The National Nonpartisan Political Campaign Committee of the A. F. of L. soon sent out a circular letter to all city centrals and state federations asking about local pressure campaigns being carried on by them, since "practically all the information now received comes from newspapers or propaganda distributed by individuals or various political parties." Particularly desired were copies of local union political literature they distributed. "Quite a number" of answers were received, a fact proving to the experimenting leaders in Washington the existence of "great interest." Among those supported for Congress by the A. F. of L. in 1928 was 45-year-old Fiorello H. La Guardia, running for re-election in the 14th New York District. In the opinion of President Green, he had been right on mining legislation, convict labor, injunctions, and railroad legislation.

> He has been steadfast in his support of remedial legislation proposed by Labor. On the floor of the House he has been one of the most active members when labor legislation or measures that would benefit all the people were up for consideration.[13]

[11] Memorandum by legislative counsel W. C. Roberts to Green, September 19, 1927. A. F. of L. Papers.

[12] Secretary Morrison forwarded "suggested statements" on three senators and two representatives to Edward Keating of the Brotherhoods on October 10, 1928.

[13] Green to President Joseph P. Ryan, Central Trades and Labor Council, N.Y.C., October 9, 1928. A. F. of L. Papers.

The Illinois Federation supported *both* Democrats and Republicans in state and national contests.[14]

As it would so often in ensuing years, the A. F. of L. urged its members to register so that they might vote. Green sent a letter on the subject to state federations and city centrals. He urged that the Presidential campaign not be allowed to overshadow the Congressional races, and that nonpartisan committees in labor bodies prevail on members to register.

> *They should not attempt to influence working men and women how to vote, but they should influence them to vote in accordance with the dictates of their consciences and in conformity with their political judgment.*

After registration, all should be urged to vote.

> Great care should be taken in carrying out the nonpartisan political policy of the American Federation of Labor. As before stated, members of organized labor cannot be compelled to vote for any candidate. The records of the candidates should be submitted and the members of organized labor can then vote as their consciences dictate.[15]

This was the official message of organizational nonpartisanship. What subordinate A. F. of L. leaders and organizations would do will now be seen.

III

After the party conventions there was partisanship for Hoover in the public utterances of some A. F. of L. leaders. This was true of those in positions of leadership in local unions, large city centrals, internationals, and state federations. John L. Lewis, President of the United Mine Workers, was the most eloquent of important A. F. of L. supporters of Hoover. He called the former Secretary of Commerce and self-made engineer "the foremost industrial statesman of modern times." [16]

---

[14] *Weekly News Letters,* October 6, 1928.
[15] President William Green to All State Federations of Labor and City Central Bodies, undated, in New York State Federation of Labor *Bulletin,* September 29, 1928. Italics added.
[16] *New York Times,* September 19, 1928.

Mr. Hoover's specific declaration in favor of high wages, free collective bargaining, restriction on the use of injunctions in labor disputes, tariff schedules protective of American labor, continuance of immigration restriction, further expansion of our foreign export trade and governmental assistance to the deprest [*sic*] textile and bituminous coal industries, constitute a program that should carry an intense appeal to every thoughtful citizen. The entire address constitutes a wholehearted recognition of the rights and ideals of labor.[17]

Moreover, Oscar T. Nelson, vice president of the Chicago Federation of Labor, and some Railroad Brotherhood officials also spoke for Hoover in a friendly way. Mrs. Gertrude Gompers, widow of the A. F. of L. founder, supported Hoover.[18] A list of alleged labor "leaders" who congratulated him on the Newark address was released by the Republican National Committee. Few were of the slightest prominence.[19]

Late in October the Republicans released a prepared statement signed by about 100 labor "leaders." [20] The document praised Republican tariff and immigration policies, and blamed the unemployment of 1921 on the Democrats. High wages and a high standard of living, low cost of government and low taxes, and administrative efficiency were also covered. Heading the list of signatories was James J. Davis, Coolidge's Secretary of Labor; another official name was that of T. V. O'Conner, chairman of the Shipping Board. An obscure editor was listed. The remainder were:

Presidents of *local* unions 17

Secretaries or treasurers of *local* unions 17

Business agents or miscellaneous officials of *local* unions 32

"Former" presidents of *local* unions 17

"Former" secretaries or treasurers of *local* unions 13

"Former" miscellaneous officials of local.
   unions and other subordinate units 14

Also among the group was a "former statistician" of a local! Concluding the listing were the names of eight officials of the "United

[17] Quoted in "Hoover's Appeal to the Workers," *Literary Digest*, LC (October 2, 1928), 10–11.
[18] *New York Times*, August 2, 1953.
[19] *Ibid.*, September 21, 1928.
[20] *New York Herald Tribune*, October 31, 1928.

States Customs Employees" group.[21] Chicago, Pittsburgh, Ohio, and Indiana men nearly monopolized the list. The Republicans were hard up for labor organization support.[22] The president of the Montana Federation was apparently a Hoover man.[23] John L. Lewis spoke under Republican auspices over a 21-station radio network on behalf of Hoover in mid-October. The leader of the hardpressed miners said that industrial prosperity was the vital issue. Hoover had "inaugurated the unprecedented industrial and business prosperity" of the times.[24]

If Lewis was partisan toward Hoover, Daniel J. Tobin, President of the Teamsters, was far more aggressive in favor of Smith. (Yet, as has been seen, he preserved a remarkable fairness of statement toward Hoover.) Long associated with Governor Smith in New York affairs, Tobin thought of him as "a man's man," human, and in favor of *organized* labor. Hoover was for labor, that is, the workingman, but what about labor *organizations?* [25] Major George L. Berry of the Pressmen, abortive Democratic vice presidential candidate in 1924 and 1928, headed the labor committee of the Democratic Party. There was idle talk of creating a "huge machine" to capture the labor vote. In no previous national campaign had the country been so systematically organized for the purpose, it was claimed.[26]

Late in August the Democrats released the names of the union officials who had consented to serve on their National Advisory Board. They had succeeded in gaining the support of *important* A. F. of L. union officials. Of the 45 names, 23 were presidents of

[21] Too small a "union" to be included in the Wolman or Reynolds and Killingsworth union lists.

[22] A master's thesis touching on this subject incorrectly observes, "Hoover had a more distinguished group of labor leaders actively engaged in working for his election than Smith had. . . ." Furthermore, "the Democratic nominee had the support of some of the high labor officials but these supporters were not as active as the labor leaders supporting the Republican nominee." Mark Odum Hatfield, "Herbert Hoover and Labor: Policies and Attitudes, 1897–1928," Stanford, 1948, pp. 82, 81.

[23] Samuel H. Rivin, State Organizer, Montana Federation, to writer, December 6, 1951.

[24] Prerelease text of the Lewis speech of October 17, 1928. A. F. of L. Papers.

[25] *Teamsters Magazine,* XXV (November, 1928), 1–5.

[26] *New York Times,* August 26, 1928.

international unions, 11 secretaries or treasurers, one a vice president, and only 10 were not identified by title.[27]

The Democrats also announced the appointment of many state labor chairmen. Again the Democratic Party had attracted important labor officials to public support of Governor Smith. Examination of names in the 36 states listed shows that seven were presidents of state federations,[28] and eight were secretaries of state federations [29]—key officials in the trade union movement. Four states had what might be called substantial officials included;[30] five had persons of moderate influence; and seven states were represented by unknowns. (In four states Chairman Berry was forced to muster brother pressmen or typographers to round out his group.) The Democrats had experienced their least success in strongly Republican states: Pennsylvania, Ohio, Wisconsin, Indiana, and Nebraska.

Chairman Berry's own partisan view of the Presidential race was that neither major party had ever offered two men of such outstanding caliber as Smith and Robinson. His Pressmen held what a newspaper account called a "Smith rally" and voted "overwhelmingly" to permit their president to function with the Democratic National Committee—many weeks after he had begun to do so.[31]

After election day the socialist-oriented League for Industrial Democracy apparently observed, "In spite of the nonpartisan

[27] Analysis by the present writer from a list printed in New York Times, August 26, 1928. International union presidents: Laundry Workers; Bricklayers; Masons and Plasterers; Metal Polishers; Theatrical Stage Employes; Flint Glass Workers; Plumbers and Steamfitters; Hotel and Restaurant Employes and Bartenders; Railway Subordinate Officials Association; Seamen's Union; Meat Cutters and Butcher Workmen; Hatters; Bookbinders; Marble Workers; Sheet Metal Workers; Brick and Clay Workers; Stereotypers and Electrotypers; Glove Workers; Bridge and Structural Iron Workers; Plasterers; Longshoremen; Paper Makers; Musicians; and the president of the Building Trades Department, A. F. of L. These were not local union officials, but presidents of the parent bodies. Absent were the names of the following presidents who opposed Davis and thereby supported Hoover in the Indiana primary: Electrical Workers, Blacksmiths, Marine Engineers, and Boilermakers. Ibid., May 1, 1928.

[28] Colorado, Georgia, Mississippi, New Hampshire, New Jersey, New York, and Virginia.

[29] Connecticut, Iowa, Nevada, North Dakota, Oklahoma, Tennessee, Texas, Utah, and West Virginia.

[30] Alabama, Kentucky, Louisiana, and Maryland.

[31] New York Times, August 30, 1928.

action of the A. F. of L. as a whole, most state federations declared for the Democrats and went down in the general defeat." [32] While this charge does not stand up under close examination, a germ of truth lay in it, as a review of the evidence will show. The NEW YORK, NEW JERSEY, NEBRASKA, and UTAH federations and the executive council of the RHODE ISLAND federation *did* endorse Smith with alacrity.[33] The NEW YORK federation sent a strongly emotional letter to all state federations urging that they follow its own endorsement example. "We call upon all organized and unorganized wage earning citizens in this State and in our sister States to enlist earnestly in this campaign to install in the White House at Washington this tested and proved champion of liberty, equality and justice for all of the people of our nation," said the New York labor leaders, sending copies broadside across the land to various union addresses.

The NEW JERSEY federation stood for repeal of the Eighteenth Amendment, prohibition being a "paramount issue"; there was said to be "little or any expression [among union men] concerning religion." [34] The president of the CONNECTICUT state federation issued a nonpartisan proclamation. Despite every radical attempt to sway convention delegates toward a labor party, the group remained officially uncommitted.[35]

The VIRGINIA federation had held its 1928 convention in May, but its officers and later its Executive Board supported and campaigned for Smith. A later effort to censure them failed.[36] A plea by the New York federation was merely filed in WISCONSIN,[37] while in MARYLAND, the resolutions committee of the state convention gained support for a nonconcurrence resolution. The Maryland group felt that an endorsement of anyone for President would jeopardize labor's legislative hopes in Congress, but Berry was

[32] Quoted in *Milwaukee Leader,* November 20, 1928.
[33] *New York Times,* September 6, 7, 8, 13 and October 9, 1928.
[34] President Louis P. Marciante, New Jersey Federation, to writer, December 12, 1951.
[35] Charles J. Moore, Secretary-Treasurer "Political Activities," and "Resolution 22," entitled "For a Labor Party"; typed copies forwarded by Joseph M. Rourke, V. P., to writer, December 6, 1951.
[36] President J. S. Smith to writer, December 6, 1951.
[37] Minutes of General Executive Board Meeting, September 17, 1928, Wis. State Fed. of Labor Papers, State Historical Society of Wisconsin.

endorsed for vice president on the Democratic ticket. Prohibition was denounced as "un-American," "wild, in theory," and impossible to enforce.[38]

In TENNESSEE, a joint nonpartisan committee of the A. F. of L. and the Brotherhoods endorsed candidates for offices other than the Presidency.[39] No action was taken by federations in ARKANSAS, MONTANA, NEBRASKA, NORTH DAKOTA, OREGON, or TEXAS.[40] Nor did SOUTH DAKOTA endorse Smith, but city centrals "decided to support Al Smith regardless of his religion," and the Democratic ticket was aided in every county where an A. F. of L. union was located. Clubs were organized and some money collected "to support him and the Democratic Party." [41] While the COLORADO federation had supported La Follette in 1924, it limited 1928 endorsements to "Democratic candidates on the state level . . . [since] the labor movement all during the 1920s in Colorado was strongly Democratic in its politics." [42] No endorsements were forthcoming in WEST VIRGINIA, VERMONT, CALIFORNIA, DELAWARE, IDAHO, KANSAS, IOWA, MICHIGAN, or OHIO.[43]

Not until 1936 would the ILLINOIS federation endorse a candidate for President. [44] Bottle blowers, teamsters, bartenders, hotel and restaurant employees, distillery workers, and some building trades workers were vigorously against prohibition at the time in Illinois, since much of their livelihood came from the beverage industry. In retrospect, the Illinois president has written

> Al Smith advocated and secured the enactment of beneficial labor legislation while Governor of New York and was regarded as friendly to labor's great cause. I think the same can be truthfully said about Herbert Hoover prior to the depression years which became accentuated with the stock crash of 1929. After that, of course, Hoover became unpopular.[45]

[38] Frank J. Coleman, Secretary to writer, December 4, 1951, enclosing a typed copy of Resolution 15.
[39] President Stanton E. Smith to writer, December 27, 1951.
[40] Letters by presidents or executive secretaries to writer, 1951–1952.
[41] President Albert J. Maag to writer, December 8, 1951.
[42] President George A. Acvender to writer, December 3, 1951.
[43] Letters by presidents or secretaries to writer, 1951–1952, confirmed in the cases of California and Ohio in particular by a minute search of printed convention proceedings. A fire in the Pennsylvania federation headquarters destroyed records on the period. President James L. McDevitt to writer, December 7, 1951.
[44] President R. G. Soderstrom to present writer, December 5, 1951.
[45] *Ibid.*

Meeting September 17-19 in Frankfort, the KENTUCKY federation took seriously the nonpartisan declaration of the A. F. of L., passing a threatening resolution.

> Any officer . . . delivering any address, writing any articles for publication in his official capacity as an executive of this Federation, whether in support or condemnation of either of the two candidates mentioned, shall be considered guilty of a breach of confidence intrusted to them as officers of this Federation.[46]

The story in INDIANA was somewhat similar, for when the request of the New York federation was received the Indiana Executive Board "voted against submitting the resolution to the convention and against the idea of endorsing Smith or Hoover." Its president subsequently told delegates to the state convention that they should support the nonpartisan policy proclaimed in Washington, not permitting the La Follette endorsement of 1924 to become a general practice. Both prohibition and religion cut deeply across political lines in Indiana, according to a contemporary who writes, "I remember considerable about that election—a most unusual one." [47]

In summary, it is apparent that only a handful of state federations ventured to endorse Alfred E. Smith in 1928, although many others were dissuaded from doing so by the nonpartisan declarations of the national Executive Council, by considerations of state politics, and by extreme emotionalism attending the religious and prohibition issues. Leaders of the 1928 trade union movement feared to seek political advantages for unions by throwing the weight of their coordinating organizations behind so controversial a figure as the New York Governor. They found the request of the New York Federation an embarrassment, however much they might agree privately with its encomiums for Al Smith.

Even in retrospect these state federation officials display in their letters the concern felt at the time over the divisionary effects of the twin ogres of 1928: religion and prohibition. Repeatedly, after

---

[46] Resolution 16, typed copy forwarded by Edward H. Weyle, Secretary, to writer, November 29, 1951.
[47] President Carl H. Mullen to writer, December 11, 1951.

talking with one or more "old timers," they wrote the present writer that union men in their states "voted for Hoover or Smith depending on their personal convictions," (Connecticut) or "tend to be like the rest of the community in which they live," (Tennessee) had their "own particular reason for voting as they did," (Arkansas) or merely voted for Smith in the South "because he was a Democrat." (Mississippi) "I believe that our votes in that year were fairly well divided," the Iowa President judged.[48]

Even in New York State the injunction issue and other economic and trade union issues were pushed to one side in workingmen's minds. One city central official, asked how the issues were shaping up in early October, replied

> . . . unfortunately the religious and prohibition issues appear at this writing to overwhelm all others, and the laboring class seems to have lost sight of the real problems in which they should be interested. In the humble opinion of this writer these two issues should have no part in the discussions, and the nonpartisan campaign committee of the American Federation of Labor should immediately warn the people that they are simply a smoke screen thrown out for the purpose of hiding the real issues such as the previous records of the various candidates and their attitude toward social and welfare legislation.

If the workingman had any sense he would vote for Smith, he concluded.[49]

IV

MINNESOTA, with its state Farmer-Labor Party, was particularly complex for orthodox trade union men. In 1926 President Green had exchanged several letters with President E. G. Hall of the Minnesota federation, hoping to woo Hall from support of the Farmer-Labor Party.[50] Its party platform hoped to gain the support of workers and farmers. Yet Smith got support from Farmer-Labor circles. Many Minnesota labor leaders were active in the Smith

[48] Ray Mills to writer, November 30, 1951.
[49] F. J. Beatty, Secretary, Geneva Federation of Labor, New York, to William Green, October 10, 1928. A. F. of L. Papers.
[50] File "Minn., 1928." A. F. of L. Papers.

campaign.[51] The A. F. of L. worked hard for Farmer-Labor Senator Shipstead, President Green keeping in close contact with Paul J. Smith, federation organizer in Minnesota. Shipstead, reported Smith, "expressed his deep appreciation for the assistance rendered him by the American Federation of Labor and expressed the belief that he could not be re-elected if it wasn't for our support of him. . . ." A candidate "practically without a party and an organization, it would be a terrific and bitter struggle" to elect him.[52] When letters of endorsement went out from Washington to local A. F. of L. unions in Minnesota, Shipstead expressed his gratitude directly to President Green.[53] The state federation thought it best not to go on record as "endorsing" Farmer-Labor nominees; instead, every union man was urged to "participate" in the campaign, and "serious consideration" of the party's nominees was urged.[54] While Smith had not been endorsed, a volunteer committee of prominent labor leaders praised him.[55] The Legislative Board of the Conductors would endorse Farmer-Labor candidates for state offices,[56] and Frank Morrison, Secretary-Treasurer of the A. F. of L., cooperated closely in Washington with the Brotherhood's Edward Keating, editor of Labor, on Minnesota politics.[57] Washington A. F. of L. headquarters went so far as to send letters endorsing one congressman to the secretaries of 102 locals in Minnesota's 8th District.[58]

So far as the pitiful national Farmer-Labor Party was concerned, with its grandiose plans and its final collapse with its secretary-treasurer resigning August 25 to support Hoover, the A. F. of L. was silent. Numerous pleading letters from Frank Lawson to Green went unanswered; when completely provoked Green finally agreed

[51] Authur Naftalin, A. History of the Farmer-Labor Party of Minnesota, Unpublished Doctoral Thesis, University of Minnesota, 1948, 154.
[52] Smith to Green, July 5, 1928. A. F. of L. Papers.
[53] Shipstead to Green, September 18, 1928. "Minn., 1928." A. F. of L. Papers.
[54] Resolution 43, in Minnesota Union Advocate, August 23, 1928, located for the writer through courtesy of the Minnesota Historical Society.
[55] Ibid.
[56] Printed open letter of F. H. Wilson, Duluth, Minn., October 10, 1928. Box 7, Teigan Papers. Minnesota Historical Society.
[57] For example, Morrison to Keating, October 11, 1928. "Minn., 1928." A. F. of L. Papers.
[58] Congressman William L. Cass. Ibid.

to spend a few minutes with the Farmer-Labor protagonist.[59] Only in Minnesota state politics had the party proven a problem in political manipulation.

In many states there was a confused pattern like that in Montana, where Senator Burton K. Wheeler was endorsed and repeal had long been advocated by organized labor. Most laborers in Butte and Anaconda were of the Catholic faith, yet "in eastern Montana the Ku Klux Klan was a powerful organization and they campaigned heavily for Hoover." [60] In the absence of a clearly delineated labor issue, nationally expounded and easy to explain, how could union leaders take *effective* stands under difficult circumstances like these?

V

The endorsements of a large number of city centrals, large local unions, and special labor groups went to Smith in 1928. Some of the organizations supported their favorite with good words in a resolution; others donated small sums of money or did small amounts of electioneering. The tiny Upholsterers International Union sent a copy of its endorsement to every one of its 1,300 members in the nation urging them to vote for Smith, and a letter in New York State praised the labor record of gubernatorial candidate Franklin D. Roosevelt. "The soul of the New York Governor, Alfred E. Smith goes out to the common people, while every throb of his heart beats with a humane spirit and for social benefit and uplift." The state Republicans had been "truly vicious in their anti labor attitude." [61] A National Association of Letter Carriers official from Brooklyn visited various locals of his 40,000-member union on behalf of the Democratic ticket.[62]

While most large international unions managed to maintain official organizational neutrality, some did not. The large unions recog-

[59] Letters in file "Farmer-Labor Party, 1928." A. F. of L. Papers. The Teigan Papers, Minnesota Historical Society, are useful on politics of the day.

[60] Samuel H. Ririn, State Organizer, A. F. of L., Montana, December 6, 1951.

[61] General Executive Board, Upholsterers, to Officers and Members, October 31, 1928; also President William Kohn to Franklin D. Roosevelt, November 2, 1928. 85.

[62] William E. Kelly to Louis H. Howe, September 12, 1928. Roosevelt Papers.

nized a threat to precarious unity in endorsements on the emotionally charged Presidential race. And national conventions were not
usually scheduled for the strategic moment. Still, the Bookbinders
endorsed Smith on July 14 in their convention.[63] State and local
union groups, especially in New York State and nearby, did likewise. The New York convention of the Bricklayers endorsed
Smith,[64] and the New York local 58 of the 26,200-member Building Service Employees, claiming to represent over twice their
number, endorsed him. The New York district council of the group
did so unanimously, while a thousand delegates of the 45,000 member Plumbers, Gas, and Steam Fitters, meeting at Atlantic City,
agreed. Like-minded groups were the Empire State Typographical
Conference, and the 15,000-member Utica Trades Assembly—
which nevertheless supported Republican candidates for state attorney general and for Congress! The New York Building Trades
Council, composed of seventy-nine unions with a claimed membership of 150,000, endorsed both the national and state Democratic
ticket. And Joint Council 16 of the Teamsters of New York not
only endorsed Smith but gave $3,000 to the Democratic National
Committee [65]—a step uncommon in those years. A most important
endorsement, and one which must have meant something to the
man who rose from the streets of New York City to run for President, was that of the city's Central Trades and Labor Council.[66]

Miscellaneous endorsements of Smith in October were: W. W.
Fitzwater of Bonham, Texas, president of the almost fictitious
Farmer-Labor Union; the Teamsters of Chicago, claiming 28,000
members; an organization of Chicago women trade unionists; the
important Chicago Building Trades Council (100,000 members);
twenty-six Jewish unions of Chicago (75,000 members); and the
"Alfred E. Smith-for-President Union Labor League," whose president was Machinist president Charles W. Fry and vice-president
was John Fitzpatrick, an important third-party enthusiast of earlier
years.[67]

[63] New York State Federation of Labor *Bulletin,* July 26, 1928.
[64] *Ibid.*
[65] *New York Times,* September 15, 21, 30, 1928; October 25, 30, 1928.
[66] *Ibid.,* October 19, 1928.
[67] *Ibid.,* October 2, 4, 6, 14, 1928.

Who can say how much effect such endorsements had on rank and file union members and their unorganized fellow workingmen? It is simply not possible to prove that the endorsements were representative of majority opinion within the groups involved, although there is, of course, a presumption in that direction. What motive influenced each of these groups to endorse the Democratic rather than the Republican candidate for President of the United States? In some cases it may have been the injunction issue. In others it may have been prohibition. In some of the endorsements in New York City the influence of Tammany Hall and patronage considerations may have been decisive. Was extensive Irish Catholicism in labor circles of consequence? Some of the organizations in New York may simply have followed the highly partisan lead of the State Federation of Labor.

The important thing is that so many and so varied a group of A. F. of L. union organizations did support the Democratic candidate in 1928 and so few endorsed the Republican. It is doubtful if the Labor Section of the Democratic National Committee should have much of the credit for these endorsements. If in restrospect the Democratic labor committee seems powerful and presumably efficient while its Republican counterpart seems inconsequential, one should bear in mind the confidential comment of highly placed Democratic leader Frank P. Walsh as he surveyed in midstream the administration of the labor committee of his party. It was "rotten," he confided.[68]

The Socialist Party and the Communist Party had little success with orthodox labor leaders or their unions, especially outside of New York City. If any key union leaders worked for the election of Norman Thomas or William Z. Foster in 1928, they did so with minimum publicity. But two unions strong in New York City called for the formation of the labor party of their dreams. The International Ladies Garment Workers Union adopted a resolution which called American labor "a political zero." Since unions combat both employers and government—the latter replete with antilabor laws, injunctions, and use of police and militia in strikes—the traditional

[68] Frank P. Walsh to Joseph B. Shannon, September 17, 1928. Walsh Papers, N.Y.P.L.

approach would not do. Surely a "great and militant political party
. . . a great Labor Party," could take government away from the
"exploiting class." Such a party would be formed of "legitimate
trade unions and for constructive purposes." [69]

The Amalgamated Clothing Workers convention heard the General Executive Board sadly report the organization of an all-
inclusive party of American labor "a dream unrealized." New York
locals failed to elect a Socialist judge. Those in Milwaukee cooperated with the Socialist Party. Locals in Twin Cities had thrown
their weight behind the Farmer-Labor Party. Financial aid had
often been given. Yet somehow the times were not yet ripe.[70] Four
resolutions calling for labor party formation were replaced by one
which merely "looked forward" to such action. The Amalgamated,
it was promised, would participate "to the utmost" when the time
might come.[71] In the 1930s in New York State, these unions would
have their chance, and in a state Liberal Party and then in a Labor
Party, they would play politics with vigor and with some transitory
effectiveness, especially as they rallied to the support of Democrat
Franklin D. Roosevelt.

VI

*The official magazines of A. F. of L. international unions avoided
official endorsements and strongly partisan political pronouncements.* Many union journals showed only a minimum of concern
with political matters.[72] Although the magazines of the postal
clerks and letter carriers contained much news of federal legislation of interest to union members, they did not cast aspersions on
any political figures. The *United Mine Workers Journal* was occupied with anti-Communist, anti-injunction, and anticompany union
material, but it took no stand on the Presidential race regardless of

[69] I.L.G.W.U. *Proceedings*, 1928, 23, 153.
[70] Report of the G.E.B., in *Amalgamated Clothing Workers Proceedings*, 1928,
Roosevelt Papers.
[71] A.C.W. *Proceedings*, 1928, 276.
[72] *Granite Cutters' Journal, Retail Clerks International Advocate, Lather, Union
Postal Clerk, Postal Record, Pattern Makers Journal, United Mine Workers
Journal, Carpenter, Shoe Workers' Journal.*

the strong personal stand of John L. Lewis for Hoover. Nor did the *Carpenter* reflect the Republican sympathies of William Hutcheson. The *Painter and Decorator* considered child labor and the injunction the important issues. The *Paper Maker's Journal* carried an editorial on the platforms and the candidates which was none too flattering to either major party but was, at any rate, quite impartial in its irritation.[73]

Some union magazines published A. F. of L.-furnished material on the candidates, the platforms, and the injunction. One quoted Hoover and Smith on the injunction and other labor matters with the observation, "These statements we print without comment. It is up to each individual to interpret them according to his understanding and knowledge of things." [74] Nor, with the clear exception of New York State Federation publications, were state federation journals heavily biased.

What was printed or mimeographed by city centrals and locals in those years on political matters would be hard to say. The editor of the *Trades Unionist,* Washington, D. C., official organ of the Washington Central Labor Union, pledged his personal aid to the Smith cause before the Houston meeting, predicting that the Federation, "in its nonpartisan political campaign" would be obliged to support him on his gubernatorial labor record.[75] Apparently the only labor paper to share in funds of the Democratic national committee in 1928 for running party material in its columns was the *Trades Council Union News,* "Official Organ of Organized Labor of St. Louis and Vicinity." Its pro-Smith editor was told that only lack of funds prevented wider use of this method of spreading the Democratic message.[76] If such tactics were questionable, so was that of a businessman who made what he called "a personal plea" to the several hundred mechanics on his payroll to support Smith.[77]

[73] *Paper Makers' Journal,* XXVII (October, 1928). 8–9.
[74] *Railway Maintenance of Way Employes Journal,* XXVII (September, 1928), 26.
[75] John B. Colpoys to Franklin D. Roosevelt, May 1, 1928. Roosevelt Papers.
[76] Correspodence between P. J. Morrison and Frank P. Walsh, Chairman of the Progressive League for Alfred E. Smith, especially Morrison to Walsh, October 20, 1928, explaining how Morrison came to print Walsh's "Why Progressives Should Vote for Alfred E. Smith." Walsh Papers.
[77] President, Kenny Bros., Inc., N.Y.C., a construction company, to Franklin D. Roosevelt, September 18, 1928. Roosevelt Papers.

It is an inescapable fact that the labor press as a whole maintained an impartial attitude toward the Presidential race. Its workingmen readers could not complain of pressure from that quarter.

VII

The Railroad Brotherhoods must not be overlooked in any study of labor politics. These nationally distributed unions had played an important part in the Progressive group which supported Robert M. La Follette for President in 1924. Two years later they obtained in the Railway Labor Act legislation which seemed to remedy many of their complaints. By 1928 these unions showed no interest in renewing third party activity. Yet they were at least as active in state politics as the American Federation of Labor.[78] That the Fireman had 104,200 members, the Engineers 82,600, the Conductors 53,100, and the Trainmen 184,300 made them impressive in some states, especially since their mobility and possession of the highly readable and pioneering weekly newspaper *Labor* made them more effective than most A. F. of L. craft unions.

The Brotherhoods took an active part in the Indiana and Ohio primaries against Charles G. Dawes, whom they regarded as the Wall Street candidate and far more conservative than Hoover.[79] This meant that long before the party conventions some Brotherhood leaders were oriented toward Hoover as a candidate for the Republican *nomination*. One Brotherhood magazine editor warned, "If we do not take part in our government through the recognized political channels, we have no moral right to complain of big business controlling the political parties." [80] A joint legislative committee in Indiana published a "Blue Book" which gave voting records of legislators, urged the election of specific friends, and suggested that union members run for precinct committeemen.[81]

The New York State Legislative Board of the Brotherhood of Locomotive Firemen and Enginemen had endorsed Governor

[78] Based on examination of their weekly newspapers, *Labor* (Washington, D.C.), and the publications of all the Brotherhood unions for the period 1823 to 1928.
[79] *New York Times,* May 1, 1928.
[80] *Railroad Trainman,* XLV (February, 1928), 136.
[81] *Ibid.,* XLV (May, 1928), 358.

Smith in 1926 in glowing terms, referring to his "consistent, courageous and successful attitude . . . in his advocacy of measures
beneficial to labor. . . ." Two years later the group endorsed him
for President, voting to spend $5,000 for the ticket. "If all the
Labor Organizations will do the same as we, "wrote its secretary-
treasurer, ". . . I know that we will carry New York State, as we
have started on a house to house voyage and before election gets
here we will have every county in the State covered." After all, "We
thank our old friend Al for being in our corner when we needed
a friend at the Capitol, and if [he] has been tried and found true
. . . he sure will have the same spirit for the poor class and the
laborer when we land him in Washington." [82]

Brotherhood political literature was enthusiastic and also argu-
mentative in tone. More forceful than A. F. of L. political material,
it said particular legislators should be elected at all costs. Cartoons
invariably labeled friends "Progressive." The word thus identified
men who would vote for laws to benefit the railroad unions. What
else these legislators might support in domestic or international
affairs does not seem to have been of primary importance to the
Brotherhood leaders. "Progressive" meant "reliable friend of the
railroad unions." The Congressional election of 1922 had been the
political ideal. Said one editorial,

> In a word, the 1922 election demonstrated that when the work-
> ers of America take the time and trouble to go to the polls and
> vote for principles and not for party, they can secure such a
> grip on their government as will enable them to compel a square
> deal. The railroad workers are largely responsible for the results
> obtined in 1922. . . . They can do it again if they will only
> organize in 1928 as they did in 1922.[83]

The Brotherhoods intended to send men to Congress who would
vote with them on key legislation. The Railway Labor Executive
Association, spokesman for the Brotherhoods, made this very
clear.[84]

[82] B. E. Jordan, its Secretary-Treasurer, to Chairman, Smith-Robinson League,
N. Y. C., October 13, 1928. Roosevelt Papers.
[83] Editorial, "Elect Your Friends, Defeat Your Enemies," *Railway Conductor,*
XLV (October, 1928), 472. See also *Machinists' Monthly Journal,* XL (October,
1928), 627-629, and *Railroad Telegrapher,* XL (September, 1928), 976-979.
[84] "Invest Your Voting Power to the Best Advantage," *Brotherhood of Locomotive Firemen and Enginemen's Magazine,* LXXXV (November, 1928), 380.

Such an opportunistic policy meant that party lines were being crossed in a way that made it ridiculous for these union leaders to try to support either the Democratic or Republican *party* in 1928. Consider the mosaic: in New York State congressional races their legislative board endorsed 21 Democrats and 4 Republicans, among the latter being both Hamilton Fish and Fiorello La Guardia. They opposed 10 Republicans but no Democrats, being neutral on the rest. In Kentucky the Brotherhoods supported 7

"Undisturbed by the Big Noise" (Drawn for *Labor* by John M. Baer)

Democrats and 2 Republicans. In New Mexico they endorsed a Republican for senator and a Democrat for congressman-at-large. And in Illinois they endorsed 10 Republicans and 5 Democrats, while they opposed one Republican and no Democrats. In Nebraska they aided a Republican senator and three Democratic and one Republican congressmen. For state executive officers they supported eight Republicans and only two Democrats and for the state senate they aided 15 Democrats and 11 Republicans. One of the legislative matters which concerned them in that state was a bill calling for "a reverse power gear in all engines." Legislative partisanship proved a complex business for trade unions!

In Massachusetts the Brotherhoods endorsed 18 Democrats and 5 Republicans, remaining neutral on the rest in state senate races. Two Republicans were opposed.[85] Since neither major party had a monopoly on U.S. senators willing to give "reasonable" support to union desires, the Brotherhoods endorsed senators from both parties. One favorite was Republican Robert M. La Follette, Jr. The railroad union executives said, "For twenty-five years or more the Progressives of the United States have looked to Wisconsin for enlightened leadership and Wisconsin has never failed them." [86]

The following senatorial candidates were also endorsed unanimously by Brotherhood chiefs:[87]

Shipstead	(F-L)	Minn.
Wheeler	(D.)	Mont.
Dill	(D.)	Wash.
Ashurst	(D.)	Ariz.
Frazier	(R.)	N. D.
Howell	(R.)	Neb.
Johnson	(R.)	Calif.
McKellar	(D.)	Tenn.
Pittman	(D.)	Nev.
Walsh	(D.)	Mass.

[85] *Brotherhood of Locomotive Firemen and Enginemen's Magazine,* LXXXV (October, 1928), 322-323, 309-310, 309; *ibid.,* LXXV (November, 1928), 395.

[86] *New York Times,* August 4, 1928.

[87] The list was frequently published. See, for example, *Railway Conductor,* VL (October, 1928), 472.

Copeland	(D.)	N. Y.
Connally	(D.)	Tex.
Stephens	(D.)	Miss.
Trammell	(D.)	Fla.
Swanson	(D.)	Va.

Most of those endorsed were Democrats, but no practical alternative existed in Southern states. Of the ten Northern and Western senators, four were Republicans. (Only a third of the Senate was up for election.)

The Brotherhoods determined on a compass course of neutrality between Hoover and Smith, and they steered it faithfully. The Railway Labor Executives Association mailed out letters to affiliated units and other labor groups in August, announcing that no nominee for President would be endorsed. Instead, active support would be given friendly congressional candidates, especially in Massachusetts, Wisconsin, Minnesota, Montana, Washington, Arizona, and Nevada.[88] No railroad union organizations seem to have aided either Presidential candidate in the general election. Members were advised:

> Every railroad worker has a vital stake in the kind of government we have in Washington. Your wages and your working conditions are largely dependent on the men who administer affairs in the nation's capital. . . . The chief executives of the standard railroad labor organizations have very wisely decided to keep hands off the Presidential contest, but they have appealed to the men and women they represent to concentrate their activities on the election of senators and congressmen.[89]

This did not mean that either individuals or unions were bound to neutrality, and it certainly did not mean, said President David B. Robertson of the Firemen, chairman of the Railway Labor Executives Association, that the neutrality policy had been devised to help Smith. For himself, he announced, he intended to support Hoover and do all he could to aid in his election. Furthermore:

[88] Letters signed by W. O. Warton, August 1928. A. F. of L. Papers.
[89] "Elect Your Friends, Defeat Your Enemies." *Railway Conductor*, VL (October, 1928), 472.

Neither the Association of Railway Labor Executives, nor their joint publication, *Labor,* will advocate the election of either Hoover or Smith, or attempt to express the opinions of the individual organizations or their memberships on the Presidential issue.[90]

A Brotherhood state body in New York endorsed Smith anyway.[91]

The Brotherhood goal of preserving official neutrality toward the Presidential race was realized to a surprising degree. One must concur with an important columnist in the Brotherhood weekly newspaper who wrote, "For weeks *Labor* has been presenting the views of Governor Smith and Mr. Hoover, and their leading lieutenants, clearly and accurately, and as fully as space permitted." [92]

Several *officials* of the Brotherhoods, including the presidents of the tiny Signalmen and the larger Trainmen, worked for the election of Hoover. One partisan called his acceptance address "the political masterpiece of the ages." A second-flight union official on being appointed to a Republican campaign post said that a Smith election would be "a menace to organized labor." He announced out of thin air that wage earners were beginning to see the absurdity of "the Al Smith promises." [93]

In addition to Brotherhood satisfaction over the enactment of the Railway Labor act, there was another factor in the decision of these unions to shy away from Smith. *Temperance* was thought the *sine qua non* of employment on railroads by many Brotherhood officials. When President Robertson of the Firemen emerged from one conference with Hoover, he said that the wet stand of Smith would not appeal, for the railway unions could never be bought with liquor.

Our organization has as one of its mottoes, "Sobriety, Charity and Industry." The railroad worker who drinks to excess loses

[90] *New York Times,* August 7, 1928. Robertson later wired Hoover his congratulations on his acceptance speech. *Ibid.,* August 13, 1928.

[91] Legislation Board of the Brotherhood of Locomotive Firemen and Enginemen, New York State. An appropriation of $5,000 was made for publicity in the state political campaign. *Ibid.,* August 30, 1928.

[92] Raymond Lonergan in *Labor,* November 3, 1928.

[93] *New York Times,* September 19 and 25; August 13, 1928.

not only his job but his membership in the union as well. Why, then, should any of them support a Presidential candidate on the illusory wet issue? [94]

This attitude had become traditional in the publications of the Brotherhoods. Exhaustive examination of their pages in the 1920s shows the effort to disassociate the railroad workers from the rest of the laboring population on the matter of drink.[95] In their fervid stand against liquor the Brotherhood leaders clearly served the interests of their members, for charges of drunkenness against railroad workers in the event of train wrecks would be tragic to their movement. To admit that railroad men might want to drink even in their own homes could bring adverse publicity against the engineers, firemen, switchmen, and others responsible for safety on the American railroads. Did the rank and file agree? That is impossible to say.

The Brotherhood unions had a better "nonpartisan" political technique than the A. F. of L. This was due in part to the newspaper *Labor,* and to their national and homogeneous character. Unified support for the Plumb Plan after World War I and active participation in the Conference for Progressive Political Action also brought unity to what was in a sense a loosely confederated industrial union. They were oriented toward Washington by the very nature of American railroad history. Government intervention in the railroad field was an old story, and to the Brotherhoods a totally unfriendly Congress was unthinkable. Thus they showed more unity than the A. F. of L., handled political publicity more

[94] *New York Times,* September 14, 1928. Robertson thought that Brotherhood men in Ohio and Pennsylvania were supporting Hoover.

[95] The *Locomotive Engineers Journal* was particularly insistent on the matter. When in 1925 the Federal Council of Churches announced that a straw vote had shown most workers opposed to prohibition, the *Journal* said it was "unrepresentative" and had been taken in "wet" cities or "foreign industrial centers." The Brotherhoods had been entirely overlooked, it said, "although their membership is overwhelmingly and emphatically 'dry.' " Most Americans, it continued, lived in small towns and cities. Editorial, "The Facts about Booze," *Locomotive Engineers Journal,* LIX (October, 1925), 727. The following year the *Journal* denied the accuracy of House hearings which indicated that labor was wet. "Nowhere in the news reports of these hearings was there the slightest intimation that the great railroad Brotherhoods are dry...." Editorial, "The Booze Issue," *ibid.,* LX (May, 26, 1926), 327. In 1927 the *Journal* asked editorially, "Does Prohibition Work?" and replied that it did. *Ibid.,* LXI (March, 1927), 168.

effectively, and displayed less hesitancy when advising members how to mark state and congressional ballots.

The Brotherhoods gave more support to Republican Party candidates than did the A. F. of L. While this was partially hidden by the use of the word "Progressives" to describe legislators of whom they approved (many of whom were Republicans) there is little doubt that the "neutrality" of the railroad unions actually inclined toward Hoover. The members of these unions were scattered over the country in accordance with the location of railroad tracks. Many lived in small towns. Less urbanized than the craft unions of the A. F. of L., the Brotherhoods depended on certain Progressive Republican legislators in the Middle and Far West. Although their deceased friend of many years, Robert M. La Follette, had been an insurgent, he had carried the Republican label. Brotherhood orientation tended to be Western rather than Eastern. William G. Mc-Adoo, a dry California Democrat and a friend from the Wilson administration, was closer to their conception of an ideal candidate than Governor Smith.[96] And Alben Barkley of Kentucky was considered their permanent friend.

VIII

Despite official pronouncements of neutrality in the Presidential campaign by the Executive Council of the A. F. of L. and by the Railway Labor Executives Association speaking for the Brotherhoods, it has been seen that innumerable labor leaders, as individuals, became publicly active in partisan politics in 1928. Many state and city labor organizations came out for one candidate or the other, but almost invariably any outspoken partisanship of A. F. of·L. leaders, unions, and organizations was exerted for Governor Smith. Several Railway Brotherhood leaders, John L. Lewis, and various obscure union leaders at a lower level spoke out for Hoover. Support came to the Democratic candidate from some state federations, from a fair number of international unions,

[96] Based on an analysis of Brotherhood periodicals from 1919 to 1928. Much attention was paid McAdoo in *Labor* previous to the Democratic convention of 1924.

from many local unions (especially those in and near New York), and from some city centrals. Such organized labor bodies as these seldom endorsed Hoover.

Trade union leaders agreed on the importance of electing friendly legislators to Congress and to state offices. The general attitude (not always this clearly expressed) was, "Your union is the most dependable weapon you can wield in your battle for economic freedom, but second only to the union is your ballot." [97] As an idea, this would gain increased attention in ensuing decades when the money and effort exerted by union bodies to influence members in the casting of ballots would reach large figures.

Political pronouncements of unions and union leaders remained on a high plane in spite of the emotional issues which marked the campaigning of some partisans of 1928. Union periodicals were almost wholly free of slurs or slanders on the personal characters of Hoover or Smith, nor was the Catholic issue stressed to the detriment of the Happy Warrior. The prohibition issue, swaying union leaders in both directions, was too tender for much union journal discussion.

Union officials called their political activity of the time "non-partisan," meaning that they did not support a *party* as such. But their policy called for maximum political pressure tactics and for comprehensive endorsements of candidates below the presidential level. Over-all, they hoped that at every level in the federal republic they were supporting "friends" and defeating "enemies."

The reluctance of many union leaders in 1928 to use the money or organizational machinery of trade unionism to further their personal preferences in the presidential contest needs to be noted. Such activity, they felt sure, would ultimately divide the labor movement to its detriment. Yet Daniel J. Tobin and many New York labor leaders correctly anticipated the opportunities ahead in forceful and partisan political action by organized labor. While some top officers agreed with Tobin and his fellow aggressive partisans on this, they did not concur with his determination that the Executive Council endorse Alfred E. Smith; his resignation from his position on that body dramatized differing viewpoints on the

[97] *Railway Conductor*, VL (October, 1928), 472.

proper role of labor in national party politics. It has been seen that Socialists in some unions, particularly in New York City, visualized larger political opportunities for the American trade union movement—even new party formation.

The majority of famous labor leaders, for whatever reasons, kept their partisan feelings on the Presidential race within close bounds in 1928. They did not convert the union press to partisanship in the national campaign, and their use of it in trying to influence races for Congress was restrained and inoffensive to the rank and file. As a result, it is only now, through minute historical investigation, that the labor movement of 1928 can be identified to some extent with the success or defeat of any party or presidential candidates of that day. This cannot be said in the case of 1924, when organized labor had become as one with La Follette and suffered public ignominy in his crushing defeat. Finally, in the 1928 election, the amount of union money spent, quantity of partisan material printed, numbers of speeches made, and degree of general effort exerted were infinitely smaller in proportion to union membership than would be true in the years to come.

That organized labor leadership (other than among the railway union hierarchy) was linked with the Democratic Party in some states, and oriented in that direction in still others, over five years before the coming of the New Deal, is inescapably evident from the record. But labor union leaders of the day were very cautious about engaging in acting aggressively on the basis of their *personal* political beliefs. Few succumbed to the temptation to use their union positions to invade the citizenship rights of individual union members—which include the right to choose between parties and candidates, free of duress. It may be said, therefore, that whatever the pattern and intensity of labor's party allegiance in the presidential election of 1928, it was accompanied by considerable respect for the special obligations incumbent on trade union leaders in a democratic society.

Chapter 12

The American
People Decide

AS ELECTION DAY came closer, the Executive Council of the American Federation of Labor announced that there would be no change in its previously announced policy of neutrality in the Presidential race.[1] The declaration was not considered very newsworthy; indeed, labor had been little in the news, inasmuch as nothing dramatic like the formation of a farmer-labor or third-party movement had taken place during the year.[2] In an editorial, the *New York Times* had observed correctly that there would be no new minor party of any importance in 1928. Farm unrest was too localized, the prohibition issue a source of dissention, third parties

[1] *New York Times,* October 20, 1928.

[2] For what little minor agrarian-labor party activity there was in 1928, see the Teigan Papers, Minnesota Historical Society, and H. G. Teigan, "Independent Political Action in Minnesota," *American Federationist,* XXXV (August, 1928), 968, which contains the allegation that the Minnesota State Federation of Labor had favored third-party action at its August, 1927, convention. In late September, 1928, a Buffalo local of the Molders asked formation of a labor party at the International's convention, but the resolutions committee recommended nonconcurrence and the convention agreed. *International Molders Journal,* Convention Number, November, 1928, pp. 139, 171. Similar resolutions often appeared in union conventions under the sponsorship of small radical groups. They were received with uniform indifference in 1928, except in certain New York unions.

See also on minor party conversation and planning the following dates in the *New York Times:* March 29; May 3; June 3, 24, 30; July 13; August 26; September 7; and October 11, 1928.

seldom popular in America anyway, and leadership lacking. Without a Colonel Roosevelt or a "Fighting Bob" La Follette, nothing could be done.

> Doubtless a large number of citizens are in the mood to cry out a plaque o' both your houses, and to wish that they had a new political agency through which to express their precise sentiments; but from that feeling to the actual work of forming a new party is a big jump which very few of them will think of making this year.[3]

The points were well taken. Another important factor was the experience union leaders had obtained from independent party activities in 1924. They would not get similarly involved soon again if they could help it.

Under the title, "Labor's Nonpartisan Political Policy," President William Green spelled out for union leaders in the *American Federationist* the political philosophy which leaders thought best for the organized labor movement. It was an eloquent manifesto.

> Throughout its existence, the American Federation of Labor has followed a policy of nonpartisan political action from which it has departed only in real emergencies. This nonpartisan policy is in accord with the voluntary principles upon which the American labor movement rests. American Labor has held the belief that a movement held together by mutual needs and interests and acting together, because they can accomplish through united action much more than as individuals, has stronger cohesive qualities and constructive possibilities than a movement which depends on any form of compulsion.
>
> The American Federation of Labor is based on a philosophy of voluntarism and distinguishes carefully between matters for individual decision and those on which the Federation should decide. Two matters which American traditions have made inviolate are the individual's rights to choose his church and cast his ballot in accord with his own best judgment.
>
> America's wage earners are from many lands and many nationalities. But though they may speak different languages, belong to different churches, advocate different political methods, they have common economic problems for which they need the labor movement. The real solidarity of wage earners depends on wisdom in not jeopardizing common interests by dealing with

[3] Editorial, "Without Leader or Issues," *ibid.*, May 23, 1928.

matters which are personal in nature. Every American citizen and therefore every trade unionist has a right to cast his ballot as his best judgment may direct.

Should the American Federation of Labor endorse a specific party representative or platform, such action would in effect constitute a notification to union members that the movement expected them to vote accordingly. Should union members exercise their rights as citizens and vote in accord with their best judgment contrary to the Federation's recommendations, the seeds of discord and alienation from the union would be sown.

The Executive Council of the American Federation of Labor in its recent meeting decided not to endorse either the Republican or Democratic candidate for President but to leave trade unionists free to act upon information furnished them. The American Federation of Labor has no votes to deliver, but it renders trade unionists the advisory service of furnishing the labor records of candidates.

Our nonpartisan policy enables our economic movement to avoid the danger of splitting into groups over partisan political issues.[4]

Teamster President Daniel J. Tobin had not agreed with the traditional nonpartisan political policy. He had a great deal to say as election day drew near. An enthusiastic Smith supporter who carefully paid tribute to many aspects of Hoover's character and career, Tobin had worked hard to get the New York State Federation of Labor to endorse Smith. Before his own union's convention, however, he refrained from outspoken views on the Presidential race and stressed the injunction abuse, ignoring personalities.[5] In the October *Teamsters Magazine* he wrote, "While the election of a suitable President is important and full discussion of this subject should be encouraged, workers must not forget that Congress is the lawmaking branch of government." [6] This did not prevent Tobin from returning to his favorite themes in the next issue just in time to reach the homes of his readers before election day. Tobin went all-out. First, he was careful to say, "No one in this organization is in any way bound to vote except in accordance with the dictates

[4] Editorial by William Green, President, American Federation of Labor, "Labor's Nonpartisan Political Policy," *American Federationist*, XXXV (September, 1928), pp. 1042-1043.

[5] *Teamsters Magazine,* XXV (November, 1928), 5-21.

[6] *Ibid.,* XXV (October, 1928), 2.

of his conscience." There would be no hard feelings. Tobin would not keep silent on politics, however, for, unlike religion, the political issues and the people in office affected everyone "in this life." And leaders should lead. Seeing and hearing more than others, they should say what was on their minds. Tobin reviewed many of his previous points about Hoover. He was "thoroughly honest," was "reputed to have made his millions honestly"; he had proven capable of most unselfish public service; and his work as Secretary of Commerce would withstand any investigation. His very "brains and courage and determination" made Tobin fear him, for having promised to carry out the policies of his predecessors he would be sure to keep his promise.

Smith was "a man's man," said Tobin, a person who had dealt with the multitude and fought for the common people. As a governor he had placed legislation on the statute books which had been helpful "to the masses of the common people." Tobin did not think that Samuel Gompers would have sat on the fence with Governor Smith in the race.[7] The man who would perform many significant services for Franklin D. Roosevelt in later years could say nothing too fine in 1928 about Alfred E. Smith. Tobin related that at a banquet given for the Executive Council by Smith at the Pennsylvania Hotel when Gompers was still alive, Smith had said, "Should I ever fail or forget the working people of America, should I ever prove untrue to the pledges I have made to the masses, should I ever believe myself to be greater than they are, in my analysis of their needs, I hope should that time ever come, life will pass from me immediately. I have always endeavored to help the workers and whatever years are left to me shall be devoted to the interests of the people of America and especially to the toilers who comprise the great bulk of our American citizenship. I firmly believe in the aims and principles of the trade union movement." Tobin said that Gompers had teemed over with enthusiasm and admiration for the great champion of the people's rights. In an emotional and oratorical style which was passing out of fashion, Tobin showed himself a partisan among partisans:

[7] *Ibid.*, XXV (November, 1928), 1-5.

In all my experiences with men in public office, and I have had some in this and other countries; meetings with ex-Presidents Wilson, Taft, Roosevelt and Harding and with President Coolidge; I have sat at luncheon with members of the House of Commons in England and the Reichstag in Germany, I have met the leaders who were considering the world problems in Geneva, Switzerland; I have sat in conference in Amsterdam with Labor officials from many of the countries in Europe, but I never met a man more human, one more sympathetic with the masses of working people, or one more desirous of helping the toilers than the governor of New York, Alfred E. Smith.[8]

II

In an election-eve radio address, Hoover paid tribute to the American two-party system. His comments contrasted sharply with the stated views of the Socialist and Communist candidates, and there is no reason to doubt that his Democratic opponent would have been in full agreement with him on certain fundamentals:

> Our two great political parties have laid before you their principles and policies. And I am a believer in party government. It is only through party organization that our people can give coherent expression to their views on great issues which affect the welfare and future of the Republic. There is no other way.
> Furthermore, it is only through party organization that we may fix responsibility for the assured execution of these promises.

Ignoring entirely the Socialist and Communist candidates, Hoover presented in a few sentences his own basic beliefs:

> We are a nation of progressives; we differ as to what is the road to progress. . . . This election is of more momentous order than for many years because we have entered into a new era of economic and moral action, not only in our own country but in the world at large. Our national task is to meet our many new problems, and in meeting them to courageously preserve our rugged individualism, together with the principles of ordered liberty and freedom, equality of opportunity with that of idealism to which our nation has been consecrated.[9]

[8] *Ibid.*, **XXV** (November, 1928), 5.
[9] *New York Times*, November 6, 1928.

In view of the savage criticism which the words "rugged individual-ism" would receive in later years, it must be observed here that most contemporaries do not appear to have found them offensive— much less humorous. They did not regard Hoover as a reactionary or the words callous or disgraceful.

Hoover's judgment on his opponent, in retrospect, was written in the spirit of true democratic liberalism which has separated self-government in the United States from that in many lands in the twentieth century:

> Governor Alfred E. Smith, the Democratic candidate, was a natural born gentlemen. Both of us had come up from the grass roots or the pavements, and from boyhood had learned the ele-ments of sportsmanship. During the campaign he said no word and engaged in no action that did not comport with the highest levels. I paid a natural tribute to him when speaking in New York during the campaign, and he did so to me when speaking in California. In after years, when I was often associated with him in public matters, we mutually agreed that we had one deep satisfaction from the battle. No word had been spoken or mis-representation made by either of us which prevented sincere friendship the day after election.[10]

III

Norman Thomas traveled from coast to coast, speaking daily on a schedule which saw him spend many nights aboard trains en-route to speaking engagements.[11] It has been judged that he could not get enough publicity to get his message a hearing,[12] and it is true that the newspapermen of 1928 did not consider the activities of a Socialist very newsworthy.[13] Thomas himself, however, is the authority for the statement that the publicity bureau of his party

[10] *Hoover Memoirs*, II, 198.

[11] *New Leader*, July 21, August 4, 18, and September 29, 1928. He covered about fifty major cities from August 4 to late October.

[12] Roy Victor Peel and Thomas C. Donnelly, *The 1928 Campaign, an Analysis* (New York, 1931), p. 96 n. This volume of analysis gives Thomas some attention.

[13] *The Literary Digest* lost interest early in the campaign. "Socialist on the Marxian Great Divide," XCVI (March 3, 1928), 18, and "Socialist Ticket," XCVII (April 28, 1928), 12, were followed the next January with "Socialist Slump," C (January 5, 1929), 9.

"handled" ten thousand or more newspaper clippings about the party during the campaign. It is significant to note the satisfied appraisal of Thomas that not a single capitalist paper confused Socialism in 1928 "with Bolshevism or Anarchy." [14] His audiences seem to have been made up of industrial laborers, old line socialists, and persons from academic life, although it would be hard to establish the proportion of each.[15] One feels that his intellectual rather than emotional appeal was better suited to the college people in his audiences.[16] He certainly lacked the earthy quality of the largely self-taught former railroad worker Eugene V. Debs; yet the animated and ministerial style of Thomas on the platform can be said to have been quite effective.

The attitudes and practices of two Socialist organs—the daily Milwaukee *Leader* and the weekly *New Leader*—need to be described momentarily. The *Milwaukee Leader* under the editorship of Victor Berger and with a front-page column by Oscar Ameringer was far from "militant" in the sense of the word often used by the far left. It firmly supported the idea of Socialism triumphant at length through electoral victories at the ballot box. It ran little on the Communists. It quietly but surely supported the national Socialist ticket, although it can quickly be sensed that no effect was being made to identify the candidacy of Berger with that of Thomas and Maurer. Pictures of the Socialist candidates were conspicuously absent from its pages. Postelection news of the defeat of Berger and the small showing made by Thomas were kept to subordinate articles when mentioned at all. Pleas for Socialism were kept on an abstract, futuristic, idealistic plane as a rule, although irony and humor, sharply pointed, were Ameringer's daily stock in trade, and the editorial page called for public power, deplored graft, and portrayed Democratic and Republican candidates as standing in identical positions as fronts for industrialists and exploiters. Oddly enough, the latter were seldom named. Neither corporations nor individuals

---

[14] Thomas, "Why Not a New Party?" p. 149.

[15] The speech in Denver was said to have drawn about five hundred persons, largely industrial workers with "a sprinkling of sociologists." *New York Times,* September 22, 1928.

[16] A judgment based on the semantics of Thomas in speeches of the day, and on comments by his colleagues in personal correspondence then and later.

were so labeled. The local city struggles of the Amalgamated Clothing Workers were given a good play, and Sidney Hillman was characterized in friendly fashion.

Thus the *Milwaukee Leader* kept its Socialism well localized. A favorite respository was the editorial page, where signed features, many of them reprints, showed ideological slant. Ameringer's column, and the sharply slanted bias of stories on Socialist Party activities, revealed the paper's sympathies. Yet party business received little space compared with other news; it is clear that innumerable non-Socialists must have read the paper without undue concern over its political and economic views. Women's activities, sports, financial news, and the usual advertising found in city dailies, were present—along with comic strips.

The *Milwaukee Leader* was a paper in 1928 without a persecution complex, although it plainly did not approve of the status quo. It was alarmed over the rise of fascism abroad. It deplored United States policies in Nicaragua, and it pointed out, on occasion, that there was unemployment and maldistributed prosperity at home in America. It was, moreover, surprisingly provincial. If the Socialist Party had important New York City leadership or financing, the reader of the paper would scarcely realize it. If the editor was a reader of the *New Leader,* Socialist weekly, his own choice of reprinted items concealed the fact. When, on rare occasions, the columns of James Oneal, editor of the *New Leader,* were reprinted in the Milwaukee organ of Socialism, it was normally without indication of their origin.

The *New Leader* was aggressive over Communist Party tactics and especially on the epithets of the Reds. The paper of Victor Berger had other concerns. Soviet Russia was not newsworthy, but the Graf Zepplein, German flyers, and certain other West European news got large headlines in Wisconsin. The U.S.S.R. was not the model. Russian "socialism," to misuse the term, was not something to be described, analyzed, praised, condemned, or simply singled out in this newspaper in 1928. Nevertheless, both of these publications were fully and avowedly organs of Socialist doctrine. E. J. Costello, editor of the *Milwaukee Leader* in 1930, wrote forthrightly to the Socialist Party of the city, ". . . in the last analysis this is a Socialist newspaper and Socialist news must have predominance." [17] In an editorial the paper told labor readers, "It is one of the sad commentaries of the labor movement in America that many workmen and women are unaware of the interdependence of trade unionism and Socialism." And Socialist Congressman Berger advised Amalgamated members, "Fight with both hands, not with one hand tied behind you. You have two hands; the trade union is one and the Socialist Party is the other. When you cling to your union but forget to vote Socialist you are fighting with only one hand." [18] Paul Douglas in a speech reported in the *Leader* called the Socialists the only "liberal political group" in the country not discouraged by the task of building a "labor party." Workers plus urban intellectuals, "the two groups which will be benefited by the new era," could readily adhere to the new framework, he said.[19]

James Maurer, Socialist vice presidential candidate, wrote in retrospect of the excitement of stumping for Socialism in those years.

> There is something fascinating about a speaking tour that never failed to get me, no matter how many I made. To meet old friends and acquaintances, to battle for the cause which I consider the one sure hope of a troubled world, to defy the myriad pigmy dictators whom custom and an easy-going people have allowed to grow up in our land—could there be a greater thrill? [20]

As the time to vote approached, the *New Leader* headlined across page one: "BOOZE—BANKNOTES—BIGOTRY. THE MOST DE-GRADED PRESIDENTIAL CAMPAIGN IN HISTORY DRAWS TO UNSAVORY CLOSE WITH REACTION TRIUMPHANT." Since Hoover would win and Smith was out of the running, said the article, "may God have mercy on all of us poor folks for the next four years." [21] Realistic Socialists had not expected miracles. Although enthusiastic comrades talked of *millions* of votes and more serious students hoped

[17] Letter of June 24, 1930, Socialist Party of Milwaukee Papers.
[18] *Milwaukee Leader,* October 3, 1928.
[19] Speech reported in *Milwaugee Leader,* October 31, 1928. See Chapter IX, Note 72.
[20] *It Can Be Done* (New York, 1938), 294, Maurer's autobiography.
[21] *New Leader,* October 20, 1928.

for *a* million, old timers whispered half a million, wrote a Socialist columnist. "Now is the time for all good, valiant men to start planning for our Party. We know most clearly what will happen two weeks from now. There will be a stupendous landslide for reaction." [22] "I should have been very glad to have been elected as Senator," said Norman Thomas two decades later, "and I should have been very glad to have been elected as President, but I never expected it." [23]

For the Socialist Party the election was no triumph, whatever it might have meant to individuals imbued with optimism. Morris Hillquit judged some years later that in 1928 the party "touched the lowest point in its downward career." [24] A myopic Communist critic who inventively described conditions in the United States for comrades in the world movement contended that the Socialist Party then had "less influence" than at any time in its history.[25] Certainly the party total of 264,608 votes [26] was unimpressive for a party which had approached the million mark eight years earlier. Yet visionary party leaders did not regard the effort as a failure or agree that the prestige of Socialism was at a new low. What if the *New York Times* called their vote "a poor showing?" [27] Hillquit said much respect had been won and considerable reorganization of the party accomplished.[28] Thomas insisted that hundreds of thousands of Americans who did not vote Socialist gained a better knowledge of the party and its aims.[29] Henceforth, he said grandiloquently, the Socialist Party would be the "official opposition," since the Democratic Party was "manifestly impotent." The only intellectual opposition to the capitalism of Herbert Hoover, he

[22] S. A. de Witt, *ibid.,* October 27, 1928. For a preconvention prediction by Hillquit between one and five million votes, see *New York Times,* April 8, 1928.
[23] Thomas to Oral History Project, Spring, 1949, p. 48.
[24] *Loose Leaves From a Busy Life* (New York, 1934), p. 323.
[25] J. Louis Engdahl, "The Capitulation of the Petty Bourgeoisie in the American (U.S.A.) Election Campaign," *International Press Correspondence,* VIII (Vienna, November 2, 1928), 1430.
[26] Edgard Eugene Robinson, *The Presidential Vote, 1896-1932* (Stanford University, 1947 edition). A total compiled by the party claimed 268,624. *The American Labor Year Book, 1929,* gives 267,835 votes. For a worthwhile study of the Socialist Party vote since 1900, see Cortez A. M. Ewing, *Presidential Elections from Abraham Lincoln to Franklin D. Roosevelt* (Norman, Okla., 1940), pp. 122-126.
[27] Editorial, "The Socialist Vote," *New York Times,* December 15, 1928.
[28] *New Leader,* November 10, 1928. Also *Loose Leaves From a Busy Life,* p. 323.
[29] *New York Times,* November 7, 1928.

claimed, had come from his party.[30] Perhaps best of all, the way had been cleared for the "realistic political alignment" his comrades sought. [31] The party was reorganized, some inactive Socialists were back in the fold, and a foundation for action had been laid.[32] Yet paid membership increased little.[33]

Crusaders and idealistic theorists in the party seemed to derive pleasure from having gone down in the course of fighting the good fight.[34] James Oneal counted on young men in college to work, *now,* to destroy the two-party alliance of "upper-class" politics. He was happy that the leaders of the unions had been carried down in the crash, since he thought (correctly!) that "most of them outside of the railroad brotherhoods" had supported Smith. A humiliating wound had been inflicted on the labor movement.[35]

To the editors of the *World Tomorrow* the Socialist candidates had won universal respect, the platform had been realistic and appealing, and the campaign had been waged with intelligence and vigor. The party might yet be the radical wing of a more general progressive party. It was just too bad the country had not been in an "experimental mood." Political revolt had just not been in the air.[36] And so it went for the Socialists with prosperity in the air. In coming years many of their ideas would come into their own.

IV

The basic statistics of the election of 1928 may be summarized quickly.[37] Hoover carried 40 states with 444 electoral votes, while Smith won in eight states with 87 electoral votes. The Smith states

---

[30] *Ibid.,* November 8, 1928.

[31] *New Leader,* November 10, 1928.

[32] Maurer, *It Can Be Done,* p. 293

[33] William H. Henry to Daniel Hoan, November 13, 1928, Hoan Papers.

[34] Note, for example, the rhapsodic air of an open letter to Thomas printed under his picture in *New Leader,* November 3, 1928, in anticipation of certain defeat.

[35] Editorial, "The Significance of the Election," *New Leader,* November 10, 1928.

[36] Editorial, "The Socialist Vote," *World Tomorrow,* XII (Feburary, 1929), 55.

[37] Official election figures by counties may be found for the period 1896 to 1944 in the following volumes by Edgar Eugene Robinson: *The Presidential Vote 1896-1932* (Stanford Univ., 1947 edition) and *They Voted for Roosevelt: The Presidential Vote, 1932-1944* (Stanford Univ., 1947). It may be noted that reviewers of these volumes in the *American Political Science Review* and the *Annals of the American Academy of Political and Social Science* intimated that election statistics should be drawn from

were Massachusetts, Rhode Island, Georgia, South Carolina, Alabama, Mississippi, Louisiana, and Arkansas. Hoover received 21,-
391,993 votes to 15,016,169 for Smith.[38] Norman Thomas polled
about 264,608 votes for the Socialist Party and William Z. Foster
obtained about 43,917 votes for the Workers (Communist)
Party.[39] All the minor parties in the campaign combined received
a total of only 397,288 votes,[40] a mediocre showing by any measurement. (See adjoining tabulation of the vote.)

The election of 1928 was a decisive and resounding Republican
victory. In every section of the nation Hoover ran ahead of Smith.[41]
Yet Governor Smith received 40.8 per cent of the vote, and in
thirty states he received more votes than any previous Democratic
candidate. This would have been more remarkable 'if it had not
been for an increase in the size of the vote from 1924 to 1928 of
about eight millions. Thus women's suffrage and increased voting
interest, rather than a mere population increase, brought the 1928
total to nearly twice that of 1916. Roosevelt found it worth re-
membering that Smith polled at least six million more votes than
any previous Democratic candidate, while the Democratic increase
over 1924 was larger than the Republican.[42] (This was a somewhat tricky evaluation in view of the C.P.P.A. inroads into the
Democrats in 1924.) A Catholic Chicagoan was less sanguine.
"Though we may have been prepared for defeat on the election
to the presidency, we surely were not prepared for so overwhelming
a rout." [43] Certainly the Democratic candidate won only 912
counties compared to Hoover's 2,172, while Hoover led in 215
counties (mostly in the South), which had never before been won

these volumes in preference to other sources. Numerous mistakes in previous compilations, even in the additions on official returns, have been corrected.

The present writer has prepared a table of election figures by states from the first
of these volumes. See Table 1.

[38] Robinson, *The Presidential Vote,* 1896-1932, p. 46.

[39] Compiled from *ibid.,* pp. 379-399. See Table 1.

[40] *Ibid.,* p. 46.

[41] Professor Robinson divided the nation into the following sections: New England,
Middle Atlantic, East North-Central, West North-Central, South Atlantic, East
South-Central, West South-Central, Mountain, and Pacific. Hoover led in each.

[42] Roosevelt to Catherine A. Broderick, Greenwich, Conn., December 8, 1928,
Roosevelt Papers.

[43] A Chicago educator to Frank P. Walsh, November 7, 1928, Walsh Papers.

Table 1. THE VOTE FOR PRESIDENT IN 1928*

State	Republican Party	Democratic Party	Socialist Party	Workers (Communist)- Party	Total
Alabama	120,725	127,808	444	...	248,977
Arizona	52,533	38,537	...	184	91,254
Arkansas	77,788	123,140	435	322a	201,685
California	1,162,323	614,365	19,595	112¹	1,796,656
Colorado	253,872	133,131	3,472	675	392,242
Connecticut	296,641	252,085	3,029	738	553,118
Delaware	68,860	35,354	329	59	104,602
Florida	144,168	101,764	4,036	3,704	253,672
Georgia	65,423	129,604	124	64	231,404
Idaho	99,848	53,271	1,329	...	154,448
Illinois	1,769,141	1,313,817	19,138	3,581	3,107,489
Indiana	848,290	562,691	3,871	321	1,421,314
Iowa	623,570	379,011	2,960h	328g	1,002,581
Kansas	513,531	192,988	6,205	320b	713,039
Kentucky	558,064	381,070	783	288	940,521
Louisiana	51,160	164,655	...	...	215,833
Maine	179,923	81,179	1,065	...	262,167
Maryland	301,479	223,626	1,701	636	528,348
Massachusetts	775,566	792,758	6,262	2,461	1,577,823
Michigan	965,396	396,762	3,516	2,881	1,372,082
Minnesota	560,977	396,451	6,774	4,853	970,976
Mississippi	26,244	124,539	...j	...	151,591
Missouri	834,080	662,684	3,739	...	1,500,845
Montana	113,300	78,578	1,667	563	194,108
Nebraska	345,745	197,950	3,433	...	547,128
Nevada	18,327	14,090	...	...	32,417
New Hampshire	115,404	80,715	465	173	196,757
New Jersey	925,285	616,162	4,866	1,240	1,548,195
New Mexico	69,707	48,211	...	158	118,076
New York	2,193,344	2,089,863	107,332	10,876	4,405,626
North Carolina	348,923	286,227	...	...	635,150
North Dakota	131,419	106,649	936	...c	239,846
Ohio	1,627,546	864,210	8,683	2,836	2,508,446
Oklahoma	393,746	219,174	3,924	...	618,127
Oregon	205,341	109,223	...k	...d	319,942
Pennsylvania	2,055,382	1,076,586	18,647	2,039e	3,159,612
Rhode Island	117,522	118,973	...	283	237,194
South Carolina	3,188	62,700	47	...	68,605
South Dakota	157,603	102,660	443	224	261,857
Tennessee	195,388	157,143	567	94	353,192
Texas	367,242	340,080	658	209	708,189
Utah	94,618	80,985	954	46	176,603
Vermont	90,404	44,440	...	...	135,191
Virginia	164,609	140,146	250	179	305,364
Washington	335,844	156,772	2,615	1,541	500,840
West Virginia	375,551	263,784	1,313	401	642,752
Wisconsin	544,205	450,259	18,213	1,528f	1,016,831
Wyoming	52,748	29,299	788	...	82,835
TOTAL	21,391,993	15,016,169	264,608	43,917	36,805,450

* Compiled from Edgar Eugene Robinson, *The Presidential Vote, 1896-1932* (Stanford University, 1947 edition), pp. 379-398, 133-379.

SPECIAL CASES

1. The Workers (Communist) Party did not appear on the ballot under its own name or any other party label in the following states: Alabama, Idaho, Louisiana, Maine, Mississippi, Nebraska, Nevada, North Carolina, Oklahoma, South Carolina, Vermont, and Wyoming.

2. The Socialist Party did not appear on the ballot under its own name or any other party label in the following states: Arizona, Louisiana, Mississippi, Nevada, New Mexico, North Carolina, Rhode Island, and Vermont.

3. None of the following state totals were included in the total given the Workers (Communist) Party by the present writer:

    a. Arkansas: Independent Party, 322

    b. Kansas: Independent Party, 320

    c. North Dakota: Farmer-Worker Party, 842

    d. Oregon: Independent Party, 1,094

    e. Pennsylvania: Labor Party, 2,687. Foster and Gitlow ran on two party tickets in this state.

4. The following figure was included in the total for the Workers (Communist) Party in spite of the fact that the party label was different:

    f. Wisconsin: Independent Workers Party, 1,528.

5. Notes (g) and (h) refer to the fact that these two figures did not appear on the official state returns used by Professor Robinson. The figures came from the *World Almanac*.

6. Notes (j) and (k) refer to the fact that neither of the following state totals was included in the Socialist Party total:

    j. Mississippi cast 264 votes for Elector Rogers.

    Some published compilations give these votes to the Socialist Party.

    k. Oregon cast 2,720 votes for a Socialist Principles—Independent Party.

7. Note 1. indicates write-in votes only.

8. Note (m) indicates that because of the above exclusions and the notes for various tiny parties the four party totals do not add to the gross total.

by a Republican.[44] Of the 409 counties won by La Follette in 1924, Smith succeeded in carrying only 43. Peel and Donnelly concluded from this that the Progressives of 1924 were "only Republicans in disguise." [45] Yet the 1924 ticket which had included

[44] *Ibid.*, pp. 34, 25, 24.
[45] Roy V. Peel and Thomas C. Donnelly, *The 1928 Campaign, An Analysis* (New York, 1931), p. 122.

Democrat Burton K. Wheeler for Vice President made inroads on both major parties, tending to pull from Democrats in the East and Republicans in the West. That its total had also included the Socialist vote is evident. Whatever was the case earlier, in 1928 it seems possible that Hoover got the bulk of the Progressive Republican vote in the Middle and Far West.

One must not laugh off certain other interpretations of the vote. An eighty-year-old Minnesotan, after a trip to Iowa, found it "most astonishing to see so many houses where the vote is divided between husbands and wives. My guess is that should Hoover be elected it will be largely due to the woman's vote." [46] The validity of this guess is unknown. That Smith succeeded at all in carrying a bloc of deep Southern states may be attributed in part to the prevalence of the reasoning of a Mississippian.

> One thing that will always keep this section in the Democratic fold is the negro. A real split between the whites would bring him back into politics, and any person who has ever been here very much and observed the question will realize the white people cannot afford to split in politics to the extent of creating two major parties here.[47]

Again, one is at a loss to pass judgment.

V

When Senator Copeland was asked why Smith had been defeated, his reply was an all-time classic: "It was simply that the Republican arguments appealed to more voters." [48] No one can quarrel with this basic fact, for the Republican position had been a strong one. The Smith candidacy had many weak points. Still, the special factors—religion and prohibition—remain and cannot be passed off lightly.

Analyses of the vote by contemporaries stressed the vital importance of prosperity, prohibition, and religion—but not always in that order. The scope of this study does not make it possible to

---

[46] L. C. Barnett to Roosevelt, October 22, 1928, Roosevelt Papers.
[47] An attorney, Lexington, Miss., to Roosevelt, October 20, 1928, Roosevelt Papers.
[48] Senator Royal S. Copeland of New York, *New York Times,* November 8, 1928.

present here a new interpretation of the relative importance of the prohibition and religion factors.[49] That they existed and were of much importance cannot be repeated too often. James D. Phelan of San Francisco, a keen observer, judged:

> The secret of the debacle, doubtless, can be traced to religious and, independently, the "dry" sentiment which was injected into the campaign. It has been said out here that Smith's weakness came from his "relatives." "Uncle" Wall Street was too friendly to awaken the enthusiasm of the radicals and progressives; moneyed support, where minds, aroused suspicion, and "Anti" Prohibition, "Anti" S lic and "Anti" Tammany created a wide-spread and hos. sentiment which did the rest.[50]

Frank P. Walsh, deeply experienced in such matters, opined, "Religion and the prosperity bunk proved Smith's undoing." [51] From a female part of the lunatic fringe in the nation came recriminations; a former Virginian, she "of course" voted for Hoover, she wrote Franklin D. Roosevelt, for "you betrayed us and your church and your own friends for your own ambitions. In your heart you knew Americans would not elect an ignorant Irishman, both wet and a Catholic. We will do the same to you in 1932." [52] (Little did she know!)

It is the opinion of the writer, in spite of such quotations, however, that *prosperity was the vital issue;* Hoover would have won regardless of the two other factors of major importance. That prosperity had meaning for union members, for example, has been evident throughout this book; it will again be discussed shortly.

[49] The following analyses of this famous election, although sometimes conflicting, are helpful: Peel and Donnelly, *The 1928 Campaign, An Analysis;* Robert M. La Follette, Jr., "Election Reveals New Forces Set in Motion," *La Follette's Magazine,* XX (November, 1928), 161-162, and "Progressive Vote in 1928," *ibid.,* XXI (February, 1929), 17-18; the following articles in *Current History,* XXIX (December, 1928): A. B. Hart, "Presidential Election of 1928" and "Aftermath of the Elections"; Patrick Henry Callahan, "Religious Prejudice in the Election"; John A. Ryan, "A Catholic View of the Election"; James Cannon, Jr., "Causes of Governor Smith's Defeat"; Fabian Franklin, "Analyzing the Election Results"; Simon Michelet, "An Analysis of the Vote in the National Election," *ibid.,* XXIX (February, 1929), 781-785; Richard Thomas Loomis, "Alfred E. Smith and Religion in Politics: 1924-1928" (Unpublished Master's thesis in History, Stanford University, 1948).

[50] Phelan to Roosevelt, February 9, 1928, Roosevelt Papers.

[51] Walsh to Joseph B. Shannon, November 13, 1928, Walsh Papers.

[52] Name withheld (an M.D.) to Roosevelt, November 16, 1928, Roosevelt Papers.

While it is important to try to answer definitively the question of how organized labor finally voted, this is manifestly an impossible question about an election which predated the polling techniques and the increase in political information that came in later years. In the 1930s and 1940s sufficient evidence existed to make it possible for one investigator to conclude that more than two thirds of union members normally voted Democratic.[53] Contemporary postelection analysts in 1928-29 were little interested in how union members voted, nor did they consider the results a victory or defeat for the unions—unlike 1920, when there was much opinion that the election marked a defeat for Samuel Gompers.[54]

It was only natural, perhaps, for postelection expressions of gratitude to be exchanged between union leaders and political figures, and their wording is poor evidence of how union men voted. Still, both Key Pittman and Burton Wheeler thanked the A. F. of L., the Montana senator saying, "the farmers, miners, railroad men, and laborers stood by me in great shape and were it not for their loyalty to me I am sure I could never have attained such a splendid victory." Copeland expressed his appreciation, and David I. Walsh told the A. F. of L., "This endorsement contributed greatly to solidifying the membership of your organizations. That has been a main factor in my election." [55] Among telegrams going the reverse direction was President Green's to governor-elect Roosevelt, "Congratulations on your election. I rejoice with your host of friends upon your great victory." [56]

Since it can be assumed that the bulk of the members of the American Federation of Labor lived in cities, the nature of the "urban vote" is therefore of particular interest. An effort was once made to determine the relative importance of some of the

[53] George Gallup, "How Labor Votes," *Annals of the American Academy of Political and Social Science,* CCLXXIV (March, 1951), 123-1924. "It is difficult, perhaps impossible, to measure precisely what effect the endorsement of a political candidate by union officials will have on the political thinking of the membership." (Page 123.) The *Literary Digest* poll was fully 9.9 per cent inaccurate, leaning Republican; this was termed a source of future "serious mischief." Fabian Franklin to *New York Times,* November 26, 1928.

[54] Based on an extensive examination of the *New York Times* for the election of 1920. See especially November 5, 6, 8, 17, 18, 1920.

[55] Letters and telegrams in A. F. of L. Papers.

[56] Green to Roosevelt, November 8, 1928, A. F. of L. Papers.

factors present in the election of 1928, including the urban factor, by utilizing statistical methods.[57] The study of Professors Ogburn and Talbot did not give direct consideration to union membership, industrialization, prosperity, the injunction, or the tariff. What it did for 173 Northern and Western counties was to consider the relative importance of five factors: prohibition, religion, urbanization, party regularity, and foreign birth. After "equalizing" the counties statistically, four of the five factors were held constant in order to study the influence of the one remaining. The idea was to see how much of an increase or decrease would appear in each case in the size of the Democratic Party vote if the factor singled out for study were to be increased by ten per cent.

The following changes were noted for each factor:

	Democratic Increase, %	Democratic Decrease, %
Prohibition	4.1	
Religion	2.8	
Party Regularity	1.8	
Foreign Birth	0.5	
Urbanization		0.8

What this means is that increasing the number of "wet" voters by ten per cent would have increased the Democratic vote by 4.1 per cent; increasing the Catholics by the same amount would have brought less of an increase. Thus prohibition was very important; religion less so. And the study seems to say that, other things being equal, urban areas would tend to support Hoover slightly more than Smith. How valid are these conclusions?

The present writer does not challenge the study on its statistical procedures, although others have done so. There is doubt about the value of the criteria the investigators used for measuring purposes. In determining urbanization, for example, they accepted the dictates of census figures available to them; that is, they considered as urban any place over 2,500 population. From the viewpoint of a

---

[57] William F. Ogburn and Nell Snow Talbot, "A Measurement of the Factors in the Presidential Election of 1928," *Social Forces,* VIII (December, 1929), 175-183. Long after my analysis of Ogburn and Talbot first appeared (1951) a sophisticated dissection of its statistical methods reduced its general validity. See Ruth C. Silva, *Rum, Religion, and Notes: 1928 Reexamined* (University Park, Pa., 1962).

student of unions, of industrialization, or of the appeal the candidate "from the city streets" might exert on fellow urban products,
the figure 2,500 is unrewarding. Nor is that all. Other criteria
were equally subject to severe questioning. The student of the election of 1928 should not use the study of Professors Ogburn and
Talbot without carefully considering such limitations in each case
and then drawing his own conclusions.

The "foreign-born" figure included persons born in every foreign
country. Those who freely predicted that Smith would be supported
by naturalized citizens had in mind a stereotype: a Catholic from
Italy or other Central and Southern European countries who was
accustomed, probably, to wine on the table—or a German who saw
no moral issue in the drinking of beer. To include immigrants from
Great Britain, Canada, Scandinavia, the British Empire countries,
Mexico, and elsewhere dilutes the factor. Moreover, what proportion of these foreign born were *registered* voters?

In obtaining their "wetness" factor the investigators enlisted the
aid of a *Literary Digest* poll taken in 1922. The serious social,
economic, and political inadequacies of these polls were not generally understood in 1931, before the poll of 1936 predicted the
victory of Governor Landon. Again, in the selection of their states,
the investigators chose those in which they could obtain an idea
of sentiment on prohibition, that is, states where division on the
question had forced a referendum. States where *less* division or
more division among the people on the matter had made such
referenda unnecessary were not used. On religion, it need only be
pointed out that the border and Southern states were excluded from
consideration.

These points are not offered as criticisms of the methods of the
pioneering *Social Forces* study, and there is no question of "error"
or misrepresentation involved. The investigators apparently used
the best figures they could find and they made the most of what
they had. It is merely suggested that the study is not clear-cut
because its sources are not clear-cut. Thus the investigators used
the Democratic vote of 1920 as a measuring stick for "party regularity," but the issues in that election cut across party lines to
some extent.

It may be noted that in spite of these objections, the study is said to have high "predictability," that is, it can be used within about six percentage points to predict the vote for counties not included in the study, so long as those counties are in the same states. Six points can cause a serious error in a country of traditionally narrow voting divisions, however, as the pollsters have since discovered.

The conclusions drawn in the study on the matter of urbanization follow:

> The urban influence was not as strong for Smith as many persons seem to think. Hoover carried many cities and large ones, including Chicago, for instance. . . . The election does not seem to have called forth any special rural or urban influence as such for either side.[58]

Against this judgment may be placed the fact that Smith carried such cities as St. Paul, St. Louis, Cleveland, San Francisco, New York, Boston, San Antonio, and New Haven. He "ran a strong race" in Philadelphia, Pittsburgh, Chicago, Detroit, Omaha, and elsewhere.[59] And one cannot safely ignore so strong a private statement as that of a Los Angeles labor official on local labor sentiment in October, 1928, "There is no Hoover sentiment apparent at all in the ranks of Labor in this city." [60] Still, since union members were in 1928 in such a small minority (even in New York), the city vote need not be considered in any real sense a measure of union membership voting.

Must the observer of labor in politics admit finally that no one knows how the rank and file of union members voted in 1928? It might be possible to shed some light on the matter if certain information were available. For example, if A. F. of L. and Brotherhood membership figures of the day were available by county residence, they might be utilized in conjunction with the county voting figures

---

[58] Ogburn and Talbot, "A Measurement of Factors in the Presidential Election of 1928," p. 117. But see Dr. Silva, pp. 42 ff.

[59] Peel and Donnelly, *The 1928 Campaign, An Analysis*, p. 121. Interesting statistical material appears in Samuel J. Eldersveld, "The Influence of Metropolitan Party Pluralities in Presidential Elections Since 1920," *American Political Science Review*, XLIII (December, 1949), 1189-1206.

[60] Secretary, Los Angeles Central Labor Council, to William Green, October 16, 1928, A. F. of L. Papers.

provided in the volume by Professor Robinson. Some interesting results might emerge. If it were to appear that the higher the union membership the higher the Smith (or the Hoover) vote, the results might have justified the great effort involved.

Entering into the realm of conjecture, it seems reasonable to believe that a fair proportion of union leaders and *interested* members were swayed toward Smith in New York City and New York State, in Chicago, and in other areas where city centrals, state federations, and large unions endorsed the Democratic candidate. But how many union men can be considered *interested?* Apparently only the handful who went through a ritualistic series of steps, that is, who attended meetings of the union, read its magazine, listened with respectful attention to the advice of union officers, and, in short, held their union membership to be of greater importance than other aspects of their daily existence, can be regarded in such a light. The present writer has absolutely no idea how many such "union-oriented" members there were in 1928 with regard to political matters. How many have there been in Presidential Elections held in the years since that time? And is the number growing or shrinking?

It is altogether probable that the working men and women of the United States divided their votes between Smith and Hoover much as did nonunion voters with similar social and economic characteristics. Judging from the sweeping Hoover victory, it is probable that a majority of union members supported him. The bare statistics show that the conceptualized American "proletariat" and "workers with hand" almost completely ignored Thomas and Foster. All in all, in the absence of any evidence to the contrary, it is impossible to conclude that in the election of 1928 the voting of union members was unique. In any case, the niggardly voting for the Socialist and Communist causes has special meaning; that is, if there was a significant class struggle in the United States in 1928, it did not show itself in the only true measurement that exists in a true democratic republic: the final count of votes secretly cast for the candidates of legal political parties in an election held in accordance with the written or unwritten constitution.

Chapter 13

The Backwash of
a Presidential Election

ON ELECTION NIGHT and the days that followed, prominent participants discussed the political meaning of what had occurred in 1928. Norman Thomas thought there had been no unmistakable mandate from the people. The major parties had not been distinguishable from one another.[1] An editorial in the *New York Times* inclined to similar views, asserting that all the traditional issues had been abandoned, platforms had read alike, candidates had spoken much the same, and foreign observers had seen nothing but prohibition separating them.[2] Just before the election, on the other hand, a Smith partisan had discerned a basic cleavage, saying, "The difference is between the conception of the Democratic candidate who believes in the regulation of business by Government, and the conception of the Republican Party which has led to control of Government by business." [3] Such narrow observations were not well made, for there were clearly discernible (and less sensationalized) differences between both candidates and parties, as has been made clear in these pages.

[1] *New York Times,* November 5, 1928.
[2] Editorial, "The Two-Party System," *ibid.,* November 15, 1928.
[3] Rabbi Stephen S. Wise, in *ibid.,* November 4, 1928.

I

The Democratic Party had been defeated by a decisive margin. Governor Smith pointed out, however, that his party was the oldest political organization in the United States. Only half a million votes "properly distributed" would have given an Electoral College majority. A ten per cent change in the popular vote would have meant a Democratic popular majority. He considered the minority to be "a live, vigorous and forceful" party.[4] The *Baltimore Sun* urged its readers to note that the worst beaten Democratic candidate of modern times in the electoral vote, had received a higher percentage of the popular vote than Cox or Davis. The party was not dead, and it would continue to dominate in the South.[5] The *New York Times* agreed, saying more truly than it knew, "At the first serious slip, whether that comes a year, two years or three years from now, an Opposition [to the Republicans] will spring from the earth again like the men of Roderick Dhu." [6] Such had been the history of the American two-party system. "The closeness of this perennial contest gives plenty of continuing hope to both parties," said the *Times* later, "and affords ample proof that there is not likely to be a perpetual majority under a single party label in this country." [7]

Progressive Republicans took pleasure in the results. Senator George W. Norris stated that the Progressive cause had been given a complete endorsement.[8] La Follette considered that his followers had the positive duty to continue their activities "unflagging and unabated," [9] for not a single Progressive candidate for the Senate had failed of re-election. He was glad that Senator Shipstead— whom he called the father of the anti-injunction bill in the Senate— had been re-elected.[10]

[4] *Ibid.*, November 14, 1928.

[5] *Baltimore Sun,* (Independent), quoted in *ibid.*, November 8, 1928.

[6] Editorial, "Future of the Democratic Party," *ibid.*, November 11, 1928.

[7] *Ibid.*, December 26, 1928.

[8] George W. Norris, "The Meaning of the Recent Election," *La Follette Magazine,* XX (December, 1928), 181. He emphasized Senatorial races, not the Presidential race. There were seeds of trouble for the new President in the attitude of some Progressives.

[9] Editorial, "Election Reveals New Forces Set in Motion," *ibid.*, XX (November, 1928), 162.

[10] *Ibid.*, pp. 161-162.

As for Al Smith, he had held his last public office. "I heaved a deep sigh of relief," he wrote a few months later, "and felt that I was coming into a new freedom it had not been my pleasure to enjoy for a long while." [11] He was in the national tradition as he said in a postelection statement, "The American people have rendered their decision. I am a democrat, and I firmly believe in the rule of the majority." [12]

Labor leaders must have viewed the results wtih mixed emotions. William Green promptly wired Hoover, "Congratulations upon your most decisive election." This was easily the most formal of the twenty-six greetings published with it. At the convention of the American Federation of Labor in New Orleans late in November, the Executive Council's report on its political activities in 1928 was approved unanimously by the delegates.[13] When it was rumored that Governor Smith, vacationing in Mississippi, might address the convention, the delegates demonstrated noisily. He sent his regrets, however.

Daniel J. Tobin, his decade of hopes for Alfred E. Smith dashed to the ground, voiced an irritated post-mortem. Readers of the *Teamsters Magazine* were told that labor's forces had been divided in the election. The workers had not been fully organized politically, and no special enemy had been singled out for defeat. Tobin explained, somewhat prophetically, how he thought a "nonpartisan" political policy should be conducted.

> Simply sending out a statement stating that a certain representative or senator voted against certain Labor measures does not get very far. Fighting an enemy of Labor means that men should be sent into the district and an intensive campaign of opposition should be started against that individual, whether he be . . . Democrat or Republican. It would be better for the people to defeat one or two of its dyed-in-the-wool enemies than to scatter whatever strength it has promiscuously over a large territory and succeed in defeating nobody. . . .

[11] *Up to Now* (New York, 1929), p. 423.

[12] *New York Times*, November 8, 1928. Although the *Times* reporters or editors chose a capital "D," the present writer will take the liberty of challenging their judgment in this instance.

[13] American Federation of Labor *Proceedings, 1928,* 248.

This sort of action, in my judgment, is sufficient to make the average member of the house or senate pay very little attention to the forcefulness of Labor or to its demands or requests. However, perhaps out of the maelstrom there may come a better understanding, a brighter day. Perhaps continued utter defeat of the aspirations of Labor may arouse the rank and file of the membership from that lethargy which seems at the present time to have absolute control of the workers. I am not discouraged. . . .[14]

John P. Frey told his Molders union that farmers made noise about their troubles; labor should do likewise. Then the injunction would get some attention.[15] In the 1930s and later, Tobin and others would have, and seize, their chance to invigorate union political activity. In the meantime, there were leaders in the Federation who emerged from 1928 without his pessimism.

When the Executive Council brought in a full report on the 1928 results at the Toronto convention in 1929, for example, a more pleasant aspect was placed on the Congressional picture. In the House, 135 representatives with 100 per cent legislative records were said to have been elected, plus 110 whose records were termed exceedingly fair. It was not generally known, said the A. F. of. L., that thirty-nine Senators boasted 100 per cent prolabor records; fourteen of these had been elected in 1928. Fifteen Senators, in addition to the 39, were said to have fair records. Yet thirty-two Senators, on the other hand, rarely voted for labor measures. "The Senate is the most democratic branch of Congress. The Executive Council does not join with the croakers who are continually denouncing the United States Senate." The real trouble in Congress was said to lie in unfavorable leadership in the House, some of it "extremely reactionary." All in all, the nonpartisan policy of the Federation was said to have proved its worth more and more each year.[16]

After the assumption of labor to power in Great Britain in coalition with the Liberal Party, William Green was invited to write an article on the political policies of American labor. He wrote decisively that while he was pleased, he could not picture similar

[14] *Teamsters Magazine*, XXVI (December, 1928), 11.
[15] *International Molders Journal*, November, 1928, 150.
[16] A. F. of L. *Proceedings, 1929*, 88-89.

independent political methods in the United States. He described the far different geographical and racial problems in his own country, and asserted that American labor had developed an effective method of meeting its political needs. Persons in *both parties* had always been willing to help labor. Furthermore, "We believe that the progress of any one group is interdependent upon progress in all other groups." [17] The election of 1928 had done nothing, it appears, to shake Green's confidence in traditional pressure methods so long as they continued to be better organized.

W. C. Roberts, A. F. of L. legislative representative, told Green in blunt language what he thought. Attacks on the policies and officers of the A. F. of L., he said, come from "socialists, communists, college professors, and the intelligencia generally." *The meat of the attacks was always the refusal to form a Labor Party.* "I think all the attacks can be answered in one article showing who it is that is objecting to labor's policy and that they are obsessed with the determined purpose to destroy the American Federation of Labor." And a Labor Party would do just that. "If the American Federation of Labor will start a Labor Party all these people now attacking us will endorse us," Roberts judged wryly.[18] It was, by and large, an astute analysis of the situation in that day, although it was silent on such matters as craft versus industrial unionization and other key differences of opinion among students of labor at the time.

Two postelection political suggestions by labor leaders retain particular interest. President Green suggested that the A. F. of L. would have to get busy and organize women workers. It would be well, he said, to profit by the fact brought out during the campaign that women had been "a determining factor." As voters, women were being recognized by the parties. A. F. of L. unions should recognize their potential political power.[19] The other vastly prophetic point was raised by Daniel J. Tobin, who recalled that his New York Teamsters had sent a check for $3,000 to Chairman

[17] William Green, [Headline]: "A Labor Party Here?—Green Says 'No,' " *New York Times,* August 4, 1929.

[18] Roberts to Green, a memorandum, February 27, 1929, A. F. of L. Papers.

[19] William Green, "Women Workers," *American Federationist,* XXXV (December, 1928), 1430-1431.

Raskob for the Smith campaign and that small amounts had been contributed by Teamster bodies around the country. *"This is a new system," Tobin said, "which in time will work to the advantage of trade unionists."* Once, unions had their hands out, palm up, in a campaign. The new idea, "my idea," said Tobin, was to have labor support its friends financially. "Only in this way can labor ever expect to get anywhere, and this does not mean that it is necessary that the candidate shall belong to any special party." [20] The years ahead would see a remarkable extension of this idea, until labor would be a financial force in presidential politics (whether publicly partisan or not). In 1928 the Washington bureau of the Republicans issued over 1,300 news and feature releases and printed 80 pamphlets in about 50 million copies; the Democrats did likewise (150 different pamphlets) in an unknown number of copies.[21] In later elections, organized labor alone would seek to exceed such totals.

II

After the election there continued to be interest in Socialist circles in somehow building a mass party. Certain liberals or progressives with pleasant memories of 1924 also felt the old urge. "What about forming a PROGRESSIVE PARTY at an early date?" wrote one of these.[22] *The building of a new party by the Socialists was to be accomplished, if possible, at the expense of the Democratic Party.*[23] But the Democratic Party organization was neither conveniently dead nor dying. It was true that the party had received only 40.8 per cent of the vote. Yet the party had polled more votes than ever before, and it actually led the Republicans in more counties in the North, Middle West, and Far West than it had in

[20] *Teamsters Magazine*, XXVI (December, 1928), inside front cover.
[21] Casey, "Party Campaign Propaganda," pp. 100-102.
[22] A manufacturer's agent to Frank P. Walsh, November 5, 1928, A. F. of L. Papers.
[23] "Labor Movement Faces the Crossroads," *New Leader*, November 17, 1928. "How About That New Political Party?" *ibid.*, November 24, 1928, Thomas, quoted in *New York Times*, November 26, 1928. Louis Stanley, "A Trade Union Movement Without Idealism," *New Leader*, December 8, 1928. Thomas, "Why Not a New Party?" *North American Review*, CCXXVII (February, 1929), 143-150.

the three-cornered contest of 1924.[24] During the campaign Senator David I. Walsh had stated after visiting national headquarters of his party, "For the first time in many years we will have a Democratic campaign organization this year to match the Republican in effectiveness and influence." [25] Chairman Raskob, Franklin Roosevelt, Mrs. Roosevelt, and others had breathed new life into the party organization, and this did not die with election day. Socialists, having themselves stressed the virtues of organization, might well have treated that of the venerable Democrats with greater awe. A leading Communist saw the truth more clearly than some in post-election weeks:

> Is the Democratic Party dead? Far from it. Mr. Smith had about 15 million votes. Fifteen million votes are not to be sneezed at in American politics. It is the biggest vote a defeated American presidential candidate ever got.[26]

A quiet meeting of Thomas supporters was held on December 15 to discuss opportunities in new party action. A form letter from Paul H. Douglas, Sherwood Eddy, and Norman Thomas said,

> It seems highly important that we begin now to plan a campaign of political education that will bear fruit at the election four years hence. It has occurred to us that it might be advisable to form an American Fabian Society under some appropriate name, composed of men and women who are equipped to write on political subjects and who are desirous of building an effective opposition party in this country.[27]

Among those at the meeting were Paul Porter, Reinhold Niebuhr, Morris L. Ernst, and Oswald Garrison Villard.[28] Thomas told the group, "It ought to be possible for Socialists and Progressives to get together." United around a Douglas-drafted statement of principles, the League for Independent Political Action was born. Douglas would soon dedicate a book, *The Coming of a New Party*

[24] Edgar Eugene Robinson, *The Presidential Vote*, 1896-1932, pp. 27, 25. While many counties were lost in the South, this was temporary.
[25] *New York Times*, July 27, 1928.
[26] Jay Lovestone, "The 1928 Elections," *The Communist*, VII (December, 1928), 744.
[27] Form letter addressed to Frank P. Walsh, October 31, 1928, Walsh Papers.
[28] James Oneal, *Some Pages of Party History* (New York, 1924?), pp. 8-9.

(New York, 1932), to Thomas. The New York State Liberal Party and Labor Party of later years were having their intellectual birth pangs.[29] Organization would be absolutely essential, wrote Thomas,[30] and the Socialists took steps to ease this by revising their constitution to make it simpler for non-Socialists to affiliate.[31] In the next election (the mayorality contest in New York City),[32] the party stressed local issues, hoping that the larger goal, the socialist state, might be realized in future years.

Norman Thomas was unable to reach the emotions of union men in 1928, although he campaigned from coast to coast and succeeded in polling a quarter of a million votes. Intense voter interest in the personalities of Hoover, "the great engineer," and Smith, the candidate from "the sidewalks of New York," had been too much for his ministerial training. He had fought like a drowning man to be heard against the tide of interest in the prohibition question and what some thought was the impending arrival of the Pope in American politics.[33] In common with many another intellectual, Thomas had deplored religious prejudice in the campaign.[34] Over and over he said the worker needed political organization. Really strong unions can only come, said the Socialist candidate, in company with philosophy and spirit which would express itself in the *political* field. Surely the workers could see that they would have to get their own party. The nation was looking to labor to bring the new and happier social order.[35] The labor party would be the "tool," the "instrument to use in erecting that city of our dreams." [36] In an essay, "The Poor Old Democratic Party," Norman Thomas continued to seek a political realignment that would bring "a conservative party representing the interests of a comparatively small class

[29] See Waldman, *Labor Lawyer*, pp. 284-299, and Hugh A. Bone, "Political Parties in New York City," *American Political Science Review*, XL (April, 1946), 272-282.
[30] Thomas, "Why Not a New Party?" p. 148.
[31] "The Socialists Loosen Up," *World Tomorrow*, XII (March, 1929), 105.
[32] Waldman, *Labor Lawyer*, pp. 179-180; *New Leader*, December 8, 1928.
[33] These two questions were "spiritous" and "spiritual" matters far removed from the real business of politics, said a party spokesman. *New York Times*, July 14, 1928.
[34] For one of his strong protests, see *New Leader*, October 6, 1928.
[35] Norman Thomas in a standard address delivered while on tour in the West. *New Leader*, September 28, 1928.
[36] Thomas to International Ladies Garment Workers convention, May 14, 1928, I.L.G.W.U. *Proceedings, 1928*, 101.

of owners" on the one side, and "a radical party representing the
interests of the producing masses both as workers and consumers"
on the other.[37] The Socialist Party would produce the latter, somehow. "Even as early as 1928, when I ran for President," said
Thomas much later, "it was with the view of creating a nucleus or
spearhead or a focal point (use any figure of speech you will) for
a grouping like the British Labour Party, adapted to American
life." And in the perspective of two decades, he judged:

> A certain number of ideas I have succeeded to a certain ex-
> tent in getting out. But the thing I wanted to do was to build a
> party, which need not necessarily have called itself the Socialist
> Party, but in it Socialism would have been the vital element. It
> would have been like the C.C.F. Party in Canada, like the British
> Labour Party, except I don't want it dominated as extensively
> by unions as in Britain. That hasn't happened. Whether what I
> wanted will be achieved in other ways by what I thought was
> impossible, namely, the transformation of the Democratic Party,
> I don't know; it's conceivable.[38]

Can we now say with precision why the Socialist Party campaigned in 1928? The evidence seems clear enough. It was to make
sure that its action in bowing to the Progressive label four years
before [39] would not make the United States forget its name. It was
to keep its methods and its beliefs separate from those of the Communists in the public mind. It was to spread the party doctrine
abroad in the land and expose "inadequacies" of capitalism. It
was to build new Socialist leadership to fill the void left by the
death of Debs. It was to try to attract the support of Progressives,
liberals, or others who might be tired of their old political homes in
the Republican and Democratic parties. It was to expose the
alleged similarity between the old parties on major economic issues.
It was to try to break organized labor away from support of the
major parties and from its traditional "nonpartisan" policy.

Above all, it was to entice labor into forming a new party in
company with farmers, and *under Socialist leadership,* thus destroy-

[37] *Milwaukee Leader* editorial page, November 20, 1928.
[38] Thomas to Oral History Project, Spring, 1949, p. 147.
[39] The C.P.P.A. got on the ballot in some states like California, however, by using
the name of the Socialist Party.

ing the traditional two-party pattern in America. In the Executive
Committee, Socialist Party, meeting of November 25, 1928, a new
Committee on Labor and Labor Organizations was formed to
"establish friendly relations between the Socialist Party and organized labor; to encourage and assist in all efforts to organize the
unorganized; to aid in Labor struggles and to state the Party's
position on all matters pertaining to Labor policy and Labor
needs." [40]

During the campaign of 1928 Norman Thomas put the over-all
goal succinctly:

> To awaken the desire for that party, to show labor what is and
> what might be, to sound forth again the trumpet call that shall
> never sound retreat, that is the purpose of the Socialist Party in
> America as in every country, in this as in every campaign.[41]

The Socialist state was the ultimate goal and the balanced two-
party system in America the chief obstacle to its attainment. A
great working-class party composed of strong trade unions but
guided in important things by Socialist leaders would be the political weapon which might one day bring the longed-for socialist state.

Norman Thomas did not get what he wanted, then or later, and
his enthusiastic admirers should weigh carefully his own retrospec-
tive appraisal: "I consider that my career in certain respects has
very definitely been a failure. The things I cared most about I have
not succeeded in doing, but I don't believe that my failure has been
utter. It's not such a terrible failure that everything is black!" [42]
When, in 1952, Thomas added specific re-evaluations, his meaning
is clarified. "The working class is not the Messiah which some of us
thought," he then said. State ownership should not be pressed too
far, for even under the most democratic theory and practice the
State will become "too huge, too cumbersome." With six Socialist
Party Presidential nominations and sixty-eight years behind him,
Thomas found that the American economy had developed "room
in it for individual ownership and individual effort." And the
Socialist Party should abandon the nominating of candidates for

---

[40] Minutes, New York City Meeting, November 24-25, 1928.
[41] *New Leader,* September 22, 1928.
[42] Thomas to Oral History Project, Spring, 1949, p. 147.

political office. Still, education of unionists would remain a worthwhile endeavor, since many modifications in the economy were
necessary despite the passage of years.[43] But these second thoughts
lay decades beyond 1928. In the light of conditions as they saw
them *at that time*, the Socialists wanted two things: frontal attacks
on the economy (Socialism), and a drastic change in the political
system (a mass party). But the year 1928 was an unfriendly environment in which Socialists might expect to maneuver their
theories into the scheme of things.

III

As American Federation of Labor leaders faced forward after
the election, the slogan "Double Union Membership in 1929" was
their curiously unrealistic watchword. The welfare activities of
automobile industry employers were severe handicaps to union
expansion. While the organization of the South was said to be
essential, this too was a dream. It was admitted that 1928 had seen
fewer injunctions than previously, but President Green promised
that "the full force and power of American labor" would be exerted
to try to influence Congress to grant relief from this major enemy.
There would be no compromise with the Communists—those who
sought "the destruction of the organized labor movement and
would substitute therefore class war and class hatred." The A. F.
of L. Executive Council told itself reassuringly, "As economic
statesmen, we are doing a constructive work second to no other
group in the country." [44] President Green stated goals before the
assembled union delegates at New Orleans:

> We are fighting that men and women might so appropriate to
> themselves the opportunities which our free institutions afford,
> that they may occupy that place in life to which their abilities
> and qualifications fit them.[45]

The election of 1928 had not altered the nature of the issues facing
labor; it had not changed the determination of the labor leaders to

[43] Norman Thomas, "Democratic Socialism—A New Appraisal," quoted in San
Francisco *Chronicle*, February 23, 1952.
[44] *New York Times*, November 18, 19, 21, 1928, A. F. of L. *Proceedings, 1928*, p. 7.
[45] *Ibid.*, p. 7.

meet them; and it had not modified to any great extent the tactics which would be used in seeking orderly change in the status quo.

In a pamphlet issued a few years later (1931) the Executive Council of the American Federation of Labor reviewed the political policies organized labor had followed for the past fifty years and found them good. The Federation was thought to have made numerous contributions to the political field. Measures advocated had been designed "to put principles of democracy to actual practice." The secret ballot, women's suffrage, primary laws, the initiative, referendum, and recall, and the direct election of senators had been labor-supported measures, according to the report.[46] While scarcely an impartial, complete, or satisfying version of American history, there can be little doubt that organized labor had been, in fact, a considerable aid to the reformers of the progressive era. In perspective of several years since 1928, the Executive Council felt that the "nonpartisan technique" had fostered both the spirit and the purposes of democracy. Wage earners had been able to secure action on vital principles "without institutionalizing" their political strength. Nonpartisan politics had brought labor a determining influence in elections and in the enactment of laws, the union leaders claimed expansively! Reactionaries who "lacked a broad vision of national progress" had been kept from office, so that "constructive representatives" might be elected.

Such bald assertions were, in their wording, typical of the long habit of union leaders to equate "unions" with "workers," and "good" government with "pro-labor" government.

The American Federation of Labor leaders claimed additionally that through the years they had exerted an influence on the selection of judges "who conceive of justice as equity in the concrete problems of life and work and not merely as a system of precedents." Much Federal and state legislation had been successfully attained; still, official labor policy in the past had been to avoid the extension of government regulation and control to private industry. Whenever government engaged in fact-finding or the presentation of services, it was a "help without hindrance." The first

[46] Pamphlet, *Fifty Years of Service* (n.p., A. F. of L., 1931), p. 14. The pamphlet consisted of part of the Report of the Executive Council for 1931.

"The Election Is Over—Now What?" From *United Mine Workers Journal*

half-century of A. F. of L. activity, in summary, was said to have helped prevent the crystallization of class barriers. The nation had been given "upstanding workers with the highest wage levels in the world and the highest standards of living." The Federation would try to solve the problem of extending those gains to backward areas while continuing to advance standards for those "in the front ranks of progress." [47]

A. F. of L. leaders had spoken out against the court injunction repeatedly in the 1920s, and in 1928 they had made it their primary rallying point. They had gone to great effort to gain passage for the Shipstead Bill in the Congress. After the election, fortified by the counsel of a battery of legal consultants (as has been seen), a new bill gradually came to supplant the old one. For this bill the Federation would rally the support of Progressive Republican Rep-

[47] *Fifty Years of Service*, pp. 14-15.

resentative Fiorello La Guardia and Progressive Republican Senator George Norris.

In 1932 the Norris-La Guardia Anti-Injunction Act was passed by a Democratic and Progressive Republican controlled Congress and signed by a Republican President.[48] The Congress contained virtually all of the legislators supported by labor leaders in 1928 and again in the Congressional elections of 1930. *The nonpartisan method had brought the grand prize.* The act in wording and in practice proved all-embracing on injunctions. It kept the Federal courts from utilizing injunctions aimed at curtailing labor activities during a dispute, by covering (allowing) almost all forms of labor conduct during a dispute, regardless of the harm it might cause. Writes Charles O. Gregory, the recognized authority on labor law, "for the first time in the federal area unions were free to exert organizational pressures against employers who did not yet recognize any union and did not employ union members." It was "the most far-reaching piece of labor legislation enacted to that time." A dozen states would subsequently enact similar laws.[49] Indeed, it was "the most pro-union piece of legislation ever enacted by Congress.[50] In two cases, Lauf vs. Skinner and Milk Wagon Drivers vs. Lake Valley Farm Products, the Supreme Court would prevent inferior courts from evading its provisions.[51]

Organized labor thus emerged victorious, for that day and time, in its long struggle to conquer the injunction, yellow-dog contracts,

[48] Some textbooks intimate that President Hoover signed the bill "with reluctance." During the campaign of 1928 he had said in his acceptance address, "We stand also pledged to the curtailment of excessive use of the injunction in labor disputes." Except that Hoover asked for and obtained the judgment of his Attorney General that the bill was constitutional (a perfectly proper action), there has been adduced no factual basis for allegations that the President longed to veto the bill.

[49] Charles O. Gregory, "Labor Law," *Encyclopaedia Britannica* (Chicago, 1957), XIII, pp. 548-9.

[50] Charles O. Gregory, *Labor and the Law* (New York, 1949, revised ed.), p. 469.

[51] A half-dozen standard books of labor history or labor economics checked by the writer give no credit to the A. F. of L. for its long fight against the injunction when they discuss passage of the Norris-La Guardia Act. Some suggest, thinly, that Felix Frankfurter deserves the credit—for writing a book on the subject. Others credit certain "experts" who helped the Congressional subcommittee. Yet each of these professors was originally asked by the A. F. of L. in summer, 1928, to interest himself in labor's problem. The bill would not have passed without A. F. of L. support, but this point is seldom mentioned by detractors. Philip Taft, *op. cit.,* presents a clear and accurate picture on the matter, fortunately.

and alleged abuses by courts and employers long decried in speeches, articles, letters, and pressure brought to bear on candidates and officeholders. In this way, in the backwash of a Presidential Election and without official national endorsement of a party or a Presidential candidate, did organized labor achieve its most emotionally expressed desires.

Chapter 14

Labor Politics in a Democratic Republic

THE YEAR 1928 had come and gone, and with it departed another of the Presidential Elections required every four years by the Constitution of the United States. At every level of government during the year, vast arrays of elective officials in office had been forced to offer themselves up to the judgment of the electorate at the ballot box, for there were other citizens who challenged their right to continue to govern; these also appealed to the electorate to help them achieve their objective. In most instances both the incumbent candidates and those who contested their future right to the administration of government office were nominees of political parties. Those parties were normally the Republican Party, born on the eve of the nation's Civil War, and the Democratic Party, descended from Jefferson and Jackson. Also contesting at the presidential level were a Socialist Party in existence since the turn of the century, and a Communist Party in its second campaign —both organized bodies with aspirations for power. All four would live on after the ballots were counted.

They consisted of small amounts of physical assets, rented buildings and typewriters, bank accounts and debts, and temporary files of correspondence in a number of parts of the nation. Additionally, the parties were composed of handfuls of salaried party workers and, more importantly, persons who held committee office in the party at national, state, county, and precinct levels. These party committeemen (and some women) were the party organization. The votes from 1928 had hardly been counted before some leaders among these politically astute people began to plan—some more actively than others—for the inevitably forthcoming Congressional Election of 1930 and the more distant but no less constitutionally inevitable Presidential Election of 1932.

The victorious party nominees of the 1928 election, meanwhile, rested briefly preparatory to being inducted into the offices they had won, or, if re-elected for new terms, they returned "to work" as had been their custom before the counting of the votes.

Elsewhere in American society in November and December the leaders of many pressure groups totaled up the election score and studied it to see whether past months of earnest effort— through meetings, resolutions, visits, letters, smiles, and threats— had resulted in net gains or losses in group prestige and power.

The voters—the "electorate"—having duly registered as party members, and thinking of themselves as somewhat partisan to party, to candidates, or to particular issues, quickly calmed themselves and waited for their elected representatives to do their duty. The voters were prepared to see victorious candidates they had opposed step forward to do their worst, confident that federal and state constitutions and laws would restrain excesses. The role of "the people" was temporarily at an end, although pen could still be taken in hand to express public discontent or enthusiasm.

Such was the nature of the American democratic republic. For many decades it had operated in this way. The people (that part of them found eligible under the Constitution and the statutory provisions of the states) had stepped forward to cast their votes for representatives of their own choosing. In the republican form of government that obtained, the persons elected were going to take office and govern by and with the consent of those who voted and those who did not, those who supported, and those who opposed.

I

Labor unions and leaders had participated in the election of 1928 in the guise of an organized pressure group, as individual spokesmen, and in the indistinguishable form of several million voters. To a severely limited extent, labor had also played some other roles on the election stage. To show the interaction of "labor" and "party" at the time it will be necessary to discuss these briefly as abstractions. In this way some truths about "labor pressure group" liaison with the "political party organizations" of 1928 may appear more clearly. The A. F. of L. and the Railway Brotherhoods were unquestionably the labor group. And the four organizations bearing party names have been central to this story from its outset.

The labor group seems to have played no part in the final selection of Smith, Hoover, Thomas, or Foster to be nominees of their parties, although the railway union men did do what they could to defeat a Hoover opponent in the primaries. Still, party leaders undoubtedly gave thought to the acceptability of Smith and Hoover to labor, for they remembered how those who built the third-party movement of 1924 had gagged at Coolidge and Davis. The state labor federations tried early and late to influence the selection of nominees for the House and Senate, for governor, and for legislative posts, but the degree of effort exerted was scarcely a semblance of that to come in later years. Union treasuries and membership were unequal to any such task at the time.

Labor leaders strove manfully to influence the wording of particular paragraphs in the platforms of the major parties. Perhaps they succeeded to some degree, negatively at least, but by their own protestations it is evident that they felt they failed in their efforts. Trying to cast major party platforms in their own image, they seemed to fail. Not caring what was in minor party platforms in 1928, they nevertheless obtained, *in absentis,* pledges of allegiance to many measures in which they believed—plus stalwart asseverations which they distrusted or detested.

It has been stressed here that political party machinery consists chiefly of elected and appointed officials who make the party label function as a reality between and during elections. The labor group

put surprisingly little effort into infiltrating the influential, but remote, world of precinct, county, and state party committees in the
late 1920s. Union journals of the day were almost wholly silent on
the importance of such action, and guidance on "how to do it" was
seldom offered by national labor headquarters or state federations
except, perhaps, in New York State. The labor group seems to
have visualized itself chiefly as negotiator with parties. The practice
of having labor leaders seek party office (precinct or county chairman, for example) was not officially furthered, although there is
little doubt that, even then, labor leaders in some cities did this
with some success.

Union leaders in several Socialist-oriented cities of the day
(Milwaukee, Bridgeport, Reading) certainly participated to the
hilt in the Socialist Party internal organization. A few subordinate
labor officials in some cities were undoubtedly members of the
Communist Party organization, despite the heated blasts against
such activity by top officials of their union hierarchy and the A. F.
of L. efforts to expel such persons in the middle 1920s.

In view of the inability of the labor leaders to agree fully *at the
outset* of the campaign of 1928 on any single political party vehicle
satisfying to their movement, it was impossible for them to have
much tangible effect on the building of either major party into a
better-organized machine for nominating labor-sensitive candidates
at the polls. A handful of individuals (Berry, Doak) did go into
action early within the national headquarters of the Democrats and
Republicans. Yet many labor leaders who publicly announced their
partisanship during the year merely lent their names—and little
else—to the party of their choice. They seemed to feel that one act
relieved them of any obligation to put time or effort at the disposal
of the candidate or party said by them to represent their choice.
Dan Tobin of the Teamsters saw clearly the futility of such limited
partisanship to a cause. Under the circumstances it is not surprising that the record shows so few instances where labor leaders were
consulted by party managers on details of party procedure. In
later years labor leaders would come to be consulted on occasion
by highly placed persons on "acceptable" Vice-Presidential candi-

dates and on party procedural matters, but in 1928 this was seldom the case.

Few, if any, plums available for party distribution came as rewards to labor leaders after 1928. Even the Labor Department cabinet post—long sought by organized labor in vain—evaded the overeager Duncan, the apparently willing Lewis, and other prominent figures in the A. F. of L. and the Brotherhoods. But Daniel Tobin was well on the way toward important position and influence in Democratic Party circles in the Roosevelt Administrations of the future, where his long-expressed philosophy calling for labor to be financially and officially aggressive on behalf of its stated needs was more than welcome.

The labor group did make some token contributions to party coffers in 1928. Here was a form of service to party destined to increase enormously in later elections.

Publicity in the form of cartoons and editorials partisan to Congressional candidates was clearly a contribution of organized labor to party success in 1928. The newspaper *Labor,* in particular, was a powerful force widely distributed and quoted in other parts of the labor press. But the Presidential candidates profited but little from trade union literature in 1928; neither were they hurt, except for the candidates of the Communist Party, who were attacked on the few occasions they were noticed.

From time to time, and in a rather matter of fact and perfunctory way, the labor group through articles in union journals urged members to *register* so that they might vote for candidates of their choice. Sources used do not report wholesale "get-out-the-vote" campaigns by city centrals, state federations, or very many unions. As William Green himself pointed out, the fact that women could and would vote and thereby might help or block union aspirations, was a factor largely ignored by the labor group.

All in all, when one looks at the influence of labor in the election year from such point of view, it is not hard to see why Smith failed to come close to carrying many cities and states where he had, on paper, the "support" of organized labor. Nor does the observer wonder at the casual attitude that major party managers and even campaigners assumed toward all but the most vigorously reiterated protests of injustice or of vital need from labor leaders who could then offer, after all, very little tangible support in a national election to a cooperative party and candidate. What believable threat could labor make at the time? When politicians spoke kindly of labor's expressed demands in that day (bearing in mind all that has been said), it is clear that they did so because they ran for office in closely contested electoral areas or because they believed, as a matter of personal principle, in the validity of labor's expressed aspirations.

II

The particular political policy eventually chosen by organized labor for use in the Presidential Election of 1928 was the traditional "nonpartisan" position. Candidates for President and Vice-President were not endorsed. Third-party formation was rejected or ignored. The fact of an American two-party system, where minor parties would come and go, was accepted without frontal challenge. An attempt was made by labor to utilize the possibilities thus offered for the bringing of pressure on parties and candidates, pressure designed to change laws and customs to accord with the desires of union leaders.

Before the conventions, Smith and Hoover were considered personally friendly to organized labor, with a decided edge going to the New York governor. The officers of the New York state federation endorsed Smith for the Democratic Party nomination and asked other state federations to follow suit. The Railroad Brotherhoods rallied to the support of Hoover in certain state primaries in order to defeat Dawes—a candidate considered unfriendly. The Executive Council of the American Federation of Labor saw to it that the problem of endorsing candidates for the major nominations did not arise prematurely.

The chief objective of the A. F. of L. in 1928 was to further the long struggle against the issuance of injunctions in labor disputes. Pressure was brought to bear on Congress in the spring to pass legislation to that effect. Although hearings were held and publicity was obtained, no law resulted at the time. *Yet the groundwork had been laid.* Articles and cartoons in the labor press, speeches by labor leaders, and attention paid the injunction by various politicians all show the significance of the injunction. In New York, Governor Smith continued in 1928, as he had in previous years, to ask the Legislature to act to remedy this injunction problem.

The leaders of the A. F. of L. appeared before the platform committees of the two major parties to present a list of their legislatives desires. Hospitably received by both parties, they obtained more in the labor planks of the Democrats than the Republicans. The minority platform presented in the Republican convention had a far stronger labor plank than the one adopted by the majority. The A. F. of L. made no gestures toward the conventions of the Socialist Party or the Communist Party.

As the close of the conventions, William Green indicated dissatisfaction with both platform planks on the injunction grievance. The next hope was for more favorable stands by the nominees in their acceptance speeches, and both Hoover and Smith were informed of this, with Smith showing the deepest interest. At the Atlantic City meeting of the A. F. of L. Executive Council, in the meantime, the next political step for the unions was hotly debated. Should Al Smith, deeply respected, be endorsed officially? (There was no chance at all for a Hoover endorsement.) Restrained by lifelong Democrat William Green but spurred on by lifelong Democrat Dan Tobin, the Council resolved to sit out the Presidential race without overt partisanship.

The appeal which Herbert Hoover made to wage earners in 1928 did not give close attention to the specific demands of union leaders. He did not go as far on the injunction as they wished, and he did not mention unions or various of their favorite legislative items. Many labor leaders shared in 1928 the fundamental beliefs of the Republican candidate on the proper relationship which should obtain between government and the individual. The A. F. of L. definitely wanted government to leave it free to settle its problems in its own way. This was in itself a rugged independence on the part of organized labor which would be abandoned gradually in the 1930s.

The appeal of Governor Smith was framed with more attention to the desires of organized labor than was that of Hoover. Smith had learned from many years as governor of an industrial state that it was worthwhile to heed the desires and complaints of state labor leaders. His speeches as a Presidential candidate showed awareness of the desires of national labor leaders, thus reflecting the influence of his experience in New York—as well as his own convictions on such matters. Smith's position on the injunction came far closer to satisfying labor leaders than did that of his leading opponent. The union leaders who supported the Republican candidate never said they did so on the injunction issue, but those supporting Smith mentioned it as a point in his favor. They often bragged about his prolabor record in New York State.

There is evidence that unemployment was quite moderate in 1928 and that it dropped steadily during the course of the campaign. The efforts of the Democrats to convince the nation that prosperity was mythical did not bring them tangible (or, in any event, measurable) results at the polls.

III

There proved to be much outright favoritism toward the Democratic Party in the nonpartisan policy of A. F. of L. and Railroad Brotherhood units in the election of 1928. Partisanship toward individual candidates was the rule rather than the exception in United States Senate and House races. The New York State Federation of Labor was almost entirely partisan to the Democratic Party in state and national races, but other states often saw labor leaders dividing their support in various national and state races. High officials of a number of state federations permitted their names to be used by the Democratic National Committee, and the presidents and other officials of key A. F. of L. unions did the same. A few union conventions endorsed Smith officially, and many city centrals and local unions did so, especially in the Northeastern section of the country where Smith was well and favorably known. There is little evidence of similar action in behalf of Hoover.

The Republican candidate had the support of a few labor leaders, especially in Railroad Brotherhood unions. Temperance sentiment was a factor in alienating some of these leaders from the

Smith candidacy, for the railroad union leaders had a long tradition of opposition to what they called "booze"; yet other union
leaders (teamsters, bartenders, etc.) found Smith attractive on the
same issue.

Considering that he had been a two-term Democratic state legis-
lator in Ohio, William Green preserved to a remarkable degree an
air of personal impartiality. His reward for abstinence was the
absence in postelection analyses and comments of catcalls that the
defeat of the Democratic candidate was a defeat for organized
labor. After the experiences of 1920 and 1924 this was a relief.
No doubt the former delegate to several Democratic national
conventions felt rewarded.

The position of Daniel J. Tobin was that of an outright Smith
partisan. Considering the enthusiastic support he would give
Franklin D. Roosevelt in later years, the kind words he had to say
about the character and abilities of Hoover have wry interest.
Tobin wanted labor to pursue a more aggressive "nonpartisanship,"
a word he clearly interpreted to mean its opposite. He urged that
unions lend financial support to his political favorites, but there
was little of this at the time. In 1928 the unions were not quite
ready to take the plunge.

The overwhelming victory of the Republican Party, its third in
a row, did not crush the Democratic Party. Its administrative machinery was, if anything, somewhat improved. Much hitherto certain ground in the South had been lost, of course, but there were
ample reasons to believe that the secessions were of the moment.
The Socialist Party and the Communist Party were able to obtain
only a small fraction of the vote, and there was no evidence in the
voting trend figures to indicate a bright future at the polls for
either organization.

It does not seem possible to determine if a "labor vote" existed
in 1928. In view of the large majorities Hoover received in every
section of the nation, however, it seems inescapable that more than
a majority of wage earners rallied to his support (or opposed his
opponents). Union members and leaders who read union publications regularly and weighed heavily the importance of the injunction and the much noted prolabor record of Governor Smith may

have been thereby inclined to vote Democratic. The number of these "interested" union men cannot be estimated.

The intra-union political propaganda circulated by A. F. of L. national headquarters to publicize its viewpoints was infinitely less than would appear in later years at the hands of labor's political committees. Its chief goal was to influence the outcome of particular Congressional races. The Brotherhoods were more aggressive, relying on their weekly newspaper *Labor* to keep their policies uniform. Extensive borrowing of cartoons and political material from this common source made Brotherhood journals take on a similarity of appearance, content, and viewpoint not always typical of A. F. of L. monthlies. The latter were united on the injunction, child labor and prison labor, immigration, and similar issues—but these had been customarily publicized for years. A. F. of L. union journals almost completely failed as a group to take stands on Congressional candidates by name. Clearly, the political persuasion machinery of the greater A. F. of L. organization was entirely inadequate to its task in 1928.

IV

The Communist political alternative was rejected by union members and by the American people in general. It was denounced by the leaders of the A. F. of L. and was scarcely mentioned by the chiefs of the Brotherhoods. Those who bore the title of Presidential or Vice-Presidential candidate were totally ignored. But Communist efforts to infiltrate or rival the orthodox unions were much noticed and loudly opposed.

The Communists referred constantly in the 1920s to "revolution" or "conflict" or "upheaval" as means whereby they would one day attain their ends. They evaded precise definitions. Their attitude toward democratic institutions—the courts, legislatures, laws, and elections—was belligerent and antagonistic. They specifically rejected any idea that they could muster the approval of majorities of voters—thus attaining power through the use of existing election machinery in the nation.

During the campaign the Communists of the United States were operating as a "section" of the Third International (Comintern). They obeyed the orders of its Executive Committee. The outspokenly expressed purposes of the Communist Party in the campaign of 1928 were to mobilize the working class, to develop increased class consciousness, to abolish capitalism, and to bring about the "overthrow" of the "present form" of society. Existing laws and courts were called obstacles to be circumvented. These were the purposes and attitudes expressed by Communist candidates and party literature. Both stressed the fact that the workers could never vote their own "emancipation." This point of view cannot be passed off as merely defeatist; though tiny, here was a recognizable menace to constitutions, compliance with laws, and the traditional machinery of self-government.

The goal of the Socialist Party was openly and repeatedly said to be *the creation of a socialist state*. The method chosen to seek this goal was the nomination of candidates and participation in democratic elections. Unequivocably rejected as pathways to power were force, violence, or revolution. When Socialist leaders stood as candidates for political office, they felt that they performed an educational function on behalf of Socialism and thereby brought the socialist state nearer. This was considered true whether they won or not. While they cherished the hope that in 1928, or before too long, they might win offices as the candidates of their beloved Socialist Party, their real hope of attaining power, of gaining control of the national and state governments, lay elsewhere.

The Socialists anticipated that an alliance or a coalition might someday be formed between themselves, the trade unions, and the farmers. A new political party might be born of such an alliance! Since class-conscious "workers of the mind" would also be included, in theory, it seemed reasonable to expect that the "new party" would so outnumber the opposition as to continue to win elections indefinitely once power might at length be obtained. The new party—a "social democratic" party like those in Europe, or a "Labour Party" like that in Britain—would derive its ideology from the Socialists and much of its organizational strength from the trade unions. This was the theory. The opposition parties would consist of any who opposed the Socialist program, presumably.

In order to facilitate formation of the new mass party, Socialists worked and hoped for the creation of trade unions with greater numerical strength. Only as union organization reached a high point could political realignment be brought to pass. Meanwhile, union leaders and members would have to be educated to accept Socialist leadership and the idea of independent party politics as superior to the "nonpartisan" or pressure paths of years past. Morris Hillquit pointed out that the Socialists would have to make their peace with the "reactionary political policies" and "other objectionable features" of the A. F. of L., for backward though it might be, it represented "the political mentality of the organized labor movement of America." The task of the Socialists was "to aid, persuade, and educate the movement and not to knock it over the head." [1] Socialists denied that as a party they had any intention of seizing power within the unions or of setting up rival or dual organizations. In these matters they contrasted sharply with the Communists.

The Socialist Party advocated extensive reforms in 1928. For this reason many of its most enthusiastic, vocal, and effective proponents were not themselves "class struggle pledge" Socialists, but amateurs in politics whose interest was to further particular reforms contained in the Socialist Party platform (including a break-up of the existing parties). These persons were not necessarily dedicated to the idea of class struggle, nor were they uniformly and aggressively in favor of state ownership and operation of the means of production, communication, distribution, and of natural resources. *Thus there was a basic Socialist doctrine.* (One must accept the Socialists at their word.) On the other hand, there was a listing of desired reforms, many of them later judged worthwhile, which the party of Debs and Thomas helped reformers to sponsor from time to time. The party sugar-coated some of its more bitter pills. Maurer told a Milwaukee audience, for example, that "under Socialism there will be more private property owned than under pres-

---

[1] Hillquit letter to editor, *Student Worker,* March 10, 1932. The editor had called the A. F. of L. part of incipient American fascism; Hillquit's letter was one of rebuke at an editorial that had been a "painful disappointment."

ent capitalism. But property used will be publicly owned." [2] This seems to be a monumental evasion.

Norman Thomas outspokenly reiterated his devotion to civil and religious liberties. There is no cause to doubt the depth of his personal belief in democratic electoral processes. He simply did not believe that the creation of a large state machinery of appointive employees might take away individual freedoms. Nor did he think it would prove inefficient. The platform on which Thomas and Maurer ran lacked "economic theology," and Thomas seldom discussed Socialism in any detail or at much length. It does not appear that Thomas really faced the enormous problems that an attempt to impose his doctrine on a highly industrialized America would have entailed. He certainly suspected that the day when he might personally have the opportunity to put words into practice was many years off. Yet there was always the British example. Power *might* be his! In any case, Norman Thomas tended to concentrate in 1928 (and also in 1929, when he ran for mayor of New York City) on particular reforms.

V

A brief analysis of some reasons why the Socialist and Communist appeals to the trade unions brought such meager response in 1928 seems in order. Socialist and Communist leaders offered through the years many reasons for their failures (*not* including the nature of their doctrines) and former party members have suggested others. This writer will present, briefly, a point of view that seems plausible.

The limited development of class consciousness in the United States was, in 1928, a primary obstacle to these two groups. Few Americans thought of themselves as "proletarians" or were willing to do so. The term "workers" was infrequently used as a class term. Largely responsible for this attitude were the size, riches, and resources of the nation compared with its population. Then there was the manner of its settlement by specially selected (often self-

[2] *Milwaukee Leader,* October 15, 1928.

selected) individuals, and the migration of its people, after arrival, into ever-expanding frontiers. Individualism had long been a national trait. The wide distribution of real and personal property among a property-conscious people made it difficult for Americans of the day to take seriously any who propagated the idea of *collective* ownership as a substitute for *individual* ownership. And *state* ownership seemed no more real as a goal. The fact that immigrants of varied habits and languages had built America forced class consciousness to compete with group consciousness and awareness of race, religion, and national origin. The curtailment of immigration, on the other hand, had by 1928 made the possessors of jobs feel more secure. The rates of naturalization were high; those just ushered into citizenship must have been loathe to attack what they had only just come to understand and respect. The basic words of American documents meant something personal to these newcomers.

Moreover, American industrial workers have long had the reputation of disliking or hating neither their jobs nor their employers to the extent common abroad. It was in 1928 that Bukharin said in the World Congress of the Comintern that the American working class is the most conservative in the world.[3] Conditions of employment in the United States were then infinitely superior to those in most lands overseas. Machinery had, by 1928, taken over much back-breaking manual labor. Increased attention by employers to the welfare of employees decreased discontent and made the organizational work of the unions difficult and that of radical groups very trying. The determined and sometimes violent opposition which radicals encountered at times in the nation's history from local police, backed up solidly by the "best elements" and orthodox unions as well, was a handicap to the Communists; to a far less degree the Socialists may also have been somewhat affected. Efforts on the local level to suppress basic freedoms did hold down the spread of radical ideas to some extent, no doubt, and this factor should not be passed over in silence. Since the Communists preached a doctrine of extralegal violence, however, it is not surprising that they reaped their share of violence.

[3] Quoted in *Daily Worker*, October 3, 1928.

Both Socialists and Communists had acute organizational difficulties. The vast size of the nation made it difficult, even in a day
of swift communications, to develop a sense of national unity in
state groups whose leaders seldom saw each other. Internal fights
and disagreements which stemmed from race differences, language
barriers, and sectional feeling hurt both movements. The Communists were rent most of the time by highly verbalized internal
factional fights—whatever the veneer of unanimity presented to the
world. Personal dislikes were common. The one primary motive of
the combatants was to be held in even momentary esteem by the
Soviet managers of the Third International. Thus at one time of
sharp argument among American Communist leaders, Joseph
Stalin himself said the key men in the United States "section"
were "guided by motives of unprincipled factionalism and place
the interests of their faction higher than the interests of the Party."
Each of the factions in the "American section," added Stalin in
this speech to a World Congress of the Third International, base
their relations with the Comintern "not on the principle of confidence but on a policy of rotten diplomacy, a policy of diplomatic
intrigue." [4] William Z. Foster was singled out by Stalin for special
castigation.

Communist organization, administration, and methods of ac-
complishing objectives were in that day not of the best. The Communists were only too obviously agitators first, organizers second.
They used a strange language peppered with unusual words, a
means of communication totally strange to the defined "proletariat." Several years after the election of 1928, one J. Tsirul wrote
a vigorous official criticism of the way the American comrades
performed their duties.[5] There had been, he said, a decline in

[4] *Stalin's Speeches on the American Communist Party* (May 6, 14, 1929) (New
York?, Central Committee, Communist Party, U.S.A., 1930), p. 12. Rival radical
groups thought it remarkable that this pamphlet should have been reprinted by those
who were criticized.

[5] S. [sic] Tsirul, *The Practice of Bolshevik Self-Criticism; How the American Communist Party Carries Out Self-Criticism and Controls Fulfillment* [sic] *of Decisions*
(New York, September, 1932). A pamphlet reprinted from the magazine *Communist
International*, IX. Inside title page: "The Central Committee of the Communist
Party of the U.S.A. wishes to give this article the widest possible circulation amongst
the Party membership and is therefore publishing it as a pamphlet." The present
writer could detect no variation from the original. Tsirul based his observations on

"factory cells" in the United States from 166 in 1927 to 111 in 1928. There had been in the latter year only 465 "street cells." Was there any guarantee, he asked, that these cells did not exist only on paper? Then there was too much "routine, officiousness, bureaucracy," and he wondered what had happened to the vaunted American efficiency. Cell meeting minutes showed that they were of a dry and bureaucratic character and contained too few political discussions of burning questions of the day.

This critic, writing in the official organ of the Executive Committee of the Communist International, charged further that "the leadership of the cells is strictly centralized and cut off from actual life." No wonder members quit after a few of these tedious and uninteresting meetings, he said. He called the membership turnover "appalling." Although ten thousand new members joined every year, the total membership still did not rise above ten thousand! There were too many "dry, formal reports . . . subscription lists to collect contributions, and newspapers to be distributed. . . ." New members joined in spite of the American Communist leadership—not because of it. Living in a fetishism of resolutions, drawing them up but not following them, Tsirul concluded that their *words* of self-criticism, at least, were "said very well." [6]

Without going to similar length, very brief reference may be made to the dispute over "militancy" which would shake the Socialist Party at the time of its Detroit Convention in 1934. Bitter words then passed between the "old guard" and the "militants" and there was ample evidence that the cleavage of the 1920s on racial and linguistic lines continued. It has already been observed that the Socialists of America were divided in 1928 between the college men and those priding themselves on being "workers." There was resentment toward Socialists who crossed over to write for "liberal" publications. James Oneal and Paul Blanshard considered such activity inconsistent with their "kind" of Socialism. Efforts to create a so-called respectable liberal front in and for the party irritated

personal inspections of American conditions. His identity cannot be determined by the present writer; but the card for the pamphlet in the Jefferson School Library, New York, is the authority for change of the author's name in my text from "S." to "J." Tsirul, since the card specifically says he is the "real" author.

[6] *Ibid.*

some who remembered Debs as an agitator, not an author. Thus James Oneal, editor of the *New Leader* in 1928, wrote in retro-spect:

> The Socialist movement is primarily a movement of working people, a class that needs no neglected geniuses of the academic and professional world to lead it; a class that must select and educate its leaders from its own ranks; a class self-directed and disciplined, relying on its own powers and ability to pilot its course to its emancipation from servitude and class rule.

In the old days, he said, the Socialist Party had been rooted in "the proletarian life of the country." [7]

There are still other reasons, of course, why both the Communist and Socialist parties failed in their efforts in 1928. Socialist Mayor J. Henry Stump of Reading, Pennsylvania, told a group of party members in Philadelphia to "Americanize" the party and "quit fighting labor, organized and unorganized." They should cease thinking in European terms. Socialists in Reading behaved decently and took the part of labor, he observed, saying that less theory and more practical effort would be a great help.[8]

The fact that the vocal "internationalism" of both Socialists and Communists which paid at least lip service to world-wide class unity went counter to the patriotic and (at the time) self-sufficient leanings of average Americans may have been an important ob-stacle to their expansion. A catastrophic weakness was the Com-munist antagonism toward religion. Observers at the Fish Com-mittee hearings of 1930, or readers of the hearings, whatever their personal beliefs, certainly experienced justifiable irritation at the handbills and songs of a group which termed Old Testament figures cowards, drunkards, and murderers. Over-all, the Communists vastly misunderstood, as have many non-Communists then and since, *the power of ideals in American history.*

[7] James Oneal, *Some Pages of Party History* (New York, pub. by author, 1934?), p. 27 *et passim.* See also Louis Waldman, *Labor Lawyer* (New York, 1944).
[8] *New York Times,* March 26, 1928.

VI

Greatest of the obstacles facing the Communist, Socialist, and other minor parties in the United States, probably, were the nation's democratic institutions. These, and especially the fluidity of major parties in the long run, have made orderly changes possible. Selig Perlman, the great labor economist, expressed the point with his usual vigor when he wrote, "In my view, the American party, especially the Democratic Party, is a remarkable shock absorber and shock deadener, and we are lucky not to have 'class parties.' " [9]

Government under law in America has been closer to the judicial ideals than the words of radicals would lead one to believe. The day-to-day administration of government on national, state, and local levels in the United States has not been typified on the whole by the extreme examples lovingly selected and then dwelt upon year after year by such organs as the *Daily Worker, The Communist,* and similar monolithic periodicals.

The working people of Seattle were told in 1928 by Vice Presidential candidate Benjamin Gitlow that Communists in the United States do not hope to carry their policies through the ballot box, but that this campaigning would "afford the opportunity to incite workers to an uprising against the capitalists, to have them rise and seize the tools of production." [10] What was supposed to be the reaction of the sons of pioneer stock in the Far West to such talk as this? William E. Borah came close to putting an important essential in a few words when he said at the time, "The American people divide into parties, but whether Democrats or Republicans, they are first and above all devoted to our Government." [11]

Because conditions have been less than perfect for many in the nation, it has been important that democratic institutions have not denied reformers the chance to agitate for change. It is not too much to say that the men and women who have sought to remove or modify capitalism's bad features while retaining its basic charac-

---

[9] Letter of December 28, 1949, to the present writer.
[10] *New York Times,* September 30, 1928.
[11] *Ibid.,* April 29, 1928.

teristics have, in the course of winning innumerable victories, kept down agitation for total change in the "system." The Populists and various types of progressives and liberals, in their turn, have stood squarely athwart the path toward violent upheaval. Conservatives, by finally concurring on the desirability of many reforms, and then helping through administration to make them work, have kept impatient reformers from achieving permanent power.

VII

There are other broad implications that arise from a close consideration of the minor party alternatives of 1928. The instrumentality through which the voice of the people has gradually come to reflect itself in governmental action in the United States is the two-party system. The two major parties have had in them substantial parts of the population from every section of the nation and from every economic level of society, despite the usually one-sided nature of party allegiance in the Deep South. Except in 1860, the parties have not been completely polarized by sections. With the vast increase in the feminine vote by 1928, they were not limited to particular strata of society, except for artificial limitations on the franchise of Negroes in certain states. And it was ordinarily possible in the nineteenth and twentieth centuries for groups in the population possessing a temporary common interest to form a new party, challenging the supremacy of the other two.

Al Smith put it this way: "Political parties are the vehicles for carrying out the popular will. We place responsibility upon the party." [12] After the election he said when contemplating the status of his defeated Democratic Party, "The existence of such a party is necessary under our system of government. The people rule negatively as well as affirmatively, and a vigorous and intelligent minority is a necessary check upon the tyranny of the majority." The minority party had a duty to formulate a program and to defend it. An educational body, it would inform the electorate. *As for one's attitude in defeat, "No matter with what party we aligned*

[12] *New York Times,* August 23, 1928.

ourselves on election day, our concern should be for the future welfare, happiness, content and prosperity of the American people." [13] Here was the credo of Alfred E. Smith, self-styled "plain, ordinary man who had received during his lifetime, to the fullest possible extent, the benefit of the free institutions of his country." [14]

One admits readily that rapid change has not been the rule under the two-party system. Yet orderly progress has been the rule rather than the exception, even if to those close to the event improvement has sometimes seemed to come by fits and starts. This progress—*not* "capitalist laws"—has kept down extreme radicalism. The responsiveness of democratic processes in America must be counted a great barrier to those who urge changing the rules of the game. This responsiveness is something which *must* be preserved, even though its preservation has often posed problems for legislators. The political methods of both the Socialist Party ("we need a labor party") and the Communist Party ("proletarians unite") might well operate to reduce or totally eliminate the opportunity to undo mistakes and bring innovations without general upheaval. This point warrants further attention.

The Communists, once in power, would not permit the maintenance of the opposition party machinery which would make possible modification or elimination of the new "system." In Soviet Russia in that day, Trotskyites found persecution and exile their assigned lot, even though they had helped make the Revolution. The result of the Communist idea of "party" in Soviet Russia after the passage of decades was rule by a tiny minority of a party minority—all in the name of the majority. This is not *democracy* as the word is used in the United States.

The Socialist Party political program then and since has been termed "democratic socialism" by its advocates. Socialist spokesmen talked the language of democracy, and many of the *reforms* advocated by them in 1928 (and at the same time by *non-*Socialists) have been adopted by the representatives of the majority of the American people through the years. In this sense they performed, though out of office, a visible educational function. But

---

[13] *Ibid.,* November 14, 1928.
[14] Alfred E. Smith, *Up to Now* (New York, 1929), p. 424.

the relation of the Socialist political and economic program to the two-party system needs brief consideration.

Polarization of the parties by economic or social classes would never lead in practice, to greater political democracy in America. The Socialist-urged mass party would include, by definition at least, the "workers," the "working" farmers, and "workers of the mind." Against it would be aligned, one must assume, all those not included in these large groups. *The Socialist presumption seems to be that their "mass party" would overwhelm all political opposition at the polls in every election.* Having defined a majority for themselves (an easier thing to do than to assemble one), they have presumed that its hitherto conflicting elements would stick together to form a permanent majority. General elections would become merely a formality, with the real contests taking place in the primaries of the new party. The result would be one-party government.

Could such a party, composed supposedly of "economic men," hang together indefinitely? Would the group vote as a group, or would labor vote as labor, farmers as farmers, and the so-called progressive faction preserve its particular characteristics into the old age of its members? The one thing that could force the various elements to hang together would be the absolute determination to get and retain governmental power to prevent the return to a private ownership system. The belief would grow that the "other party" would have to be kept from office at all costs. The results would be a "we" and "they" psychology in the land and the opposition party would in time bear the appearance of—not fellow countrymen—but "the enemy." An election defeat would seem (and might be) a *total* defeat.[15]

Eventually the day might come when a great emotional issue would divide the *entirely different* polarized parties—parties with "real" differences. It would not be the extension of slavery into the territories or the preservation of the union—the ante-bellum issues —but some issue unlike those but similar in impact—perhaps

[15] Could it then be said of America, "No decision is final; no verdict not subject to revision; no guide to doctrine fixed and eternal except in the continuous functioning of the human mind"? Edgar Eugene Robinson, "Leadership in America," *Stanford Review,* April, 1962, p. 41.

denationalization of partially Socialized industry. To class parties, compromise might seem utterly impossible. The result of election day, therefore, could turn out to be civil conflict between those who had *won all* and those who had *lost all*. Who then would say with the Dan Tobin of 1928, "As good Americans it is our duty to give our full support to the newly elected President, Herbert Hoover," [16] or words to that effect? Is the inability to lose gracefully the inevitable end of party realignments intended in the first instance only to bring "democratic socialism" or increased "party responsibility"? Such is the view offered here. Said Senator George Norris in 1928, when an election is over "every lover of human liberty, every defender of justice, and every believer in our form of Government must accept the result as final and conclusive." [17]

XII

The trade union leaders of the United States chose in 1928 the road of political pressure on the major parties rather than third-party action by themselves, in alliance with farmers or "progressives," or with the Socialists or Communists. They also rejected the Communist appeal.

The idea of ignoring political matters altogether was not considered within the realm of possibilities, for the nonpartisan program of the unions was a heritage of the past. Labor as pressure goup was a recognition of the variegated party and personal interests of the individual members of the trade unions. Labor leaders recognized that they represented a group whose political unity was doubtful, and they were quite aware that they were themselves partially divided on at least the Presidential race. They felt that the political policy they chose was well suited to the facts of the case. Thus they rejected political alternatives whose immediate practicality was felt to be dubious and whose eventual consequences on their movement and themselves they could not predict and might not be able to control.

[16] *Teamsters Magazine*, December, 1928, 10-12.
[17] George Norris, "The Meaning of the Recent Election," *La Follett's Magazine*, XX (December, 1928), 185.

These labor leaders recognized that if the path they chose should not be completely effective in 1928, there would be, under the American electoral system, other elections and further opportunities. They would have done nothing to close the door on the means of orderly change in the nation.

In this acceptance of the American party system they followed the farewell advice of Samuel Gompers. He first urged union men to keep the faith and not to forget their trade union obligations. To this he added that they were to *remember* that "a union man carrying a card is not a good citizen unless he upholds the institutions of our country. . . ."

The union leaders of 1928 did not feel called on to apologize for their occasional efforts to further through modest amounts of political activity the economic interests of their movement. In later years, some union leaders would bring on themselves the wrath of rival groups in the population because of overly enthusiastic use of union office virtually to force (or brainwash) political unity among the dues-paying rank and file. William Green in 1928 recognized fully the restraints on his power in the political arena. To the Secretary of the Jamestown, New York, Central Labor Council he wrote that any effort to sway one way or the other the prospective appointment of a state jurist would be out of keeping with his office. "I do not believe that the President of the American Federation of Labor should enter into a political scramble in any state unless requested to do so by the State Federation of Labor." [18]

But the A. F. of L. president did not feel apologetic about his role as leader of one of many pressure groups in the nation. He probably would have applauded the dictum of a later student of labor in politics who wrote

. . . pressure groups are not just unfortunate incrustations on the party process. They are the live steam that sets the party mechanism in motion. Americans should not be surprised to find a maze of cross-pressures inside their parties. America is a land of conflicting interests. The party is a legitimate battle-field, where such conflicts can be expressed, tested, and settled with a modicum of physical violence.[19]

[18] William Green to Harry A. Hartman, December 13, 1928, A. F. of L. Papers.
[19] Fay Calkins, *The CIO and the Democratic Party* (Chicago, 1952), pp. 154-155.

The labor leaders who, as citizens, announced themselves Demo-
cats or Republicans and said they supported Smith or Hoover,
were on equally firm ground, even when they urged their rank and
file and friends of the union movement to concur in their judgment.
It was the Republican candidate of 1928 who declared as well as
it has ever been expressed the *right* of free Americans, as individuals, to engage in political partisanship. Said Herbert Hoover
to a Maryland delegation on September 22, 1928,

> Membership in a political organization is no disgrace. Funda-
> mentally, we can only conduct this government with a definite
> party organization. It is the only way through which the people
> can express their will upon issues and men. It goes to the very
> roots of organization of our form of government and of de-
> mocracy itself, for without organization the will of the majority
> upon public issues could not find expression, so those who take
> part in party organization are engaged in a public service,
> whether they belong to our party or to the opposition.[20]

To these words might well be added the judgment of two other
Americans of differing viewpoints. Norman Thomas, repeatedly
defeated for President, nevertheless adjudged in retrospect, "I've
always believed, especially in America, in the two-party system. . . .
I believe that the philosophy on which men divide permits two
parties with variations in *both*—neither of them being monolithic—
but an honest division which permits either side to draw up a
platform and in its major items to hold its officials to it." [21] And
twice-defeated Presidential candidate Thomas E. Dewey concluded
about the same time,

> For more than a century and a half the two-party system has
> served our country well. Thus far we have survived every kind
> of crisis. We are still the strongest nation on earth. We have pre-
> served our liberties. As against the single party or the multi-party
> system, I think it is clear that our two-party tradition, despite
> occasional failures, has been the most effective instrument of
> government yet devised and should be vigorously supported.[22]

[20] *New York Times,* September 23, 1928.
[21] Thomas to Oral History Project, July, 1950, pp. 176-177. By this time he also
felt that he would want "very little to do with a party that is just a plaything for labor
leaders." p. 163.
[22] Thomas E. Dewey, "The Two-Party System of Government," *Vital Speeches,*
XXI (June 1, 1950), 491.

XIII

As for the significance of third parties, there is the educated opinion of Professor Cortez A. M. Ewing: "An honest evaluation of minor parties should not be that they are intruders in sacred precincts, but that they are the only democratic means by which the American people can retain the system of two great major parties and at the same time reach for solutions of emergent political problems." [23]

Having expressed distaste for the core of the Socialist solution in 1928 and dismay over the challenge in the Communist solution, one may yet observe that both of these groups contained leaders who dreamed dreams of perfectionism and thought they could see just over the horizon a better land and a better world. The editorial "May Day Thoughts," in the *Milwaukee Leader* of Socialist Victor Berger looked forward to the day "that poverty will be abolished, that employment will be guaranteed, that hours of labor will be shortened and incomes raised, that war will be abolished, that kindness will take the place of hatred, and brotherhood will be substituted for strife." [24] To these words, on which all readers could unite, the Socialist paper added that working for Socialism was the one way to bring these things to pass. In "The Message of May Day" on the same page, James Oneal wrote that the Socialists stood for "working-class interests"; described the "age-old struggle of the working class"; said workers should organize their voting power "for their own claims, interest and program"; and said it was, in 1928, the working class versus "the exploiters." [25] The Socialist Party was a threat to private ownership of property, to the continuing existence of a balanced two-party system, and to the continuation of a society more interested in opportunity than class consciousness. It did not, on fundamentals, deserve the support of the American electorate. No amount of admiration which some may want to give to individuals, reformist program, or occasional ideal-

[23] Cortez A. M. Ewing, *Presidential Elections* (Norman, Okla., 1940), p. 130. See also William B. Hesseltine, *The Rise and Fall of Third Parties* (Washington, D.C., 1948) for interesting points of view.
[24] *Milwaukee Leader*, May 1, 1928.
[25] *Ibid.*

ism of individual expression should wave aside these plain and altogether vital facts.

In final summary on the nature of the American party system in 1928, it may be said that the Republican and Democratic Parties stood for *moderation;* the Socialist Party was inescapably representative of *division;* and the Communists were plainly symbolic of *disruption.*

As for the union leaders of 1928, they did not call for the destruction of parties or of governmental units—executive offices, legislatures or courts. They accepted the full force of the laws but, as was their right, they urged the modification of particular ones. Union members went to the polls as citizens; they chose sides, when holding union office, in the effort to accomplish designated ends on behalf of the labor movement. Partisanship could thus be found in many places. In New York, the "Organized Labor Committee for the Election of Smith, Roosevelt, and Copeland" contained in 1928 the names of the State Federation, the New York Central Trades and Labor Council, the State Building Trades Council, the State Printing Trades Council, and the names of seventy-three labor leaders—among them (obscurely at the time) that of one George Meany.[26] Thus did labor leaders choose to support candidates, take sides on issues, and gain a hearing. They respected the two-party system as an instrument through which they, in company with other citizens, could influence government to refrain from harmful action and take steps which would be helpful to the trade union movement.

XIV

Nearly all Americans who had participated in the election as candidates, as workers for parties, or as voters, agreed that the counting of the votes and announcement of results ended the spirited contest of 1928. This had long been an entirely safe assumption. And so it was in this instance; but in one important sense the episode was not quite at an end. As the winning candi-

[26] From the letterhead of the group. Copy in Box 13, FDR Campaign Correspondence. Roosevelt Papers.

date, and then after taking the Oath of Office, Herbert Hoover left no doubt that the transition in power would be routine and orderly, and that basic institutions would remain intact. In his Inaugural Address on March 4, 1929, he did not fail to state that among his important mandates was "the maintenance of the integrity of the Constitution." And under the heading *Party Responsibilities* in his first address as President of the Unitèd States, Mr. Hoover stated fundamentals:

> In our form of democracy the expression of the popular will can be effected only through the instrumentality of political parties. We maintain party government not to promote intolerant partisanship but because opportunity must be given for expression of the popular will, and organization provided for the execution of its mandates and for accountability of government to the people. It follows that the Government both in the executive and the legislative branches must carry out in good faith the platforms upon which the party was intrusted with power. But the government is that of the whole people; the party is the instrument through which policies are determined and men chosen to bring them into being. The animosities of election should have no place in our Government, for government must concern itself alone with the common weal.[27]

The election, a political contest—not a battle, struggle, or ideological war—was thus declared at an end.

The detailed story of labor politics in a democratic republic, of unions, parties, and leaders in the Presidential Election of 1928, can now be brought to a close. Much of the political spectrum of the time has been on display. Although that contest of men, ideas, and emotions lies decades in the past, it may offer lessons for citizens of many lands in the deeply troubled present. The most important heritage of the American people is, above all, the story of free men and women engaging in one of the central experiences of mankind: the inexact but vital science of peaceful self-government.

[27] Inaugural Address, March 4, 1929, in *The State Papers and Other Public Writings of Herbert Hoover* (New York, 1934), I, pp. 10-11.

BIBLIOGRAPHY

Bibliography

THIS BIBLIOGRAPHY contains most of the materials the writer consulted during the period covered by the writing of this book. The manuscript collections were particularly important to the work, of course. All the newspapers, books, articles, pamphlets, and other materials (unless noted to the contrary) have been examined by the writer. This is not true of all the doctoral dissertations and master's theses.

The list is not intended as an exhaustive bibliography of the 1920s, nor of the 1928 election. Neither does it contain the hundreds of articles on religion, prohibition, and various personalities that may be easily found through use of the standard reference guides. Books and articles on the C. I. O., the Knights of Labor, labor in the nineteenth century, and British and European labor are, among other subjects generally excluded. Political materials which are chiefly or entirely concerned with elections in the United States both before and after 1928, unless they served a particular purpose, are also missing. Finally, a few works given only passing mention in the text are omitted. Items used in researching material not included in the final book do appear in the bibliography. (Omitted chapters covered the first decade of the Communist Party of America, the New York State Federation of Labor in 1928, and Franklin D. Roosevelt's campaign for governor.) It is hoped that by bringing together scattered materials this bibliography will ease the research of others in several areas.

Materials on Socialism and Communism listed below may often be found in the Hoover Library of War, Revolution, and Peace. Nearly all of the trade union journals and proceedings are present in the library of the Wisconsin State Historical Society and the Main Library of the University of California at Berkeley, while the Hopkins Transportation Library at Stanford contains almost all Railway Brotherhood publications.

A. MANUSCRIPTS

American Federation of Labor Papers, A. F. of L. Headquarters, Washington, D. C

Cigar Makers' International Union, Local No. 98 (St. Paul), Papers. Volume 66, "Registry of Unemployed Members," 1927ff. Minnesota Historical Society.

Calvin Coolidge Papers. Library of Congress.

Conference for Progressive Political Action. Stenographic Minutes of Meetings, 1924-1925. Library of Congress.

Democratic National Campaign Committee Correspondence, 1928. Franklin D. Roosevelt Library

Mary W. Dewson Papers, 1928. Franklin D. Roosevelt Library.

William Green Papers. American Federation of Labor Library.

Samuel Gompers Papers. American Federation of Labor Library.

E. George Hall Papers. Minnesota Historical Society.

Morris Hillquit Papers. Wisconsin State Historical Society.

Daniel Webster Hoan Collection. Milwaukee County Historical Society.

Louis McHenry Howe Papers. Franklin D. Roosevelt Library.

David Fulton Karsner Papers. New York Public Library.

League of Women Voters Papers. Library of Congress.

George B. Leonard Papers. Minnesota Historical Society.

George H. Lommen Papers. Scrapbook. Minnesota Historical Society.

William McKinley Papers. Library of Congress.

Tom Mooney Papers. Bancroft Library, University of California.

National Civic Federation Papers Relating to Communism, 1920-1939. Library of Congress

National Women's Trade Union League of America Papers. Library of Congress.

Oral History Project, Columbia University; various transcribed interviews by Allan Nevins and Dean Albertson.

Franklin D. Roosevelt Papers. Roosevelt Library, Hyde Park, N. Y. Among collections used: Speeches of F. D. R., Drafts and Reading Copies, 1921-1929; 1928 Campaign Correspondence; General Political Correspondence, 1921-1928; Private Correspondence, 1928-1932; Gubernatorial Papers, 1929-1933; Lieutenant Governor's Papers; 1929-1933; Addresses, October-November, 1928; Drafts of Houston, Texas, speech, June 27, 1928; American Federation of Labor Correspondence, 1923-1928.

A. M. Simons Papers. Wisconsin State Historical Society.

Socialist Party of Milwaukee Collection. Milwaukee County Historical Society.

Socialist Party, Minutes of National Executive Committee Meetings, 1928. In Daniel W. Hoan Papers. Milwaukee County Historical Society.

Socialist Party Papers. Duke University.

Norman Thomas Papers. New York Public Library.

Henry George Teigan Papers. Minnesota Historical Society.

Alexander Trachtenberg Papers. New York Public Library.

U. S. Department of Labor Papers. National Archives.

Frank Walsh Papers. New York Public Library.

Wisconsin State Federation of Labor Papers, Minutes of Executive Board Meetings, Jan., 1927 to Dec., 1933 (typed). Wisconsin State Historical Society.

B. BIBLIOGRAPHICAL AIDS

ADAMS, FREDERICK B., JR. *Radical Literature in America.* Stamford, Conn., 1939.

AMERICAN FEDERATION OF LABOR. *Guide to Sources of Information,* (Wash., D. C., 1923).

BEGINNINGS OF POLITICAL ACTION BY LABOR GROUPS IN THE UNITED STATES. New York State School of Industrial and Labor Relations, Cornell University. Cornell List No. 1. Ithaca, Oct., 1948. Mimeographed.

BORNET, VAUGHN DAVIS. "The New Labor History: A Challenge for American Historians," *The Historian,* XVIII (Autumn, 1955), 1-24. (Contains the first inventory of the A. F. of L. papers.)

COMMONWEALTH COLLEGE. Henry Black, compiler. *A List of Recent References on a Farmer-Labor Party.* May 20, 1936.

DEPARTMENT OF LABOR LIBRARY. Brief List of References on Labor and the New Deal. Washington, March 18, 1947. Mimeographed by the Institute of Labor and Industrial Relations, University of Illinois.

HAMER, PHILIP. *A Guide to the Archives and Manuscripts in the United States.* New Haven, 1961. (Not available for my use.)

Index to Labor Articles. New York, Rand School of Social Science, 1926+.

Labor and the '48 Political Campaign. A Selected Bibliography. New York State School of Industrial and Labor Relations, Cornell University. Cornell List No. 2. Ithaca, Oct., 1948. Mimeographed.

Labor's Library; A Bibliography. New York, Workers Education Bureau, 1945.

NAAS, BERNARD G. AND CARMELITA S. SAKER. *American Labor Union Periodicals: A Guide to Their Location.* Ithaca, N. Y., 1956.

REYNOLDS, LLOYD G. AND CHARLES C. KILLINGWORTH. *Trade Union Publications.* 3 vols. Baltimore, 1944.

STEELE, HELEN M. "The Library of the United States Department of Labor." *Special Libraries,* 41 (1950), 93-97.

THOMPSON, L. A., compiler. "Injunction in Labor Disputes," *Monthly Labor Review,* XXVII (Sept., 1928), 631-650.

A Trade Union Library, 1949. Princeton, 1949.

What to Read on Socialism. Chicago, C. H. Kerr, 1902.

C. GOVERNMENT DOCUMENTS

Congressional Record. 1900-1936.

New York State. *The Governor's Message to the Legislature, Jan. 5, 1921.* New York Legislative Document No. 3. Albany, 1921. Similar documents. 1923-1928.

New York State. *Legislative Manual.* Albany, 1920-1940.

New York State. Legislature. Joint Committee Investigating Seditious Activities (Lusk Committee). *Revolutionary Radicalism: Its History, Purpose and Tactics.* 4 vols. Albany, 1920.

New York State. *Message of Governor Franklin D. Roosevelt to the Legislature, Jan. 2, 1929.* New York Legislative Document No. 3. Albany, 1929. Similar documents, 1930-1932.

New York State. *Message of Governor Herbert H. Lehman to the Legislature, Jan. 4, 1933.* New York Legislative Document No. 3. Albany, 1933. Similar documents, 1934-1936.

New York State. *Public Papers of Alfred E. Smith. Fourth Term, 1928.* Albany, 1938.

New York State. *Public Papers of Franklin D. Roosevelt, Second Term, 1932.* Albany, 1939.

U. S. Congress. House of Representatives. Special Committees To Investigate Communist Activities in the United States (Fish Committee). *Investigation of Communist Propaganda.* 6 Parts. 71st Cong., 2nd Sess. Washington, 1930.

U. S. Congress. Senate. Commission on Industrial Relations. *Final Report and Testimony.* 11 vols. 64th Cong., 1st Sess. Washington, 1916.

U. S. Congress. Senate and House. *Robert M. La Follette Memorial Addresses.* 69th Cong., 1st Sess. (Proceedings in House, Feb. 20, 1927; proceedings in Senate, June 20, 1926.) Washington, 1927.

U. S. Congress. Senate. Committee on Education and Labor. *Investigation of Strike in Steel Industries.* 2 parts. 66th Cong., 1st Sess. Washington, 1919.

U. S. Congress. Senate. Committee on Education and Labor. *Violations of Free Speech and Rights of Labor.* (La Follette Hearings.) 64th Cong., 1st Sess. Washington, 1936. 65th Cong., 1st Sess. Washington, 1937.

U. S. Congress. Senate. Committee on Foreign Relations (Lodge Committee). *Relations With Russia.* Hearings. 66th Cong., 3rd Sess. Washington, 1921.

U. S. Congress. Senate. Subcommittee of the Committee on the Judiciary. *Limiting Scope of Injunctions in Labor Disputes.* Hearings. 70th Cong., 1st Sess. Washington, 1928.

U. S. Congress. Senate. Special Committee to Investigate Campaign Expenditures of Presidential, Vice Presidential, and Senatorial candidates in 1936. *Investigation of Campaign Expenditures in 1936.* (Lonergan Report.) 75th Cong., 1st Sess. Washington, 1936.

U. S. Congress. Senate. Subcommittee of the Committee on Foreign Relations (Borah Committee). *Hearings on Recognition of Russia.* 68th Cong., 1st Sess. Washington, 1924.

U. S. Congress. Senate. Subcommittee of the Committee on Foreign Relations (Moses Committee). *Hearings on Russian Propaganda.* 13 parts. 66th Cong., 2nd Sess. Washington, 1920.

U. S. Department of Labor. Bureau of Labor Statistics. *Brief History of the American Labor Movement.* Prepared by John M. Brumm *et al.* Washington, 1947.

U. S. Department of Labor. Bureau of Labor Statistics. Labor Relations in the United States: Summary of Historical Events in the World War Period, 1912-1920. Washington, Feb., 1941. Mimeographed.

U. S. Department of Labor. Bureau of Labor Statistics. World War I, Chronology of Important Events, August, 1914—December, 1918. Washington, Jan., 1941, Mimeographed.

U. S. Department of Labor. Bureau of Labor Statistics. World War I. Source Materials for Research. Washington, Jan., 1942. Mimeographed.

D. NEWSPAPERS

America For All, 1928. Chicago, Socialist Party.

Christian Science Monitor, 1920-1929. Boston.

Daily Worker, 1924-1929. Chicago and New York. Communist Party.

Farmer-Labor Press Service. Irregular, 1928. Minneapolis. (In Teigan Papers, Box 7.)

Labor, 1922-1929, Washington. Railroad Brotherhoods.

Labor Clarion. 1927-1928. San Francisco. San Francisco Labor Council.

Militant, 1928-1930. New York. Title varies. Socialist Workers Party (Trot-skyist).

Milwaukee Leader, 1927-1929. Also Scrapbook of Socialist Party Clippings, 1926-1929, chiefly from the *Leader.* (In Milwaukee Hist. Soc. Library.)

New York Call, 1920. Socialist Party. New York.

New York Times, 1919-1929. New York.

Official Bulletin of the Communist Party of America, March 31, 1921.

San Diego Evening Tribune, 1928. San Diego, California.

San Francisco Chronicle, 1928. San Francisco, California.

San Francisco Examiner, 1928. San Francisco, California.

San Jose Mercury-Herald, 1928. San Jose, California.

Socialist Labor Party Vote Ticket, 1928. New York.

Socialist Party, The Bulletin, 1919-1920. Chicago.

Weekly Press News. Socialist Party, 1928. Mimeographed. (In Hoan Papers.)

Worker, 1922-1923. New York. Workers Party.

E. PAMPHLETS

Trade Union Pamphlets

This section includes only official publications of the American Federation of Labor and other trade union organizations.

American Federation of Labor. *American Federation of Labor* (Washington, n.d., 1939?).

————. *American Labor's Position in Peace or in War* (Washington, 1917).

————. *Correspondence between Mr. Newton D. Baker . . . and Samuel Gompers . . .,* February, 1923 (Washington, 1923).

————. *Disarmament; the American Federation of Labor, its Declarations and Actions in Support of Disarmament and International Peace* (Washington, 1921).

————. *55 Questions and Answers on Campaign Issues* (Washington, 1920).

————. *For President Harding or Cox? Read! Think! Choose! Report of the Platform Committee . . .* (Washington, 1920).

————. *Forty Years of Action; Non-Partisan Political Policy, American Federation of Labor* (Washington, 1920).

————. *From Politics to Industry . . . an Editorial from the American Federationist* dated May, 1923.

————. *Industrial Unionism in its Relation to Trade Unionism* (Washington, 1912).

————. *Instructions to Organizers* (Washington, 1928).

————. *An Interesting Discussion at the Tenth Annual Convention . . . upon the question: "Should a Charter be Issued by the American Federation of Labor to a Central Labor Union Which has a Political Party Represented Therein?"* (New York, 1891).

————. *Labor and the Courts; Statement Adopted by the El Paso Convention of 1924* (Washington, 1924).

————. *Labor Planks in the Political Platforms.* . . . (Washington, 1928).

————. *Labor Planks in the Political Platforms.* . . . (Washington, 1932).

————. *Labor Planks in the Political Platforms.* . . . (Washington, 1936).

————. *Labor Planks in the Political Platforms.* . . . (Washington, 1940).

————. *Manual of Common Procedure.* . . . (Washington, 1927).

————. *A Verbatim Report of the Discussion on the Political Programme at the Denver Çonvention of the American Federation of Labor, Dec. 14, 15, 1894. Reported by an Expert Stenographer.* (N. Y., 1895.)

————. *Why the Peace Treaty Should be Ratified. American Labor's Reasons for Supporting the League of Nations Covenant with its Labor Provisions.* (Washington, n.d.)

A. F. of L. vs. C. I. O., The Record (Washington, A. F. of L., 1939).

Fifty Years of Service (n.p., A. F. of L., 1931.)

GOMPERS, SAMUEL. *The American Labor Movement, Its Makeup, Achievements and Asperations* (Washington, A. F. of L., 1915).

————. *Collective Bargaining: Labor's Proposal to Insure Greater Industrial Peace* (Washington, A. F. of L., 1920).

————. *Samuel Gompers' Creed* (Washington, A. F. of L., 1934). Reprint of the El Paso speech. Introduction by William Green.

GREEN, WILLIAM, *American Labor in Politics* (Washington, 1929).

————. *A Great American Institution* [the A. F. of L.] (Washington, A. F. of L., 1930).

————. *An Outline of Labor's Principles and Policies.* Speech delivered to the International Kiwanis Convention, Boston, June 20, 1939. Mimeographed.

————. *President Green Extols Labor Movement as Shield of Democracy and Relentless Foe of Dictatorships* (Washington, A. F. of L., 1936?). Speech delivered April 3, 1936.

————. *The Right to Work* (Washington, A. F. of L., 1931). Speech to Vancouver Convention, A. F. of L.

————. *Unions Reduce Industrial Waste* (Washington, A. F. of L., 1925).

————. *Wage Theories* (Washington, A. F. of L., 1926). Address at Princeton University, Feb. 26, 1926.

————. *We Work for the Future; American Federation of Labor and National Defense* (Washington, A. F. of L., 1941).

Industrial Unionism. Report of the Executive Council to the Rochester, New York, Convention, 1912 (Washington, A. F. of L., n.d.).

Labor and the Courts (n.p., A. F. of L., 1924). Declaration of the El Paso Convention.

Non-Partisan Declarations: Fifty-Six-Year Political Policy (n.p., A. F. of L., n.d., 1936?).

POPE, FREDERICK RUSSELL. *Samuel Gompers: A Character Appreciation* (Washington, A. F. of L., 1930).

Labor Speeches of William Jennings Bryan (Chicago, Ill., Sept. 7, 1908).

Ten International Unions Affiliated with the A. F. of L. Stand Automatically Suspended for Failure to Withdraw from Committee on Industrial Organization (n.p., A. F. of L., n.d., 1936?).

Text Book of Labor's Political Demands (Washington, A. F. of L., 1906).

THORNTON, SIR HENRY. *The Partner. The New Labor Era* (Washington, A. F. of L., 1930). Speech by the president, Canadian National Railways to A. F. of L. Toronto Convention, 1929.

TRANT, WILLIAM. *Trade Unions, Their Origin and Objects, Influence and Efficacy.* 21st ed. (Washington, A. F. of L., 1928). Contains the statement, "carefully edited to fit American conditions."

Unemployment: American Labor's Problem (n.p., A. F. of L., 1931). A. F. of L., 1931. Extracts from reports at the Vancouver Convention, A. F. of L., 1931.

United Mine Workers of America. *Attempt by Communists to Seize the American Labor Movement* (Washington, Government Printing Office, by order of 68th Cong., 1st Sess., 1924).

Yellow Dog Contracts Condemned by Experts (Washington, A. F. of L., 1930). Introduction by William Green. Extracts from noted persons.

Communist Pamphlets

This section includes only pamphlets which by their authorship, subject matter, or publisher are adjudged publications of the Workers Party, the Workers (Communist) Party, or the Communist Party. Where there was doubt the pamphlet was included under Miscellaneous Pamphlets.

Acceptance Speeches: William Z. Foster, Candidate for President and Benjamin Gitlow, Candidate for Vice President of the Workers (Communist) Party (New York, 1928).

ARNOLD, JOHN. *The Jewish People Today* (New York, Communist Party, n.d., 1940?).

BARTON, ANN. *Mother Bloor* (New York, Workers Publishers, February,. 1935).

BROWDER, EARL. *Democracy or Fascism: Report to the Ninth Convention of the Communist Party* (New York, Workers Publishers, 1936).

————. *The Democratic Front: For Jobs Security, Democracy and Peace* (New York, Workers Library, June, 1938).

————. *A Message to Catholics* (New York, Workers Library, June, 1938).

BUDENZ, LOUIS. *Red Baiting: Enemy of Labor* (New York, Workers Library, 1937).

————. *Save Your Union!* (New York, 1940).

CAMPION, MARTHA. *Who Are the Young Pioneers?* (New York, New Pioneer Publishing Co., Oct., 1934).

Communist International. 6th Congress, Moscow, 1928. *Communism and the International Situation* (New York, Workers Library, Jan., 1929).

For a Labor Party; Recent Revolutionary Changes in American Politics (New York, Workers Party, Oct. 15, 1922).

FOSTER, WILLIAM Z. *Halt the Railroad Wage Cut* (New York, 1938).

————. *A Manual of Industrial Unionism* (New York, 1937).

————. *Organizing Methods in the Steel Industry* (New York, 1936).

————. *Railroad Workers, Forward!* (New York, 1937).

————. *The Rankin Witch Hunt* (New York, Dec., 1945).

————. *What Means a Strike in Steel* (New York, 1937).

————. *What's What About the War* [World War II] (New York, July, 1940).

League of Professional Groups for Foster and Ford. *Culture and the Crisis: An Open Letter to the Writers, Artists, Teachers, Physicians, Engineers, Scientists, and other Professional Workers of America* (New York, Workers Library, Oct., 1932). Back cover contains a list of supporters.

PEPPER, JOHN. *For a Labor Party: Recent Revolutionary Changes in American Politics.* 3rd ed. (New York, Workers Party, 1923). See above for earlier copy without author credit.

Stalin's Speeches on the American Communist Party [May 6, 14, 1929] (New York?, Central Committee, Communist Party, U.S.A., 1930?).

TSIRUL, S. *The Practice of Bolshevik Self-Criticism; How the American Communist Party Carries Out Self-Criticism and Controls Fulfillment* [sic] *of Decisions* (New York, Sept., 1932). Reprint from *Communist International*, IX.

WARE, CLARISSA S. *The American Foreign-Born Workers* (New York, Workers Party, 1923).

Socialist Pamphlets

This section includes only pamphlets which by their authorship, subject matter, or publisher are adjudged publications of the Socialist Party. Where there was doubt the pamphlet was included under Miscellaneous Pamphlets.

A. B. C. of Socialism: Declaration of Principles of the Socialist Party [July, 1924] (Chicago, S. P., 192?). Thin leaflet.

Constitution of the Socialist Party of Wisconsin (Milwaukee, Wis., State S. P., 1932).

The Crisis in the Socialist Party: The Detroit Convention Appeal by the Committee for the Preservation of the Socialist Party (New York, Com. for the Pres. of the S. P., 1934?). Issued by a right wing faction (James Maurer, Louis Waldman, etc.).

[Program of] *The Eighteenth Convention of the Socialist Party of America. . . . Detroit, Michigan, May 30-June 3, 1934* (Chicago, S. P., 1934).

GASSON, REV. FATHER. *The Menace of Socialism. An Address Delivered in Boston . . . and the Reply Thereto . . . by James F. Carey* (Milwaukee, 1912).

GERMER, ADOLPH. *Report of Executive Secretary. Emergency National Convention* (St. Louis, Mo., April 7, 1917?).

HILLQUIT, MORRIS. *Foundations of Socialism* (Chicago, S. P. Natl. Hdqtrs., 1934). Chapters 1, 2, and 4 of Hillquit's book *Present Day Socialism* (1920).

————. *The Immediate Issue* [inside title: *The Socialist Task and Outlook*] (New York, 1920?).

HUNTER, ROBERT. *Labor in Politics* (Chicago, S. P., 1915), 202 pages.

The Intelligent Voter's Guide: Official 1928 Campaign Handbook of the Socialist Party (New York, 1928).

Journal For the Eleventh National Convention of the Socialist Party of the United States (New York, May, 1923).

KORNGOLD, RALPH. *Are There Classes in America?* (Chicago, S. P., 1914).

KRZYCKI, LEO [sic]. *The Unions and the Socialists* (Chicago, S. P., 1936?).

LAIDLER, HARRY W. *An Appeal to White Collar Workers and the Professions* (New York, S. P., n.d., 1920s?).

LOWE, CAROLINE A.*The Teacher and Socialism* (Chicago, S. P., 191?).

LYNCH, DANIEL. *Socialism and Trade Unionism* (Chicago, C. H. Kerr, 1900). Also contains Max S. Hayes, *Trade Unions and Socialism*.

MALKIEL, THERESA S. *To the Union Man's Wife* (Chicago, S. P., n.d., 1911?).

Manifesto and Program of the Left Wing Section, Socialist Party, Greater New York (New York, Left Wing Section, S. P., 1919). Issued by left wing faction.

A Militant Program for the Socialist Party of America: Socialism in Our Time (New; York, n.p., 1932?). Issued by left wing or "militant" faction.

Minutes of the National Convention, Socialist Party, New York City, April 13-17, 1928 (Chicago, 1928?). Also printed in the *New Leader* in April, 1928.

National Platform of the Socialist Party, 1926 (Chicago, S. P., 1926).

"Not Guilty." Charge of Federal Judge Clarence W. Sessions in the Conspiracy Case Against Adolph Germer, et al. . . . (Chicago, S. P., 1917?).

ONEAL, JAMES. *Labor and the Next War* (Chicago, S. P., 1927).

————. *The Next Emancipation* (New York, United Colored Socialists of America, 1929).

100 Years—For What? (Chicago, S. P., 1920?).

OPPENHEIMER, MOSES. *Outlawing Socialism* (Chicago, S. P., 1920).

O'REILLY, MARY. *The Boy Scout Movement* (Chicago, S. P., 191?).

PANNEKOCK, ANTON. *Marxism and Darwinism* (Chicago, C. H. Kerr, n.d.).

A Plan for America: Official 1932 Campaign Handbook of the Socialist Party (Chicago, S. P., 1932).

Platform of the Socialist Party for the Presidential Election of 1928 (Washington, U. S. Government Printing Office, 1928). Reprint from Congressional Record of April 23, 1928.

Platform, Socialist Party (Chicago, National Campaign Committee, S. P., 1928?).

A Political Guide for the Workers: Socialist Party Campaign Book, 1920 (Chicago, S. P., 1920).

PORTER, PAUL. *Which Way for the Socialist Party?* (Milwaukee, Wis., S. P. of Wis., 1937).

RUSSELL, CHARLES EDWARD. *Socialism the Only Remedy* (New York, S. P., 1912?).

SCHAFFER, LOUIS. *Stalin's Fifth Column on Broadway* (New York, Rand School, 1940).

Should the Workers Form a Party of Their Own? A Debate. Morris Hillquit, Yes; Matthew Woll, No. (New York, Rand School, 1932.)

Socialist Handbook, 1916 (Chicago, S. P., 1916).

Socialist Handbook, 1937 (Chicago, S. P., 1937).

STEDMEN, SEYMOUR, *Socialism and Peace* (Chicago, S. P., n.d., 1917?).

Thirty-Fifth Anniversary Journal . . . Nineteenth Convention, Cleveland, Ohio, May 23-26, 1936 (Chicago, S. P., 1936).

THOMAS, NORMAN. *Collective Security and War* (Milwaukee, Wis., S. P., 1938?). Radio address, Jan. 2, 1938.

————. *Emancipate Youth from Toil—Old Age From Fear* (Chicago, S. P., 1936). Speech to a Townsend Plan convention.

————. *Is the New Deal Socialism? An Answer to Al Smith and the American Liberty League* (Chicago, S. P., 1936?). Speech over C.B.S., Feb. 2, 1936.

————. *Martin Dies and Socialism* (New York, S. P., 1943?). Radio Address, March 6, 1943.

————. *The New Deal:A Socialist Analysis* (Chicago, S. P., Dec. 15, 1933).

————. *To Huey Long and Father Coughlin: An Open Letter* (Chicago, S. P., 193?).

————. *What Socialism Is and Is Not* (Chicago, S. P., 1932?). A leaflet.

————. *Why I Am a Socialist* (Chicago, 1932).

Towards a Militant Program for the Socialist Party of America: Socialism in Our Time (New York, 1934). Issued by the left wing, "militant," faction.

TYLER, AUGUST. *The United Front* (New York, Rand School, 1933).

Which Road for American Workers, Socialist or Communist? Norman Thomas vs. Earl Browder. A Debate (New York, Socialist Call, Jan., 1936). Madison Square Garden, New York, Nov. 27, 1935.

WILSHIRE, GAYLORD. *Why a Workingman Should Be a Socialist* (New York, 191?).

WORK, JOHN M. *What's So and What Isn't* (Chicago, C. H. Kerr, 1912). First issued, 1905.

YOUNG, ART. *The Socialist Primer* (Chicago, S. P., 1930).

Miscellaneous Pamphlets

American Fund for Public Service, Inc., Reports of (New York, 1925-1931). The Garland Fund.

An Appeal to the Membership of the Socialist Party (n.p., Revolutionary Policy Committee, n.d., 1934?). Contains the Statement, "We make no fetish of legality. . . ."

BOECKEL, RICHARD. *Presidential Politics, 1928* (Editorial Research Reports, 1928).

Bolshevism: Second Report of the Committee of the Union League Club of New York (n.p., March 13, 1919).

BROWNE, STUART (pseudonym). *A Professor Quits the Communist Party* (n.p., n.d.). Reprint from *Harper's Magazine,* July, 1937, by the Industrial Association of San Francisco.

A Catechism of Communism for Catholic High School Students (New York, Paulist Press, 1936). "By a Passionist Father." Anti-Communist pamphlet.

CLAESSENS, AUGUST. *A Manual for Trade Union Speakers* (New York, I.L.G. W.U., Rand School copyright, 1936).

COWAN, WILLIAM WALLACE. *The Red Hand in the Professor's Glove* (Manchester, N. H., 1933).

DANNENBERG, KARL. *Reform or Revolution* (New York, Radical Review Publishers, 1918).

DILLING, MRS. ALBERT W. *Red Revolution: Do We Want It?* (Wilmette, Ill., 1932). Reprints of articles.

Doctor Matthews' Amazing Statement Before the Dies Committee . . . (New York, 193?).

DOUGLAS, PAUL. *Why a Political Realignment?* (New York, League for Independent Political Action, 1930).

EASTMAN, MAX. *The Trial of Eugene Debs* (New York, Liberator Publishers, 1919?).

HICHBORN, FRANKLIN. *The Case of Charlotte Anita Whitney* (San Jose, Calif., 1920).

HOWARD, SIDNEY. *The Labor Spy* (New York, 1921). Reprint from the *New Republic.*

Labor in Politics (Washington, Chamber of Commerce of the United States, 1950). Prepared by the Employer-Employee Relations Division, U. S. Chamber of Commerce, April 28, 1950.

Labor Record of Franklin D. Roosevelt (New York, National Dem. Camp. Com., 1932-1933).

Labor Research Association. *Arsenal of Facts* (New York, International Publishers, 1938).

LITTLETON, M. W. *The Revolution Against American Government* (New York, 1924).

MANLEY, BASIL M. *Where La Follette Stands* . . . (Chicago, 1924).

MICHELET, SIMON. *Third Party Vote in the Election of 1924* (Washington, 1925).

MORGENTHAU, HENRY. *Why I Supported Alfred E. Smith* (New York, 1928).

MOULTON, HAROLD G. *Public Works or Public Charity?* (Chicago, Union League Club, 1919). Deals with postwar unemployment problem..

MUSTE, A. J. *Why a Labor Party?* (New York, 1929).

National Civil Liberties Bureau. *War-time Prosecutions and Mob Violence* . . . *from April 1, 1917 to May 1 1918* (New York, N.C.L.B., July, 1918).

National Industrial Conference Board. Numerous pamphlets on economic conditions, stock purchase plans, the 1929 crash, mechanization of industry, wages, world economy, industrial lunch rooms, etc. (At N.I.C.B.).

NEARING, SCOTT, et al. *Can the Church Be Radical? Debate* . . . *Feb. 12, 1922* [between] *John Haynes Holmes* [and] *Scott Nearing* (New York, Hanford Press, 1922).

NEARING, SCOTT. *A Nation Divided or Plutocracy versus Democracy* (Chicago, S. P., 1920). Stresses international socialism in final paragraph, issued during intra-party strife.

NEARING, SCOTT, et al. *A Public Debate: "Capitalism vs. Socialism." Prof. Edwin R. A. Seligman vs. Prof. Scott Nearing* (New York, Fine Arts Guild, 1921).

New York State. *Labor Laws Enacted in 1928.* Bulletin 155 (N. Y., 1928).

OCHS-OAKES, GEORGE W. *The Menace of Communism* (n.p., n.d.,). Address delivered on Flag Day, 1931, to D.A.R., Chattanooga, Tenn., by the editor of *Current History.*

ONEAL, JAMES. *Some Pages of Party History* (New York, published by the author, 1934?).

————. *Resolved: That the Terms of the Third International are Inacceptable to the Revolutionary Socialists of the World. A Debate. James Oneal vs. Robert Minor* (New York, Academy Press, 1921).

PATCH, BUEL W. *Industrial Unionism and the A. F. of L.* (Washington, Editorial Research Reports, Vol. II, no. 17, Nov. 11, 1936).

PETERSON, ARNOLD. *W. Z. Foster—Renegade or Spy?* (New York, N. Y. News Co., 1932). Socialist Labor Party Pamphlet.

PLAVNER, MURRAY. *Is the American Youth Congress a Communist Front?* (New York, Murray Plavner, 1939).

The Politics of Labor. (A Radio Discussion by Neil Jacoby, Raymond Walsh, and Leo Wolman. N.B.C., Jan. 9, 1944.) University of Chicago Roundtable.

RUSHMORE, HOWARD. *Rebirth of an American* (New York, 1940). Reprint from *American Magazine*, April, 1940.

SAPOSS, DAVID J. Structure of A. F. of L. Unions. Washington, N. L. R. B. Division of Economic Research, May 15, 1939. Mimeographed pamphlet.

SNOW, JOHN HOWARD. *America ... Which Way?* (New York, 1945).

SOKOFSKY, GEORGE E. *Is Communism a Menace?* (n.p., n.d.,). Address made in debate with Earl Browder, New York, March 21, 1943.

SOLITIN, J. *The Struggle Against Anti-Semitism* (New York?, Communist Party?, 1938?).

SOULE, GEORGE HENRY. *The Intellectual and the Labor Movement* (New York, League for Ind. Dem., 1923).

STARK, LOUIS. *Labor and the New Deal* (Washington, Public Affairs Committee, 1936).

STAROBIN, JOSEPH. *It's Up to You* (New York, New Age Publishers, 1940?). By the editor of the *Young Communist Review*.

WHITNEY, R. M. *La Follette, Socialism, Communism* (New York, 1924).

WILLIAMS, DAVID C. *Labour in the U. S. A.* (London, Bureau of Current Affairs, 1947).

F. PERIODICALS AND MAGAZINES

Trade Union Journals

The following are illustrative only. The writer used all labor periodicals for 1928 housed in the University of California and Wisconsin State Historical Society Libraries.

American Federationist, 1906-1951.

Bricklayer, Mason and Plasterer, 1928.

Brotherhood of Locomotive Firemen and Enginemen's Magazine, 1924-1928.

Carpenter, 1928.

Cigar Makers' Journal, 1928.

Granite Cutters' Journal, 1928.

Illinois State Federation of Labor Bulletin, 1928.

International Molders Journal, 1928.

International Stereotypers and Electrotypers Union Journal, 1928.

Lather; Official Journal of the Wood, Wire and Metal Lathers International Union, 1928.

Locomotive Engineers Journal, 1924-1928.

Machinists Monthly Journal, 1928.

Minnesota State Federation of Labor Bulletin. 1928.

Motorman and Conductor, 1928.

New York State Federation of Labor Bulletin. 1928.

Official Magazine, International Brotherhood of Teamsters, Chauffeurs, Stablemen and Helpers of America, 1916-1929.

Paper Makers Journal, 1928.

Painter and Decorator: Official Journal of the Brotherhood of Painters, Decorators and Paperhangers of America, 1928.

Pattern Makers Journal, 1928.

Postal Record: A Monthly Journal of the National Association of Letter Carriers, 1928.

Railroad Telegrapher, 1924-1928.

Railway Clerk, 1928.

Railway Conductor, 1924-1928.

Railway Maintenance of Way Employes Journal, 1928.

Railway Carmen's Journal, 1928.

Retail Clerks International Advocate, 1928.

Shoe Workers' Journal, 1928.

Union Postal Clerk, 1928

United Mineworkers Journal, 1928.

Trade Union Convention Proceedings

Amalgamated Clothing Workers of America, 1928. (Includes Report of the General Executive Board, New York, 1928.)

Journeyman Barbers International Union, 1929.

American Federation of Labor, 1906-1936.

American Federation of Musicians, 1928.

Bricklayers, Masons and Plasterers' International Union of America, 1928.

Building Trades Department, American Federation of Labor, 1920-1928.

California State Federation of Labor, 1928.

Glass Bottle Blowers, 1927.

United Brotherhood of Carpenters and Joiners of America, 1928.

International Brotherhood of Electrical Workers, 1927, 1929.

International Association of Firefighters, 1928.

International Ladies' Garment Workers' Union, 1928.

National Marine Engineers' Beneficial Association, 1928.

New York State Federation of Labor, 1920-1932.

Brotherhood of Painters, Decorators and Paperhangers, 1929.

International Brotherhood of Paper Makers, 1927.

International Photo-Engravers' Union, 1928.

Ohio State Federation of Labor, 1928.
International Seamen's Association of America, 1927.
United Mine Workers, 1927, 1930.

Miscellaneous Periodicals and Magazines

(Other than learned journals)

American Federation of Labor, Legal Information Bureau, *Legal Information Bulletin*, 1924-1928.

American Labor Legislation Review, 1920-1928.

The Communist, 1928-1932. New York.

The Communist International, 1925-1932. London.

International Press Correspondence (English edition), 1928. Vienna. Publication of the Third International. Contains the statement, "Unpublished Manuscript—Please reprint."

International Trade Union Movement, 1921-1925. Amsterdam. Review of the International Federation of Trade Unions.

The Labor Herald, May, 1922—Oct., 1924. Chicago. "Official Organ of the Trade Union Educational League."

La Follette's Magazine, 1925-1929.

Law and Labor, 1919-1928. New York. League for Industrial Rights (American Anti-Boycott Association).

Liberator, 1918-1924. New York.

National Industrial Conference Board Bulletin, 1927-29. Also other N.I.C.B. publications.

New Leader and American Appeal, 1927-1929. Name changed to *New Leader* after October, 1928.

New Masses, 1927 to April, 1928; Oct., 1928 to 1929.

The Open Forum. 1928. Southern California Branch, Amer. Civil Liberties Union.

Proceedings, National Association of Manufacturers, 1928.

The Workers Monthly, 1924-1927. Chicago.

World Tomorrow, 1928-1929. New York.

G. ARTICLES

The following abbreviations are used in this section:
A. E. R.   *American Economic Review*
A. P. S. R.   *American Political Science Review*
C. H.   *Current History*

J. P. E.   *Journal of Political Economy*
M. V. H. R.   *Mississippi Valley Historical Review*
P. S. Q.   *Political Science Quarterly*

Trade Union Articles

Includes the following: articles by union leaders; articles about unions; articles on legal and economic topics directly concerning unions. Does not include the subject "labor in politics." Excludes most *general* articles on unions, especially those exclusively devoted to conditions in the 1930s and later.

"American Trade Unionists' Interview with Joseph Stalin; With a Comment by Matthew Woll," *C. H.*, XXVII (Feb., 1928), 691-692.

ANDREWS, JOHN B. "Labor Legislation in 1928," *A. P. S. R.*, XXIII (May, 1929), 417-421.

BARBASH, JACK. "Ideology and the Unions," *A. E. R.*, XXXIII (Dec., 1943), 868-876.

BARNETT, GEORGE E. "American Trade Unionism and Social Insurance," *A. E. R.*, XXIII (Mar., 1933), 1-8.

BERMAN, EDWARD. "The Supreme Court Interprets the Railway Labor Act." *A. E. R.*, XX (Dec., 1930), 619-639.

"Bills and Legislation of Interest to Labor in the First Session of the Seventieth Congress, 1927-28," *Monthly Labor Review*, XXVII (Aug., 1928), 298-305.

BRISSENDEN, PAUL F. "The Labor Injunction," *P. S. Q.*, XLVIII (Sept., 1933), 413-450.

COMMONS, JOHN ROGERS. "Karl Marx and Samuel Gompers," *P. S. Q.*, XLI (June, 1926), 281-286.

———. "Labor and Politics," *National Civic Federation Report on Municipal and Private Ownership,*. Vol. I, Part I.

COOPER, LYLE W. "The American Federation of Labor and the Intellectuals," *P. S. Q.*, XLIII (Sept., 1928), 388-407.

———. "The American Labor Movement in Prosperity and Depression," *A. E. R.*, XXII (Dec., 1932), 641-659.

———. "The Tariff and Organized Labor," *A. E. R.*, XX (June, 1930), 210-225.

CUTLER, ADDISON T. "Labor Legislation in Thirteen Southern States," *Southern Economic Journal*, VII (Jan., 1941), 297-316.

CUMMINS, E. E. "The National Board for Jurisdictional Awards and the Carpenters' Union," *A. E. R.*, XIX (Sept., 1929), 363-377.

———. "Political and Social Philosophy of the Carpenters' Union," *P. S. Q.*, XLII (Sept., 1927), 397-418.

DOUGLAS, DOROTHY W. "American Minimum Wage Laws at Work," *A. E. R.*, IX (Dec., 1919), 701-738.

DOUGLAS, PAUL H. "American Labor Relations Acts," *A. E. R.,* XXVII (Dec., 1937), 735-761.

DOUTY, H. M. "The Trend of Industrial Disputes, 1922-1930," *Journal of the American Statistical Association,* XXVII (June, 1932), 168-172.

EBY, KERMIT. "Why Labor Leaders are Human," Mimeographed reprint (place?, date?).

FISHER, WALDO E. "Wage and Hour Policies and Employment," *A. E. R.,* XXX (June, 1940), 290-299.

FISHER, WILLARD C. "American Experience with Workmen's Compensation," *A. E. R.,* X (March, 1920), 18-47.

FURUSETH, ANDREW. "Shall Government by Injunction Rule?" *La Follette's Magazine,* XX (March, 1928), 44.

GALIARDO, DOMENICO. "Strikes in a Democracy," *A. E. R.,* XXXI (March, 1941), 47-55.

GILBERT, A. B. "Non-Partisan vs. Party Politics," *Amercian Federationist,* XXXIV (Nov., 1927), 1350-1353.

GITLOW, A. L. [*sic*] "The Communist Threat to Labor," *Southern Economic Journal,* XVI (April, 1950), 458-470.

"Green vs. Red in the A. F. of L.," *Literary Digest,* LXXXVII (Oct. 24, 1925), 12-13.

KILLINGSWORTH, CHARLES C. "Public Regulation of Labor Relations—The Wisconsin Experiment," *A. E. R.,* XXXIII (June, 1943), 247-263.

KING, JOSEPH J. "The Durham Central Labor Union," *Southern Economic Journal,* V (July, 1938), 55-70.

KLEMM, MARY. "The Rise of Independent Unionism and the Decline of Labor Oligopoly," *A. E. R.,* XXIV (March, 1944), 76-86.

"Labor's Neutral Strategy," *Literary Digest,* XCVIII (Aug. 25, 1928), 15.

LEWIS, EDWARD E. "The Southern Negro and the American Labor Supply," *P. S. Q.,* XIVIII (June, 1933), 172-183.

LONIGAN, EDNA. "The Effect of Modern Technological Conditions Upon the Employment of Labor," *A. E. R.,* XXIX (June, 1939), 246-259.

MASON, ALPHEUS T. "Labor, the Courts, and Section 7(A)," *A. P. S. R.,* XXVIII (Dec., 1934), 999-1015.

McNATT, E. B. "Labor Again Menaced by the Sherman Act," *Southern Economic Journal,* VI (Oct., 1939), 190-208.

MILLIS, HARRY A. "The Union in Industry: Some Observations on the Theory of Collective Bargaining," *A. E. R.,* XXV (March, 1935), 1-13.

NORTHRUP, HERBERT R. "The Negro and the United Mine Workers of America," *Southern Economic Journal,* IX (April, 1943), 313-326.

PERLMAN, JACOB. "Labor's New Head is Real Leader," *La Follette's Magazine,* XVII (Feb., 1925), 21.

PERLMAN, SELIG. "Labor in the New Deal Decade." Lectures before the I. L. G. W. U. Institute, 1943. Mimeographed.

QUARLES, JAMES. "Labor Unions in Peace and War," *P. S. Q.,* LIX (June, 1944), 264-274.

ROSE, CAROLINE BAER. "Morale in a Trade Union," *American Journal of Sociology*, LVI (Sept., 1950), 167-174.

ROURKE, FRANCIS E. "The Department of Labor and Trade Unions," *Western Political Quarterly*, VII (Dec., 1954), 656-672.

SAYRE, FRANCIS B. "Does American Labor Stand to Win or Lose By Trade Agreements?" *P. S. Q.*, LIV (June, 1939), 175-186.

SEAGER, HENRY R. "Company Unions vs. Trade Unions," *A. E. R.*, XIII (March, 1923), 1-13.

SOROKIN, P. A. and others. "Leaders of Labor and Radical Movements in the United States and Foreign Countries," *American Journal of Sociology*, XXXIII (Nov., 1927), 382-411.

STALEY, EUGENE. "Sources for Labor Historians," *American Federationist*, XXXV (March, 1928), 282-286.

STANLEY, LOUIS. "The Collapse of the A. F. of L.," *Nation*, CXXXI (Oct. 8, 1930), pp. 367-369.

STEWART, ETHELBERT. "Conditions of Labor and Labor Organizations," *American Year Book, 1928* (New York, 1929), pp. 521-525.

STEVENS, HAROLD (pseudonym). "How Unions are Run," *Personnel Journal*, XXVIII (Jan., 1950), 279-284.

SULLIVAN, MARK S. "A. F. L. Winds Up Convention," Seattle *Times*, Oct. 19, 1941.

TAFT, PHILIP. "The Problem of Structure in American Labor," *A. E. R.*, XXVII (March, 1927), 4-16.

————. "Some Problems of the New Unionism in the United States," *A. E. R.*, XXIX (June, 1939), 313-324.

"Tariff, a Labor Question," *National Republic*, XVII (Nov., 1929), 12-13.

TROXELL, JOHN P. "Protecting Members' Rights Within the Union," *American Economic Review Supplement* (Mar., 1942).

WARE, NORMAN J. "Labor Movements of Great Britain and the United States," *A. E. R.*, XXIX (June, 1939), 237-245.

WOLMAN, LEO. "The Area of Collective Bargaining," *P. S. Q.*, LIX (Dec., 1944), 481-488.

————. "Issues in American Industrial Relations," *P. S. Q.*, LII (June, 1937), 161-173.

————. "The Turning Point in American Labor Policy," *P. S. Q.*, LV (June, 1940), 161-175.

Politics, and Labor in Politics

AGAR, HERBERT. "Why Have a Labor Party?" *Atlantic Monthly*, CLXXXVI (Oct., 1950), 25-28.

BARCLAY, THOMAS S. "The Publicity Division of the Democratic Party, 1929-30," *A. P. S. R.*, XXV (Feb., 1931), 68-73.

344   ☒ **LABOR POLITICS IN A DEMOCRATIC REPUBLIC**

BERDAHL, CLARENCE A. "Party Membership in the United States," *A. P. S. R.*, XXXVI (Feb. and Apr., 1942).

————. "Some Notes on Party Membership in Congress," *A. P. S. R.*, XLIII (April, June, August, 1949).

BERNSTEIN, IRVING. "John L. Lewis and the Voting Behavior of the C. I. O." *Public Opinion Quarterly*, V (1941), 233-249.

BONE, HUGH A. "Political Parties in New York City," *A. P. S. R.*, XL (April, 1946), 272-282.

CANNON, JAMES, JR. (Bishop). "Causes of Governor Smith's Defeat," *C. H.*, XXIX (Dec., 1928), 373-377.

CARGILL, OSCAR. "Lincoln Steffens: Pied Piper of the Kremlin," *Georgia Review*, V (Winter, 1951), 430-443.

CASEY, RALPH D. "Party Campaign Propaganda," *Annals*, 179 (May, 1935), 96-105.

————. "Scripps-Howard Newspapers in the 1928 Campaign," *Journalism Quarterly*, VII, 207-31.

CLARK, LINDLEY. "Labor in Politics," *American Year Book, 1928* (New York, 1929), pp. 526-527.

COMMONS, JOHN R. "Is Class Conflict in America Growing and Is it Inevitable?" *Amer. Jour. of Sociol.* XIII (May, 1908), 756-783. Plus discussion.

————. "Labor Organization and Labor Politics," *Quarterly Journal of Economics*, February, 1907.

CUNIFF, M. G. "Labor in Politics. The Campaign Against Littlefield," *World's Work*, XII (1906), 8130-8135.

DAVID, HENRY. "Labor and Political Action After World War I: 1919-1924," *Labor and Nation*, I (Feb.-March, 1946), 27-32.

————. "Labor's Bi-Partisan Political Thinking. . . ." *Ibid.*, V (Sept.-Oct., 1949), 50-55.

————. "One Hundred Years of Political Action by Labor," *Labor and Nation*, V (Nov.-Dec., 1946), 36-40.

DEWEY, THOMAS E. "The Two-Party System of Government," *Vital Speeches*, XVI (June 1, 1950), 489-496.

DICKSON, EVERETT M. and WALTER P. REUTHER (a debate). "Should Political Activities of Labor Unions Be Restricted?" *Town Meeting Bulletin*, X (June 22, 1944).

DOHERTY, HERBERT J., JR., "Florida and the Presidential Election of 1928," *Florida Historical Quarterly*, XXVI, 174-186.

DREISER, THEODORE. "Theodore Dreiser on the Elections," *New Masses*, IV (Nov., 1928), 17.

DOUGLAS, PAUL H. "The Prospects for a New Political Alignment," *A. P. S. R.*, XXV (Nov., 1931), 906-914.

————. "Why a Political Labor Party is Slow in Forming in the United States," *American Labor Monthly*, II (Feb., 194), 21-27.

ELDERSVELD, SAMUEL J. "The Influence of Metropolitan Party Pluralities in Presidential Elections Since 1920," *A. P. S. R.*, XLIII (Dec., 1949), 1189-1206.

FREY, JOHN P. "Labor in Politics," *American Federationist*, 39 (Sept., 1932), 1012-21.

FORD, H. "Radicalism in American Politics," *Yale Review*, IX (July, 1920), 759-770.

FRANKLIN, FABIAN. "Analyzing the Election Results," *C. H.*, XXIX (Dec., 1928), 370-373.

HART, A. B. "Aftermath of the Election," *C. H.*, XXIX (Dec., 1928), 483-486.

————. "Cross-Currents in the Election," *C. H.*, XXIX (Dec., 1928), 367-370.

————. "The Presidential Election of 1928," *American Year Book, 1928* (New York, 1929), pp. 1-6.

HAYNES, FRED E. "The Collapse of the Farmer-Labor Bloc," *Social Focus*, IV (Sept., 1925) 148-156.

————. "The Significance of the Latest Third Party Movement," *M. V. H. R.*, XII (Sept. 1925), 177-186.

HERRING, E. PENDLETON. "The Political Context of the Tariff Commission," *P. S. Q.*, XLIX (Sept., 1934). 421-440.

"Hoover's Appeal to the Workers," *Literary Digest*, XCIX (Oct. 6, 1928), 10-11.

HOXIE, ROBERT. "President Gompers and the Labor Vote," *J. P. E.*, XVI (Dec., 1908), 693-700.

HOTELLING, HAROLD. "Why We Have the Two-Party System," *American Journal of Economics and Sociology*, X (Oct., 1950), 13-15.

HUDSON, R. A. and H. ROSEN. "Union Political Action: The Union Member Speaks," *Industrial and Labor Relations Review*, VII (1954), 404-18.

HUNTINGTON, SAMUEL P. "A Revised Theory of American Party Politics," *A. P. S. R.*, XLIV (Sept., 1950), 669-677.

KAMPLEMAN, MAX M. "Labor in Politics," In: *Interpreting the Labor Movement* (Madison, 1952).

KARSON, MARC. "The Catholic Church and the Political Development of American Trade Unionism, 1900-1918," *Industrial and Labor Relations Review*, IV (1951), 527-542.

KEARNEY, JOHN J. "A. F. of L. Political Policy Proven Sound," *American Federationist*, 37 (July, 1930), 798-802.

KIPLINGER, W. M. "The Political Role of Labor," *Annals*, 184 (Mar., 1936), 124-129.

KNAPPEN, THEODORE M. "Business and the Campaign," *Magazine of Wall Street*, XLII (July 14, 1928), 453-455.

"Labor Party Not Wanted by Labor," *Literary Digest*, LXXXIII (Dec. 6, 1924), 10-11.

"Labor Strategy," *Nation*, CXXVII (Sept. 19, 1928), 259.

LA FOLLETTE, ROBERT M., JR. "Progressive Vote in 1928," *La Follette's Magazine*, XXI (Feb., 1929), 17-18.

LEEDS, MORTON. "The A F L in the 1948 Elections," *Social Research*, XVII (June, 1950), 207-218.

"Matthew Woll." Obituary. *New York Times,* June 2, 1956.

McCoy, Donald R. "The Records of the Democratic and Republican National Committees," *American Archivist,* XIV (Oct., 1951), 313-321.

McGoldrick, Joseph. "The New York City Election of 1929," *A. P. S. R.,* XXIV (Aug., 1930), 688-691.

Michelet, Simon. "An Analysis of the Vote in the National Election," *C. H.,* XXIX (Feb., 1929), 781-785.

Naftalin, Arthur. "The Failure of the Farmer Labor Party to Capture Control of the Minnesota Legislature," *A. P. S. R.,* XXXVIII (Feb., 1944), 71-79.

Norris, George W. "The Meannig of the Recent Election," *La Follette's Magazine,* XX (Dec., 1928), 181.

Ogburn, W. F. and Estelle Hill. "Income Classes and the Roosevelt Vote in 1932," *P. S. Q.,* L (June, 1935), 186-193.

Ogburn, William F. and Nell Snow Talbot. "A Measurement of the Factors in the Presidential Election of 1928," *Social Forces,* VIII (Dec., 1929), 175-183.

Overacker, Louis. "Dirty Money and Dirty Politics," *New Republic,* CXXIII (Sept. 11, 1950), 11-13.

————. "Labor's Political Contributions," *P. S. Q., LIV* (March, 1939), 56-58.

Pollock, James K., Jr. "Campaign Funds in 1928," *A. P. S. R.,* XXIII (Feb., 1929), 59-69.

"Presidential Campaign of 1928; Symposium," *C. H.,* XXVIII (June, 1928), 335-372.

"Presidential Election of 1928," *C. H.,* XXIX (Dec., 1928), 353-355.

Ratchford, B. U. "Certain Bases of Power Politics," *Southern Economic Review,* XI (July, 1944), 20-33.

Robinson, Edgar Eugene. "The Place of Party in the Political History of the United States," *Proceedings of the Pacific Coast Branch of the American Historical Association, 1928,* pp. 11-36.

————. "Realities in Politics," *New Republic,* XXIV (Nov. 3, 1920), 237-239.

————. "Role of Political Parties in American Public Life," *Information Please Almanac, 1948* (New York, 1947), 24-29.

Ryan, John A. "A Catholic View of the Election," *C. H.,* XXIX (Dec., 1928), 377-381.

Sheppard, Harold L. and Nicholas Masters. "The Political Attitudes and Preferences of Union Members: The Case of the Detroit Auto Workers," *A. P. S. R.,* LIII (June, 1959), 437-447.

————. "Union Political Action and Public Opinion Polls in a Democratic Society," *Social Problems,* V (July, 1957), 14-20.

Shideler, James H. "The La Follette Progressive Campaign of 1924," *Wisconsin Magazine of History,* XXXIII (June, 1950), 444-457.

"Shall We Vote for Al?" Editorial, *World Tomorrow,* XI (August, 1928), 323-324.

STARR, JOSEPH R. "The Legal Status of American Political Parties," *A. P. S. R.*, XXXIV (June, August, 1940).

TAFT, PHILIP H. "Labor's Changing Political Line," *J. P. E.*, XLV (Oct., 1937), 634-650.

TIBBETTS, CLARK. "Majority Votes and the Business Cycle," *American Journal of Sociology*, XXXVI (Jan., 1931), 596-606.

WHITE, WILLIAM ALLEN. "The Farmer's Votes and Problems," *Yale Review* (Spring, 1939), 433-448.

WILLIAMSON, HUGH. "Evils of the American Two-Party System," *American Journal of Economics and Sociology*, IX (July, 1950), 405-417.

WOLMAN, LEO. "Labor in Politics," *Freeman*, I (Nov. 13, 1959), 105-106.

Communism, Communists, Communist Party, Third International, and Communist Propaganda

BECKNER, E. R. "Trade Union Educational League and the American Labor Movement," *J. P. E.*, XXXIII (Aug., 1925), 410-431.

BITTLEMAN, ALEXANDER. "A Conference of Progressive Reactionaries," *The Workers Monthly*, IV (Feb., 1925), 166-167. Refers to C. P. P. A.

BORNET, VAUGHN DAVIS. "Historical Scholarship, Communism, and the Negro," *Journal of Negro History*, XXXVII (July, 1952), 304-324.

COMMONS, JOHN R. "Communism and Collective Democracy," *A. E. R.*, XXV (June, 1935), 212-223.

ENGDAHL, J. LOUIS. "The Capitulation of the Petty-Bourgeoisie in the American (U. S. A.) Election Campaign," *International Press Correspondence*, VIII (Nov. 2, 1928), 1430-1431.

————. "The Presidential Elections in the United States," International Press Correspondence, VIII (June 28, 1928), 641-642.

ENGDAHL, J. LOUIS. "Sam Gompers is Not Dead," *The Workers Monthly*, V (Nov., 1925), 10-14.

————. "The Victors in the American Elections," *International Press Correspondence*, VIII (Nov. 16, 1928), 1499-1500.

FOSTER, WILLIAM Z. "The Crisis in the Labor Movement," *The Communist*, VII (Jan., 1928), 10-20.

————. "The Workers (Communist) Party in the South," *The Communist*, VII (Nov. 1928), 675-681.

GITLOW, BENJAMIN. "Big Business Can't Lose in 1928," *The Communist*, VII (Aug., 1928), 467-472.

————. "Hoover and Smith—Mouthpieces of Big Business—Accept the Nomination," *The Communist*, VII (Sept., 1928), 531-537.

GREEN, P. "Eight Years of Proletarian Dictatorship," *The Workers Monthly*, V (Nov., 1925), 3-4.

LENIN, V. I. "The Presidential Elections in the United States," *The Communist*, VII (Jan., 1928), 67-68. Reprint from *Pravda*, Nov. 9, 1912.

LOVESTONE, JAY. "Class Divisions in the United States," *The Workers Monthly*, V (Nov., 1925), 18-20.

————. "The 1928 Elections," *The Communist*, VII (Dec., 1928), 734-755.

————. "Practical Phases of the Labor Party Campaign," *The Communist*, VII (April, 1928), 205-218.

————. "The Present Situation in the Labor Movement," *The Communist*, VII (May, 1928), 265-278.

————. "The Sixth World Congress of the Communist International," *The Communist*, VII (Nov. 1928), 659-675.

————. "Some Immediate Party Problems," *The Communist*, VII (July, 1928), 421-433.

MOORE, BENJAMIN, JR. "The Communist Party of the U. S. A.," *A. P. S. R.*, XXXIX (Feb., 1945), 31-41. Begins about 1935.

NEARING, SCOTT. "Democracy," *Labour Monthly*, X (Nov., 1928), 681-685.

————. "The Political Outlook for the Workers (Communist) Party," *The Communist*, VII (Dec., 1928), 756-759.

NEIKIND, CLAIRE. "U. S. Communism: Its Secret Business Empire," *The Reporter*, IV (Jan. 23, 1951), 5-8.

NEUMAN, HEINZ. "Marx and Engels on the Role of the Communists in America," *The Workers Monthly*, V (Nov., 1925), 32-36; (Dec., 1925), 86-90. Extracts from correspondence.

OLGIN, MOISSAYE J. "Politics and the Fly Hunt," *The Communist*, VII (Sept., 1928), 538-547.

————. "The Socialist Party Offers Itself," *The Communist*, VII (Oct., 1928), 595-604. Detailed criticism of the S. P. program for 1928.

PENNIMAN, HOWARD. "Communist Party," *Collier's Encyclopedia*, V (New York, 1950), 537-538.

PEPPER, JOHN. "America and the Tactics of the Communist International," *The Communist*, VII (April, 1938), 219-227.

————. "Certain Basic Questions of Our Perspective," *The Communist*, VII (May, 1928), 297-306.

————. "A Program of Action for America," *The Communist*, VII (June, 1928), 327-339.

"Red Presidential Ticket," *Literary Digest*, XCVII (June 16, 1928), 14.

ROTHSTEIN, ANDREW. "Sixth Congress of the Communist International," *Labour Monthly*, X (Dec., 1928), 728-737.

RUTHENBERG, C. E. "Progressive, But Not Labor," *The Workers Monthly*, III (Nov., 1924), 21-23.

STOLBERG, B. "Peter Pans of Communism; Study of Bolshevism in America, 1919-1925," *Century*, CX June, 1925), 219-227.

SWABECK, ARNE. "The Presidential Elections of 1928," *The Communist*, VII (Sept., 1928), 548-554.

TANIN, J. "The Leading Party of the American Capitalists [the Republican Party] on the Eve of the Elections," *International Press Correspondence*, VIII (June 21, 1928), 623-624.

TRACHTENBERG, ALEXANDER. "Eugene Victor Debs," *The Communist,* VII (Nov., 1928), 700-713.

WARBASSE, J. P. "The Communist Religion," *World Tomorrow,* XI (Dec., 1928), 507-509.

WEINSTONE, WILLIAM W. "Al Smith and the New Tammany Hall," *The Communist,* VII (April, 1928), 229-235.

WICKS, H. M. "Herbert Hoover," *The Communist,* VII (Jan., 1928), 69-74.

WOLFE, BERTRAM D. "The Right Danger in the Comintern," *The Communist,* VII (Dec., 1928), 723-735. Wolfe's final article as editor.

Socialism, Socialists, Socialist Party, Second International, and Socialist Propaganda

BESTOR, ARTHUR EUGENE, JR. "The Evolution of the Socialist Vocabulary," *Journal of the History of Ideas,* IX (June, 1948), 259-302.

GHENT, W. J. "Collapse of Socialism in the United States," *C. H.,* XXIV (May, 1926), 242-246.

HECHT, DAVID. "Plekhanov and American Socialism," *Russian Review,* IX (April, 1950), 112-123.

HILLQUIT, MORRIS. "Marxism Essential Evolutionary," *C. H.,* XXIX (Oct., 1928), 29-35.

JOHANNET, R. "Why America Isn't Socialist," *Living Age,* CCCIV (Jan. 1, 1928), 33-35.

MATSON, NORMAN. "The Split in Italy," *The Liberator,* IV (March, 1921), 16-21.

ONEAL, J. "American Socialist Party's New Activities," *C. H.,* XXIV (Aug., 1926), 753-755.

ONEAL, J. "Changing Fortunes of American Socialism," *C. H.,* XX (April, 1924), 92-100.

————. "A Socialist View of American History," *New Leader* (Newspaper), Sept. 22, 1928, p. 4:1-7.

PAGE, KIRBY. "Why I Shall Vote for Norman Thomas," *World Tomorrow,* XI (Nov., 1928), 449-452.

PEPPER, JOHN. "The Transformation of the American Socialist Party," *International Press Correspondence,* VIII (May, 1928), 484. A Communist analysis.

"Socialist Ticket," *Literary Digest,* XCVII (April 28, 1928), 12.

"Socialist Slump," *Literary Digest,* C (Jan. 5, 1929), 9.

"The Socialist Vote," Editorial, *World Tomorrow,* XII (Feb., 1929), 55.

"Socialists Loosen Up," Editorial, *World Tomorrow,* XII (March, 1929), 105.

SPARGO, P. "The Foe of Liberty and Progress," *North American Review,* CCXXV (April, 1928), 476-484.

"The Split in the Socialist Party," *C. H.,* XIII (Jan., 1921), 37-43.

STEDMAN, MURRAY S., JR. " 'Democracy' In American Communal and Social-ist Literature," *Journal of the History of Ideas*, XII (Jan., 1951), 147-154.

THOMAS, NORMAN. "Eugene Victor Debs," *C. H.*, XXV (Dec., 1926), 373-376.

————. "Why Not a New Party?" *North American Review*, CCXXVII (Feb., 1929), 143-150.

YELLEN, S. "Socialist Boyhood," *American Mercury*, XXI (Oct., 1930), 199-207.

Miscellaneous Articles

BEER, MAX. "Communism," *Encyclopedia of the Social Sciences* (New York, 1930).

BERGLUND, ABRAHAM. "The Tariff Act of 1930," *A. E. R.*, XX (Sept., 1930), 467-479.

BRISSENDEN, PAUL F. "The Campaign Against the Labor Injunction," *A. E. R.*, XXIII (March, 1933), 42-54.

COMMONS, JOHN R. "Marx To-day: Capitalism and Socialism," *Atlantic*, CXXXVI (Nov., 1925), 682-693.

————. "Passing of Samuel Gompers," *C. H.*, XXI (Feb., 1925), 670-676.

DEWEY, JOHN. "The Future of Radical Political Action," *Nation* (Jan. 4, 1933).

————. "The Need for a New Party," *New Republic* (Mar. 18-Apr. 8, 1931).

————. "Prospects for a Third Party," *New Republic* (Jan. 27, 1932).

"Dewey's Third Party," *Outlook* (Jan. 7, 1931).

"Dr. Dewey and the Insurgents," *World Tomorrow* (Feb.,1931).

FITE, GILBERT C. "The Agricultural Issue in the Presidential Campaign of 1928," *M. V. H. R.* (March, 1951), 653-672.

FLORINSKY, MICHAEL T. "Stalin's New Deal for Labor," *P. S. Q.*, XVI (March, 1941), 38-50.

HEWES, AMY. "The Transformation of Soviet Trade Unions," *A. E. R.*, XXII (Dec., 1932), 605-619.

HINSHAW, A. W. "Story of Frances Perkins; Her Fight Against Selfishness, Prejudice and Vested Interests," *Century*, CXIV (Sept., 1927), 596-605.

HOCKETT, H. C. "The Influence of the West on the Rise and Fall of Political Parties," *M. V. H. R.*, *IV* (Mar., 1918), 459-469.

HOWENSTEIN, E. J., JR. "The High-Cost-of-Living Problem after World War I," *Southern Economic Journal*, X (Jan., 1944), 222-234.

LE ROSSIGNOL, J. E. "Labor Governments and the Social Revolution," *A. E. R.*, XV (June, 1925), 267-274.

LORWIN, LEWIS W. "Communist Parties," and "Class Struggle," *Encyclopedia of the Social Sciences* (New York, 1930).

MACDONALD, LOIS. "The National Labor Relations Act," *A. E. R.*, XXVI (Sept., 1936), 412-427.

MAY, HENRY F. "The End of American Radicalism," *American Quarterly,* II (Winter, 1950), 291-302.

MERRIAM, CHARLES E. "The Assumptions of Democracy," *P. S. Q.,* LIII (Sept., 1938), 328-349.

MUSTE, A. J. "American Labor, the International Labor Movement and Peace," *International Trade Union Review,* IV (July/Sept., 1924).

NORTHRUP, HERBERT R. "Literature of the Labor Crisis," *P. S. Q.,* LXI (Sept., 1946), 420-433.

"Present Status of the Anti-Injunction Bill in Congress," *Monthly Labor Review,* XXVII (Nov., 1928), 955-959.

RICH, EDGAR J. "The Transportation Act of 1920," *A. E. R.,* X (Sept., 1920), 507-527.

SCHILPP, PAUL ARTHUR. "Is Western Civilization Worth Saving?" *World Tomorrow,* XI (Sept., 1928), 369-371.

"Socialist on the Marxian Great Divide," *Literary Digest,* XCVI (March 3, 1928), 18.

TAFT, PHILIP. "A Rereading of Selig Perlman's A Theory of the Labor Movement," *Industrial and Labor Relations Review,* IX (Oct., 1950), 70-77.

H. PRINTED COLLECTIONS OF PUBLIC PAPERS, SPEECHES, LETTERS, AND REPORTS

BERGER, VICTOR L. *Voice and Pen of Victor L. Berger: Congressional Speeches and Editorials* (Milwaukee, 1929).

BUNYAN, JAMES and H. H. FISHER. *The Bolshevik Revolution, 1917-1918; Documents and Materials.* Stanford Univ., 1934.

CHAMBERLAIN, WILLIAM HENRY. *Blueprint for World Conquest.* Washington and Chicago, Human Events, 1946. Collection of documents of the Third International.

COMMONS, JOHN R., *et al. Documentary History of American Industrial Society.* 11 volumes. Cleveland, 1910-1911.

COOLIDGE, CALVIN. *The Price of Freedom: Speeches and Addresses.* New York, 1924.

DEBS [*Eugene V.*]: *His Life, Writings and Speeches.* Chicago, C. H. Kerr, 1908.

DE LEON, DANIEL. *Industrial Unionism: Selected Editorials.* New York, Socialist Labor Party, 1920.

FOSTER, WILLIAM Z. *American Trade Unionism . . . Selected Writings.* New York, 1947.

GANKIN, OLGA HESS and H. H. FISHER. *The Bolsheviks and the World War; the Origin of the Third International.* Stanford Univ., 1940.

HOOVER, HERBERT. *The New Day. Campaign Speeches of Herbert Hoover, 1928.* Stanford Univ., 1928.

Interborough Rapid Transit Company Against William Green, et al. Brief for Defendants. . . . New York, 1928.

Interchurch World Movement. *Public Opinion and the Steel Strike. Supplementary Reports of the Investigators to the Commission of Inquiry, the Interchurch World Movement.* New York, 1921.

————. *Report on the Steel Strike of 1919.* New York, 1920.

JOHNSON, WALTER, ed. *Selected Letters of William Allen White: 1899-1943.* New York, 1947.

Official Report of the Proceedings of the Democratic National Convention, Houston, Texas, June 26-29, 1928. Indianapolis, 1928.

Official Report of the Proceedings of the Republican National Convention, Kansas City, Missouri, June 12-15, 1928. New York, 1928.

PORTER, KIRK H., ed. *National Party Platforms.* New York, 1924.

The Public Papers and Addresses of Franklin D. Roosevelt. Volume I. *The Genesis of the New Deal, 1928-1932.* New York, 1938.

SAPOSS, DAVID J. *Readings in Trade Unionism.* New York, 1927.

SMITH, ALFRED E. *Campaign Addresses of Governor Alfred E. Smith, Democratic Candidate for President, 1928.* Washington, Democratic National Committee, 1929.

A Symposium on Andrew Furuseth. New Bedford, Mass., 1948.

WINTER, ELLA and GRANVILLE HICKS, editors. *The Letters of Lincoln Steffens.* 2 vols. New York, 1932.

WOLMAN, LEO. "The Meaning of Employment and Unemployment," "Labor Relations Since the War," and "Industrial Democracy," speeches collected in *The State and Society.* Toronto, 1940.

Writings and Speeches of Eugene V. Debs. With an introduction by Arthur M. Schlessinger, Jr. New York, 1948.

I. MEMOIRS AND BIOGRAPHIES

ALINSKY, SAUL. *John L. Lewis, An Unauthorized Biography.* New York, 1949.

ANDERSON, MARY. *The Autobiography of Mary Anderson as told to Mary N. Winslow.* Minneapolis, 1951.

BUDENZ, LOUIS FRANCIS. *This is My Story.* New York, 1947.

COLEMAN, MCALISTER. *Eugene V. Debs: A Man Unafraid.* New York, 1930.

DREIER, MARY E. *Margaret Dreier Robins: Her Life, Letters and Work.* New York, 1950.

FARLEY, JAMES A. *Behind the Ballots.* New York, 1938.

FAY, BERNARD. *Roosevelt and His America.* Boston, 1934.

FOSTER, WILLIAM Z. *From Bryan to Stalin*. New York, 1937.

————. *Pages from a Worker's Life*. New York, 1939.

FREEMAN, JOSEPH. *An American Testament; a Narrative of Rebels and Romantics*. New York, Farrar and Rinehart, 1936.

GERARD, JAMES W. *My First Eighty-Three Years in America*. New York, 1951.

GINGER, RAY. *The Bending Cross: A Biography of Eugene Victor Debs*. New Brunswick, N. J., 1949.

GITLOW, BENJAMIN. *I Confess: The Truth About American Communism*. New York, 1940.

GOMPERS, SAMUEL. *Seventy Years of Life and Labor: An Autobiography*. New York, 1925. (One volume reprint, 1948.)

HANDLIN, OSCAR. *Al Smith and His America*. New York, 1958.

HARVEY, ROLAND HILL. *Samuel Gompers, Champion of the Toiling Masses*. Stanford Univ., 1935.

HILLQUIT, MORRIS. *Loose Leaves from a Busy Life*. New York, 1934.

HOFSTADTER, RICHARD. *The American Political Tradition and the Men Who Made It*. New York, 1948.

HOWE, FREDERICK C. *Confessions of a Reformer*. New York, 1925.

KARSNER, DAVID. *Debs Goes to Prison*. New York, Irving Kaye Davis and Co., 1919.

KEATING, EDWARD. *Story of Labor: Thirty-three Years on the Rail Workers Fighting Front*. Washington, 1953.

LINDLEY, EARNEST K. *Franklin D. Roosevelt, A Career in Progressive Democracy*. Indianapolis, 1931.

MADISON, CHARLES A. *American Labor Leaders*. New York, 1950.

MANCHESTER, WILLIAM. *Disturber of the Peace: The Life of H. L. Mencken*. New York, 1950.

MATTHEWS, J. B. *Odyssey of a Fellow Traveler*. New York, Mt. Vernon Publishers, 1938.

MAURER, JAMES HUDSON. *It Can Be Done*. New York, 1938.

MERRITT, WALTER GORDON. *Destination Unknown: Fifty Years of Labor Relations*. New York, 1951.

MINTON, BRUCE. *Men Who Lead Labor*. New York, 1937.

MOLEY, RAYMOND. *27 Masters of Politics*. New York, 1949.

MORGAN, H. WAYNE. *Eugene V. Debs: Socialist for President*. Syracuse, N. Y., 1962.

NORRIS, GEORGE W. *Fighting Liberal*. New York, 1945.

RICHBERG, DONALD. *My Hero*. New York, 1954.

————. *Tents of the Mighty*. New York, 1930.

ROBINSON, EDGAR EUGENE. *The Roosevelt Leadership, 1933 to 1945*. Phila. 1955.

————, and Paul C. Edwards, eds. *The Memoirs of Ray Lyman Wilbur*. Stanford, 1960.

SALTER, JOHN THOMAS, editor. *The American Politician*. Chapel Hill, 1938.

SCHENKOFSKY, HENRY. *A Summer with the Union Men.* San Francisco, 1918.

SEIDLER, MURRAY. *Norman Thomas, Respectable Rebel.* Syracuse, 1961.

SMITH, ALFRED E. *Up to Now.* New York, 1929.

SOULE, GEORGE HENRY. *Sidney Hillman, Labor Statesman.* New York, 1939.

SULLIVAN, MARK. *The Education of an American.* New York, 1938.

VILLARD, OSWALD GARRISON. *Fighting Years: Memoirs of a Liberal Editor.* New York, 1939.

WALDMAN, LOUIS. *Labor Lawyer.* New York, 1944.

WECHSLER, JAMES A. *Labor Baron.* New York, 1944.

J. MONOGRAPHS AND SPECIAL STUDIES

ANDERSON, PAUL H. *The Attitude of the American Leftist Leaders Toward the Russian Revolution (1917-1923).* Notre Dame, Ind., 1942.

BARBASH, JACK. *Unions and Telephones.* New York, 1952.

BESTOR, ARTHUR EUGENE. *Backwoods Utopias; the Sectarian and Owenite Phases of Communitarian Socialism in America, 1663-1829.* Philadelphia, 1950.

BRAND, CARL F. *British Labour's Rise to Power.* Stanford Univ., 1941.

BRAZEAL, B. R. *The Brotherhood of Sleeping Car Porters, its Origin and Development.* New York, 1946.

CALKINS, FAY. *The C. I. O. and the Democratic Party.* Chicago, 1952.

CARROLL, MOLLIE RAE. *Labor and Politics: the Attitude of the American Federation of Labor Toward Legislation and Politics.* New York, 1923.

DRAPER, THEODORE. *The Roots of American Communism* (New York, 1957) and *American Communism and Soviet Russia* (New York, 1960).

DOUGLAS, PAUL H. *Real Wages in the United States, 1890-1926.* Boston, 1930.

ERNST, MORRIS L. and DAVID LOTH. *Report on the American Communist.* New York, 1952.

EWING, CORTEZ ARTHUR MILTON. *Congressional Elections, 1896-1944; the Sectional Basis of Political Democracy in the House of Representatives.* Norman, Okla., 1947.

————. *Presidential Elections. From Abraham Lincoln to Franklin D. Roosevelt.* Norman, Okla., 1940.

FAINSOD, MERLE. *International Socialism and the World War.* Cambridge, Mass., 1935.

FITCH, JOHN ANDREWS. *The Causes of Industrial Conflict.* New York, 1924.

FLORINSKY, MICHAEL T. *World Revolution and U. S. S. R.* New York, 1930.

FRANKFURTER, FELIX and NATHAN GREENE. *The Labor Injunction.* New York, 1930.

GREEN, MARGUERITE. *The National Civic Federation and the American Labor Movement, 1900-1925.* Washington, 1956.

HECHT, DAVID. *Russian Radicals Look to America.* Cambridge, Mass., 1947.

HERRING, E. PENDLETON. *Group Representation Before Congress,* Baltimore, 1929.

HILL, SAMUEL E. *Teamsters and Transportation: Employee-Employer Relationships in New England.* Washington, American Council on Public Affairs, 1942.

JENKIN, THOMAS PAUL. *Reactions of Major Groups to Positive Government in the United States, 1930-1940.* Berkeley, California, 1945.

KAMPELMAN, MAX M. *The Communist Party vs. the C. I. O.* New York, 1957.

KIPNIS, IRA. *The American Socialist Movement, 1897-1912.* New York, 1952.

KNOLES, GEORGE HARMON. *The Jazz Age Revisited.* Stanford, Univ., 1955.

KORNHAUSER, A., HAROLD L. SHEPPARD, and ALBERT S. MAYER. *When Labor Votes: A Study of Auto Workers.* New York, 1956.

LEEK, JOHN H. *Government and Labor in the United States.* New York, 1952.

LEITER, ROBERT D. *The Musicians and Petrillo.* New York, 1953.

LOGAN, HAROLD A. *The History of Trade-union Organization in Canada.* Chicago, 1928.

MCCALEB, WALTER F. *Brotherhood of Railroad Trainmen; with Special Reference to the Life of Alexander F. Whitney,* New York, 1936.

MCCRACKEN, DUANE. *Strike Injunctions in the New South.* Chapel Hill, 1931.

MACKAY, KENNETH C. *The Progressive Movement of 1924.* New York, 1947.

MCKELVEY, JEAN TRAPP. *A. F. L. Attitudes Toward Production, 1900-1932.* Ithaca, N. Y., 1952.

MASON, ALPHEUS T. *Organized Labor and the Law.* Durham, N. C., 1925.

MIDDLETON, PHILLIP H. *Railways and Organized Labor.* Chicago, 1941.

MILLS, C. WRIGHT. *The New Men of Power: America's Labor Leaders.* New York, 1948.

MOSCOW, WARREN. *Politics of the Empire State.* New York, 1948.

MURCHISON, CARL A. *Social Psychology; the Psychology of Political Domination.* Worcester, Mass., 1929.

OVERACKER, LOUISE. *Money in Elections.* New York, 1932. Based on Material gathered by Victor J. West.

PEEL, ROY VICTOR and THOMAS C. DONNELLY. *The 1928 Campaign, an Analysis.* New York, 1931.

PERLMAN, SELIG. *Theory of the Labor Movement.* New York, 1928.

PETERSON, FLORENCE. *Strikes in the United States, 1880-1936.* Washington, U. S. Bureau of Labor Statistics, Bulletin No. 651, 1937.

QUINT, HOWARD H. *The Forging of American Socialism.* Columbia, S. C., 1953.

REED, LOUIS SCHULTZ. *The Labor Philosophy of Samuel Gompers.* New York, 1930.

RICE, STUART A. *Farmers and Workers in American Politics.* New York, 1924.

ROBINSON, DWIGHT E. *Collective Bargaining and Market Control in the Women's Coat and Suit Industry*. New York, 1949.

SAPOSS, DAVID J. *Communism in American Unions* (New York, 1959).

————. *Communism in American Politics* (Washington, 1960).

SCHATTSCHNEIDER, ELMER ERIC. *Politics, Pressures and the Tariff*. New York, 1935.

SCHNEIDER, DAVID MOSES. *The Workers' (Communist) Party and American Trade Unions*. Baltimore, 1928.

SEIDMAN, JOEL ISAAC. *The Yellow Dog Contract*. Baltimore, 1932.

SHANNON, DAVID A. *The Socialist Party of America*. New York,1955.

————. *The Decline of American Communism*. New York, 1959.

SILVA, RUTH C. *Rum, Religion, and Votes: 1928 Re-Examined* (University Park, Pa., 1962).

STEDMAN, MURRAY S., JR., and SUSAN W. *Discontent at the Polls: A Study of Farmer and Labor Parties, 1827-1948*. New York, 1950.

STETLER, HENRY GRUBER. *The Socialist Movement in Reading [Penna.], 1899-1936*. Storrs, Conn., 1943.

STIMSON, GRACE HEILMAN. *The Rise of the Labor Movement in Los Angeles*. Berkeley, 1955.

STUCKEY, LORIN. *The Iowa State Federation of Labor*. Iowa City, 1916.

TANNENBAUM, FRANK. *The Labor Movement; Its Conservative Functions and Social Consequences*. New York, 1921.

THOMPSON, PHILLIPS. *The Politics of Labor*. New York, 1887.

WALSH, WILLIAM J. *The United Mine Workers of America as an Economic and Social Force in the Anthracite Territory*. Washington, 1931.

WOLMAN, LEO. *Ebb and Flow in Trade Unionism*. New York, 1936.

ZARETZ, CHARLES E. *The Amalgamated Clothing Workers of America*. New York, 1934.

ZELLER, BELLE. *Pressure Politics in New York; a Study of Group Representation Before the Legislature*. New York, 1937.

K. GENERAL WORKS

ALLEN, FREDERICK LEWIS. *Only Yesterday*. New York, 1931.

ANDERSON, HOBSON DEWEY and PERCY DAVIDSON. *Ballots and the Democratic Class Struggle*. Stanford Univ., 1943.

BAILEY, THOMAS A. *America Faces Russia: Russian-American Relations From Early Times to Our Day*. Ithaca, 1950.

BEAN, LOUIS H. *How to Predict Elections*. New York, 1948.

BEARD, CHARLES A. *The American Party Battle*. New York, 1928.

————, editor. *Whither Mankind: A Panorama of Modern Civilization.* New York, 1929.

BEARD, CHARLES A. and MARY R. *America in Mid-Passage.* New York, 1939.

BEARD, MARY. *The American Labor Movement.* New York, 1931.

BERNSTEIN, IRVING. *The Lean Years.* New York, 1960.

BINKLEY, WILFRED E. *American Political Parties, Their Natural History.* New York, 1943.

BLOOM, GORDON F. and HERBERT R. NORTHRUP. *Economics of Labor and Industrial Relations.* Philadelphia, 1950.

BONN, MORITZ JULIUS. *Economics and Politics.* New York, 1932.

BROOKS, R. R. R. *When Labor Organizes.* New Haven, 1937.

BROWN, P. S., ed. "The Second Industrial Revolution and Its Significance," *Annals of the American Academy of Political and Social Science,* CXLIX (May 1930), 1-197.

CATLIN, WARREN B. *The Labor Problem in the United States and Great Britain.* New York, 1926.

CHAMBERLAIN, JOHN. *Farewell to Reform.* New York, 1933.

COMMONS, JOHN R. *History of Labor Legislation.* 4th rev. ed. New York, 1936.

————. *History of Labour in the United States.* 2 vols. New York, 1926.

COTTRELL, WILLIAM F. *The Railroader.* Stanford Univ., 1940.

DULLES, FOSTER REA. *Labor in America.* New York, 1949.

FELDMAN, HERMAN. *Racial Factors in American Industry.* New York, 1931.

GHENT, W. J. *The Reds Bring Reaction.* Princeton, N. J., 1923.

GINZBERG, ELI. *The Labor Leader.* New York, 1948.

GOSNELL, HAROLD F. *Grass Roots Politics.* Washington, 1942.

GREER, THOMAS H. *American Social Reform Movements; Their Pattern Since 1865.* New York, 1949.

GREGORY, CHARLES O. *Labor and the Law.* New York, 1946.

HACKER, LOUIS M. *et al. The New Industrial Relations.* Ithaca, N. Y., 1948.

HADLEY, ARTHUR TWINING. *The Conflict Between Liberty and Equality.* Boston, 1925.

HARDMAN, J. B. S., editor. *American Labor Dynamics.* New York, 1928.

HAYNES, FREDERICK EMORY. *Social Politics in the United States.* Boston, 1924.

HERRING, PENDLETON. *The Politics of Democracy.* New York, 1940.

HESSELTINE, WILLIAM B. *The Rise and Fall of Third Parties.* Washington, 1948.

HICKS, JOHN D. *The Republican Ascendency, 1921 to 1933.* New York, 1960.

HOLCOMBE, A. N. *The New Party Politics.* New York, 1933.

————. *Our More Perfect Union.* Cambridge, Mass., 1950.

KEY, VALDIMER ORLANDO. *Politics, Parties and Pressure Groups.* New York, 1942.

LAZARSFELD, PAUL FELIX. *The People's Choice; How the Voter Makes Up His Mind in a Presidential Campaign.* New York, 1948.

358 ⊠ **LABOR POLITICS IN A DEMOCRATIC REPUBLIC**

LEIGHTON, JOSEPH A. *Social Philosophies in Conflict.* New York, 1937.

LEISERSON, WILLIAM M. *Right and Wrong in Labor Relations.* Berkeley, Calif., 1938.

LESCOHIER, DON D. and ELIZABETH BRANDEIS. *History of Labor in the United States, 1896-1933. Working Conditions.* New York, 1935.

LEUCHTENBURG, WILLIAM E. *The Perils of Prosperity, 1914-1932.* Chicago, 1958.

LEWIS, STUART. *Party Principles and Practical Politics.* New York, 1928.

LINDBLOM, CHARLES E. *Unions and Capitalism.* New Haven, 1949.

LYND, ROBERT S. and HELEN. *Middletown.* New York, 1929.

McKEAN, DAYTON DAVID. *Party and Pressure Groups.* Boston, 1949.

MERRIAM, CHARLES E. *The American Party System.* 4th edition. New York, 1949.

MERRIAM, CHARLES E. and LOUISE OVERACKER. *Primary Elections.* Chicago, 1928.

MILLIS, HARRY A. and EMILY CLARK BROWN. *From the Wagner Act to Taft-Hartley: A Study of National Labor Policy and Labor Relations.* Chicago, 1950.

MILLIS, HARRY A. and ROYAL E. MONTGOMERY. *Labor's Progress and Some Basic Labor Problems.* New York, 1938.

————. *Labor's Risks and Social Insurance.* New York, 1938.

MILLIS, HARRY A. and ROYAL E. MONTGOMERY. *Organized Labor.* New York, 1945.

MITCHELL, BROADUS. *Depression Decade: From New Era Through New Deal, 1929-1941.* New York, 1947.

National Industrial Conference Board. The Economic Almanac. New York, various dates.

ODEGARD, PETER H. and E. ALLEN HELMS. *American Politics; A Study in Political Dynamics.* New York, 1938.

OGBURN, WILLIAM F., ed. *Social Changes in 1928.* Chicago, 1929.

PENNIMAN, HOWARD R. *Sait's American Parties and Elections.* 4th ed. New York, 1948.

PERLMAN, SELIG and PHILIP TAFT. *History of Labor in the United States, 1896-1932. Labor Movements.* New York, 1935.

PETERSON, FLORENCE. *American Labor Unions.* New York, 1945.

Recent Economic Changes in the United States. 2 vols. New York, 1929.

Recent Social Trends in the United States. 2 vols. New York, 1933.

ROBINSON, EDGAR EUGENE. *The Evolution of American Political Parties.* New York, 1924.

————. *The New United States.* Stanford Univ., 1946.

————. *The Presidential Vote, 1896-1932.* Stanford Univ., 1947 ed.

————. *They Voted for Roosevelt: The Presidential Vote, 1932-1944.* Stanford Univ., 1947.

SCHATTSCHNEIDER, ELMER ERIC. *Party Government.* New York, 1942.

SCHLESINGER, ARTHUR M. *The American as Reformer*. New York, 1950.

SCHRIFTGIESSER, KARL. *This Was Normalcy*. Boston, 1948.

SELEKMAN, BENJAMIN M. *Labor Relations and Human Relations*. New York, 1947.

SEIDMAN, JOEL. *The Needle Trades*. New York, 1942.

SIEGFRIED, ANDRE. *America Comes of Age*. Translated by H. H. and Doris Hemming. New York, 1927.

SLOSSEN, PRESTON W. *The Great Crusade and After, 1914-1928*. New York, 1935.

SOULE, GEORGE. *Prosperity Decade, From War to Depression: 1917-1929*. New York, 1947.

————. *Economic Forces in American History*. New York, 1950.

STOLBERG, BENJAMIN. *Tailor's Progress: The Story of a Famous Union and the Men Who Made It*. New York, 1944.

STEWART, PAUL W. *Market Data Handbook*. Washington, 1929.

SULLIVAN, MARK. *Our Times*. 6 vols. New York, 1926-1935.

TAFT, PHILIP. *Economics and the Problems of Labor*. Harrisburg, Penn., 1942.

Twentieth Century Fund. *Labor and Government*. New York, 1935.

WATKINS, GORDON S., ed. "Labor in the American Economy," *Annals of the American Academy of Political and Social Science*, CCLXXIV (March, 1951), 1-205.

WEBB, WALTER PRESCOTT. *Divided We Stand; the Crisis of a Frontierless Democracy*. New York, 1937.

YELLEN, SAMUEL. *American Labor Struggles*. New York, 1936.

L. SUPPLEMENTARY WORKS

BALDWIN, ROGER N., editor and author of a biographical sketch. *Kropotkin's Revolutionary Pamphlets*. New York, Vanguard, 1927.

————. *Liberty Under the Soviets*. New York, Vanguard, 1928. Copy used contained an "Author's Note" dated January, 1930.

BIMBA, ANTHONY. *The History of the American Working Class*. New York, 1927.

CANNON, JAMES P. *History of American Trotskyism*. New York, Pioneer Press, 1944. Semiautobiographical.

CHASE, STUART. *Prosperity, Fact or Myth*. New York, Dec., 1929. Designed to prove the latter.

Communist International. *The Communist International; Between the Fifth and the Sixth World Congresses—1924-1928*. London, Communist Party of Great Britain, 1928. "A report on the position in all sections of the World Communist Party."

————. 6th Congress, Moscow, 1928. *Program of the Communist International.* New York, Workers Library, 1929.

Communist Party of the U. S. A. *On the Road to Bolshevization.* New York, 1929. Reprints of various decisions, theses of the movement, etc.

Democratic Party. New York (County) Committee. *The Story of Tammany.* New York, 1928.

Doan, Edward J. *The La Follettes and the Wisconsin Idea.* New York, 1947.

Douglas, Paul H. *The Coming of a New Party.* New York, New York, 1932. Urges a new party alignment.

Dyche, John A. *Bolshevism in American Labor Unions.* New York, Boni and Liveright, 1926. An attack on the I. L. G. W. U. by an employer.

Fay, Charles Norman. *Labor in Politics or Class versus Country; Considerations for American Voters.* n.p., The University Press, 1920. By a retired employer.

Fine, Nathan. *Labor and Farmer Parties in the United States, 1828-1928.* New York, Rand School, New York, 1928.

Foster, William Z. *Misleaders of Labor.* New York, 1927.

————. *Toward Soviet America.* New York, 1932.

————, J. P. Cannon, and E. R. Browder. *Trade Unions in America.* Chicago, Trade Union Educational League, 1925?

Frey, John P. *The Labor Injunction; An Exposition of Government by Judicial Conscience and Its Menace.* Cincinnati, Ohio, 1923?

Gompers, Samuel. *Labor in Europe and America.* New York, 1910. Unfavorable picture of conditions in Europe.

Green, William. *Labor and Democracy.* Princeton, N. J., 1939.

Greenway, John. *American Folksongs of Protest.* Philadelphia, 1953.

Hillquit, Morris. *History of Socialism in the United States.* New York, 1903.

James, C. L. R. *World Revolution, 1917-1936. The Rise and Fall of the Communist International.* London, 1937. A Trotskyist view.

Kent, Frank R. *The Democratic Party, a History.* New York, 1928.

————. *Political Behavior.* New York, 1928.

Laidler, Harry W., ed. *New Tactics in Social Conflict, [a] Symposium.* New York, 1926.

Laski, Harold. *Communism.* New York, 1927.

Levinson, Edward. *Labor on the March.* New York, 1938.

Lovestone, Jay. *The Government—Strikebreaker.* New York, Workers Party. 1923.

Lyons, Eugene. *The Red Decade.* New York, 1941.

Marvin, Fred R. ("The Senator From Alaska"). *Fools Gold. An Expose of Un-American Activities and Political Action in the United States since 1860.* New York, 1936.

Myers, William Starr. *The Republican Party, a History.* New York, 1928.

Olds, Marshall. *Analysis of the Interchurch World Movement Report on the Steel Strike.* New York, 1923. By the author of a volume entitled *The High Cost of Strikes.*

ONEAL, JAMES and G. A. WERNER. *American Communism*. New and revised edition. New York, Dutton, 1947. A Socialist view.

PAGE, KIRBY. *Individualism and Socialism*. New York, 1933.

PAINTER, LEONARD. *Through Fifty Years with the Brotherhood of Railway Carmen of America*. Kansas City, Mo., 1941.

Political Issues of 1928. The Sixth Commonwealth Conference, State University of Iowa, July 9-11, 1928. Iowa City, Iowa, 1928.

Republican Campaign Textbook, 1928.

SARRN, PAUL. *The Lawless Decade*. New York, 1957.

SAPOSS, DAVID J. *Left Wing Unionism: a Study of Radical Policies and Tactics*. New York, International Publishers, 1926.

————. *Readings in Trade Unionism*. New York, 1927. Extracts reprinted for the most part from labor union journals.

SEIDMAN, HAROLD. *Labor Czars; a History of Labor Racketeering*. New York, 1938.

SULLIVAN, J. W. and HAYES ROBBINS. *Socialism as an Incubus on the American Labor Movement*. New York, B. H. Tyrrel, 1918. Sullivan's part (pp. 1-100) first published in 1909.

SYMES, LILLIAN and TRAVERS CLEMENT. *Rebel America: the Story of Social Revolt in the United States*. New York, 1934.

THOMAS, NORMAN. *America's Way Out: A Program for Democracy*. New York, 1931.

————. *The Choice Before Us: Mankind at the Crossroads*. New York, 1934.

————. *What Is Industrial Democracy?* New York, 1925.

UMINSKI, SIGMUND. *The Progress of Labor in the United States*. New York, House of Field, 1939.

WALLING, WILLIAM ENGLISH. *American Labor and American Democracy*. New York, 1926.

WEISBORD, ALBERT. *Passaic; the Story of a Struggle Against Starvation Wages and for the Right to Organize*. Chicago, 196.

WHITNEY, RICHARD M. *Reds in America*. New York, 1924.

M. WORKS OF REFERENCE, YEARBOOKS, AND MISCELLANEOUS

American Catholic Who's Who. Grosse Pointe, Mich., 1946-1947. (Volume VII.)

American Civic Annual. Washington, 1929.

American Labor Who's Who. New York, Rand School, 1925.

CASSELMAN, P. H. *Labor Dictionary*. New York, 1949.

Current Biography. New York, 1942-1949. Contains sketches of William Z. Foster (1945), William Green (1942), George MacGregor Harrison (1949), William Hutcheson (1943), John L. Lewis (1942), Norman Mattoon Thomas (1944), Daniel J. Tobin (1945), Matthew Woll (1943).

Memoranda for the Baltimore Meeting of the National Executive Committee of the Socialist Party, Dec. 9-11, 1932. Dated Dec. 4, 1932. Mimeographed. Main Library, Stanford Univ.

Poor's Railroad Section, Banks and Insurance Companies. New York, 1928.

Socialist Party, National Committee. Miscellaneous Campaign Material, 1928. Main Library, Stanford Univ.

Who's Who in Labor. New York, 1946.

N. DOCTORAL DISSERTATIONS AND MASTER'S THESES

BALMER, RONALD GORDON. The Taft-Hartley Act: A Case Study of Congressional Procedures and Political Strategy. M. A. Thesis, Univ. of Washington, 1949.

BARTLETT, GEORGE R. Use of the Injunction by Organized Labor. M.A. Thesis, Univ. of California, 1928.

BELFER, BERNICE SHOUL. American Labor in Politics; Preface to the Labor Party. M.A. Thesis, Columbia Univ., 1943.

BELLUSH, BERNARD. Apprenticeship for the Presidency: Franklin D. Roosevelt as Governor of New York. Doctoral Dissertation, Columbia Univ., 1950.

BORNET, VAUGHN DAVIS. Labor and Politics in 1928. Doctoral Dissertation, Stanford Univ., 1951.

BRUBAKER, OTIS. Trends in Federal Labor Legislation. 2 volumes. Ph.D. Dissertation, Stanford Univ., 1940.

BRUCKNER, MOLLY ACREMAN. The Role of Labor in the Conduct of United States Foreign Affairs. Ph.D. Dissertation, Univ. of Chicago, 1950.

CASEY, RALPH. Campaign Techniques in 1928. Ph.D. Dissertation, Univ. of Wisconsin, 1929.

CONRAD, FREDERICK A. Agrarian Discontent: A Study of Class Conflict Based on Farmer Movements in the United States, 1860-1930. Ph.D. Dissertation, Stanford Univ., 1932.

ERGBERT, GEORGE BARKER. The Rise of Organized Labor in Minnesota, 1850-1890. M.A. Thesis, Univ. of Minnesota, 1939.

FELIZ, GEORGE COMTE. Organized Labor and Higher Education in the United States. Ph.D. Dissertation, Stanford Univ., 1939.

FIBUSH, KENNETH MORRIS, The American Federation of Labor Since Gompers. M.A. Thesis, Univ. of California, 1934.

FITZPATRICK, MARY BLANCHE. The Changing Character of Labor Leadership. M.A. Thesis, Stanford Univ., 1950.

GOODMAN, T. WILBAIN. The Presidential Campaign of 1920. Ph.D. Dissertation, Ohio Univ., 1951.

HARVEY, ROLAND HILL. A Comparison of the Approach Toward Socialism of British and American Labor Since 1900. Ph.D. Dissertation, Stanford Univ., 1923.

HINDS, JOHN LOUIS. A History of the Communist Party of America, 1919-1933. M.A. Thesis, Stanford Univ., 1933.

HATFIELD, MARK ODUM. Herbert Hoover and Labor: Policies and Attitudes, 1897-1928. M.A. Thesis, Stanford Univ., 1948.

ISAACS, WILLIAM. Contemporary Marxian Political Movements in the United States. 2 volumes. Ph.D. Dissertation, New York Univ., 1939.

IVERSON, ROBERT W. Morris Hillquit: American Social Democrat, a Study of the American Left from Haymarket to the New Deal. Ph.D. Dissertation, Univ. of Iowa, 1951.

JACKSON, HOYT MILTON. The Political Ideas and Tactics of Sidney Hillman, M.A. Thesis, Univ. of California, 1950.

JOHNSTON, SCOTT DORAN. The Socialist Party in the Conference for Progressive Political Action. Ph.D. Dissertation, Univ. of Minnesota, 1952.

JONES, DALLAS LEE. The Wilson Administration and Organized Labor, 1912-1919. Ph.D. Dissertation, Cornell Univ. 195?

JONES, HERMON W. The Role of the Company Union in the American Labor Movement. M.A. Thesis in Economics, Stanford Univ., 1949.

KIERNAN, CHARLES J. The Labor Injunction and American Trade Unionism. M.A. Thesis, Columbia Univ., 1934.

KREPS, JUANITA M. Developments in the Political and Legislative Policies of Organized Labor, 1920-1947. Ph.D. Dissertation, Duke Univ., 1948.

LEONARD, SISTER JOAN DE LOURDES. Catholic Attitude Towards American Labor 1884-1919. M.A. Thesis, Columbia Univ., 1940.

LOOMIS, RICHARD THOMAS. Alfred E. Smith and Religion in Politics: 1924-1928. M.A. Thesis, Stanford Univ., 1948.

McCOY, ROBERT EDWIN. Labor in Politics: The C I O-P A C in California, 1943-1948. M.A. Thesis, Stanford Univ., 1949.

NAFTALIN, ARTHUR. A History of the Farmer-Labor Party of Minnesota. Ph.D. Dissertation, Univ. of Minnesota, 1948.

OLSON, FREDERICK. The Milwaukee Socialists, 1897-1941. Ph.D. Dissertation, Harvard Univ., 1952.

OTTINI, VIRGINIA. The Socialist Party in the Election of 1920. M.A. Thesis, Stanford Univ., 1948.

PLESHER, MICHAEL A. A Comparison of the Political and Economic Policies, and the Administration of the Socialist Party and the Socialist Labor Party of the United States. Ph.D. Dissertation, Univ. of Pittsburgh, 1951.

PRETTYMAN, E. COURTNEY. The Trial of the Eleven Communist Leaders in New York, 1949: An Examination of the Testimony of the Witnesses for the Prosecution. M.A. Thesis, Stanford Univ., 1950.

RUNKEL, HOWARD WILLIAM. Hoover's Speeches During His Presidency. Ph.D. Dissertation, Stanford Univ., 1950.

SEYLER, WILLIAM C. The Socialist Party of the United States: Its Rise and Decline, 1901-1951. Ph.D. Dissertation, Duke Univ., 1952.

SEYMOUR, JOHN B. The Unemployable. M.A. Thesis, Stanford Univ., 1922.

SHANNON, DAVID A. The Decline of the American Socialist Party. Ph.D. Dissertation, Univ. of Wisconsin, 1951.

SHIDELER, JAMES HENRY. The Neo-Progressives: Reform Politics in the United States, 1920-1925. Ph.D. Dissertation, Univ. of California, 1945.

SHOTT, J. G. A Paper in Answer to the Contention that the Supreme Court Has Nullified the Labor Provisions of the Clayton Anti-Trust Law. M.A. Thesis, Stanford Univ., 1930.

THISTLEWAITE, ROBERT L. The Labor Press: A Critical Examination and Appraisal of its Policies, Needs, Progress, and Opinions of Labor Editors on Topics Vital to the Labor Movement. Ph.D. Dissertation, Univ. of Iowa, 1951.

VILLAUME, WILLIAM J. The Federal Council of Churches of Christ in America on Labor Problems in the United States, 1908-1933. Ph.D. Dissertation, Hartford Seminary, 1951.

WACHMAN, MARVIN. History of the Social-Democratic Party of Milwaukee, 1897-1910. Ph.D. Dissertation, Univ. of Illinois, 1942.

WEINSTEIN, LEO. The Control of Labor-Management Relations in World War I and the Postwar Decade. M.A. Thesis, Univ. of Chicago, 1949.

WEINTRAUB, HYMAN. The I. W. W. in California, 1905-1931. M.A. Thesis, U.C.L.A., 1947.

WILENSKY, HAROLD L. Local 166: A Study of a Union's Influence on the Political Orientation of its Membership. M.A. Thesis, Univ. of Chicago, 1949.

WILLIAMS, ROBERT F. The Railroad Shopmen's Strike of 1922. M.A. Thesis, Univ. of California, 1950.

ZICKEFOOSE, PAUL WESLEY. Protestant Churches and the Labor Movement in the Twentieth Century. M.A. Thesis, Univ. of Washington, 1949.

INDEX